The Book of Asian Proverbs

Unabridged collection of ancient sayings and teachings from across Asia.

D1637147

by

Steven Howard

The Book of Asian Proverbs

ISBN: 978-1-943702-10-7 (Print edition)
          978-1-943702-11-4 (Kindle edition)

For reprint permission, please contact:
    Steven Howard
    c/o Caliente Press
    1775 E Palm Canyon Drive, Suite 110-198
    Palm Springs, CA   92264
    U.S.A
    Email: stevenhoward@verizon.net

Published by:
    Caliente Press
    1775 E Palm Canyon Drive, Suite 110-198
    Palm Springs, CA 92264
    U.S.A.
    Email: CalientePress@verizon.net

Cover Design: Lee Chee Yih

Asian Words of Wisdom Series

The *Asian Words of Wisdom* series comprises the following titles:

Asian Words of Success — *Thoughts, quotations and phrases on leadership, marketing and personal development from Asia's leading thinkers.*

Asian Words of Meaning — *Reflections and thoughts on success, self-understanding and spiritual guidance from Asia's leading thinkers.*

Asian Words of Inspiration — *Thoughts, motivational quotes and wisdom from Asia's leading thinkers on personal and professional success and the journey of life.*

The Book of Asian Proverbs —*Unabridged collection of ancient sayings and teachings from across Asia.*

Indispensable Asian Words of Knowledge — *Words of wisdom from Asia's leading sages, philosophers, and statesmen.* (October 2016)

The Book of Asian Proverbs

Dedication

This book is dedicated to

Masahiro Miki

Long-time colleague and friend.

Devotee of knowledge. Enthusiast of experiences.

Keen wearer of cowboy hats.

And,

like myself,

a lover of all things Japanese and Texas.

Table of Contents

Introduction

The widespread interest in proverbs throughout the world is well documented.

Ancient sayings and proverbs offer insights and understanding about many aspects of the cultural traditions of the societies from which they emanate. Additionally we find proverbs that have been borrowed or exchanged between similar languages and cultures, and thus reach us today through more than one language. This is particularly true within Asia, where common cultures and traditions often transcend political boundaries and lines drawn on maps.

Proverbs usually originate from humble indigenous people, who handed down their wise sayings and life lessons from generation to generation and from century to century. But they also come from ancient thinkers like Buddha and Confucius.

While we believe all of our sources for these proverbs to be reliable, readers should not interpret *The Book of Asian*

Proverbs as a highly researched, authoritative reference book. This is not what we set out to do and it is certainly not what we have delivered.

What we have set out to do is gather and share the proverbs and sayings that moved us, impressed us, or got us thinking a bit harder, deeper, or even more lightly. In achieving this endeavor, we trust you will agree, *The Book of Asian Proverbs* does deliver.

While technically the continent of Asia extends all the way west to Turkey, most people today seem to cut Asia off at the western border of Pakistan. In truth, the boundaries of Asia are more culturally determined that geographic lines on maps and globes. As such, I have elected to include a handful of proverbs from Afghanistan, Persia (modern Iran), as well as the Arabian Peninsula.

The word proverb comes to us from the Latin *proverbium* and is typically a single, concrete statement or saying expressing what the originators saw as a truth or common sense advice regarding life experiences. Often expressed as metaphors they become commonly known and popularly repeated, both orally and in writing.

Ancient proverbs, particularly from Asia, tend to condense the experiences and habits of life into the fundamental lessons for our respective life journeys. As such, they enable us to set our personal bearings for traversing the vast realms and depths of our individual hopes, desires, dreams, plans, and pursuits.

Truly inspirational proverbs reflect the deepest wisdom about life culled from the experiences, knowledge, and wisdom of past generations. They help us crystallize our own understanding of life; benefitting from the experiences, understanding, knowledge, and wisdom of those who have gone before us.

When these pithy sayings and short maxims resonate with our personal inner beliefs and truths, we are uplifted, motivated, and strengthened in our resolve to hurdle the obstacles life throws at us and pursue our chosen paths.

May the Asian Proverbs in this book become inspirational dictums and teachings that open up new perspectives for you that help reframe your personal experiences of life, reality, and spirituality.

Steven Howard
August 2016

Afghan Proverbs

Don't show me the palm tree, show me the dates.

Afghan Proverb

In bad things be slow; in good things be quick.

Afghan Proverb

No one says his own buttermilk is sour.

Afghan Proverb

Only stretch your foot to the length of your blanket.

Afghan Proverb

What you see in yourself is what you see in the world.

Afghan Proverb

The Book of Asian Proverbs

Arabian Proverbs

Do not stand in a place of danger trusting in miracles.

Arabian Proverb

He who has health has hope, and he who has hope has everything.

Arabian Proverb

The willing contemplation of vice is vice.

Arabian Proverb

When you have spoken the word, it reigns over you. When it is unspoken you reign over it.

Arabian Proverb

Ashanti Proverb

You must act as if it is impossible to fail.

Ashanti Proverb

Balinese Proverb

Goodness shouts. Evil whispers.

Balinese Proverb

Bengali Proverbs

The highest goes hand in hand with the lowest. It is only the commonplace that walks at a distance.

Bengali Proverb

Unless a man is simple, he cannot recognize God, the Simple One.

Bengali Proverb

Buddhist Proverbs

Given careful attention, any activity may become a window on the universe and a doorway to understanding.

Buddhist Proverb

God gives every bird its food, but He does not throw it into its nest.

Buddhist Proverb

Good people shine from afar, like the highest peaks of Himalayas.

Buddhist Proverb

If you want to know your past, look into your present conditions. If you want to know your future, look into your present actions.

Buddhist Proverb

Laughter is the language of the Gods.

Buddhist Proverb

Loneliness is better than friendship of a fool.

Buddhist Proverb

Lovely flowers without fragrance are sweet words without sweet action.

> Buddhist Proverb

No suffering befalls the man who calls nothing his own.

> Buddhist Proverb

Tell no lies and deceive no one.

> Buddhist Proverb

The present is the offspring of the past and parent of the future.

> Buddhist Proverb

The search for God is like riding around on an ox hunting for the ox.

> Buddhist Proverb

To know the mind is the most important task of your life. And to know the mind is to know the world.

> Buddhist Proverb

Victory breeds hatred. He who has given up both victory and defeat, he is contented and happy.

> Buddhist Proverb

When the mind discriminates, there is manifoldness of things; when it does not, it looks into the true state of things.

Buddhist Proverb

When the student is ready, the master appears.

Buddhist Proverb

Burmese Proverbs

A hero only appears once the tiger is dead.

Burmese Proverb

A stupid act entails doing the work twice over.

Burmese Proverb

Beware of a man's shadow and a bee's sting.

Burmese Proverb

If you take big paces you leave big spaces.

Burmese Proverb

If you truly want honesty, don't ask questions you don't really want the answer to.

Burmese Proverb

If you trust before you try, you will repent before you die.

Burmese Proverb

One sesame seed won't make oil.

Burmese Proverb

Only with a new ruler do you realize the value of the old.

Burmese Proverb

Only your real friends will tell you when your face is dirty.

Burmese Proverb

Seven days is the length of a guest's life.

Burmese Proverb

Sparrows who emulate peacocks are likely to break a thigh.

Burmese Proverb

The blind person never fears ghosts.

Burmese Proverb

The learned are apt to be taciturn.

Burmese Proverb

The least and weakest man can do some hurt.

Burmese Proverb

The least boy always carries the biggest fiddle.

Burmese Proverb

Cambodian Proverb

Cultivate a heart of love that knows no anger.

Cambodian Proverb

Chinese Proverbs

A bird does not sing because it has an answer; it sings because it has a song.

Chinese Proverb

A bit of perfume always clings to the hand that gives the rose.

Chinese Proverb

A book holds a house of gold.

Chinese Proverb

A book is a garden carried in the pocket.

Chinese Proverb

A diamond with a flaw is worth more than a common stone that is perfect.

Chinese Proverb

A dog in a kennel barks at his flea; a dog hunting does not notice them.

Chinese Proverb

A fool judges people by the presents they give him.

Chinese Proverb

A great man can bend and stretch.

Chinese Proverb

A hundred men may make an encampment, but it takes a woman to make a home.

Chinese Proverb

A journey of a thousand miles must begin with a single step.

Chinese Proverb

A little impatience will spoil great plans.

Chinese Proverb

A single conversation across the table with a wise man is worth a month's study of books.

Chinese Proverb

The Book of Asian Proverbs

A person who doesn't know, but knows that he doesn't know, is a student; teach him. A person who knows, but doesn't know that he knows, is asleep; awaken him. But a person who knows and knows that he knows is wise; follow him.

Chinese Proverb

A sly rabbit will have three openings to its den.

Chinese Proverb

A smile will gain you ten more years of life.

Chinese Proverb

A watched flower never blooms, while a carelessly planted willow grows into shade.

Chinese Proverb

A weasel comes to say "Happy New Year" to the chickens.

Chinese Proverb

Add legs to the snake after you have finished drawing it.

Chinese Proverb

All the flowers of all of the tomorrows are in the seeds of today.

Chinese Proverb

An army of a thousand is easy to find, but, how difficult it is to find a general.

Chinese Proverb

An inch of time is an inch of gold, but you can't buy that inch of time with an inch of gold.

Chinese Proverb

An iron rod can be ground down to become a needle.

Chinese Proverb

Be not afraid of going slowly; be afraid only of standing still.

Chinese Proverb

Be the first to the field and the last to the couch.

Chinese Proverb

Before enlightenment chop wood and carry water. After enlightenment chop wood and carry water.

Chinese Proverb

Better to do a good deed near at home than to go far away to burn incense.

Chinese Proverb

Better to light a candle, than to curse the darkness.

> Chinese Proverb

Cautious, careful people, always casting about to preserve their reputations, can never effect a reform.

> Chinese Proverb

Climb mountains to see lowlands.

> Chinese Proverb

Crows everywhere are equally black.

> Chinese Proverb

Deal with the faults of others as gently as with your own.

> Chinese Proverb

Deep doubts, deep wisdom; small doubts, little wisdom.

> Chinese Proverb

Dig a well before you are thirsty.

> Chinese Proverb

Do not look where you fell, but where you slipped.

> Chinese Proverb

Dream different dreams while on the same bed.

> Chinese Proverb

Enjoy yourself; it's later than you think.

Chinese Proverb

Even a hare will bite when it is cornered.

Chinese Proverb

Even for a tree of 10,000 feet, its leaves return to the root when they fall.

Chinese Proverb

Every child's life is like a piece of paper on which every person leaves a mark.

Chinese Proverb

Every day cannot be a feast of lanterns.

Chinese Proverb

Fool me once, shame on you. Fool me twice, shame on me.

Chinese Proverb

For every hundred men hacking away at the branches of a diseased tree, only one will stoop to inspect the roots.

Chinese Proverb

The Book of Asian Proverbs

Giving your son a skill is better than giving him one thousand pieces of gold.

> Chinese Proverb

Govern a family as you would cook a small fish – very gently.

> Chinese Proverb

Great souls have wills; feeble ones have only wishes.

> Chinese Proverb

Happiness is like a sunbeam, which the least shadow intercepts, while adversity is often as the rain of spring.

> Chinese Proverb

Have a mouth as sharp as a dagger but a heart as soft as tofu.

> Chinese Proverb

He who asks is a fool for five minutes, but he who does not ask remains a fool forever.

> Chinese Proverb

He who governs by his moral excellence may be compared to the pole star which abides in its place while all other stars bow towards it.

> Chinese Proverb

He who restrains his appetite avoids debt.

Chinese Proverb

He who rides the tiger can never dismount.

Chinese Proverb

He who sacrifices his conscience to ambition burns a picture to obtain the ashes.

Chinese Proverb

He who takes medicine and neglects to diet wastes the skills of his doctors.

Chinese Proverb

I dreamed a thousand new paths. I woke and walked my old one.

Chinese Proverb

I was angered, for I had no shoes. Then I met a man who had no feet.

Chinese Proverb

If a man does more than is required of him, he is a free man. If a man does only what is required of him, he is a slave.

Chinese Proverb

If heaven made him, earth can find some use for him.

Chinese Proverb

If I keep a green bough in my heart, then the singing bird will come.

Chinese Proverb

If there is light in the soul, there will be beauty in the person. If there is beauty in the person, there will be harmony in the house. If there is harmony in the house, there will be order in the nation. If there is order in the nation, there will be peace in the world.

Chinese Proverb

If you always give you will always have.

Chinese Proverb

If you are patient in one moment of anger, you will escape a hundred days of sorrow.

Chinese Proverb

If you are planning for one year, grow rice. If you are planning for 20 years, grow trees. If you are planning for centuries, grow men.

Chinese Proverb

The Book of Asian Proverbs

If you are poor, though you dwell in the busy marketplace, no one will inquire about you; if you are rich, though you dwell in the heart of the mountains, you will have distant relatives.

Chinese Proverb

If you chase two rabbits, both will escape.

Chinese Proverb

If you don't stand for something, you will fall for something.

Chinese Proverb

If you don't want anyone to know, don't do it.

Chinese Proverb

If you must play, decide on three things at the start: the rules of the game, the stakes and the quitting time.

Chinese Proverb

If you want happiness for an hour, take a nap.
If you want happiness for a day, go fishing.
If you want happiness for a year, inherit a fortune.
If you want happiness for a lifetime, help somebody.

Chinese Proverb

If you wish your merit to be known, acknowledge that of other people.

Chinese Proverb

If your strength is small, don't carry heavy burdens. If your words are worthless, don't give advice.

Chinese Proverb

In the midst of great joy, do not promise anything. In the midst of great anger, do not answer anyone's letter.

Chinese Proverb

It is not the knowing that is difficult, but the doing.

Chinese Proverb

Laws control the lesser man. Right conduct controls the greater one.

Chinese Proverb

Learning is a treasure that will follow its owner everywhere.

Chinese Proverb

Learning is like rowing upstream: not to advance is to drop back.

Chinese Proverb

Learning is weightless, a treasure you can always carry easily.

> Chinese Proverb

Life's journey is the reward.

> Chinese Proverb

Man fools himself. He prays for a long life, yet fears an old age.

> Chinese Proverb

Men trip not on mountains, they trip on molehills.

> Chinese Proverb

Never was good work done without much trouble.

> Chinese Proverb

No wind, no waves.

> Chinese Proverb

Not the cry but the flight of the wild duck leads the flock to fly and follow.

> Chinese Proverb

Not the fastest horse can catch a word spoken in anger.

> Chinese Proverb

Of all the stratagems, to know when to quit is the best.

Chinese Proverb

Once a word leaves your mouth, you cannot chase it back even with the swiftest horse.

Chinese Proverb

One generation plants the trees; another gets the shade.

Chinese Proverb

One joy scatters a hundred griefs.

Chinese Proverb

One moment of patience may ward off great disaster. One moment of impatience may ruin a whole life.

Chinese Proverb

One monk shoulders water by himself; two can still share the labor among them. When it comes to three, they have to go thirsty.

Chinese Proverb

One never needs their humor as much a when they argue with a fool.

Chinese Proverb

One step in the wrong direction will cause you a thousand years of regret.

> Chinese Proverb

Only the man who crosses the river at night knows the value of the light of day.

> Chinese Proverb

Paper can't wrap up a fire.

> Chinese Proverb

Patience is power; with time and patience the mulberry leaf becomes silk.

> Chinese Proverb

Person who says it cannot be done should not interrupt person doing it.

> Chinese Proverb

Plan the whole year in the spring.

> Chinese Proverb

Problems are sent to us as gifts.

> Chinese Proverb

Pure gold does not fear furnace.

> Chinese Proverb

Rotten wood cannot be carved.

> Chinese Proverb

Small ills are the fountains of most of our groans. Men trip not on mountains, they stumble on stones.

> Chinese Proverb

Sometimes you lose a forest through the trees.

> Chinese Proverb

Sour, sweet, bitter, pungent, all must be tasted.

> Chinese Proverb

Take chances. When rowing forward the boat might rock.

> Chinese Proverb

Talk doesn't cook rice.

> Chinese Proverb

Tao points out, "The snow goose need not bathe to make itself white." Neither need you do anything but be yourself. If a man does only what is required of him, he is a slave. If a man does more than is required of him, he is a free man.

> Chinese Proverb

The Book of Asian Proverbs

Teachers open the door, but you must enter by yourself.

Chinese Proverb

Tell me and I'll forget, show me and I may remember, involve me and I'll understand.

Chinese Proverb

Tension is who you think you should be. Relaxation is who you are.

Chinese Proverb

That the birds of worry and care fly over your head, this you cannot change, but that they build nests in your hair, this you can prevent.

Chinese Proverb

The beginning of wisdom is to call things by their right names.

Chinese Proverb

The best time to plant a tree is twenty years ago.

Chinese Proverb

The butterfly becomes only when it is entirely ready.

Chinese Proverb

The gem cannot be polished without friction, nor man perfected without trials.

Chinese Proverb

The gods cannot help those who do not seize opportunities.

Chinese Proverb

The greatest conqueror is he who overcomes the enemy without a blow.

Chinese Proverb

The journey of a thousand miles must begin with a single step.

Chinese Proverb

The longer the night lasts, the more our dreams will be.

Chinese Proverb

The man who strikes first admits that his ideas have given out.

Chinese Proverb

The mind that turns forever outward will have no end to craving. Only the mind turned inward will find a still-point of peace.

Chinese Proverb

The more you sweat in Peacetime, the less you bleed during War.

> Chinese Proverb

The net of Heaven is large and wide, but it lets nothing through.

> Chinese Proverb

The palest ink is better than the best memory.

> Chinese Proverb

The person who removes a mountain begins by carrying away small stones.

> Chinese Proverb

The sun will shine on those who stand, before it shines on those who kneel under them.

> Chinese Proverb

The wise adapt themselves to circumstances, as water molds itself to the pitcher.

> Chinese Proverb

The woman who tells her age is either too young to have anything to lose or too old to have anything to gain.

> Chinese Proverb

There are always ears on the other side of the wall.

Chinese Proverb

There are many paths to the top of the mountain, but the view is always the same.

Chinese Proverb

There are three truths: my truth, your truth, and the truth.

Chinese Proverb

There are two perfect men: one dead and the other unborn.

Chinese Proverb

There is no economy in going bed early to save candles if the result is twins.

Chinese Proverb

There is no one to sweep a common hall.

Chinese Proverb

Those who bully the weak are cowards before the strong.

Chinese Proverb

Those who do not read are no better off than those who cannot.

Chinese Proverb

Those who say it cannot be done, should not interrupt those doing it.

Chinese Proverb

Those whose palm-kernels were cracked for them by a benevolent spirit should not forget to be humble.

Chinese Proverb

Thousands of candles can be lighted from a single candle, and the life of the candle will not be shortened. Happiness never decreases by being shared.

Chinese Proverb

Tigers don't eat grass.

Chinese Proverb

To be uncertain is to be uncomfortable, but to be certain is to be ridiculous.

Chinese Proverb

To chop a tree quickly, spend twice the time sharpening the axe.

Chinese Proverb

To forget one's ancestors is to be a brook without a source, a tree without a root.

Chinese Proverb

To listen well is as powerful a means to influence as to talk well, and is as essential to all true conversations.

Chinese Proverb

To talk goodness is not good. Only to do it is.

Chinese Proverb

To understand your parents' love, bear your own children.

Chinese Proverb

Too many captains will steer the ship up a mountain.

Chinese Proverb

Vicious as a tigress can be, she never eats her own cubs.

Chinese Proverb

Virtue never dwells alone; it always has neighbors.

Chinese Proverb

We are not so much concerned if you are slow as when you come to a halt.

Chinese Proverb

What you cannot avoid, welcome.

Chinese Proverb

When a finger points at the moon, the imbecile looks at the finger.

Chinese Proverb

When a man says yes, his *chi* says yes also.

Chinese Proverb

When a question is posed ceremoniously, the universe responds.

Chinese Proverb

When drinking water remember the source.

Chinese Proverb

When the moon is shining the cripple becomes hungry for a walk.

Chinese Proverb

When you bow, bow low.

Chinese Proverb

When you have only two pennies left in the world, buy a loaf of bread with one, and a lily with the other.

Chinese Proverb

When you want to test the depths of a stream, don't use both feet.

Chinese Proverb

Who is not satisfied with himself will grow; who is not sure of his own correctness will learn many things.

Chinese Proverb

With time and patience the mulberry leaf becomes a silk gown.

Chinese Proverb

With virtue you can't be entirely poor; without virtue you can't really be rich.

Chinese Proverb

Without rice, even the cleverest housewife cannot cook.

Chinese Proverb

You cannot prevent the birds of sorrow from flying over your head, but you can prevent them from building a nest in your hair.

Chinese Proverb

Confucian Proverbs

Be not ashamed of mistakes and thus make them crimes.

Confucian Proverb

Choose a job you love and you will never have to work a day in your life.

Confucian Proverb

Formerly men studied for self-improvement; today men study for the sake of appearances.

Confucian Proverb

If thy strength will serve, go forward in the ranks; if not, stand still.

Confucian Proverb

If today will not, tomorrow may.

Confucian Proverb

If two ride on a horse, one must ride behind.

Confucian Proverb

Leading an uninstructed people to war is to throw them away.

> Confucian Proverb

Learning without thought is labor lost. Thought without learning is perilous.

> Confucian Proverb

Study as if you were never to master it.

> Confucian Proverb

To engage in gossip is to cast aside excellence.

> Confucian Proverb

To see what is right, and not do it, is want of courage, or of principle.

> Confucian Proverb

Hindu Proverbs

A man in this world without learning is as a beast of the field.

Hindu Proverb

Among the blind, the squint rules.

Hindu Proverb

Anger has no eyes.

Hindu Proverb

Be good yourself, and the world will be good.

Hindu Proverb

Can the monkey know the taste of ginger?

Hindu Proverb

Dig a well every day to drink water every day.

Hindu Proverb

Eating while seated makes one of large size; eating while standing makes one strong.

Hindu Proverb

Help thy brother's boat across, and lo! — thine own has reached the shore.

Hindu Proverb

It is better to walk than to run; it is better to stand than to walk; it is better to sit than to stand; it is better to lie than to sit.

Hindu Proverb

Kill a cow to donate shoes.

Hindu Proverb

Lifespan is measured in breaths, not years.

Hindu Proverb

Like the body that is made up of different limbs and organs, all moral creatures must depend on each other to exist.

Hindu Proverb

Many dogs kill a hare, no matter how many turns it makes.

Hindu Proverb

Of what use is the veil if you are going to dance.

Hindu Proverb

Saints fly only in the eyes of their disciples.

Hindu Proverb

Sleep after selling horses and elephants.

Hindu Proverb

There are hundreds of paths up the mountain, all leading to the same place, so it doesn't matter which path you take. The only person wasting time is the one who runs around the mountain, telling everyone that his or her path is wrong.

Hindu Proverb

There is nothing noble in being superior to some other man. The true nobility is in being superior to your previous self.

Hindu Proverb

These three take crooked ways: carts, boats, and musicians.

Hindu Proverb

They who give have all things; they who withhold have nothing.

Hindu Proverb

Those who travel unworn paths find the rarest flowers.

Hindu Proverb

To control the mind is like trying to control a drunken monkey that has been bitten by a scorpion.

Hindu Proverb

Wash your hands in the flowing Ganges.

Hindu Proverb

Waste makes want. Waste not want not.

Hindu Proverb

When a camel is at the foot of a mountain then judge of his height.

Hindu Proverb

When an elephant is in trouble even a frog will kick him.

Hindu Proverb

When anger comes, wisdom goes.

Hindu Proverb

Whose stick, his buffalo.

Hindu Proverb

Hindustani Proverbs

Bathe early every day and sickness will avoid you.

Hindustani Proverb

Dictators ride to and fro upon tigers which they dare not dismount.

Hindustani Proverb

Diet cures more than the lancet.

Hindustani Proverb

Give your ears to words but do not give your words to ears.

Hindustani Proverb

It is a cart if it goes well, otherwise it is but timber.

Hindustani Proverb

No sooner have you spoken than what you have said becomes the property of another.

Hindustani Proverb

Once out of the throat it spreads over the world.

Hindustani Proverb

The adult looks to deeds, the child to love.

Hindustani Proverb

Indian Proverbs

A bandicoot is lovely to his parents; a mule is pretty to its mate.

Indian Proverb

A fly, a harlot, a beggar, a rat, and gusty wind; the village-boss and the tax collector — these seven are always annoying to others.

Indian Proverb

A fool who knows he is a fool has a little intelligence, but a fool that thanks he is intelligent is really a fool.

Indian Proverb

A good well-lived today makes every yesterday a dream of good future, and every morning is a vision of hope.

Indian Proverb

A house without a child is like a tomb.

Indian Proverb

A man in this world without learning is a beast of the field.

Indian Proverb

A person who misses a chance and the monkey who misses its branch can't be saved.

Indian Proverb

A sin that is confessed is less heavy to bear.

Indian Proverb

A thief thinks everybody steals.

Indian Proverb

A woman talks to one man, looks at another, and thinks about a third.

Indian Proverb

Abstinence is the best medicine.

Indian Proverb

Agriculture is best, enterprise is acceptable, but avoid being on a fixed wage.

Indian Proverb

Agreement with two people, lamentation with three.

Indian Proverb

All we can hold in our cold dead hands is what we have given away.

Indian Proverb

Among the blind, the squint rules.

> Indian Proverb

Anger ends in cruelty.

> Indian Proverb

Anger has no eyes.

> Indian Proverb

As day breaks, the glowworms say "We've lit up the world!"

> Indian Proverb

As people go their own way, destiny goes with them.

> Indian Proverb

As the spokes of a wheel are attached to the hub, so all things are attached to life.

> Indian Proverb

Before you build a house you have to dig a pit.

> Indian Proverb

Blaming your faults on your nature does not change the nature of your faults.

> Indian Proverb

Blow the wind ne'er so fast, it will lower at last.

Indian Proverb

By slitting the ears and cutting the tail, a dog is still a dog, not a horse, not an ass.

Indian Proverb

Call on God, but row away from the rocks.

Indian Proverb

Clouds that thunder seldom rain.

Indian Proverb

Do not blame God for having created the tiger, but thank him for not having given it wings.

Indian Proverb

Don't bargain for fish which are still in the water.

Indian Proverb

Drops join to make a stream; ears combine to make a crop.

Indian Proverb

Eat fire and your mouth burn; live on credit and your pride will burn.

Indian Proverb

Eating while seated makes one of large size; eating while standing makes one strong.

Indian Proverb

Eleven persons take eleven paths.

Indian Proverb

Empty vessels make much noise.

Indian Proverb

Even a cat is a lion in her own lair.

Indian Proverb

Even an elephant can slip.

Indian Proverb

Even the devil needs a friend.

Indian Proverb

Fate and self-help share equally in shaping our destiny.

Indian Proverb

Fear is the fever of life.

Indian Proverb

Garlic is as good as ten mothers.

Indian Proverb

Giving advice to a stupid man is like giving salt to a squirrel.

Indian Proverb

Great anger is more destructive than the sword.

Indian Proverb

He who allows his day to pass without practicing generosity and enjoying life's pleasures is like a blacksmith's bellows: he breathes but does not live.

Indian Proverb

He who loves the truth has many enemies.

Indian Proverb

I bought the nettle, sowed the nettle, and then the nettle stung me.

Indian Proverb

I have lanced many boils, but none has pained like my own.

Indian Proverb

If a man's heart be impure, all things will appear hostile to him.

Indian Proverb

If they don't exchange a few words, father and son will never know one another.

Indian Proverb

If you are buying a cow, make sure that the price of the tail is included.

Indian Proverb

If you forsake a certainty and depend on an uncertainty, you will lose both the certainty and the uncertainty.

Indian Proverb

If you have planted a tree you must water it too.

Indian Proverb

It is better to be blind than to see things from only one point of view.

Indian Proverb

Justice is better than admiration.

Indian Proverb

Keep five yards from a carriage, ten yards from a horse, and a hundred yards from an elephant; but the distance one should keep from a wicked man cannot be measured.

Indian Proverb

Kind words conquer.

Indian Proverb

Large desire is endless poverty.

Indian Proverb

Learn about the future by looking at the past.

Indian Proverb

Life is a bridge. Cross over it, but build no house on it.

Indian Proverb

Life is like a lamp flame; it needs a little oil now and then.

Indian Proverb

Life is not a continuum of pleasant choices, but of inevitable problems that call for strength, determination, and hard work.

Indian Proverb

Love is a crocodile in the river of desire.

Indian Proverb

Never strike your wife, even with a flower.

Indian Proverb

No strength within, no respect without.

Indian Proverb

No sweet without sweat.

Indian Proverb

Nonviolence is the supreme law of life.

Indian Proverb

One spark is enough to burn down the whole forest.

Indian Proverb

Only mad dogs and Englishmen go out in the noonday sun.

Indian Proverb

Only the cure you believe in cures.

Indian Proverb

Our faults provide opportunities for others.

Indian Proverb

Our shadow will follow us.

Indian Proverb

Popular agitation leads to justices.

Indian Proverb

Separation secures manifest friendship.

Indian Proverb

September blow soft till the fruit's in the loft.

Indian Proverb

Sit on the bank of a river and wait: Your enemy's corpse will soon float by.

Indian Proverb

Snakes turn milk into poison.

Indian Proverb

Sorrow for the death of a father lasts six months; sorrow for a mother, a year; sorrow for a wife, until another wife; sorrow for a son, forever.

Indian Proverb

Speak like a parrot; meditate like a swan; chew like a goat; and bathe like an elephant.

Indian Proverb

Take a close look at today, because yesterday is but a dream and tomorrow is barely a vision.

Indian Proverb

The beggar is not afraid of the drawbacks of being rich.

Indian Proverb

The beggar who asks for crumbs gets more than the one who asks for bread.

Indian Proverb

The danger past, and God forgotten.

Indian Proverb

The diamond in your belly sparkles on your face.

Indian Proverb

The fall is nobody's sire.

Indian Proverb

The greatest hero is one who has control over his desires.

Indian Proverb

The one who teaches is the giver of eyes.

Indian Proverb

The three great mysteries: air to a bird, water to a fish, mankind to himself.

Indian Proverb

The tip of a finer cannot be touched by itself.

Indian Proverb

The water from the river becomes salty when it reaches the ocean.

Indian Proverb

The way to overcome the angry man is with gentleness, the evil man with goodness, the miser with generosity, and the liar with truth.

Indian Proverb

The weakest go to the wall.

Indian Proverb

The wind sweeps the road clean.

Indian Proverb

The wise must be respected, even when the advice they give is not suitable.

Indian Proverb

There are none so deaf as those who will not hear advice.

Indian Proverb

There are three things that refresh the heart and reduce your grief: water, flowers, and a beautiful woman.

Indian Proverb

They know not their own defects who search for the defects of others.

Indian Proverb

They who give have all things; they who withhold have nothing.

Indian Proverb

This is wisdom you cannot learn; you must become it.

Indian Proverb

Those who hunt deer sometimes raise tigers.

Indian Proverb

To quarrel with a man of good speech is better than to converse with a man who does not speak well.

Indian Proverb

To the mediocre, mediocrity appears great.

Indian Proverb

Truth has but one color, a lie has many.

Indian Proverb

Under the mountains is silver and gold, but under the night sky hunger and cold.

Indian Proverb

Walking slowly, even the donkey will reach Lhasa.

Indian Proverb

War is to men, childbirth is to women.

Indian Proverb

We can't change the direction of the wind, but we can adjust the sails.

Indian Proverb

What was hard to bear is sweet to remember.

Indian Proverb

You can never enter the same river twice.

Indian Proverb

You can often find in rivers what you cannot find in oceans.

Indian Proverb

You can only lean against that which resists.

Indian Proverb

You cannot cook one half of the chicken and leave the other lay eggs.

Indian Proverb

You may look up for inspiration or look down in desperation but do not look sideways for information.

Indian Proverb

You sometimes forget the harm that was done to you, but never the harm you have done to others.

Indian Proverb

Indonesian Proverbs

Different fields, different grasshoppers; different seas, different fish.

Indonesian Proverb

Different men have different opinions; some like apples, some onions.

Indonesian Proverb

If you enter a goat stable, bleat; if you enter a water buffalo stable, bellow.

Indonesian Proverb

Nothing is difficult if you are used to it.

Indonesian Proverb

Rippling water shows lack of depth.

Indonesian Proverb

The shadow should be the same length as the body.

Indonesian Proverb

The shallower the brook, the more it babbles.

Indonesian Proverb

Islamic Proverb

To you your religion and to me my religion.

Islamic Proverb

Japanese Proverbs

A fog cannot be dispelled by a fan.

Japanese Proverb

A good husband is healthy and absent.

Japanese Proverb

A good Jack makes a good Jill.

Japanese Proverb

A good sword is the one left in its scabbard.

Japanese Proverb

A man in love mistakes a pimple for a dimple.

Japanese Proverb

A mended lid to a cracked pan.

Japanese Proverb

A merchant's happiness hangs upon chance, winds, and waves.

Japanese Proverb

A merry companion on the road is as good as a nag.

Japanese Proverb

The Book of Asian Proverbs

A pig used to dirt turns its nose up at rice.

Japanese Proverb

A round egg can be made square according to how you cut it; words would be harsh according to how you speak them.

Japanese Proverb

A single arrow is easily broken, but not ten in a bundle.

Japanese Proverb

A tongue three inches long can kill a man six feet tall.

Japanese Proverb

A wise hawk hides its claws.

Japanese Proverb

Adversity is the foundation of virtue.

Japanese Proverb

Affinity is a mysterious thing, but it is spicy!

Japanese Proverb

After victory, tighten your helmet chord.

Japanese Proverb

All married women are not wives.

> Japanese Proverb

An accomplishment sticks to a person.

> Japanese Proverb

An excess of courtesy is discourtesy.

> Japanese Proverb

Bad and good are intertwined like rope.

> Japanese Proverb

Beginning is easy. Continuing is hard.

> Japanese Proverb

Better go without medicine than call in an unskilled physician.

> Japanese Proverb

Better than a thousand days of diligent study is one day with a great teacher.

> Japanese Proverb

Darkness reigns at the foot of the lighthouse.

> Japanese Proverb

Deceive the rich and powerful if you will, but don't insult them.

Japanese Proverb

Deceiving a deceiver is no knavery.

Japanese Proverb

Difficulties make you a jewel.

Japanese Proverb

Don't stay long when the husband is not at home.

Japanese Proverb

Dumplings are better than flowers.

Japanese Proverb

Duty knows no family.

Japanese Proverb

Even a fool has one talent.

Japanese Proverb

Even a sheet of paper has two sides.

Japanese Proverb

Even a thief takes ten years to learn his trade.

Japanese Proverb

Even monkeys fall from trees.

Japanese Proverb

Every worm to his taste.

Japanese Proverb

Fall seven times, stand up eight.

Japanese Proverb

Fast Ripe, Fast Rotten.

Japanese Proverb

First the man takes a drink, then the drink takes a drink, then the drink takes the man.

Japanese Proverb

First things first.

Japanese Proverb

Follow the villagers when you are in the new village.

Japanese Proverb

Forgiving the unrepentant is like drawing pictures on water.

Japanese Proverb

Getting money is like digging with a needle. Spending it is like water soaking into the sand.

Japanese Proverb

Had the pheasant not screamed, it wouldn't have been shot.

Japanese Proverb

He is poor who does not feel content.

Japanese Proverb

He who buys what he needs not, sells what he needs.

Japanese Proverb

He who smiles rather than rages is always the stronger.

Japanese Proverb

He who would go a hundred miles should consider ninety-nine as halfway.

Japanese Proverb

If a man be great, even his dog will wear a proud look.

Japanese Proverb

If a man deceive me once, shame on him; if he deceive me twice, shame on me.

Japanese Proverb

If man has no tea in him, he is incapable of understanding truth and beauty.

Japanese Proverb

If money be not thy servant, it will be thy master.

Japanese Proverb

If my shirt knew my design, I'd burn it.

Japanese Proverb

If neither animal nor vegetable you be, then mineral you are.

Japanese Proverb

If one man praises you, a thousand will repeat the praise.

Japanese Proverb

If the father is a frog, the son will be a frog.

Japanese Proverb

If you believe everything you read, better not read.

Japanese Proverb

If you look up, there are no limits.

Japanese Proverb

If you never climb Mt. Fuji, you're a fool; and if you climb it more than once, you're a crazy fool.

Japanese Proverb

If you see Mt. Fuji, a hawk, and an eggplant on New Year's Day, you will be forever blessed.

Japanese Proverb

If you understand everything, you must be misinformed.

Japanese Proverb

If you want a thing done well, do it yourself.

Japanese Proverb

If you wish to learn the highest truths, begin with the alphabet.

Japanese Proverb

It is a beggar's pride that he is not a thief.

Japanese Proverb

It is a blessing in disguise.

Japanese Proverb

Knowledge without wisdom is a load of books on the back of an ass.

Japanese Proverb

Laughter cannot bring back what anger has driven away.

Japanese Proverb

Laughter is the hiccup of a fool.

Japanese Proverb

Let each child follow his own path even if it takes him to the edge of a cliff.

Japanese Proverb

Let the past drift away with the water.

Japanese Proverb

Life is for one generation; a good name is forever.

Japanese Proverb

Life without endeavor is like entering a jewel-mine and coming out with empty hands.

Japanese Proverb

Life's not all beer and skittles.

Japanese Proverb

The Book of Asian Proverbs

Luck is like having a rice dumpling fly into your mouth.

Japanese Proverb

Money grows on the tree of persistence.

Japanese Proverb

Money has no smell.

Japanese Proverb

My skirt with tears is always wet: I have forgotten to forget.

Japanese Proverb

My son is my son till he gets him a wife, but my daughter's my daughter all the days of her life.

Japanese Proverb

Never rely on the glory of the morning or the smiles of your mother-in-law.

Japanese Proverb

Never trust the advice of a man in difficulty.

Japanese Proverb

No branch is better than its trunk.

Japanese Proverb

One dog yelping at nothing will set ten thousand straining at their collars.

> Japanese Proverb

One kind word can warm three winter months.

> Japanese Proverb

One kindness is the price of another.

> Japanese Proverb

One written word is worth a thousand pieces of gold.

> Japanese Proverb

Only lawyers and painters can turn white to black.

> Japanese Proverb

Passionate love and a cough cannot be concealed.

> Japanese Proverb

Silence surpasses speech.

> Japanese Proverb

Silent worms dig holes in the walls.

> Japanese Proverb

Sleeping people can't fall down.

Japanese Proverb

Some people like to make of life a garden, and to walk only within its paths.

Japanese Proverb

The absent get further off every day.

Japanese Proverb

The bamboo that bends is stronger than the oak that resists.

Japanese Proverb

The beginning of sin is sweet; its end is bitter.

Japanese Proverb

The crow that mimics a cormorant is drowned.

Japanese Proverb

The day you decide to do it is your lucky day.

Japanese Proverb

The fallen blossom doesn't return to the branch.

Japanese Proverb

The go-between wears out a thousand sandals.

Japanese Proverb

The inarticulate speak longest.

Japanese Proverb

The jellyfish never dances with the shrimp.

Japanese Proverb

The mouth is the door of evil.

Japanese Proverb

The nail that sticks its head up is the one that gets hit.

Japanese Proverb

The nail that sticks out is hammered down.

Japanese Proverb

The pebble in the brook secretly thinks itself a precious stone.

Japanese Proverb

The reputation of a thousand years may be determined by the conduct of one hour.

Japanese Proverb

The reverse side also has a reverse side.

Japanese Proverb

The slug always leaves a trail to follow.

Japanese Proverb

The smaller the margin, the greater the turnover.

Japanese Proverb

The smallest good deed is better than the grandest good intention.

Japanese Proverb

The strong will protect the weak and, in return, the weak will serve the strong.

Japanese Proverb

The tongue is more to be feared than the sword.

Japanese Proverb

The winds may fell the massive oak, but bamboo, bent even to the ground, will spring upright after the passage of the storm.

Japanese Proverb

There is always light behind the clouds.

Japanese Proverb

There is no flower that remains red for ten days, and no power that lasts for ten years.

Japanese Proverb

Tigers die and leave their skins; people die and leave their names.

Japanese Proverb

Time spent laughing is time spent with the gods.

Japanese Proverb

To teach is also to learn.

Japanese Proverb

To wait for luck is the same as waiting for death.

Japanese Proverb

Transactions in Hell also depend upon money.

Japanese Proverb

True words are not always pretty; pretty words are not always true.

Japanese Proverb

You cannot see the whole sky through a bamboo tube.

Japanese Proverb

Unless you enter the tiger's den you cannot take the cubs.

Japanese Proverb

Virtue is not knowing but doing.

Japanese Proverb

Vision without action is a daydream. Action without vision is a nightmare.

Japanese Proverb

Walls have ears, bottles have mouths.

Japanese Proverb

Walls have ears, paper sliding doors have eyes.

Japanese Proverb

We are no more than candles burning in the wind.

Japanese Proverb

We learn little from victory, much from defeat.

Japanese Proverb

We're fools whether we dance or not, so we might as well dance.

Japanese Proverb

We've arrived, and to prove it we're here.

Japanese Proverb

The Book of Asian Proverbs

When the character of a man is not clear to you, look at his friends.

Japanese Proverb

When the time comes, even a rat becomes a tiger.

Japanese Proverb

When your companions get drunk and fight, Take up your hat, and wish them good night.

Japanese Proverb

When you're thirsty it's too late to think about digging a well.

Japanese Proverb

While we consider when to begin, it becomes too late.

Japanese Proverb

Who travels for love finds a thousand miles not longer than one.

Japanese Proverb

Wisdom and virtue are like the two wheels of a cart.

Japanese Proverb

Work the fields on a fine day, study on a rainy day.

Japanese Proverb

Kannada Proverb

A colt you may break, but an old horse you never can.

Kannada Proverb

Kashmiri Proverbs

Agreement with two people, lamentation with three.

Kashmiri Proverb

Eleven persons take eleven paths.

Kashmiri Proverb

Empty vessels make much noise.

Kashmiri Proverb

Giving advice to a stupid man is like giving salt to a squirrel.

Kashmiri Proverb

I bought the nettle, sowed the nettle, and then the nettle stung me.

Kashmiri Proverb

Ignorance is the peace of life.

Kashmiri Proverb

Life is like a lamp flame; it needs a little oil now and then.

Kashmiri Proverb

No strength within, no respect without.

Kashmiri Proverb

No sunshine but hath some shadow.

Kashmiri Proverb

No sweet without sweat.

Kashmiri Proverb

O daughter, I'm telling you. O daughter-in-law, listen to it.

Kashmiri Proverb

One and one are sometimes eleven.

Kashmiri Proverb

One man can burn water, whereas another cannot even burn oil.

Kashmiri Proverb

One man cut the barrage, and a thousand people fell into the river.

Kashmiri Proverb

One man's beard is on fire, and another man warms his hands on it.

Kashmiri Proverb

One man's breath's another man's death.

Kashmiri Proverb

Saving mustard seeds in hand, while a watermelon escapes.

> Kashmiri Proverb

Service is greatness.

> Kashmiri Proverb

The customers are known to the shopkeepers.

> Kashmiri Proverb

The fall is nobody's sire.

> Kashmiri Proverb

The gardener had not yet dug out the radish, when the beggar held the alms-bowl in front of him.

> Kashmiri Proverb

When pumpkins are watered, brinjals also get watered.

> Kashmiri Proverb

When rogues fall out, honest men come by their own.

> Kashmiri Proverb

Where there is sunshine, there is also shade.

> Kashmiri Proverb

Korean Proverbs

A kitchen knife cannot carve its own handle.

Korean Proverb

A nobleman's calf does not know how a butcher kills.

Korean Proverb

Carve the peg by looking at the hole.

Korean Proverb

Cast no dirt into the well that gives you water.

Korean Proverb

Cast not pearls to swine.

Korean Proverb

Catch not at the shadow, and lose the substance.

Korean Proverb

Cross even a stone bridge after you've tested it.

Korean Proverb

Even a fish wouldn't get into trouble if it kept its mouth shut.

Korean Proverb

Even children of the same mother look different.

Korean Proverb

He is not strong and powerful who throws people down, but he is strong who withholds himself from anger.

Korean Proverb

If there is a rich man in the area three villages are ruined.

Korean Proverb

If you starve for three days, there is no thought that does not invade your imagination.

Korean Proverb

Man's affairs are evaluated only after his coffin is closed.

Korean Proverb

Man's extremity, God's opportunity.

Korean Proverb

Put off for one day and ten days will pass.

Korean Proverb

The bad ploughman quarrels with his ox.

Korean Proverb

The deeper the waters are, the more still they run.

Korean Proverb

Where there are no tigers, a wildcat is very self-important.

Korean Proverb

Words have no wings but they can fly a thousand miles.

Korean Proverb

You will hate a beautiful song if you sing it often.

Korean Proverb

Laotian Proverbs

Flee from the elephant and meet the tiger; Flee the tiger and meet a crocodile.

Laotian Proverb

If you like things easy, you'll have difficulties; if you like problems, you'll succeed.

Laotian Proverb

Live with vultures, become a vulture; live with crows, become a crow.

Laotian Proverb

Some are brave in the village but cowards in the forest.

Laotian Proverb

Ten mouths speaking are not as good as seeing with one's own eyes; Ten eyes that see are not as good as what one has in one's hand.

Laotian Proverb

The cat is absent and the mice dance.

Laotian Proverb

To judge an elephant, look at its tail; To judge a girl, look at her mother.

Laotian Proverb

When the water level rises, the fish eat the ants.

Laotian Proverb

When you enter the city of people with one eye closed, you must also close one eye.

Laotian Proverb

Malay Proverbs

A fool is like the big drum that beats fast but does not realize its hollowness.

Malay Proverb

An ox with long horns, even if he does not butt, will be accused of butting.

Malay Proverb

An unasked excuse infers transgression.

Malay Proverb

Ants die in sugar.

Malay Proverb

Clapping with the right hand only will not produce a noise.

Malay Proverb

Do not measure another man's coat on your body.

Malaya Proverb

Don't use an axe to embroider.

Malay Proverb

Fear to let fall a drop and you will spill the lot.

Malay Proverb

Feasting is the physician's harvest.

Malay Proverb

He who has learned to steal, must learn how to hang.

Malay Proverb

If there is no reason, why would the *tempua* bird nest on the low branches?

Malay Proverb

If you have, give; if you lack, seek.

Malay Proverb

One can pay back the loan of gold, but one dies forever in debt to those who are kind.

Malay Proverb

Smack a tray of water and you get to wash your face.

Malay Proverb

The body pays for a slip of the foot, and gold pays for a slip of the tongue.

Malay Proverb

The Book of Asian Proverbs

The existence of the sea means the existence of pirates.

> Malay Proverb

The more shoots, the more leaves.

> Malay Proverb

The more sorrow one encounters, the more joy one can contain.

> Malay Proverb

The turtle lays thousands of eggs without anyone knowing, but when the hen lays an egg the whole country is informed.

> Malay Proverb

To bend a bamboo, start when it is a shoot.

> Malay Proverb

When one holds a split bamboo, hold it firmly or it will cut your hand.

> Malay Proverb

Where there is sugar, there are bound to be ants.

> Malay Proverb

You can't get at the precious sago without first breaking the bark.

Malay Proverb

Nepal Proverb

Wealth is both an enemy and a friend.

Nepal Proverb

Okinawan Proverbs

Be as hard as the world requires you to be, and as soft as the world allows you to be.

Okinawan Proverb

One cannot live in this world without the support of others.

Okinawan Proverb

The Book of Asian Proverbs

Persian Proverbs

A bad wound heals but a bad word doesn't.

Persian Proverb

A broken hand works, but not a broken heart.

Persian Proverb

A broken sleeve holdeth the arm back.

Persian Proverb

A stone thrown at the right time is better than gold given at the wrong time.

Persian Proverb

A thief is a king till he's caught.

Persian Proverb

A thief knows a thief as a wolf knows a wolf.

Persian Proverb

Be a lion at home and a fox abroad.

Persian Proverb

By a sweet tongue and kindness, you can drag an elephant with a hair.

Persian Proverb

Courteous men learn courtesy from the discourteous.

Persian Proverb

Courtesy is cumbersome to them that ken it not.

Persian Proverb

Courtesy on one side can never last long.

Persian Proverb

Do men gather grapes of thorns, or figs of thistles?

Persian Proverb

Do well the little things now; so shall great things come to thee by and by asking to be done.

Persian Proverb

Epigrams succeed where epics fail.

Persian Proverb

Every man goes down to his death bearing in his hands only that which he has given away.

Persian Proverb

Go and wake up your luck.

Persian Proverb

Go as far as you can see, and when you get there you'll see further.

Persian Proverb

Go further and fare worse.

Persian Proverb

He gives a party with bath water.

Persian Proverb

He gives him roast meat and beats him with the spit.

Persian Proverb

He who want a rose must respect the thorn.

Persian Proverb

He who wants content can't find an easy chair.

Persian Proverb

I used to feel sorry for myself because I had no shoes until I met a man who was dead.

Persian Proverb

If a man would live in peace, he should be blind, deaf, and dumb.

Persian Proverb

If fortune turns against you, even jelly breaks your tooth.

Persian Proverb

If one has to jump a stream and knows how wide it is, he will not jump. If he does not know how wide it is, he will jump, and six times out of ten he will make it.

Persian Proverb

If the teacher be corrupt, the world will be corrupt.

Persian Proverb

Luck is infatuated with the efficient.

Persian Proverb

No lamp burns till morning.

Persian Proverb

One pound of learning requires ten pounds of common sense to apply it.

Persian Proverb

Taking the first step with the good thought, the second with the good word, and the third with the good deed, I enter paradise.

Persian Proverb

The best memory is that which forgets nothing but injuries. Write kindness in marble and write injuries in the dust.

Persian Proverb

The best mode of instruction is to practice what we preach.

Persian Proverb

The best of friends must part.

Persian Proverb

The best of men are but men at best.

Persian Proverb

The blind man is laughing at the bald head.

Persian Proverb

The doctor must heal his own bald head.

Persian Proverb

The loveliest of faces are to be seen by moonlight, when one sees half with the eye and half with the fancy.

Persian Proverb

The wise man sits on the hole in his carpet.

Persian Proverb

Thinking is the essence of wisdom.

Persian Proverb

Use your enemy's hand to catch a snake.

Persian Proverb

Walls have mice and mice have ears.

Persian Proverb

What is brought by the wind will be carried away by the wind.

Persian Proverb

Whatever is in the heart will come up to the tongue.

Persian Proverb

Whatever you sow, you reap.

Persian Proverb

When the cat and mouse agree, the grocer is ruined.

Persian Proverb

Who does not beat his own child will later beat his own breast.

Persian Proverb

You can't pick up two melons with one hand.

Persian Proverb

You can't please everyone.

Persian Proverb

You can't push on a rope.

Persian Proverb

You can't put an old head on young shoulders.

Persian Proverb

You can't put new wine in old bottles.

Persian Proverb

You can't squeeze blood from a rock.

Persian Proverb

You can't take blood from a stone.

Persian Proverb

Philippine Proverbs

A clear conscience is far more valuable than money.

Philippine Proverb

A fly that lands on a carabao feels itself to be higher that the carabao.

Philippine Proverb

Alertness and courage are life's shield.

Philippine Proverb

Don't empty the water jar until the rain falls.

Philippine Proverb

Don't trust in fortune until you are in heaven.

Philippine Proverb

He who boasts of his accomplishments will heap ridicule on himself.

Philippine Proverb

He who gives alms to the poor faces heaven.

Philippine Proverb

It is advantageous to follow advice, for you will succeed in life.

Philippine Proverb

Loyalty is more valuable than diamonds.

Philippine Proverb

People who do not break things first will never learn to create anything.

Philippine Proverb

The pain of the little finger is felt by the whole body.

Philippine Proverb

Punjabi Proverb

If you live in the river you should make friends with the crocodile.

Punjabi Proverb

Sanskrit Proverb

Yesterday is a dream, tomorrow but a vision. But today well lived makes every yesterday a dream of happiness, and every tomorrow a vision of hope. Look well, therefore to this day.

Sanskrit Proverb

Singhalese Proverbs

By committing foolish acts, one learns wisdom.

> Singhalese Proverb

Eat coconuts while you have teeth.

> Singhalese Proverb

Even the fall of a dancer is a somersault.

> Singhalese Proverb

If you had teeth of steel, you could eat iron coconuts.

> Singhalese Proverb

Sufi Proverb

Before you speak, let your words pass through three gates. At the first ask, "Is it true?" At the second ask, "Is it necessary?" At the third ask, "Is it kind?"

> Sufi Proverb

Tamil Proverbs

Abstinence is the best medicine.

Tamil Proverb

Anger ends in cruelty.

Tamil Proverb

Kind words conquer.

Tamil Proverb

Popular agitation leads to justice.

Tamil Proverb

Taoist Proverbs

A truly good person functions without ulterior motives.

Taoist Proverb

Always the teacher, always the student.

Taoist Proverb

Do not look only at your self and you will see much.

Taoist Proverb

If you realize that you have enough, you are truly rich.

Taoist Proverb

No one can see their reflection in running water. It is only in still water that we can see.

Taoist Proverb

Overcoming others requires force, overcoming yourself requires strength.

Taoist Proverb

The journey is the reward.

Taoist Proverb

The world is lost to those who try to win it.

Taoist Proverb

There are no coincidences.

Taoist Proverb

Those who use weapons will be harmed by them.

Taoist Proverb

To act sincerely with the insincere is dangerous.

Taoist Proverb

Thai Proverbs

Bald people can always find a comb.

Thai Proverb

Life is so short we must move very slowly.

Thai Proverb

Wait until the tree has fallen before you jump over it.

Thai Proverb

With one stump you cannot make a good fire.

Thai Proverb

Tibetan Proverbs

A child without education is like a bird without wings.

Tibetan Proverb

A father deserted by a wise son is like being caught in a shower without a felt.

Tibetan Proverb

A man is wealthy when he knows that he has enough.

Tibetan Proverb

Eat according to the limits of your provisions; walk according to the length of your step.

Tibetan Proverb

Even if you have failed at something nine times, you have still given it effort nine times.

Tibetan Proverb

Excellent people are honored wherever they go.

Tibetan Proverb

Goodness speaks in a whisper, evil shouts.

Tibetan Proverb

The wise understand by themselves, fools follow the reports of others.

Tibetan Proverb

The wish is father to the thought.

Tibetan Proverb

When with yourself watch your thoughts. When with others watch your speech.

Tibetan Proverb

Vietnamese Proverbs

A day of traveling will bring a basketful of learning.

Vietnamese Proverb

A fair face may hide a foul heart.

Vietnamese Proverb

All cats are grey in the dark.

Vietnamese Proverb

All chili is hot; all women are jealous.

Vietnamese Proverb

Because the caterpillar exists, there exists also a bird to eat it.

Vietnamese Proverb

Better a lean peace than a fat victory.

Vietnamese Proverb

Catch the bear before you sell his skin.

Vietnamese Proverb

Eat as small as a cat.

Vietnamese Proverb

Hunger brings the wolf to the fold.

Vietnamese Proverb

If a father eats a lot of salt, his children will be thirsty.

Vietnamese Proverb

If you want to gather a lot of knowledge, act as if you are ignorant.

Vietnamese Proverb

Many a good father has but a bad son.

Vietnamese Proverb

Never forget benefits done you, regardless how small.

Vietnamese Proverb

One often gets what one disdains.

Vietnamese Proverb

Once the fish is caught, the net is let aside.

Vietnamese Proverb

People live with their own idiosyncrasies and die of their own illnesses.

Vietnamese Proverb

The higher you climb, the heavier you fall.

Vietnamese Proverb

The husband eats turtle soup, the wife eats spring roll.

Vietnamese Proverb

The rich eat. The poor smoke.

Vietnamese Proverb

The rich worry over their money, the poor over their bread.

Vietnamese Proverb

There is one fish in the pond, and ten anglers on the bank.

Vietnamese Proverb

Venture all; see what fate brings.

Vietnamese Proverb

When eating a fruit, think of the person who planted the tree.

Vietnamese Proverb

When the tree falls, any child can climb it.

Vietnamese Proverb

Zen Proverbs

Be master of mind rather than mastered by mind.

> Zen Proverb

Better to see the face than to hear the name.

> Zen Proverb

Better to sit all night than to go to bed with a dragon.

> Zen Proverb

Better to struggle with a sick jackass than carry the wood by yourself.

> Zen Proverb

Coming or going, always at home.

> Zen Proverb

Do not seek the truth, only cease to cherish your opinions.

> Zen Proverb

From the withered tree, a flower blooms.

> Zen Proverb

How you do one thing is how you do everything.

Zen Proverb

If you understand, things are just as they are; if you do not understand, things are just as they are.

Zen Proverb

If we are facing in the right direction, all we have to do is keep on walking.

Zen Proverb

In studying the way, realizing it is hard. Once you have realized it, preserving it is hard. When you can preserve it, putting it into practice is hard.

Zen Proverb

Kites harness the force of the wind. They express our intent, but they cannot change the wind.

Zen Proverb

Knock on the sky and listen to the sound!

Zen Proverb

Man stands in his own shadow and wonders why it's dark.

Zen Proverb

Miso with the smell of miso is not good miso. Enlightenment with the smell of enlightenment is not the real enlightenment.

Zen Proverb

My barn having burned down, I can now see the moon.

Zen Proverb

No snowflake ever falls in the wrong place.

Zen Proverb

Only when you can be extremely pliable and soft can you be extremely hard and strong.

Zen Proverb

Sitting quietly, doing nothing, spring comes, and the grass grows by itself.

Zen Proverb

The fruit drops when it is ripe.

Zen Proverb

The infinite is in the finite of every instant.

Zen Proverb

The man who's drunk water knows if it's cool or warm.

Zen Proverb

The most difficult battle you will ever face is the battle within yourself.

Zen Proverb

The obstacle is the path.

Zen Proverb

Unformed people delight in the gaudy and in novelty. Cooked people delight in the ordinary.

Zen Proverb

When the source is deep, the stream is long.

Zen Proverb

When you reach the top, keep climbing.

Zen Proverb

About the Author

Steven Howard
Global Leadership Development and Facilitation
Leadership Coach | Keynote Speaker

Steven Howard specializes in creating and delivering Leadership Development curriculum for frontline leaders, mid-level leaders, senior leaders and high-potential leaders.

An author with 36 years of international senior sales, marketing, and leadership experience, his corporate career covered a wide variety of fields and experiences, including Regional Marketing Director for Texas Instruments Asia-Pacific, South Asia & ASEAN Regional Director for TIME Magazine, Global Account Director at BBDO Advertising handling an international airline account, and VP Marketing for Citibank's Consumer Banking Group.

Since 1988 he has delivered leadership development training programs in the U.S., Asia, Australia, Africa, Canada, and Europe to numerous organizations, including Citicorp, Covidien, DBS Bank, Deutsche Bank, DuPont Lycra, Esso Productions, ExxonMobil, Hewlett Packard Enterprise,

Micron Technology, Motorola Solutions, SapientNitro, Standard Chartered Bank, and many others.

He has been a member of the training faculty at MasterCard University Asia/Pacific, the Citibank Asia-Pacific Banking Institute, and Forum Corporation. He brings a truly international, cross-cultural perspective to his leadership development programs, having lived in the USA for 26 years, in Singapore for 21 years and in Australia for 12 years.

In addition to his leadership facilitation work Steven has served on several Boards in both the private and non-profit sectors. He has also chaired a strategic advisory group for a local government entity and a national sporting organization that is a member of the Australian Olympic Committee.

Steven is the author of 16 marketing, management, and leadership books and is the editor of three professional and personal development books in the *Project You* series.

His books are:

Corporate Image Management: *A Marketing Discipline*

Powerful Marketing Minutes: *50 Ways to Develop Market Leadership*

MORE Powerful Marketing Minutes: *50 New Ways to Develop Market Leadership*

The Book of Asian Proverbs

Asian Words of Wisdom

Asian Words of Knowledge

Essential Asian Words of Wisdom

Pillars of Growth: *Strategies for Leading Sustainable Growth* (co-author with three others)

Motivation Plus Marketing Equals Money (co-author with four others)

Marketing Words of Wisdom

The Best of the Monday Morning Marketing Memo

Powerful Marketing Memos

8 Keys To Becoming A Great Leader *(With Leadership Lessons and Tips from Gibbs, Yoda and Capt'n Jack Sparrow)*

Asian Words of Success

Asian Words of Meaning

Asian Words of Inspiration

The Book of Asian Proverbs

Contact Details

Email: steven@CalienteLeadership.com

Twitter: @stevenbhoward | @GreatLeadershp

LinkedIn: www.linkedin.com/in/stevenbhoward

Facebook: www.facebook.com/CalienteLeadership

Website: www.CalienteLeadership.com

Blog: CalienteLeadership.com/TheArtofGreatLeadershipBlog

Reader Reviews Appreciated

Thank you for reading this book. I hope you found some useful nuggets of wisdom that are relevant to your current and future life journey.

One favor to ask, if I may. Please take a few minutes, go to this book's page on Amazon and leave a reader review. Here's the link: http://www.amazon.com/dp/B01LM18XJA.

As an author I sincerely appreciate hearing from my readers. And I know other readers often use these reviews in determining whether a book might meet their needs.

Thank you in advance.

And best wishes for continued success in your professional and personal endeavors.

The Book of Asian Proverbs

Made in the USA
Middletown, DE
20 November 2023

43080709R00076

CONVERSATIONS
WITH DURITO

CONVERSATIONS WITH DURITO

Stories of the Zapatistas and Neoliberalism

Subcomandante Marcos

Edited and introduced by
ACCIÓN ZAPATISTA EDITORIAL COLLECTIVE

AUTONOMEDIA

Autonomedia
P. O. Box 568
Williamsburgh Station
Brooklyn, NY 11211-0568

www.autonomedia.org
email: info@autonomedia.org

ISBN 1-57027-118-6

Book design & typesetting: Kernow Craig
Thanks to Erika Biddle, Lea Johnson,
Carla Verea Hernandez, Ben Meyers

Printed in Canada

TABLE OF CONTENTS

STORIES FOR A SUFFOCATING NIGHT

STORIES FOR A SLEEPLESS SOLITUDE

STORIES OF VIGILANCE BY CANDLELIGHT

Preface

Since 1994 when they emerged as a political force in Chiapas, the Zapatista Army of National Liberation, or EZLN, has repeatedly addressed grassroots movements in Mexico and around the world about new forms of political action. Under an indigenous leadership, the Zapatista military commander and spokesperson Subcomandante Marcos has issued hundreds of communiqués that form a broad political discourse illuminated with poetry, humor, and storytelling.

Through the forty-four stories collected here, in which the beetle and quixotic knight-errant Don Durito de la Lacandona befriends and advises Subcomandante Marcos, we learn about the shifting political terrain on which the Zapatistas struggle and about their history as an organization and movement. The political analysis and strategy embodied in the Durito stories and in the communiqués in which they appear has engaged not only Zapatista supporters, but also the broader international movement against neoliberalism and capitalist globalization.

The idea for this book grew out of an earlier project that originated in Chiapas during the First Continental Encounter Against Neoliberalism and For Humanity in April 1996. Prompted by international solidarity discussions, that project assembled thirteen Durito stories in a chapbook quickly produced for circulation to those interested in learning more about the Zapatista rebellion. In 1998, as the number of Durito stories continued to grow, the Acción Zapatista Editorial Collective began work on this collection. Regrettably, the original intent to publish a bilingual volume was thwarted by the large and growing number of stories and the need to disseminate them as soon as possible. This compilation ends in 2002, but the Durito stories continue to appear regularly in the magazine *Rebeldía*.

While most other Durito collections have excerpted these stories from the communiqués in which they originally appeared, *Conversations With Durito* presents each one within the original Zapatista communiqué, presenting them not simply as stories, but as documents of particular moments in the Zapatista struggle. To further this understanding, we have supplemented the communiqués with a historical overview, brief introductions to each story, integrated footnotes and bibliographic resources. Where necessary, the footnotes include comments on translation, but primarily add critical political, historical, and cultural information.

Translation & Editing Notes

The stories of Durito are some of the most literary and complex EZLN communiqués. Their narratives combine political critique, satire, historical debate, literary seduction, and poetry, and regularly change register from elevated theoretical language to popular Mexican word play or *albures*, indigenous and foreign languages, archaic and peninsular Spanish, and Caló (a hybrid language spoken along the U.S.-Mexico border). They are a formidable challenge to translate.

Compiling and editing the stories into a cohesive collection also posed the challenge of crafting linguistic, stylistic, and narrative consistency. Most of the communiqués were originally disseminated through the Mexican newspaper *La Jornada* and then over the Internet. Most had previously been translated by various persons, usually in a matter of hours or days. Given the complexity of the task, our editing process consisted of two stages. Each member of the collective took responsibility for the initial edits of a story: either reviewing and revising an existing translation or creating a new one, and then adding preliminary footnotes. This stage was followed by subsequent collective edits that incorporated discussion of footnotes, additional research, and a line-by-line translation review.

We hope that our liberties with translation have made the text more fluid for the English reader while remaining true to the meaning of the original documents. On the one hand, we sought to avoid interpreting the text for the reader any more than is implicit in any translation. On the other, we sought to capture the literary resonance and multi-narrative that takes place across the communiqués. In attempting to make them as accessible and rewarding in English as they are in the original Spanish, we have sometimes rendered the Spanish into idiomatic phrases common to English speakers.

At times we chose to retain the use of some Spanish terms. In this, we were guided by three principles: 1) the terms had specific cultural and historical significance that was fairly widely known, e.g., *cacique*; 2) there was no direct equivalent in English, e.g., *pozole*; and 3) there were poetic, metaphorical or thematic elements that would be lost in translation. A notable example of the latter is the use of *vale* and *salud* at the end of each communiqué in that these terms have a number of possible translations and interpretations. Because their function as closings was clear, but the play and emphasis impossible to determine, we chose to leave both untranslated.

Gendered terms were also a subject of discussion, for example, the customary use of the male plural to signify both men and women. Letters are sometimes addressed to *"hermanos"* and at other times to *"hermanos y hermanas."* Our choice was to simply translate both as "brothers and sisters."

When confronted with text quoted by Subcomandante Marcos from other writers, we tried to locate existing standardized translations of the text and provide a citation for further investigation. However, there were some quotations for which we chose to provide our own translation, and others that we chose to leave in the language in which they appeared in the original.

Acknowledgements

This volume is a project of Acción Zapatista (AZ) of Austin, Texas, a small collective dedicated to providing information about the Zapatista movement, the low-intensity war against the Zapatistas, and the struggle against neoliberalism in Mexico. Acción Zapatista is also part of a network involved in the struggle against capitalist globalization. The AZ Editorial Collective consists of a core group of editors who share a history of studying and documenting the Zapatista struggle since its inception: Manuel Callahan, Harry Cleaver, Rebecca Gamez, Virginia Grise, Marco O. Iñiguez Alba, and Tamara Villarreal Ford.

We would like to thank those friends, colleagues, and comrades who provided invaluable assistance with translation, political analysis, cultural critique, and historical interpretation: Vik Bahl, Antonio Cabral, Elaine Cohen, Ignacio Corona, Gustavo Esteva, Adria Frizzi, H. Esperanza Garza, Catarina Giménez, Jorge González, Douglas Kellner, Frank Levine, Pancho McFarland, Anita Pantin, Alessandro Pascolini, Roberto Pérez Valenzuela, Marissa Ramírez, Bret Ratcliffe, John Ross, Stanton Sky, and Hugo Trujillo.

It would have been virtually impossible to complete our translation and footnote research without access to a substantial amount of information archived on the Internet. We made extensive use of the archives of *La Jornada* and the LANIC directory of Latin American websites. Other valuable resources have been those that emerged as a result of the Zapatista struggle. Two of the most comprehensive archives are Chiapas95, a project begun by Harry Cleaver and later supported by Acción Zapatista and other volunteers, and EZLN.org, begun by Justin Paulson, which hosts a comprehensive archive of Zapatista communiqués in Spanish. Other significant resources on the web include sites maintained by the FZLN, the Irish Mexico Group, CIEPAC, and SIPAZ.

The Collective wishes to acknowledge those who provided the first English versions of these communiqués for Internet circulation: Peter Haney, irlandesa, Monique Le Maitre, Leslie Lopez, Cecilia Rodríguez, Esther Rodríguez, Susana Saravia, Bonnie Schrack, Eduardo Vera and Robin Yeamans. All together, they provided translations for twenty-two of the stories. The majority of the later communiqués were first translated by irlandesa, some specifically for this volume, and the remaining translations were provided by members of the Collective.

The first Durito chapbook, prepared by Brendan Guilfoyle, Vik Bahl, and Manuel Callahan, featured drawings by John Dolley and other illustrations taken from the Internet. This book includes some of those drawings as well as photographs and illustrations from *La Jornada*, and original artwork from Beatriz Aurora, Alonso Álvarez de Araya, Erica Chappuis, John Dolley, Durito Productions, Arturo Kemchs, Rogelio Naranjo, Anita Pantin, Leah Robinson, Subcomandante Marcos, Pedro Valtierra, and unknown artists who posted their work to the Internet.

Finally, we are grateful to Jim Fleming of Autonomedia for his enthusiasm for this volume and his endless patience in waiting for this manuscript.

Historical Overview

"And you, what is your name?" I asked him.
"Nebuchadnezzar," he said, and continued, "but my friends call me Durito."
I thanked him for the courtesy and asked him what it was that he was studying.
"I'm studying neoliberalism and its strategy of domination for Latin America," he told me.
"And what *good* is that to a beetle?" I asked him.
And he replied, very annoyed, "What good is it?! I have to know how long your struggle is going to last, and whether or not you are going to win. Besides, a beetle should care enough to study the situation of the world in which it lives, don't you think, Captain?"

Don Durito of the Lacandon Jungle — a knight-errant beetle from the Southern Mexican state of Chiapas — first became known to the world in the spring of 1994 through the writings of Subcomandante Marcos, a spokesperson for the Zapatista Army of National Liberation, or EZLN (Ejército Zapatista de Liberación Nacional). The EZLN itself emerged suddenly into public view on January 1st of that year when, as the armed wing of an indigenous uprising, it took over several towns and declared war on the Mexican government (First Declaration of the Lacandon Jungle).

Durito's Appearance in a Turbulent Year

When the Zapatista rebellion broke out, the Mexican government responded violently with some 15,000 troops, torture, summary executions, and general repression. But as EZLN communiqués carrying the Zapatista message reached the world and observer reports of state brutality multiplied, hundreds of thousands of people in Mexico and other countries rallied to the Zapatista cause, demanding that the government negotiate with the just demands of the rebels instead of responding with brutal force. As a result, the government was forced to declare a ceasefire, to pull back the troops and enter into negotiations.

The first negotiations began on February 21, 1994 and were held in the Catholic cathedral in San Cristóbal de las Casas, the old colonial capital of the state and a contemporary tourist center. Bishop Samuel Ruiz García of the diocese of San Cristóbal mediated negotiations between the ski-masked Zapatistas and government bureaucrats—a process that quickly became a media event with daily coverage by independent Mexican and foreign press correspondents. When the government finally came up with a proposal that addressed the rebels' demands, the Zapatistas returned to their communities to discuss the government's offer. It was during this period that Marcos first presented Durito to the world.

In a letter to Mariana, a young girl who wrote to him shortly after the onset of the rebellion, Marcos related how one day he discovered a beetle making off with his bag of tobacco. Angry about the military invasion and the threat of so many soldiers' boots to such small creatures as himself, the beetle told Marcos that he was "studying neoliberalism and its strategy of domination for Latin America" in order to discover how long the Zapatista, and by extension his own, struggle would last. In a parody of left-wing methodology, he explained that "Many things have to be taken into account: the objective conditions, the ripeness of the subjective conditions, the correlation of forces, the crisis of imperialism, the crisis of socialism, etcetera, etcetera." Although he introduced himself as Nebuchadnezzar, in a gesture of friendship he allowed Marcos to call him by his nom de guerre: Durito. Although the meeting was friendly and Durito invited Marcos to come and chat at any time, it would be almost a year before they would meet again. (**The Story of Durito and Neoliberalism**)

The course of that first year of the rebellion was a turbulent one. Although the ceasefire held throughout the year, Mexican political life was profoundly affected by the Zapatista uprising. The rebellion itself demonstrated to the world the profound poverty and desperation that was common in Mexico. The widespread mobilization of grassroots support within Mexico for the Zapatista demands of Justice, Equality and Democracy revealed the existence of equally widespread dissatisfaction with the Mexican political system.

For almost 50 years Mexico had been ruled by a single political party, the Institutional Revolutionary Party, or PRI (Partido Revolucionario Institucional). The PRI had ruled as a virtual dictatorship through the careful wielding of both the velvet glove (buying off opponents) and the mailed fist (striking down those too expensive or impossible to buy). The year 1994 would have been a year of tension in Mexico even without the Zapatista uprising because it was the sixth and final year of the presidential term of Carlos Salinas de Gortari and new elections were scheduled for August. Salinas had come to office during the last national election in 1988 through electoral fraud. Popular resentment of that fraud and subsequent repression by the government fed the continued growth of opposition parties, especially on the "Left" with the Party of the Democratic Revolution, or PRD (Partido de la Revolución Democrática), and on the "Right" the National Action Party, or PAN (Partido de Acción Nacional). Attacked from all sides, internal conflicts over how to deal with these challenges began to tear the PRI apart. A series of shocking assassinations wiped out several of its main figures, including Salinas' handpicked presidential candidate Luis Donaldo Colosio who had to be replaced by a substitute candidate: Ernesto Zedillo Ponce de León.

Within this volatile context, the EZLN and the Zapatista communities from which it emerged had considerable leverage to pursue their demands. After many weeks of discussing the government proposals that came out of the negotiations in San Cristóbal, the communities rejected them and continued their mobiliza-

2

tion. When the leadership of the PRD came to Chiapas to attempt to draw the Zapatistas into party politics, they refused.

In what would prove to be the first of a series of innovative, non-violent, political moves that would capture popular imaginations and catch both government and professional politicians off guard, the Zapatistas issued the Second Declaration of the Lacandon Jungle calling on Mexican civil society—by which they meant grassroots movements for change—to gather in Chiapas prior to the national elections in a National Democratic Convention, or CND (Convención Nacional Democrática). The CND was proposed as a space where all those truly interested in serious political change could gather to discuss strategies for achieving democracy and justice in Mexico. This unprecedented national gathering was held in the remote Zapatista community of Guadalupe Tepeyac in a vast meeting site carved from the jungle. They called it "Aguascalientes" after the place where Emiliano Zapata, Pancho Villa and Venustiano Carranza met during the Mexican Revolution to discuss the formation of a new government. From August 5-9, 1994 over 6,000 representatives of grassroots groups, independent intellectuals and even foreign supporters participated in a unique and provocative democratic "encounter" —observed and reported by a considerable contingent of reporters whose attentions were diverted from the spectacle of formal electoral politics. Although not immediately recognized by either reporters or many participants, this Zapatista "encounter" was new, not only in being the first such national gathering of the pro-democracy movement, but in being structured as a space of discussion and exchange of experience rather than as a meeting designed to reach a consensus or pass a resolution.

At that encounter, the Zapatistas met directly with the civil society that had mobilized in their defense. They explained themselves and their demands, paraded their troops—a few with automatic weapons, many more with carved wooden sticks—and called for the generalization of their own rebellion in whatever forms the diverse groups represented found appropriate to their own situations. The political success of this gathering bolstered the Zapatista communities still threatened by the presence of thousands of government troops, inspired activists in their support of the Zapatistas and became a model for even broader encounters.

In August of 1994, despite the presence of thousands of observers trying to keep the elections clean, the PRI once again not only retained the presidency but stole dozens of local elections, including the state elections in Chiapas. The response was widespread protest, but in Chiapas the protests went further than elsewhere. The editor of the newspaper *El Tiempo*, Amado Avendaño, had run for governor on the PRD ticket, and his supporters created a Revolutionary Government of Transition parallel to the official PRI-controlled state government. This creation of an autonomous institution of self-government intensified the democratic movement in Chiapas and would later prove to have been a forerunner of the formation of autonomous Zapatista municipalities.

3

Salinas' successor, Ernesto Zedillo, inherited not only the Zapatista rebellion and an increasingly unmanageable pro-democracy movement but also an untenable economic situation. Throughout 1994, under pressure from nervous foreign investors to hold the international value of the peso constant, the Salinas government had been secretly running down its reserves of foreign exchange. Informed again and again by his economic advisors that a devaluation of the peso was unavoidable, Salinas had refused, seeking to maintain the illusion of economic stability, and with it his chances to be appointed the first head of the new World Trade Organization by his U.S. patrons.[1]

Therefore, one of the first acts of the new Zedillo administration had to be some devaluation of the peso. The efforts of Zedillo's team to bring about a slight downward adjustment in its value, however, were dramatically undermined by angry foreign investors and the Zapatistas. Just as news of the devaluation was being released, the Zapatistas announced that they had broken out of military encirclement and taken action in over 30 surrounding communities. Investors panicked, started dumping pesos, and its value plunged. Instead of a marginal downward adjustment, the value of the currency dropped precipitously. "Hot money" invested in the short-term Mexican capital market fled the country and created a "Peso Crisis," the reverberations of which ("the Tequila Effect") shook other emerging capital markets around the world.

Durito Returns Amidst the Thunder of War

The response of international capital and the Mexican government to this crisis and to the evidence of Zapatista political strength was severe. On January 13, 1995, Riordan Roett, a consultant to Chase Manhattan Bank (and former director of Latin American Studies at the Johns Hopkins School of Advanced International Studies) sent a newsletter to Chase's investors in emerging markets stating that "the [Mexican] government will need to eliminate the Zapatistas to demonstrate their effective control of the national territory and security policy."[2] Within weeks, Zedillo unilaterally terminated discussions for new negotiations, ruptured the yearlong ceasefire and launched a new military offensive against the Zapatistas.

The government orchestrated press conferences and a media campaign claiming to have evidence of Zapatista plans for urban guerrilla attacks and proof that the "real" identity of Subcomandante Marcos was Rafael Sebastián Guillén Vicente, a former university professor from Tampico. Zedillo issued arrest warrants against him and other alleged Zapatista leaders. To enforce these warrants and to eliminate the Zapatista movement, he ordered 60,000 troops into the mountains of Chiapas.

---

1 Not only would Salinas not get the post, but he would also wind up in exile after revelations of his family's corruption forced him to flee Mexico.
2 Alexander Cockburn and Ken Silverstein, "Major U.S. Bank Urges Zapatista Wipe-out: 'A Litmus Test for Mexico's Stability.'" *Counterpunch* 2:3 (February 1995), 1, 3.

More broadly, the Zedillo government launched a devastating economic attack against Mexican civil society for its support of the Zapatistas and their demands for greater democracy. Backed by a $50 billion package organized by the Clinton administration to bail out the Mexican capital market, the Mexican government and foreign investors, the Zedillo administration imposed a brutal austerity of high interest rates, rising unemployment and falling wages, while accelerating sales of the nation's assets to foreign investors. The collateral to the bailout loans was Mexico's national oil reserves.

As brutal army offensives burned their homes and destroyed whatever they left behind, the Zapatista army and thousands of people from their base communities fled into the jungle, enduring great hardships as refugees. Their urban supporters and the broader grassroots pro-democracy movement, however, mobilized hundreds of thousands of protesters who took to the streets of Mexico City and other major cities around the world, demanding an immediate end to the military offensive and a withdrawal of the troops. Supporters of the Zapatistas, recognizing a common struggle against the same kind of neoliberal policies they themselves suffered, demonstrated in over 40 countries at Mexican embassies, consulates and, in some cases, Chase Manhattan Bank branches.

It was during the Zapatistas' "strategic withdrawal" from the military offensive that Marcos, once again, stumbled across Durito. After recuperating from the shock of learning about the threat posed to beetles by 60,000 pairs of boots tromping around the jungle, Durito shared his analysis of the Mexican regime and its neoliberal program. Neoliberalism, he argued, is an ad hoc, improvised response to the crisis of the capitalist order. The inconsistency of Mexican government, negotiating one day, sending in the military the next, he explained, is symptomatic of such improvisation. "Well," Durito concluded, "it turns out that 'neoliberalism' is not a theory to confront or explain a crisis. It is the crisis itself made theory and economic doctrine! That is, 'neoliberalism' hasn't the least coherence; it has no plans or historic perspective. In the end, pure theoretical shit." (**Durito II**)

As the military offensive continued, worries about the possibilities of being bombed by the Mexican airforce led, on the 12th day of the withdrawal, to a discussion between Marcos and Durito about the possibilities of hiding in caves. In this context Marcos told Durito a story about a very particular cave. (**The Cave of Desire**) The story recounted the trials and tribulations of an ugly man who lived alone in the mountains but who one day fell passionately in love with a young woman whom he happened to see bathing and washing clothes in a stream. When a fierce storm drove him to take refuge in a cave, he found strange things and never returned. Durito's expedition to find the cave was washed out by a torrential downpour.

By April 1995, two months of protests forced the government to agree to a new ceasefire and a new round of negotiations mediated by two groups. The first was the National Intermediation Commission, or CONAI (Comisión Nacional de Intermediación), made up of independent and respected individuals organized in late 1994 by Bishop Ruiz. The second was the Commission on Concordance and Pacification, or COCOPA (Comisión de Concordia y Pacificación), consisting of representatives of the various political parties in the Mexican National Assembly (House of Representatives). These two groups arranged for negotiations between the EZLN and the government to take place at San Andrés Larrainzar (renamed by the Zapatistas "San Andrés Sacamch'en de los Pobres"), a Tzotzil community in the Chiapas highlands north of San Cristóbal.

Unlike the ceasefire a year earlier, however, the Mexican Army did not withdraw but remained entrenched in the Zapatista areas they had invaded. The continued military presence—which included the proliferation of new bases, roadblocks and check points, increasing acts of intimidation and the beginnings of government financed and armed paramilitary terrorism—created a highly tense backdrop to the new negotiations. During the preparations for these negotiations, Durito proclaimed himself "the knight-errant Don Durito de la Lacandona," and appointed Marcos his squire, much to the latter's astonishment. **(Durito Names Marcos His Squire)**

In another memorable moment of light-hearted interaction between Durito and Marcos during this period, they played at being bullfighters while high in a ceiba—a very tall tropical tree common in Chiapas. After Marcos used his bandana as a cape to make passes at a crescent moon, Durito showed him some of his own moves that, he claimed, were taught to him by Federico García Lorca, the famous Spanish poet. Unfortunately, just when Durito thought he had found a real bull to fight, it turned out to be a swarm of wasps from which he fled, leaving Marcos to be attacked and stung. **(On Bullfighting, Détente and Rock)**

On April 20th, on the eve of talks between the EZLN and the government, thousands of people from Zapatista base communities and groups of supporters gathered in San Andrés to form a human chain as a security cordon to protect their leadership. Embarrassed by this outpouring of popular support, the government demanded they leave; it was only after the EZLN asked most of them to return to their communities that the talks proceeded. The talks ended on April 23rd with essentially no progress towards resolving the conflict in Chiapas. It was agreed that a second round of negotiations would begin on May 12, 1995.

Meanwhile, Durito traveled to Mexico City on his valiant steed Pegasus (a turtle) to challenge Fidel Velázquez, general secretary of the Confederation of Mexican Workers since 1941, to a duel. **(Durito III)** Fearful of rank and file anger over the government's austerity program, Velázquez had canceled the traditional May Day Parade for the first time in 75 years. Despite his efforts, the parade took place as hundreds of thousands of rank and file union workers and their supporters (including Durito), took to the streets of Mexico City in a tremendous expression of protest.

Although the ire of the protesters was directed primarily at the austerity imposed by the Zedillo administration, the people in the streets also expressed solidarity and support for Zapatista demands, further embarrassing the government. Shortly thereafter, Marcos received a postcard from Durito describing his participation in the demonstrations. Struck by the power and enthusiasm of the sheer number of workers protesting, Durito wrote that, "the only thing missing was a revolution." (**May Day Postcard**) Damning the union bureaucrats for not standing up for the workers, Durito announced he would seek out those trying to create a truly independent labor movement.

The second round of negotiations, from May 12-16, also produced very little. Although the government promised to withdraw its troops from selected areas, the military occupation and daily harassment of communities continued. Through the use of regular troops and paramilitary forces, the Zapatista communities were surrounded and terrorized as part of a "low intensity war" strategy of the sort taught at the infamous "School of the Americas" in the U.S. These efforts to break the Zapatista will and ability to resist involved not only land occupations, insults, interrogations and repeated low-level flyovers, but also theft, the destruction of property, dissemination of false information, forced eviction, imprisonment, rape, torture, disappearances, and murder. Frustration at the hypocrisy and duplicity of the government and its unwillingness to seriously discuss issues at the national level while conducting a low-intensity war, led the Zapatistas to imagine once again a creative initiative that would outflank the Mexican state.

The Zapatistas' new initiative called for a National Plebiscite for Peace and Democracy (Consulta Nacional por la Paz y la Democracia) in which they took their struggle directly to the Mexican people. Asking civil society to express an opinion of the demands being made by the Zapatista rebellion—without the mediation of the government or recognized political parties—the Consulta, like the convening of the National Democratic Convention a year earlier, was an unprecedented form of direct democracy. "Never before in the history of the world or the nation," Marcos explained, "had a peaceful civil society dialogued with a clandestine and armed group." (Fourth Declaration from the Lacandon Jungle)

The organization of this Consulta occupied the Zapatistas and their supporters during most of the summer of 1995. A successful appeal to the non-governmental, pro-democracy Mexican group Civic Alliance (Alianza Cívica) meant thousands of voting booths were installed all over Mexico to facilitate widespread participation. The massive organizing effort by Zapatista supporters carried the word of this initiative not only throughout Mexico but also around the world, allowing foreigners an opportunity to express their opinion in writing or via the Internet.

To provide a political explanation for why such efforts to bypass the current political system were necessary, Marcos passed on, through a communiqué pub-

Petro chemical fertilizers Word hanger

rate

lished in early June, a letter written by Don Durito to a university professor at the Autonomous University of Mexico, or UNAM (Universidad Nacional Autónoma de México). (**Durito IV**) This letter, written while Durito accompanied a 41-day protest march from Tabasco to Mexico City, presented the Zapatista critique of the Mexican political system. In this missive, Durito made three points that clearly differentiated Zapatista politics from those of the traditional Leninist Left. First, he argued that no one formula, organization, method or leader can succeed in bringing about the changes that are needed; it must be a collective anti-vanguard process that includes many approaches. Second, the goal of the revolution is not the seizure of power or the construction of a new order; it is, instead, the creation of the conditions necessary to build new worlds. Third, the conditions that the revolution must create are democracy, liberty and justice. From these premises, Durito critiqued the fragmentation of the forces fighting against the party-state that enable the PRI to divide and conquer the opposition and remain in power. He concluded by calling for a national dialogue on how to overcome this fragmentation.

After arriving with the Tabasco protest march in Mexico City, Durito wandered its streets, a solitary Humphrey Bogart-like character complete with trench coat and fedora, depressed by the loneliness of its inhabitants and the useless, stultifying "game of mirrors" that constitutes so much of its political life. (**Durito V**) At one point, through a series of magical gestures, Durito brought to life a music-box ballerina behind a storefront window who danced while he played the piano, and who, after he left to return to Chiapas, escaped from her captivity.

Upon his return from Mexico City, and against the background of preparations for the Consulta, Durito joined Marcos, Camilo and Marcos' "Other Self" in a round of self-criticism. In describing the scene Marcos evoked an Italian film about family infighting. The whole situation playfully mocked a traditional Leftist ritual, in contrast to the Consulta in which the Zapatistas went beyond self-criticism in favor of seeking the opinions of the men and women of civil society. (**Durito's Return**)

Some time later, Durito announced to Marcos that, using the method he once taught Sherlock Holmes, he had deduced the real force spreading the plague of neoliberalism in Mexico. Behind a public pretense at theoretical and policy clarity and the actual contradictory policies of the Zedillo administration lurks, he declared, a shadowy figure named Stupid Improvisation. With the folly Zedillo and his technocrats learned in their studies in U.S. universities, they have pretended to know what they are doing and what will happen as they hand the country over to unregulated, chaotic market forces. So neoliberalism, he argued, is not only the economic chaos of unregulated markets, it's also "chaotic theory" and "catastrophic management" as well. When Marcos worried about the possibilities of neoliberalism perpetuating itself indefinitely, Durito reassured him that the chaos of its own internal battles, assassinations and contradictory actions will certainly help undermine it. "Neoliberalism," Durito concluded, "is the chaotic theory of economic chaos, the stupid exaltation of social stupidity and the cata-strophic political management of catastrophe." (**Durito VI**)

During the month of August, the EZLN sent a "Durito Productions" video to Mexico City in which Marcos appeared with Durito to explain Zapatista conceptions of the upcoming Consulta. The plebiscite, Durito explained through Marcos' translation, was intended as one step in an ongoing dialogue with civil society that began with the National Democratic Convention a year earlier. The Consulta, Durito insisted, should not be conceived as a singular act but as a process, one moment of an unfolding encounter and dialogue. He plead-ed for this view, noting that the Zapatistas had also originally conceived of the CND in this manner but, because it was viewed by too many as an institution, it died. Durito also insisted that this Consulta, this moment of broad dialogue with civil society, not only sought the participation of self-proclaimed revolutionaries but of all those who want a transition to democracy in Mexico. (**Durito, Chibo, and La Consulta**)

On August 27, 1995, as the Consulta began, Durito sent a letter to members of a European Encounter working in solidarity with the struggle in Chiapas. In that letter, he told a story of a little mouse who, after repeated frustrated attempts, finally discovered how to deal with a menacing cat. In clear appreciation of the international solidarity of those to whom he was writing, Durito denounced nationality as mere "circumstantial accident," and let them know that he was thinking about invading Europe, possibly in January. (**The Story of the Little Mouse and the Little Cat**)

With over a million Mexicans and over 80,000 foreigners participating, the vote was overwhelmingly in support of the Zapatistas' demands including democracy, liberty, justice and equal rights for women. Beyond supporting the Zapatista demands, those participating also voted in large majority for the Zapatistas to transform themselves into a political, rather than military, force. Accepting this mandate without giving up their weapons, the Zapatistas renounced further armed actions in favor of non-military political struggle.

Peace talks resumed at San Andrés on October 12, 1995. This time, the Zapatistas outflanked government efforts to keep the dialogues narrowly focused on Chiapas by inviting over one hundred independent intellectuals, activists and representatives of various political, social and indigenous organizations from all over Mexico to convene as "advisors" to the EZLN. The talks were divided into working groups on various sub-themes, such as community and autonomy, jus-tice for indigenous people, the rights and culture of indigenous women and access to the means of communication. The first phase ended on October 22, after eleven days of work.

The next day, the government provoked a crisis by ordering the arrest of Fernando Yáñez Muñoz, who had previously been targeted by the government as being "Comandante Germán" of the EZLN. Fearing that this direct violation of the Law for Dialogue and Reconciliation (which explicitly prohibited arrests

9

of EZLN leaders as long as negotiations continued) heralded another military offensive such as the one launched the previous February, the Zapatistas declared a "Red Alert." Angered by the undermining of its attempts at reaching a peace settlement, the legislators of COCOPA pressured the government into releasing Muñoz. In return the EZLN suspended the "Red Alert" and agreed to resume talks with the second round on Indigenous Rights and Culture, which lasted from November 13-18.[3]

During the second period of negotiations, Durito gave Marcos a copy of cultural critic Carlos Monsiváis' book, *The Rituals of Chaos*. The book prompted Marcos to draft a long letter to Monsiváis concerning the role of intellectuals in Mexican political life. The book and the discussion between Marcos and Durito provided the occasion for a critique of those intellectuals who propagated and defended the chaos of Salinas' neoliberal program. In the process, Marcos critiqued the neoliberal ethical mantra of "efficiency" and the propaganda that an alternation of the party in power (e.g., the PRI or the PAN) amounts to democracy. Wielding the metaphor of the mirror, he also extended his critique to the Left and its debilitating illusion of replacing "bad guys" with "good guys." "The inversion of the image," he pointed out, "is not a new image, but [only] an inverted image." The Zapatistas, he wrote to Monsiváis, do not pretend to embody a higher morality (they did, after all, take up arms and use them) or to offer a better world after seizing power (like the Left). They argue instead for "the necessity of fighting for the creation of a space in which a new political morality can be born." (**Of Trees, Transgressors and Ondontology**) Durito, meanwhile, punctuated Marcos' analysis with his own musings on art, the Consulta and the fate of Pegasus, who ran off with a Ruta 100 bus—who had taken part in the big strike in Mexico City.

During this period, there were renewed tensions between the PRD and the Zapatistas due to the EZLN's refusal, once again, to support them at the polls. The EZLN responded to PRD complaints by asserting that the EZLN did not declare war on the government in order to support the PRD or any other political party. Musing on the dangers of a fragmented resistance, Durito told Marcos a story that evoked the historical process whereby the Spanish conquistadors were able to defeat indigenous populations by exploiting the divisions among them. (**The Story of the Hot Foot and the Cold Foot**)

As the year 1995 neared its end, just days before the second anniversary of the Zapatista uprising, Durito mused on Love. In response to Toñita, a little girl who suggested that love is like a teacup that is repeatedly broken and patched back together again, Durito suggested that it can also be thought of in terms of a scale where the good outweighs the bad. But it is a scale, Durito warned, that bears watching, for even trivial things can tip the balance toward indifference. (**On Love, Indifference, and Other Foolishness**)

---

3 When the Zapatistas marched into Mexico City in the spring of 2001, Muñoz would be appointed primary negotiator with the new Fox government.

On Christmas Day, Marcos wrote to civil society about just how important Durito is, with his energy, his stories and his wonders, in lightening the oppressive conditions of life for the rebels living in the mountains of the Mexican Southeast. In the communiqué he recounted a story told to him by Old Antonio—an indigenous elder who played a key role in teaching Marcos about local customs and wisdom. Old Antonio's story told how the Gods created dreams so the people of the corn could be better and a mirror called dignity so they could see themselves as equals, and so that those who spread hierarchy and darkness across the land could see themselves as emptiness and be undone. (**The Story of Dreams**)

Durito, Accords and Encounters

The year 1996 began with a flurry of successful Zapatista initiatives. In the "Fourth Declaration of the Lacandon Jungle," issued on January 1, 1996, the EZLN lamented the failure of the CND—torn apart by internal conflicts and sectarian politics—and called for the formation of a broad-based "front," a network of autonomous groups outside party politics or government sanctioned institutions. The creation of the Zapatista Front for National Liberation, or FZLN (Frente Zapatista de Liberación Nacional) was another step in the Zapatista effort to find concrete forms for radical democratic politics.

On January 3, 1996 the Zapatistas convened the first National Indigenous Forum, or FNI (Foro Nacional Indígena) in San Cristóbal. Nearly five hundred representatives from all over Mexico gathered to give vitality to a network of interrelationships whereby indigenous peoples would support and reinforce one another and their struggles, including, but not limited to, those of the Zapatistas. In the closing statement to the forum, Marcos thanked all of those who had supported the Zapatista movement, those who came and those who could not, but whose hearts were with them, including Durito. To the assembly, he recounted a story that Durito told him of a horse who escaped a dire fate by slipping away to another story. (**The Story of the Bay Horse**) By year's end, the dialogues begun in San Cristóbal would congeal in the formation of a new, ongoing National Indigenous Congress, or CNI (Congreso Nacional Indígena).

The Zapatistas also issued a call for the organization of a series of continental encounters of grassroots movements against neoliberalism in April to be followed by an Intercontinental Encounter in Chiapas in August of 1996. This was an audacious call for a level of organization that had never been achieved anywhere before. Nation-states and even well funded non-governmental organizations (e.g., Rio in 1992 and Beijing in 1995) have often organized such global meetings but never before had any grassroots movement had the power to convoke such a comprehensive gathering. These encounters, the Zapatistas suggested, could provide times and spaces where those opposed to neoliberalism and seeking better worlds could come together to compare experiences and ideas. Such actions would constitute the beginnings of an "international of hope" to be

11

pitted against the neoliberal "international of terror."(First Declaration of La Realidad) The proposed agenda would examine the economic, political, social and cultural aspects of "how one lives under neoliberalism, how one resists, how one struggles and proposals of struggle against it and for humanity." Their call was answered with an enthusiasm that far exceeded their expectations.

At San Andrés, government representatives finally agreed to a series of Accords on Indigenous Rights. As in early 1994, these Accords were carried by EZLN representatives to Zapatista communities for discussion. They represented a symbolic, if controversial, step forward for the indigenous movement. For the first time, the government of Mexico appeared to accept the principle of indigenous autonomy. Despite later government claims, there is no hint of secession in either the spirit or the letter of the Accords, but rather the recognition and valorization of indigenous traditions and institutions. As Marcos would later explain: "The Zapatistas think that the defense of the national state is necessary in view of globalization and that the attempts to slice Mexico to pieces comes from the governing group and not from the just demands for autonomy for the indigenous peoples. The EZLN, and the best of the national indigenous movement, does not want the indigenous people to separate from Mexico, but to be recognized as part of the country with their differences." (Seven Loose Pieces of the Global Jigsaw Puzzle)

Zapatista advisor Gustavo Esteva notes that the Zapatistas did not put forward a specific definition of autonomy as a program, but a claim that would validate already existing notions of autonomy such as that of a Yaqui leader who stated: "Autonomy is not something that we need to ask someone or that someone can give to us. We occupy a territory, in which we exert government and justice in our own way, and we practice self-defense. We now claim respect and recognition for what we have conquered."[4] The Accords were controversial because they did not include all of the indigenous demands put forth before or during the negotiations. But through a prolonged period of examination and discussion, the Zapatista communities came to view them not as an unsatisfactory final compromise, but as a step forward in an ongoing struggle. These Accords, which the government signed but later refused to implement, would become a key point of reference for the Zapatistas in the years to follow.

The First American Continental Encounter Against Neoliberalism and for Humanity began on April 3, 1996 and paralleled similar gatherings in Europe and other parts of the world. Hundreds of grassroots activists arrived in the village of La Realidad under the noses of the Mexican police, army and intelligence services to discuss continued resistance to neoliberalism. "The most sophisticated and modern war technology," Subcomandante Marcos declared, "is set forth against wooden weapons, the broken feet and the ancestral philosophy of the Zapatistas, which declares, without shame or fear that the place of knowledge,

---

4   Gustavo Esteva, "The Zapatistas and People's Power" *Capital and Class* 68 (Summer 1999): 163.

truth and speech is in the heart. Modern death against ancestral life. Neoliberalism against Zapatismo." (Opening Speech to American Encounter)

Despite army patrols and flyovers by military aircraft, the participants spent almost a week in intense discussions. For his own presentation, Marcos turned to Durito for help and the latter provided, along with side comments on rock bands and dance styles, a critique of the way history too often appears as a deceptive and badly told tale in which government leaders are the only actors and the people and their dignity disappear completely. (**Durito IX**)

In the European Encounter, several thousand activists gathered in Berlin. Marcos sent a letter explaining that the continuing discussion of the San Andrés Accords made it impossible for any Zapatista representative to attend the European meetings, but he appended a postscript warning NATO that Durito was considering setting off for the conquest of Europe. (**Durito to Conquer Europe**) This warning later proved to have been portentous. At the end of 1996, Durito would disappear and remain mysteriously absent for three years, returning in the fall of 1999, as a pirate just back from Europe.

The talks at San Andrés were followed by another round of meetings on issues of Democracy and Justice. Ironically, the behavior of the government representatives exemplified Marcos and Durito's worst views of its spokespersons. In a contribution to the Mexican political humor magazine *El Chamuco*, they had agreed that Mexico would be better off if ruled by cartoonists than by the current corps of caricatures in its government. (**Durito on Cartoonists**) At San Andrés, instead of genuinely participating in the discussion, government representatives sat stone-faced and silent, making a farce of the proceedings. At the same time, the police and military intensified their harassment of Zapatista communities. The dramatic combination of silence in the negotiating room and active repression beyond its walls made the real, and very unfunny, intentions of government's "negotiators" quite clear. The state had brought its pretense of negotiations to an end while accelerating its efforts at repression.

Undeterred, during this period the Zapatistas responded with events such as the gathering in San Cristóbal of over 5,000 indigenous women from all over Chiapas to celebrate International Women's Day and to protest governmental repression and its effects on women. In early March, against the backdrop of closed-door negotiations among professional politicos from the PRI, the PAN and the PRD over the "reform of the state" in Mexico City, the Zapatistas announced a new list of advisors, once more over a hundred, making the talks into a national forum that included, rather than excluded, civil society.

Later in March, the atmosphere of intimidation took a turn for the worse when the government sentenced Javier Elorriaga and Sebastián Entzin to prison for "terrorism." It also unleashed paramilitary forces—that it had been covertly arming and training—against Zapatista communities. In Bachajon, paramilitaries known as los Chinchulines, attacked anti-PRIista families, killing several people and burning down their houses. The survivors fled into the hills, becoming the

13

first of thousands of refugees from this particular phase of the low intensity war. In the midst of such violence, Marcos wrote to European supporters that although "the horizon is becoming overcast, with a gray fading to black," liberty still waits. Indeed, Durito points out that sometimes one must walk through the night to reach the dawn. (**Durito on Liberty**)

Days after an appellate court exonerated Elorriaga and Entzin and revoked their sentences, another government-funded paramilitary group Paz y Justicia intensified the gathering darkness by attacking Zapatista base communities, burning down villages and driving over 2,000 people into the mountains. Remaining steadfast in their promise to civil society after the Consulta, the Zapatistas did not respond militarily to these murderous attacks but continued to seek peace.

In a letter to the National Campaign for Peace and Against Hunger, Marcos explained that the EZLN would not counter the government's violence and death with more violence, but with renewed efforts to construct a better world. Instead of war, they would embrace peace; instead of hunger and death they would continue to struggle for the corn harvest. Drawing on Old Antonio, Marcos likened the present period to the annual food shortages and the hunger that face peasants in the difficult weeks before harvest. Durito, for his part, dreamed of an anti-hunger campaign that would bring him ice cream! (**Durito's Comment on Hunger**) At month's end, stymied by government refusal to participate in real discussions about Democracy and Justice and in dramatic contrast to a series of closed-door negotiations being held by the main political parties, the Zapatistas organized a Special Forum on the Reform of the State, to which they invited a wide variety of participants from civil society.

When in June a new, armed guerrilla group, the Popular Revolutionary Army, or EPR (Ejército Popular Revolucionario), appeared in the state of Guerrero, the Zapatistas denied any knowledge of or contact with them. In a series of communiqués issued during the summer the Zapatistas affirmed that, unlike the EPR, their politics were not about "taking power" but about creating a political space in which civil society could undertake the restructuring of Mexican politics and society. (This is evoked again in **Magical Chocolates**)

The most dramatic mobilization of the summer of 1996, the First Intercontinental Encounter for Humanity and Against Neoliberalism convened in Oventic where over 3,000 grassroots activists from over 40 countries gathered to discuss how to resist and transcend neoliberalism. This gathering mobilized on the scale of a military operation, and was convened despite the increased presence of the military forces of the state. Amidst government roadblocks and delays intended solely to harass, participants traveled to five Zapatista communities previously organized as new Aguascalientes—after the original Aguascalientes built in Guadalupe Tepeyac for the CND in 1994 (and destroyed in the government offensive of 1995). In all five communities, which had built meeting spaces, mess halls, shelters and latrines, thousands organized themselves into workshops for

14

intense discussion. Although ski-masked Zapatista soldiers were in attendance everywhere, they had not organized the meetings to disseminate their own ideas. Instead, they had built concrete expressions of their politics: spaces in which representatives of civil society could seek new paths of resistance and creativity among themselves.

Accords, Encounters and the "Low Intensity War"

In preparation for this momentous gathering, Marcos prepared a series of interventions, two of which drew on the advice and contributions of Durito. In an effort to assist Marcos in preparing a presentation for the workshop on culture and media, Durito showed him a story written by Bertold Brecht (which Durito claimed to have dictated to Brecht) about sharks. While "Brecht's" story is a rather dark parable of oppression, exploitation, competition and war, Durito brightens it with a tale of revolt and the creation of a new culture in which different kinds of people coexist without division, war, or jails. (**Big Sharks and Little Fishes**)

In a paper presented to the workshop on politics, Marcos recounts Durito's juxtaposition of the values of neoliberalism and those of resistance and struggle. Playing on the Spanish word *bolsa* that can mean either financial assets such as stocks and bonds, or alternatively vessels for carrying such as pockets, bags, or backpacks, Durito denounces the "value" of the former, while poetically evoking the values of the Zapatistas and the thousands who had come with backpacks to Chiapas:

Can I speak? Can I speak about our dead at this celebration? After all, they made it possible. It can be said that we are here because they are not. Can't it? I have a dead brother. Is there someone here who doesn't have a dead brother? I have a dead brother. He was killed by a bullet to his head. It was before dawn on the 1st of January 1994. Way before dawn the bullet was shot. Way before dawn death kissed the forehead of my brother. My brother used to laugh a lot but now he doesn't laugh anymore. I couldn't keep my brother in my pocket, but I kept the bullet that killed him. On another day before dawn, I asked the bullet where it came from. It said: "From the rifle of a soldier of the government of a powerful person who serves another powerful person who serves another powerful person who serves another in the world. The bullet that killed my brother has no nationality. The fight that must be fought to keep our brothers with us, rather than the bullets that have killed them, has no nationality either. For this purpose we Zapatistas have many big pockets in our uniforms. Not for keeping bullets. For keeping brothers." (Presentation in **Seven Voices Seven**)

After days of discussion, debate and amusement, the encuentro, which Durito had nicknamed the "Intergaláctica," ended with Marcos delivering the "Second Declaration of La Realidad." This pivotal document called for those who attended the encounter to return home and build new intercontinental networks of communication, and to interconnect and interweave all moments of resistance against neoliberalism to build a better world together.

As the delegates to the Intergaláctica returned to their countries, the Zapatistas resumed their efforts to negotiate with the government at San Andrés over issues of Democracy and Justice. When the final plenary meeting of those negotiations ended with no progress, the Zapatistas returned to their communities for critical dialogues. At the end of August, they announced their withdrawal from the peace talks, pointing to the absence of any action on the San Andrés Accords, to the mockery of the government negotiators' silence at the second round of talks, and to the continuing military and paramilitary terrorism against their communities.

In the absence of any peace talks and amidst a climate of terror, Durito figured prominently in two September communiqués. In the first (**Love and the Calendar**), Marcos found a bottle that had floated to the top of his ceiba tree with a message recounting the fate of a man who was always late and who missed his own death. The second, which also arrived at the ceiba in a bottle (**The Story of the Magical Chocolates**), told of three boys and their different responses to the same options. It also warned Marcos that his ceiba made an excellent military target and told him how to get down from his exposed position.

At the National Indigenous Forum organized in Chiapas the previous January, the Zapatistas and many other indigenous groups had laid the groundwork for a National Indigenous Congress, to be held October 8-12, 1996. Intended as the first of many assemblies of indigenous organizers from all over Mexico, the Congress was scheduled to take place in Mexico City. When the EZLN declared its intention to send representatives, the government threatened to arrest any Zapatistas who dared to leave Chiapas. Pro-Zapatista lawyers pointed out that existing laws protected such travel. Political commentators wrote multiple polemics for and against and the COCOPA engaged in shuttle diplomacy. Amidst tremendous publicity and the threat of reprisals by the government, the Zapatistas sent Comandanta Ramona, well known for her prominent role in the 1994 negotiations in the San Cristóbal Cathedral (and in desperate need of medical treatment in the capital). Her speech at the forum was a moment of public victory for the Zapatistas.

In the wake of the National Indigenous Congress and during a series of "tripartite" talks among the EZLN, COCOPA and the CONAI over the possibility of restarting peace talks, Marcos sent a new communiqué to civil society. It contained a story by Durito about the architectural poetry of the first Zapatista Aguascalientes built at Guadalupe Tepeyac for the 1994 National Democratic Congress. In that story, Comandante Tacho points out to Marcos how the illiterate indigenous of Guadalupe Tepeyac had constructed the buildings of the Aguascalientes so that all together they formed a huge seashell, a giant spiral with an amphitheater at the center. This seashell, Durito pointed out, was symbolic of Zapatista politics in which the beginning and the end are ambiguous and the focus is not the goal but the search. Durito contrasted this perspective and the ethics it implied with those of Power—evoking the government destruction of the Aguascalientes of Guadalupe Tepeyac in 1995. (**The Seashell and the Two People**)

During the last months of the year, against a backdrop of increasing violence against NGOs working for peace in Chiapas, EZLN representatives met repeatedly with the COCOPA and the CONAI to produce a concrete legislative initiative for the implementation of constitutional reforms in the spirit of the San Andrés Accords. The final draft by the COCOPA was accepted by the EZLN, with reservations since it did not include all of the points previously agreed to in the Accords. Despite the EZLN's good faith efforts, the Zedillo administration rejected the draft and offered an alternative completely at odds with the original content and spirit of the Accords, making explicit the hypocrisy of its pretended interest in a negotiated peace in Chiapas. There would be no more stories of Durito in Zapatista communiqués for nearly three years.

1997 - 1998: In Durito's Absence: Growing State Terrorism and the Mobilizations of Civil Society

Early in 1997, COCOPA's attempt to push through legislation to implement the San Andrés Accords failed in the face of the Zedillo administration's intransigence and its deliberate expansion of paramilitary violence against Zapatista communities. The government's counterproposal, which the EZLN rejected, made it clear to all that the government had negotiated in bad faith. The Zapatista communities responded with marches in January and February demanding that the government honor its agreements.

Instead of responding to these appeals to good faith, government-backed paramilitaries increased their attacks, especially in Northern Chiapas. In Sabanilla, families supporting the PRD were forced to flee their homes by PRIista supporters backed by the police. Near Palenque, the police violently drove 65 families belonging to the indigenous organization Xi'Nich from their homes and communities. The state judicial police arrested and tortured four persons, including two Jesuit priests. A week later, public security forces, the judicial police and the Mexican Army joined forces to attack the community of San Pedro Nixtalucum in the municipality of San Juan de la Libertad. Four were killed and 29 beaten, detained or disappeared. The rest were driven from their homes and forced to flee. Once again there were mass protests. 20,000 joined a Pilgrimage for Peace to Tila to call for an end to the attacks. 150 traveled to Tuxtla Gutiérrez and staged a sit-in before the State Capitol. The government responded with increased attacks by the paramilitaries and continued build-up of military forces around Zapatista communities.

The months of July and August were marked by a dramatic juxtaposition of state and grassroots politics. In August, Federal mid-term elections were held and the victory of opposition parties deprived the PRI of an absolute majority in the Chamber of Deputies for the first time in over 50 years. This political opening was widely heralded as a major step forward in Mexico's transition to democracy. Parallel to these events in the "Spectacle of the Parties," the Zapatistas organized a very different kind of politics. First, the Zapatista communities boycotted the elections, rejecting the notion that anything approaching democracy can occur under conditions of state militarization and terrorism. Second, the Zapatistas threw their support behind another Intercontinental Encounter Against Neoliberalism and For Humanity that was organized by a coalition of European groups and held in Spain at the end of July. Over 4,000 activists from dozens of countries participated in a mobilization begun the previous summer at the Intergaláctica in Chiapas. Third, the Zapatistas organized a delegation of 1,111 representatives to Mexico City for the founding Congress of the Zapatista National Liberation Front (FZLN) and for the Second National Assembly of the CNI in September. They achieved this despite adamant government opposition and military repression in their communities, which prevented many Zapatistas from traveling within and beyond Chiapas. This trip amounted to a political "breakout" even more dramatic in some ways than the military maneuver of December 1994.

The government's response to these dramatic actions by the Zapatistas was violent. In early November the PRI-backed paramilitary group Paz y Justicia used automatic weapons to attack a caravan of church workers that included the Bishops Samuel Ruiz and Raúl Vera, wounding three in their party. On December 22, 1997 some 70 paramilitaries equipped with automatic weapons, attacked the community of Acteal murdering 45 people. The victims, members of the religious community "Las Abejas" (the Bees), were mostly women and children, attacked while holding prayer services in their church. During this nearly five-hour long slaughter, the only actions taken by the local police were to close the highway so the massacre would not be interrupted. Afterwards, they attempted to conceal the killings by burying the bodies in hastily dug shallow graves and removing any signs of the attack. Their efforts of concealment were, however, unveiled by human rights activists.

The revelation of the Acteal massacre prompted widespread protests demanding an end to state-sponsored violence in Chiapas and calling for an investigation and prosecution of those responsible for the murders. In response, the government increased its military presence in the State, claiming to "disarm" civilian groups. More than 6,000 troops were moved into previously unoccupied areas of the highlands. The Zedillo administration's strategy for misdirection and concealment through increased militarization and harassment, however, was repeatedly exposed by human rights groups who demonstrated how Zapatista communities were being besieged while the paramilitary groups were allowed to operate with impunity. The World Bank contributed financial support to the government's repression by approving a 47 million dollar credit line the day after the massacre. In the euphemistic language of the Bank and the Mexican government, the money was designated for "Development Programs in Marginalized Areas."

In the early months of 1998, state repression increased with the assassination of peasant leaders and the invasion of several important Zapatista communities by combined operations of the military, the various police forces and paramilitaries. Two of the most notable acts of terror revealed the level of repression and the logic of low-intensity warfare. In January, Rubical Ruiz Gamboa, a leader of the Independent Campesino Organization of Villa Corzo and of the Democratic State Assembly of the People of Chiapas, or ADEPECH (Asamblea Estatal del Pueblo Chiapaneco) was killed in Tuxtla Gutiérrez. In February, José López García from Tila in Northern Chiapas was assassinated after testifying about human rights violations.

In April, the Mexican Army along with state and federal police invaded the tzeltal town of Taniperla in the autonomous municipality of Ricardo Flores Magón. Among the most infamous acts during that invasion was the destruction of a community center decorated with a magnificent mural created by artists from 12 different communities—a mural later celebrated and recreated in various sites on the Internet and around the world. A week later, the same forces invaded the community of Diez de Abril, arresting, torturing and imprisoning notable community members while stealing their money and goods. The same kind of action was repeated in May in the autonomous municipality of Tierra y Liberatad. In June, 30 families of Zapatista sympathizers were driven out of Nabil, Tenejapa in a joint action of paramilitaries and public security police. The next day, the municipality of Nicholás Ruiz, legally governed by the PRD, was occupied by a combined force of 3,000 army troops, state and federal police and members of the Chinchulines paramilitary group. Over 150 people were arrested and jailed.

Faced with the absolute unwillingness of the Mexican government to seek a peaceful solution to the conflicts in Chiapas, on June 7, 1998 Bishop Samuel Ruiz resigned in protest from the mediating group CONAI, forcing the organization to dissolve itself. The government's only response was to attack the communities of the autonomous municipality of San Juan de la Libertad three days later. More than a thousand federal troops, judicial police and state security forces invaded the villages. Houses were burned, six Zapatistas were killed and over 50 were arrested. Many residents fled. Several of those taken prisoner were subsequently executed extra-judicially, and after a series of protests their mutilated bodies were returned to San Juan de la Libertad by the state in decorative caskets. Some of the bodies were so badly decomposed that they could not be identified.

Following the Acteal massacre and amidst these widespread state attacks on Zapatista communities, the influx of foreign human rights observers into

Definition of a Terrorist and a combatant

19

Chiapas noticeably expanded. There were many observers from many different groups but the most striking, by their large numbers, were those from Europe, where the Mexican government was being openly critiqued in the Parliament. In February, 200 participants in the International Civil Commission for Human Rights Observation arrived from all over Europe to spend ten days in Chiapas visiting communities and talking to NGOs to gather information regarding the Mexican government's low-intensity war. A second group of 135 Italian human rights observers arrived in May, demanding access to communities that were being subjected to violent repression, such as Taniperla. In clear violation of international law, the Italians were denied immigration permits, but having been invited as humanitarian observers by a community in dire need, they went anyway, to the great consternation of the Mexican government.

The state's response to the negative publicity resulting from these visits was to accelerate their campaign of obstruction and expulsion of human rights observers under the xenophobic rhetoric of defending Mexican "sovereignty." In February, a parish priest of French origin, who had been serving in the Chenalhó diocese for over 30 years, was deported for declaring to the press that the government was responsible for the Acteal massacre. During the April attack on Diez de Abril, Norwegian peace observers were arrested and deported. 85 Italians who visited Taniperla were accused of violating the terms of their visa and barred from returning to Mexico for ten years. 40 more were banned for life. The National Immigration Institute of Mexico announced new regulations for international human rights observers designed to dramatically reduce the number of observers (maximum of ten per group) and freedom of observation (detailed itineraries and a time limit of ten days). The move, coupled with the accelerating number of deportations and denials of visas, constituted an obvious attempt to hide the government's multiplying crimes from the critical eyes of the world.

For approximately four-and-a-half months of this drama, Subcomandante Marcos and the General Command of the Clandestine Revolutionary Committee of the EZLN, or CCRI-CG (Comité Clandestino Revolucionario Indígena-Comandancia General) maintained a long and unprecedented silence. In the place of their voice arose those of the communities that were under attack and whose own spokespersons began to produce detailed "denunciations" of the aggressions against them. In what was later revealed to have been a strategy to break the vision of the Zapatista movement as directed by Marcos and only a handful of "leaders," the EZLN created the space and opportunity for local communities to find and develop their own voice to speak of their plight to the world. The success of this strategy was demonstrated by the large number of local statements distributed internationally via the Internet by groups such as Enlace Civil in San Cristóbal de las Casas and the FZLN in Mexico City.

On July 19, 1998 the EZLN issued the Fifth Declaration of the Lacandon Jungle, once again taking the government, and the world, by surprise with a call for a renewal of the Zapatista dialogue with Civil Society. They proposed a new national plebiscite or consulta, "For the Rights of Indian Peoples and an End to the War of Extermination" (Por el Derecho de los Pueblos Indios y el Fin de la Guerra de Exterminio). Bypassing the state, the Zapatistas appealed directly to the people of Mexico, and ultimately the world, to participate in the organization of a formal nationwide vote for or against the objectives of the San Andrés Accords as embodied in COCOPA's legislative proposal.

In the autumn of 1998, Chiapas suffered torrential rains and flooding that drowned hundreds and displaced over 18,000 people. The flooding was particularly bad because of earlier forest fires that had denuded the hillsides. Many believed that those fires had been started by government forces. The rains brought not only more death and suffering but also more army troops, ostensibly to help the victims. At the national level, Zedillo presented his fourth State of the Nation address in September, making no reference to Chiapas but fueling the anti-foreign-observer propaganda by announcing a no-tolerance policy for outside intervention in Mexico's internal affairs. At the state level, the elections were postponed until October when a combination of Zapatista abstention and electoral fraud delivered the bulk of the official municipalities into the hands of the PRI. The PRD demanded the annulment of the elections arguing fraud. The PRIista governor Roberto Albores Guillén denied any irregularities and made an additional and incredible claim that no political prisoners were in Chiapas jails. On November 10, 1998 he issued an amnesty to paramilitaries whose existence the state had systematically denied.

On November 20-22, 29 Zapatista delegates, including well-known figures like Major Moisés and Comandantes Tacho, David and Zebedeo, accompanied by members of the Red Cross, joined over 2,000 people from 28 states and 300 international observers for an Encounter in San Cristóbal de las Casas. This gathering was in preparararation for the Consulta Nacional on indigenous rights scheduled for the following March. At that Encounter, the Zapatistas announced that over 5,000 of their representatives would travel to all the municipalities of Mexico to spread word of the Consulta and to explain the Zapatistas' position to potential voters.

At year's end the Mexican government released the "White Book on Acteal," a report that attempted to conceal government involvement in the Acteal massacre. Bishop Ruiz celebrated a commemorative mass in Acteal in memory of those slaughtered. The mass was joined by a number of foreigners who were harassed en route by immigration officials and thousands of indigenous Zapatista sympathizers who marched from the refugee camps in Polhó.

1999–2000: Durito Returns to the Struggles of the "Little Ones"

Increasingly desperate to crush the Zapatistas, whose courage and resistance continued to inspire the pro-democracy movement undermining the PRI's diminishing hold on power, the government pursued its dual offensives against Zapatista communities and the international observers who came to bear witness to repeated human-rights abuses. On New Year's Day 1999, the Army sought to intimidate the Zapatista community of La Realidad with hours of low-level reconnaissance flights and troop convoys driving through the village while both military and immigration officials stopped a group of human rights observers organized by the San Francisco-based Global Exchange. The group was detained and photographed, their bus inspected for "explosives," and several individuals were ordered to appear before immigration officials. A week later, a member of the group was accused of interfering in domestic politics and was expelled from Mexico for life. Undeterred, the U.S. Mexico Solidarity Network announced a delegation of medical personnel to assess the health needs in indigenous villages. Not long after, Peace Action announced a separate delegation to investigate human rights abuses in a number of communities. When a large delegation of Italians went to Acteal and Polhó despite being told not to, they were deported by the Mexican government. Meanwhile, foreign support for the building of an autonomous school in Oventic continued. So too did police, army and paramilitary terror.

Despite such harassment, the Zapatista communities prepared 5,000 delegates to travel throughout Mexico for a national Consulta on Indigenous Rights and For an End to the War of Extermination, while also working to bring in the winter coffee harvest. As in 1995, Alianza Cívica assisted the Zapatistas in their organization of the Consulta. As a result, the group found its San Cristóbal offices vandalized and their computer equipment stolen. The coffee harvest, so essential to the base communities' economic survival, was protected from paramilitary interference by the presence of observers from the Mexican Red Cross and Human Rights Commission.

As the state's repression widened and more and more people from Zapatista communities were arrested on false charges, the struggle spread to the prisons in Chiapas. In February, 30 Zapatista political prisoners from the organization the Voice of Cerro Hueco (La Voz de Cerro Hueco) initiated a hunger strike inside prisons in Tuxtla Gutiérrez and San Cristóbal. The words of this new collective voice began to be heard far beyond the walls of their cells as these unbowed campesinos added their denunciations of unjust and illegal imprisonment to the communiqués flowing with regularity from their communities onto the Internet and throughout the world.

In March, the Zapatistas achieved two very public victories: the Consulta on Indigenous Rights and the further exposure of Mexico's abysmal human rights record. Although the ultimate impact of the consulta process was impossible to measure, the very large numbers of people involved was striking. Over 120,000 people took part in organizing the Consulta throughout Mexico. 5,000 Zapatistas visited 1,299 municipalities across the country talking with millions of Mexicans. As a result over 2.8 million voted, more than double the number participating in the Consulta of 1995. The Consulta was also organized in 29 foreign countries where over 58,000 also participated in the voting. This huge mobilization and the resounding embrace of indigenous peoples' rights struck directly at the government's refusal to implement the San Andrés Accords. The Mexican government's human rights record was publicly denounced twice: first in a report by Amnesty International titled "Mexico: the Shadow of Impunity," and then by a Mexico City Federal Judge who ruled against the expulsion of foreign observers carried out the previous year during the attack on Taniperlas.

In mid-March, the Zapatistas unexpectedly received publicity on the front page of *The New York Times*. In El Paso, Texas, Cinco Puntos Press was set to publish a bilingual edition of *The Story of Colors* by Subcomandante Marcos, as told to him by Old Antonio. This short book about how the gods had created colors to enliven the world, illustrated by indigenous artist Domitila Domínguez, had been awarded funding from the National Endowment for the Arts (NEA). *Times* reporter Julia Preston—long infamous for her anti-Zapatista bias—drew NEA chief William Ivey's attention to the author and the book's connection to the Zapatistas. Ivey promptly canceled the funding and Preston had front-page news. Outraged by the censorship, individuals, independent presses and the Lannan Foundation donated amounts well in excess of the NEA grant to Cinco Puntos Press, allowing for the distribution of thousands of copies of the book. It sold out the entire first printing (5,000), prompting a quick second (7,000) and third (5,000) production runs. The book quickly rose to 25th on the Amazon.com "best-seller" list and at the time of this writing more than 17,000 copies have been printed.

At the end of March, in a feeble, almost comical, attempt to recoup public relations ground lost because of the Acteal massacre and the Consulta, the PRI-appointed Governor of Chiapas, Roberto Albores Guillén staged the first in a series of theatrical productions. 14 fake Zapatista soldiers in crisp new uniforms and brand new ski masks turned in their arms to Albores, members of his cabinet and Army officials in exchange for "amnesty" and 20 head of cattle. The Zapatistas immediately identified each of the false Zapatistas by name as members of the paramilitary Anti-Zapatista Revolutionary Indigenous Movement, or MIRA (Movimiento Indígena Revolucionario Anti-Zapatista) from the community of La Trinidad. They also assured readers that these terrorists would soon be getting their weapons back, courtesy of the Army.

In April, in what seemed like a response to the Consulta's support for indigenous rights, 200 Judicial Police, Public Security Police, Military Intelligence and CISEN (Centro de Investigación y Seguridad Nacional) agents were sent into

San Andrés Larrainzar (where negotiations had led to the San Andrés Accords) to crush the autonomous municipality of San Andrés Sakamch'en de Los Pobres. Filmed by Televisa and Azteca reporters, the police took over the municipal building from the autonomous authorities in order to install a PRI mayor. The next day, however, 3,000 unarmed Zapatistas from throughout the municipality pushed the police out of the community and reoccupied the municipal offices, once again reestablishing the autonomous authorities. The state government immediately signed arrest warrants for those authorities. Two days later, when thousands more indigenous EZLN supporters from all over the state converged in San Andrés to commemorate the assassination of Emiliano Zapata, Albores canceled the arrest warrants and ordered the police to withdraw. The governor then shifted his efforts to the PRI-controlled state legislature, where he introduced a law to re-draw the boundaries of the state's municipalities to undercut autonomous organizations set up by the Zapatista communities.

On April 20, student protests against planned increases in tuition and a government-proposed privatization of the university and in favor of the right of the poor to higher education, congealed into a general strike that shut down the National Autonomous University of Mexico or UNAM (Universidad Nacional Autónoma de México) in Mexico City. This strike closed Mexico's largest university (over 250,000 students attending a scattered collection of schools) and quickly became a central terrain of struggle against the government's neoliberal policies, and would last into the next year. The strikers formed a General Strike Committee, or CGH (Consejo General de Huelga) of over 100 students, called for a national debate over the future of higher education and entered into negotiations with the university administration. The CGH also adopted the Zapatista approach to negotiations, i.e., all questions for decision were taken to the various schools for discussion and vote. The CGH also moved the strike into cyberspace with regular Internet updates and appeals for support from students and professors in other countries. Not surprisingly, the Zapatistas raised their voices in support of the students.

A huge May Day protest march and demonstration in Mexico City's Zócalo was highlighted by the arrival of several Zapatistas to celebrate the raising of a 26-foot high, black bronze sculpture titled "Pillar of Shame," commemorating the massacre at Acteal and condemning the government for its responsibility in the incident. The sculpture was brought to the Zócalo by the National Indigenous Congress and CLETA (Centro Libre de Experimentación Teatral y Artística), an organization of politically active artists. Later this artwork was permanently installed in Acteal, and its creator, Jens Galschiot, was promptly expelled by immigration authorities. Two days later, Global Exchange, Miguel Agustín Pro Juárez Human Rights Center, the Mexican Commission for the Defense and Promotion of Human Rights, and the "All Rights for Everyone" Human Rights Network released a joint report titled "Foreigners of Conscience: The Mexican Government's Campaign Against International

24

Human Rights Observers," detailing the sanctioning or expulsion of some 300 foreigners over the previous five years. Time and again, the report pointed out, the Mexican government had violated its own laws in its frantic attempts to keep the world from learning about its campaign of terror in Chiapas.

The summer of 1999 was marked by three developments. First, the government stepped up its program of road-building in Chiapas, a standard feature of counter-insurgency programs in rural areas with rebellious populations and difficult terrain for military countermeasures. This road building was rationalized in the standard way: as a dimension of economic development to help farmers get their products to market. The road building was financed in part with World Bank funds made available immediately after the massacre at Acteal. The hypocrisy of the road building became obvious during the confrontations between the Army, the road builders and the people of the community of Amador Hernández in the Montes Azules region. As the Army moved in, cutting down trees, building a heliport, flying in more and more soldiers and stringing more and more razor-edged barbed wire, the local "beneficiaries" protested continuously. Even those who had previously thought a road might be useful spoke out and carried petitions against what was clearly a military invasion. Soon people from other adjacent communities joined the protests. Students from as far away as Mexico City made the trek through the forest on foot to join the opposition to this project. Faced with this spreading opposition the government backed off and renounced building the road. But the soldiers remained in their camp—a continuing threat that the project might be resumed.

Second, in May a Second Encuentro between the EZLN and Civil Society took place in La Realidad. More than 1,500 people, including striking students and militant industrial workers, met with a hundred Tojolabal, Tzotzil, Tzeltal and Chol Zapatista delegates to assess the experience of the Consulta Nacional and to continue the dialogue begun the previous November. Organized into five workshops, the participants shared their experiences of the Consulta and discussed the current situation in Chiapas and future plans. Making his first public appearance in two years, Marcos read the EZLN's opening address using Federico García Lorca's poetry to evoke the possibilities of changing the "laws" and defying "fate."

Third, in August a National Encounter for the Defense of Mexico's Cultural Heritage was convened by the EZLN and by students from the National School of Anthropology and History, or ENAH (La Escuela Nacional de Antropología e Historia). The motivation for the gathering was a recent move in the federal legislature to extend privatization of the nation's wealth to the cultural sphere by handing over many of Mexico's great Aztec and Mayan ruins to private entrepreneurs. The encounter, however, dealt with a much broader range of issues, including workshops not only on legislation of cultural heritage but also on cultural diversity and identity, tourism, education, and the relationship between academics and indigenous peoples. Some of the students and professors who attended this encounter also organized trips to Amador Hernández as civil observation teams to bolster that community's resistance to the military incursion.

In the shadow of the UNAM strike, the first Democratic Teachers and the Zapatista Dream Encuentro took place in La Realidad July 31–August 1, 1999. The EZLN invited primary and secondary school teachers to reflect on the growing privatization that threatened public education, on the interconnections between teaching and the Zapatista principles of "laterality, inclusion, tolerance, diversity, and democracy," and on the struggle for democracy inside teachers' unions. In a series of communiqués to the gathering, Marcos called for teachers to play key roles in building bridges among their own struggles and many others, including those of the students at UNAM, those of electricians against the privatization of the electrical industry, and those of the indigenous in Chiapas.

The UNAM strike continued throughout the summer and fall. The government and anti-strike forces sought repeatedly to play upon differences among the striking students to split the student movement between moderates and "ultras."

In October, in the first of a five-part communiqué (**The Hour of the Little Ones**), Marcos announced the return of Durito from a long sojourn in Europe. Dressed as a pirate and calling himself "Black Shield" Durito arrived unexpectedly at Marcos' ceiba in a sardine-can frigate. To explain both his appearance and his absence, he recounted a surreal voyage through Europe in which he was recruited by the shade of the 16th-century pirate Barbarossa to carry on the tradition of true piracy (as opposed to corporate and government piracy). In that voyage he also met with European cultural icons including Dario Fo, José Saramago, Joaquín Sabina and Manuel Vázquez Montalbán.[5]

The second part of the communiqué denounced government corruption and the paucity of help for the victims of recent natural disasters in Chiapas, while the third part supported the struggles of undocumented Mexican workers and Latinos more generally in the United States. The fourth part was dedicated to "lesbians, homosexuals, transsexuals and transvestites" and included a Durito retelling of the story of the 18th-century pirates Mary Read and Anne Bonny.

The last part of the communiqué dealt with the UNAM strike through a letter to a newspaper photograph of police beating two young students demonstrating against press coverage of the strike. The students had been peacefully blocking a highway when they were violently assaulted by Mexico City police under orders of the PRDista mayor Rosario Robles. Marcos thanks the photograph for revealing what the Mexican government-controlled press would have

---

5 Dario Fo is a Nobel Prize-winning (1997) Italian author and performer. José Saramago is a Nobel prize-winning (1998) Portuguese author and outspoken Zapatista supporter (and contributor of a preface to a collection of Durito stories published in Chiapas). Joaquín Sabina is a well-loved Spanish musician. Manuel Vázquez Montalbán is a famous Spanish mystery writer, essayist and author of a book on the Zapatistas.

hidden and how much the current PRD city government is like the previous PRI one.

As the year 1999 moved into its final month, the anti-neoliberal shockwave started by the Zapatistas in 1994 and promulgated by the Intercontinental Encounters in 1996 and 1997 made headlines once again when 30,000 demonstrators from all over the world swept into Seattle, Washington to protest and ultimately block the meetings of the World Trade Organization. Protests against the WTO had begun in Geneva, Switzerland the year before, organized by an alliance of pro-Zapatista solidarity groups and peasant organizations from India, but it was the failure of the local and federal government in the U.S. to stem the protests and keep the WTO meetings on track that brought global news coverage and elite outrage. Some demanded that the next meetings should be held on ships at sea far from such harassment and embarrassing opposition.

To contribute to the building of the anti-neoliberal globalization shockwave the city of Belem in northern Brazil—ruled by the Workers' Party, or PT (Partido dos Trabalhadores)—hosted the Second American Encounter Against Neoliberalism and For Humanity that same December (the first was in April 1996). The momentum would continue to build in the coming year with demonstrations against elite policy-makers in Davos, Switzerland and Washington, D.C.

The millennial and election year 2000 began with the formal political parties (the PRI, the PAN, and the PRD) cranking up their campaign machines to prepare for the July elections. But offstage from this public spectacle, two attacks on the real pro-democracy movement were launched.

First, the Catholic Church announced that Raúl Vera—who most expected to replace Bishop Samuel Ruiz upon his retirement and who had proved sympathetic to indigenous demands for justice—would be transferred out of Chiapas to Coahuila. The transfer of Vera outraged indigenous members of the church in Chiapas and was celebrated by conservatives in San Cristóbal and reactionary clergy elsewhere in Mexico who immediately began suggesting counter-revolutionary Bishops for his replacement. Liberation theology and a real "option for the poor," they hoped, would soon be replaced by good conservative church doctrine. However, they were sadly disappointed when the Pope named Felipe Arizmendi from Tapachula as the new Bishop of the diocese of San Cristóbal. Although not known as a great advocate of the downtrodden, he was not the kind of bishop the conservatives had hoped for. The indigenous with words, and the government and their paramilitaries by their actions, set about re-educating the new Bishop in the bloody realities of his new diocese.

Second, the UNAM strike was violently broken by a new militarized police force: the Federal Preventive Police, or PFP (Policía Federal Preventiva), patched together with troops from the CISEN, the Federal Highway Patrol and the Military Police. On February 6th thousands of them were sent to invade and re-occupy the university and to arrest more than 250 students, charging them with terrorism. Despite massive protests, the police would not relinquish their control over the university; the strike was over and the student movement was reduced to trying to defend their imprisoned comrades.

In response to the breaking of the strike, Marcos wrote to Don Pablo González Casanova, former rector at UNAM who had resigned from the university in protest of the student arrests, and shared some texts written by Durito that targeted lying, self-serving politicians and sycophantic Catholic clergymen and intellectuals. In these, Durito mocks government representations of the economy that praise growth and ignore suffering. He blasts the Catholic hierarchy that cultivates state power (by doing things like exiling Raúl Vera from Chiapas) and derides right-wing intellectuals who lose the battle of ideas (with people like González Casanova) but who win seats at the tables of the powerful by their willingness to rationalize and justify injustice. Durito also denounces the media for presenting only what suits the wealthy and powerful while keeping the embarrassing struggles of the little ones, such as the continuing efforts of students in Mexico City and the indigenous in Chiapas, out of public view. But it is there, "far from the front page" Durito asserts, where the real story of Mexico is being played out. (**Off the Record: La Realidad**)

On March 8, 2000, in celebration of International Women's Day, several thousand Zapatista women occupied the XERA radio station in San Cristóbal de las Casas, demanding rights for the indigenous and women. In their honor, Marcos describes both the difficulties women have faced in the EZLN because of male prejudice and the importance of their work. In response to Marcos' sadness at having drifted apart from one woman in particular, Durito gives him advice on lovesickness that leads him to share with her Old Antonio's account of how the old gods created things to accompany each other: air and birds, words and night, men and women. (**Story of the Air and the Night**)

The government offensive against the Zapatistas took a new turn during the winter and spring of 2000, as a campaign was opened against Zapatista communities in the Lacandon jungles of the Montes Azules biosphere. Spearheaded in the press by Secretary of the Environment Julia Carrabias, and on the ground by military and police forces, the government falsely accused the communities of ecological destruction and announced their imminent removal. But those communities were dedicated to the preservation of the environment and not its destruction, certainly not the wanton cutting of the forest for commercial profit ignored by the government in the past. Many determined that the government's real aim was the destruction of the Zapatistas, on the one hand, and clearing the way for multinational corporate exploitation on the other. As a result, the defensive self-mobilizations of the communities to resist eviction drew support from environmentalists and other civil society activists.

The political summer of 2000 was successfully usurped by the formal electoral spectacle as it became clear that the PRI might lose the elections because of the successes of the pro-democracy movement's fight to reduce electoral fraud.

The Zapatistas, for the most part, stood apart from both the spectacle and from participation. Neither the danger that the rabidly anti-Zapatista PRI candidate Francisco Labastida might come to power and unleash the military against their communities nor the declaration by the PAN candidate Vicente Fox Quesada that he would end the conflict in Chiapas "in fifteen minutes" by ordering a military withdrawal and sending the San Andrés Accords to Congress for approval were enough to draw the Zapatistas onto the electoral stage. Despite the PRI's expenditure of millions of pesos in vote-buying, on July 2nd it was swept out of presidential power by voters whose demands for at least minimal democracy had been growing for the last six years. The PAN candidate, Vicente Fox, won the elections, eclipsing both PRI and the PRD.

With state elections coming up in August and Fox not due to take office until December, the Zedillo government continued its war against the Zapatistas with paramilitary attacks on the community of Tierra y Libertad. Wanting to extend the change in Mexico City into Chiapas, eight political parties joined together to support a common anti-PRI candidate: the ex-PRIista and pro-Fox Pablo Salazar Mendiguchía. Salazar's campaign promised to end PRI corruption and violence and to bring real peace to Chiapas. In tune with Fox's intention to continue neoliberal economic policies, Salazar voyaged north to talk to U.S. business and government leaders about how his administration would open Chiapas to more foreign investment. Openly backed by the recently elected Fox and seen as a marginal improvement over the PRI by voters in Chiapas, Salazar easily won the election.

Upon taking office in December of 2000, Fox ordered a partial military withdrawal in Chiapas and called on the Zapatistas to return to peace talks. In response, the Zapatistas laid out their conditions for re-engaging in talks: the fulfillment of the San Andres Accords, the release of all Zapatista political prisoners, and the beginnings of serious demilitarization, i.e., the withdrawal of the military from seven of the 279 positions then occupied by the army. Those seven were all in or close to Zapatista communities and included Amador Hernández, Guadalupe Tepeyac (occupied since 1995) and four of the new Aguascalientes. The Zapatistas also announced that they would come to Mexico City the following year to lay their case for indigenous rights, democracy, justice and the implementation of the San Andrés Accords before the Mexican Congress and people.

2001: The Zapatista March for Indigenous Dignity
With the New Year the Zapatistas began organizing their march to Mexico City. The Zapatistas did not ask permission from the government, political parties or local authorities to travel; they simply announced their intentions and began organizing. For years the Salinas and Zedillo administrations had tried to confine them to the jungle, threatening to arrest any who tried to leave. It was only through great political pressure that Ramona was allowed to travel unmo-

29

lested to the founding of the CNI in 1996. But the new Fox administration—whose leader had sworn to end the conflict in Chiapas in 15 minutes—would take no action to stop the Zapatistas from traveling.

On January 3rd, Marcos issued a communiqué announcing the formation of a new Zapatista Information Center and calling for the mobilization of Mexican activists and allies in other countries. The Information Center would disseminate regular news about organization and itinerary; the call for mobilization invited supporters to either accompany the Zapatistas on their march or to meet them when they would arrive in Mexico City. Within days the Zapatistas announced that they would leave their communities on February 24th and pass first through San Cristóbal and Tuxtla Gutierrez and then through the states of Oaxaca, Puebla, Veracruz, Tlaxcala, Hidalgo, Michoacán, Morelos, and the State of Mexico, arriving in Mexico City on March 11, 2001. During the march they met with as much of civil society as organizers could arrange—including the Third National Indigenous Congress in the village of Nurio, Michoacán.

The march was a kind of rolling encounter for the Zapatista delegates, who traveled in buses, accompanied by many supporters and the press. And as they were greeted by cheering crowds in town after town, stopping to meet dozens of delegates from local grassroots communities, explaining their demands and listening to what those who greeted them had to say, it became impossible to ignore the vast base of support that the Zapatistas had generated over the previous seven years. The Zapatistas had requested the participation of the International Red Cross for their own protection, but when Fox refused to allow this, local and international observers, such as the Tute Bianche (or White Overalls) Collective joined the march to guard the Zapatista encampments from the numerous threats and provocations they experienced throughout the trip.

The Third National Indigenous Congress, from March 2-4, was attended by over 3,300 delegates from 41 out of Mexico's 57 indigenous communities, over 6,400 observers, and over 700 invited guests. All of these greeted, hosted, and dialogued with the Zapatistas upon their arrival. These representatives of Mexico's indigenous peoples declared from Nurio their full support for the COCOPA law to implement the San Andrés Accords. They joined with the Zapatistas in denouncing the treatment of the indigenous and in condemning as potentially devastating for local communities the large-scale Puebla-Panamá Plan (PPP) aimed at turning southern Mexico into an industrial-trade corridor. They declared their intention to follow the Zapatista lead in transforming indigenous communities into autonomous municipalities all over Mexico.

As the Zapatistas traveled along their 3,000 kilometer route to Mexico City, the government continued to partially meet the EZLN's three preconditions for talks: they withdrew the military from a few positions, they liberated a few more Zapatista prisoners and Fox reiterated his promise to present the COCOPA law to the Congress. While recognizing these moves as steps in the right direction, the Zapatistas continued to demand the vacating of all seven military positions, the freeing of all imprisoned Zapatista sympathizers, and the actual passage of the law on indigenous rights.

When the Zapatistas arrived in Mexico City, they were greeted in the Zócalo by more than 250,000 people. The faculty, staff and student body of the National School of Anthropology and History, or ENAH (Escuela Nacional de Antropología e Historia), put their school in the service of the Zapatista comandancia during their stay in the capital.

In the days following their arrival, the Zapatistas took part in many informal consultations, gatherings with grassroots groups and conferences. Among these many meetings was the March 12, 2001 intercultural meeting of intellectuals at the ENAH on: "Paths of Dignity: Indigenous Rights, Memory and Cultural Heritage" that included Zapatista supporters such as José Saramago, Manuel Vázquez Montalbán, Carlos Monsiváis, Elena Poniatowska, Carlos Montemayor, and Pablo González Casanova. In his presentation Marcos complained about Durito interrupting his efforts to prepare his speech, but passed on Durito's pirate-like view of the buses used by the Zapatistas as ships sailing through a supporting sea of resistance and rebellion. He also told a story of an indigenous man who interrupted a chess game among his would-be "betters." In an unusual manner, Marcos interpreted his story, explaining that the key aspect of the story was not the interruption per se, but the understanding by the indigenous man that the game was missing players both now and in the future: himself and other indigenous people. This ability to dream the future, to imagine other worlds, he juxtaposed to the blindness of the neoliberal declaration of the end of history. (**The Other Player**)

In another talk, this time to children in the neighborhood surrounding the ENAH, Marcos recounted a story dictated to him by Durito for just that occasion. The story concerned a neglected wind-up toy that made itself useful in generating electricity when the power failed. Because not everyone has such a toy, Marcos explained, it would be better not to privatize the electrical industry (a move begun by Zedillo and continued by Fox) and cause a crisis in the availability of electricity. (**The Story of the Little Dented Car**)

One of the Zapatista goals in Mexico City was to formally address the national congress—something no indigenous community had ever been allowed to do. A central theme of this presentation would be their arguments as to why the Congress should pass the COCOPA proposal into law, giving legal form to at least some of the agreements on indigenous rights reached at San Andrés years before. The Congress was split over allowing the Zapatistas to address them. Although the PRD delegates generally supported such a presentation, the majority PRI and PAN delegates at first refused the Zapatistas the right to speak. The popular reaction was outrage; public debate flared, and political pressure began to build.

During those days of controversy, at a meeting with university students at the Azcapotzalco campus of the Autonomous Metropolitan University, or UAM

31

(Universidad Autónoma Metropolitana), Marcos revealed that he had just discovered that Durito was once a student and then a teacher at UAM, and moonlighted at a nearby refinery, first to be able to pay his tuition and later to supplement his low professorial income. Given Durito's experience and knowledge of Mexico City, Marcos asked him to explain why the PRIista and PANista "hard-liners" were blocking the Zapatistas from addressing the Congress. Durito told him that it was because politicians think life is like writing with a pencil and anything you don't like can simply be erased and rewritten to get rid of anything uncomfortable. They write, erase, and rewrite even though nothing changes but the shape of their words. But what matters, Marcos suggests, is not the pencil but the dream that guides the hand. (**The Hand That Dreams When It Writes**)

Eventually, under tremendous popular and even presidential pressure—fueled by a Zapatista denunciation of racist and "caveman" politicians and a threat to return home—Congress narrowly approved, by a vote of 220 to 210, a resolution to allow Zapatista representatives to speak about the Law on Indigenous Rights and Culture. The presentation was set for March 28, 2001. On that day four Zapatista leaders—Comandantes Esther, David, Tacho, and Zebedeo—spoke to the Congress, explaining the situation of the indigenous and the reasons why a law should be passed recognizing and legalizing indigenous autonomy. A few days later, the Zapatistas returned to Chiapas and Congress passed such a watered-down version of the COCOPA proposal as to make a mockery of the demand for indigenous autonomy and kill any chance for a renewal of peace talks. The EZLN formally denounced the new legislation, recalled Fernández Yáñez Muñoz from his negotiations with the Fox government and said they would refuse any further peace talks until the Congress's acts were reversed.

As the Zapatistas withdrew from negotiating with the government, they turned their efforts to rebuilding and renewing their struggle. Among those places to be rebuilt was the village of Guadalupe Tepeyac. Abandoned in the face of the military offensive of February 1995, the community had been in exile for over five years because of continued military occupation. When the army withdrew as part of Fox's partial meeting of the Zapatista conditions for peace talks, the community returned. In April, the ejidal authorities issued a communiqué announcing their desire to rebuild their destroyed houses and their intention to refuse any official aid, but also their willingness to accept the support of civil society. A construction project that would finally bear fruit in October of 2001 was the installation of an electricity-generating turbine in the Zapatista community of La Realidad. Conceived at the First Intercontinental Encounter in 1996, the project was realized by the donations of Italian communities and the efforts of the Mexican Electricity Unionists working together with community volunteers. Thus, through national and international solidarity, one community was able to overcome the supreme irony that Chiapas generates much of Mexico's hydroelectric power while thousands of its villages have no electric service!

The government's reaction to the Zapatista withdrawal was to return to a policy of military and paramilitary harassment during the summer of 2001. Military patrols were increased, helicopter flyovers multiplied and soldiers began stopping and interrogating individuals inside their own communities. Part of this harassment was the intensification of road building. Not surprisingly, as the Zapatista communities pointed out, such roads were often driven right through crops and coffee plantations with no concern or compensation for the losses of the local owners. Another part of the government's renewed offensive was an effort, within the process of privatization begun under Salinas, to divide ejidal lands that had been collectively owned by the communities in favor of pro-government factions. Finally, in the summer and fall, paramilitary attacks increased in number and intensity; lands were seized and members of Zapatista communities were injured or killed. All of these actions were described and denounced in communiqués publicly issued by the various affected communities.

Repression of the struggle for democracy, liberty and justice came at the national level in the assassination of prominent human rights activist and lawyer Digna Ochoa y Plácido on October 19, 2001, in Mexico City. Ochoa had previously been kidnapped and left to die for defending those tortured by the military and police, and had recently received numerous death threats. Despite the Inter-American Court for Human Rights' request that she be protected, the threats had been largely discounted and ignored by the government. Along with her body, riddled with 22-caliber bullets, was found yet another death threat, this time against her colleagues at the Miguel Agustín Pro Human Rights Center. Unlike the daily outrages perpetuated in indigenous communities, her murder brought public outcries and made it clear that such vicious repression continued unabated under the Fox government.

The year ended with continuing repression in Chiapas and the refusal of the Mexican government to recognize and accept demands for indigenous autonomy that the Zapatistas had brought to the Capitol early in the year. It also ended with the celebration of the eight years of struggle since January 1, 1994 and renewed determination of Zapatista communities to continue their own self-organization and resistance.

2002: Rebeldía, Terrorism and Apples

Although the EZLN did not officially attend, July witnessed an important gathering in San Cristóbal de las Casas intended to revive a dialogue regarding peace in Chiapas. More than a thousand people participated in the National Encounter for Peace with Justice and Dignity from July 5-7, including many people from the Zapatista base communities. Those gathered represented activists, indigenous and non-indigenous, from 285 organizations, 23 states of the Republic and 13 countries.

Paramilitary violence persisted throughout the year. The Autonomous municipality of Ricardo Flores Magón decried the emergence of the

Organization for the Defense of Indigenous and Campesino Rights, or OPDIC (Organización por la Defensa Indígena y Campesina). This new paramilitary force was alleged to be under the direction of Pedro Chulín, a PRI congressman who also had links to Revolutionary Indigenous Anti-Zapatista Movement, an earlier paramilitary group with a history of violent activities. On July 31st, OPDIC attacks wounded seven members of the ejido La Culebra. On August 7th, José López Santiz from the autonomous municipality of 17th of November (Altamirano) was assassinated. Less than two weeks later nine members of Crucero Quexil (autonomous municipality of San Manuel) were wounded. On August 25th, two officials of Ricardo Flores Magón were gunned down at Amaytik village (Ocosingo) and another was killed at the autonomous municipality of Olga Isabel (Chilón).

While Zapatista municipalities were being subjected to lethal levels of paramilitary violence, the National Supreme Court of Justice, or SCJN (Suprema Corte de Justicia de la Nación) deliberated over 3,000 challenges to the legitimacy of the indigenous law reforms, approved by Congress in April 2001. Those challenges argued that the reforms ran drastically counter to the spirit of the San Andrés Accords, to which the government had previously agreed. On September 6th, 2002, the SCJN rejected all of the challenges—a move seen by many as further evidence of the government's lack of commitment to change.

During October, a number of gatherings and direct actions occured throughout the region as part of the growing mobilization against the Puebla-Panamá Plan. The First Chiapas Meeting Confronting Neo-liberalism convened in San Cristóbal de las Casas from October 9–12. As the meeting ended, direct actions, including roadblocks, demonstrations and other actions along borders, protested against increased privatization, biopiracy, militarization and maquiladorization associated with the PPP and the Free Trade Agreement of the Americas (FTAA). Opposition also took root nationally as the National Consultation Against the FTAA was inaugurated throughout Mexico.

In November, the PGR disbanded the Special Unit for the Handling of Crimes Committed by Armed Civil Groups, a special division established immediately following the massacre at Acteal. Despite Governor Pablo Salazar's very public efforts to prosecute prominent figures responsible for violence, the decommissioning of the investigative unit underscored doubts regarding the government's commitment to address the widespread aggressions being carried out by paramilitary forces.

The official silence of the Zapatistas during this period led some to pronounce the EZLN a political force weakened by its failure to achieve the implementation of the San Andrés Accords, and quickly fading as a factor in Mexican politics. On November 17th, Subcomandante Marcos broke that silence by responding to Zapatista critics in a communiqué published in the recently established magazine *Rebeldía*. Included in that communiqué was an account of Durito's musings on apples. While some eat ripe apples and others eat green or rotten apples, Durito suggested, the Zapatistas take the seeds and plant them so that some day everyone will be able to eat apples in whatever form they choose. (**Apples and the Zapatistas**)

On November 25th *La Jornada* published another communiqué, this one written a month earlier and sent to Ángel Luis Lara, or El Ruso, celebrating the inauguration of a new Aguascalientes in Madrid. The communiqué addressed the struggles of the Basque people against Spanish colonialism and criticized King Juan Carlos, Prime Minister José María Áznar, ex-Prime Minister Felipe González Márquez and Judge Baltazar Garzón for their repression of the Basque people. When Garzón replied with a vituperative letter challenging him to a debate, Marcos—claiming the traditional rights of the challenged—named the Canary Island of Lanzarote and set as a condition that Garzón attend an encuentro to be called "The Basque Country: Paths" that would be organized and attended by all the parties involved in the political struggle in Euskal Herra (Basque). He also wrote to the Basque separatist organization ETA, or Euskadita Askatasuna, requesting them to consent to a ceasefire for 177 days and to attend the encuentro. Finally, he wrote to the Spanish Left and to Spanish civil society asking them to participate in pressuring the ETA and the Spanish state to participate in the encuentro.

Marcos' letter, calling for the replacement of terrorism (both by the state and by the ETA) by encounter, debate and political negotiation, caused an enormous stir in Spain. The State tried to use its ambiguous language about the ETA to accuse the Zapatistas of supporting terrorism. For its part, the ETA denounced this Zapatista intervention, accusing Marcos of not respecting them and thus not respecting the Basque people. On the other hand, over 57 academics, journalists and artists responded positively by organizing a Civil Forum for the Word on December 22 as part of the preparation for a larger Encounter scheduled for April 22.

In a follow-up communiqué to the ETA, Marcos pointedly remarked that both they and Garzón accused the Zapatistas of disrespecting the people they represented. Does the ETA really represent the Basque people, he wondered? Does Garzón represent the Spanish people? The Zapatistas, he pointed out, represent no one but themselves. Moreover, he unambiguously denounced the killing of innocent civilians and those who disagree, whether this killing is carried out by the state or by some self-proclaimed "revolutionary vanguard." In the strongest language he has ever used to denounce groups like the ETA, Marcos ended his communiqué with the statement: "I shit on all the revolutionary vanguards of this planet."

During the winter of 2002 the government continued its low-intensity war with an increase in officially sanctioned, forced evictions. On December 19th, the people of the small community of Arroyo San Pablo were forced to abandon their homes. Government spokesmen such as Jaime Alejo Castillo of the Ministry of the Environment, or SEMARNAT (Secretaría de Medio Ambiente y Recursos Naturales), revived the oft-used argument that the indigenous communities in the Montes Azules Biosphere damage the environment by using outdated farming methods such as slash and burn. Such arguments, however, ignored not only the environment-friendly practices of the communities in question, but also the ambitions of multinational corporations eager to exploit the rich resources of timber, petroleum, water and biologically diverse fauna and flora. Barely hidden in the shadows of the free-market policies and privatization articulated in the PPP and FTAA—and promoted by the World Bank, IMF, Inter-American Development Bank, European Union and USAID—are a legion of corporations ready to exploit the Biosphere. Among those accused of such intentions are: EXXON, Shell, Mobil, Dow Chemicals, Boise Cascade, Smurfit, International Paper, Hyundai, Samsung, Monsanto, Sandoz and the Pulsar Group.

The next year began with a massive mobilization by the EZLN and their communities to demonstrate that their movement was alive and well, and that government repression and their resistance to it continues. At six in the evening of December 31, 2002, over 20,000 Zapatistas from 40 autonomous municipalities marched into the main plaza of San Cristóbal de las Casas. They were armed with machetes and lit bonfires all around the central plaza. The indigenous rebels listened to speeches by seven comandantes: Tacho, David, Brus Li, Fidelia, Omar, Míster and Esther. The comandantes declared their commitment to continue resistance and condemned President Vicente Fox and the rest of the Mexican government for its duplicity and failure to pursue peace. Underscoring their right to speak on issues outside of Chiapas, the Comandancia voiced support for Subcomandante Marcos in his recent exchange with the spokespersons of the Spanish state and the ETA.

At the time of this writing, the Zapatista resistance to government repression continues, as do their efforts to build their own autonomous communities and to develop new and better ways of life. Within that resistance and amidst those efforts, the ever resourceful knight-errant and pirate Don Durito de la Lacandona continues to provide ideas to illuminate the confused and humor to push back the ever-threatening darkness. With a little luck, his squire, scribe and sometimes resentful student, Subcomandante Marcos, will also continue to pass along to us, in his letters and communiqués, whatever enlightenment Durito may have to offer in the future.

Durito says that this is the difference between the Zapatistas and the rest of humanity:

Where everyone sees an apple, the Zapatista sees a seed, goes and cultivates the land, plants the seed and guards it.

March 2003
Austin, Texas

Postscript that adds two notes as this manuscript goes to press.

Note #1: We are pleased to see that the magazine *Rebeldia*, from whose first issue we drew the last story in this volume, continues to pass along stories from and about Durito. For those who, having read the stories that we have prepared here, can't wait to read more, we recommend them to you. *Rebeldia* is available both in hard copy and on the web at www.revistarebeldia.org.

Note #2: During August of 2003, the Zapatistas held one of the most important encounters of recent years. They organized a giant fiesta, inviting their friends and supporters from all over Mexico and the world to celebrate the creation of new forms of organization, both among their communities and between themselves and the world.

Tired of waiting for government recognition of the San Andrés Accords on indigenous autonomy, they have proceeded to elaborate that autonomy in the form of regional autonomous "good governments" to facilitate cooperation among the various autonomous municipalities they had already created. These regional governments will work to overcome imbalances among the municipalities, to mediate relationships between those municipalities and official state municipal governments, to deal with complaints against Autonomous Councils and to monitor the enforcement of rebel law and the carrying out of community projects within the autonomous regions. Finally, these regional bodies will be located within the Aguascalientes, which were built as zones of encounter between the Zapatistas and the larger Mexican and international civil society.

However, these Aguascalientes are also being transformed into "Caracoles" (or seashells) that will not only continue to be places of encounter but will now become the required portals through which supporters must bring any and all proposals for projects. This is aimed at allowing the representatives of the larger regional community to make sure that such outside resources are more evenly distributed throughout the autonomous municipalities rather than accentuating inequalities in income and opportunities.

Thus, these new regional governments represent another innovative step in the Zapatista project of transforming their own world and their relationships with those of us from other worlds. Already, indigenous communities in other parts of Mexico are formally studying these innovations and discussing how they might be adapted to their own needs. The revolution continues.

37

STORIES FOR A
SUFFOCATING NIGHT

The Story of Durito and Neoliberalism

Responding to a letter from ten-year-old Mariana Moguel, Subcomandante Marcos shares the story of his first conversation with Durito, thus marking the beginning of an ongoing dialogue between them. During the period in which this communiqué appeared, the fighting of January 1994 had given way to negotiations and the Zapatistas had returned to their base communities to discuss a set of peace proposals offered by the government.

April 10, 1994
To: Mariana Moguel
From: Subcomandante Insurgente Marcos

Subcomandanta Mariana Moguel,
I greet you with respect and congratulate you for the new rank you acquired with your drawing. Permit me to tell you a story that, perhaps, you will understand someday. It is the story of . . .

First published in *La Jornada*, April 17, 1994. Original translator unknown.

DURITO

The story I am going to tell you came to me the other day. It is the story of a small beetle who wears glasses and smokes a pipe. I met him one day as I was looking for my smoking tobacco and I couldn't find it. Suddenly, on one side of my hammock, I saw that a bit of tobacco had fallen and formed a small trail. I followed it to see where my tobacco was and to see who the hell had taken it and was spilling it. A few meters away, behind a rock, I found a beetle sitting at a little desk, reading some papers and smoking a tiny pipe.

"Ahem, ahem," I said, so that the beetle would notice my presence, but he paid no attention to me.

Then I said, "Listen, that tobacco is mine." The beetle took off his glasses, looked me up and down, and told me angrily, "Please, Captain, I beseech you. Do not interrupt me. Do you not realize that I am studying?"

I was a bit surprised and was going to give him a good kick, but I calmed myself and sat down to one side to wait for him to finish studying. In a little while, he gathered up his papers, put them away in the desk, and, chewing on his pipe, said to me, "Well, now, what can I do for you, Captain?"

"My tobacco," I replied.

"Your tobacco?" he said to me. "You want me to give you a little?"

I started to get pissed off, but the little beetle passed me the bag of tobacco with his little foot and added, "Don't be angry, Captain. Please understand that you can't get tobacco around here and I had to take some of yours."

I calmed down. The beetle was growing on me and I told him, "Don't worry about it. I've got more around somewhere."

"Hmmm," he answered.

"And you, what is your name?" I asked him.

"Nebuchadnezzar," he said, and continued, "but my friends call me Durito.[1] You can call me Durito, Captain."

I thanked him for the courtesy and asked him what it was that he was studying.

"I'm studying neoliberalism and its strategy of domination for Latin America," he told me.

"And what good is that to a beetle?" I asked him.

And he replied, very annoyed, "What *good* is it?! I have to know how long your struggle is going to last, and whether or not you are going to win. Besides, a beetle should care enough to study the situation of the world in which it lives, don't you think, Captain?"

"I don't know," I said. "But, why do you want to know how long our struggle will last and whether or not we are going to win?"

---

1 Nebuchadnezzar, the second king of the Chaldean dynasty of Babylonia (605–562 BC), was known as a skilled field commander who conquered Jerusalem in 597 BC. During his reign, he built the "hanging gardens" of Babylon, one of the Seven Wonders of the World. He is referenced in the Bible in Jeremiah, Ezekiel, and Daniel, where he is characterized as a champion warrior-king divinely chosen by God. Durito literally means "little hard one."

"Well, you haven't understood a thing," he told me, putting on his glasses and lighting his pipe. After letting out a puff of smoke, he continued, "To know how long we beetles are going to have to take care that you do not squash us with your big boots."

"Ah!" I said.

"Hmmm," he said.

"And to what conclusion have you come in your study?" I asked him.

He took out the papers from the desk and began to leaf through them. "Hmmm . . . hmmm," he said every so often as he reviewed them. After having finished, he looked me in the eye and said, "You are going to win."

"I already knew that," I told him. I added, "But how long will it take?"

"A long time," he said, sighing with resignation.

"I already knew that, too . . . Don't you know exactly how long?" I asked.

"It cannot be known exactly. Many things have to be taken into account: the objective conditions, the ripeness of the subjective conditions, the correlation of forces, the crisis of imperialism, the crisis of socialism, etcetera, etcetera."

"Hmmm," I said.

"What are you thinking about, Captain?"

"Nothing," I answered. "Well, Mr. Durito, I have to go. It was a pleasure to have met you. Know that you may take all the tobacco you want, whenever you like."

"Thank you, Captain. You can be informal with me if you like."[2]

"Thank you, Durito. Now I'm going to give orders to my *compañeros* that it is prohibited to step on beetles. I hope that helps."

"Thank you, Captain. Your order will be very useful to us."

"But regardless, be very careful, because my compañeros are very distracted, and they don't always watch where they're going."

"I'll do that, Captain."

"See you later."

"See you later. Come whenever you like, and we'll talk."

"I'll do that," I told him, and went back to headquarters.

That's all Mariana. I hope to know you personally someday and be able to trade ski masks and drawings. *Mask does not signify evil*

Vale. Salud, and more colored markers, because the ones you used surely must have run out of ink.

From the mountains of the Mexican Southeast
Subcomandante Insurgente Marcos

* * *

2 In Spanish, "puedes tutearme" (you can be informal with me) is an invitation to use the familiar form of address, "tú," instead of the formal "usted."

Durito II: Neoliberalism Seen From La Lacandona

Almost a year after their first encounter, Marcos once again meets Durito. Some weeks earlier, the Zedillo government had launched a two-pronged attack on the Zapatista communities. While press agents claimed to have discovered Marcos' "true identity," tanks rolled into Chiapas. Faced with an attack by some 60,000 soldiers, the EZLN and over 26,000 people from Zapatista communities retreated into the mountains. The conversation in this new encounter dwelt particularly on the inhabitants of Prado Pacayal who, after enduring great hardship in the mountains, returned to find their possessions, provisions, and houses destroyed by the Army. Following this vivid account of the havoc wrought by the army, Durito and Marcos examine the neoliberal policies behind the army offensive. Here Durito puts forth his critical "metatheoretical" observation that neoliberalism is a social crisis made theory and doctrine, and is thus "pure theoretical shit."

First published in *La Jornada*, March 17, 1995. Original translator unknown.

To *Proceso, El Financiero, La Jornada, Tiempo*
To the National and International Press
March 11, 1995

Sirs:
Here is a message demonstrating that man is the only animal that risks falling into the same trap twice. Indeed, it would be good if you would send a copy of the much-mentioned law to the federal troops.[1] They don't seem to have been informed, because they keep advancing. If we keep withdrawing we're going to run into a sign saying: "Welcome to the Ecuador-Peru border." It's not that we wouldn't enjoy the trip to South America, but being in the middle of three fires like that must not be very pleasant.[2]

We are well. Here in the jungle one can appreciate, in all its rawness, the transformation of man into monkey (anthropologists, abstain).

Vale. Salud, and one of those crystals that lets you see the present and the future.

From the mountains of the Mexican Southeast
Insurgente Subcomandante Marcos

P.S. that asks just out of curiosity: What is the name of the general of the Federal Army who, before retreating from the *ejido* Prado, ordered the destruction of everything useful in the houses of the indigenous people and the burning of several huts?[3] In Prado they earn, on average, 200 new pesos a month per family; how much does the general earn for such a "brilliant" military action? Will they promote him in rank for "meritorious service"? Did the general know that one of the houses he ordered destroyed was Toñita's house? Will this general tell his children and grandchildren about this "shining entry" in his record of service?

What is the name of the officer who, days after having invaded and destroyed houses in the *ejido* Champa San Agustín, came back with candy and had himself photographed as he gave it to the children?

---

1 The "Law for Dialogue, Reconciliation and Dignified Peace in Chiapas," approved by the Mexican Congress on March 11, 1995 and accepted by the EZLN on March 16, 1995, protected the EZLN against arrest and harassment during the peace process.
2 A long-standing border dispute between Ecuador and Peru flared into armed conflict in 1995.
3 *Ejido* refers to communally held land recognized in Article 27 of the Mexican Constitution. The film *Prado Pacayal* chronicles the return of people to the destroyed village (see Bibliography).

What is the name of the officer, who, emulating the protagonist of Mario Vargas Llosa's novel *Pantaleón y las visitadoras*, brought dozens of prostitutes to "attend" to the garrison that occupies Guadalupe Tepeyac?[4] How much do the prostitutes charge? How much does the general in charge of such a "risky" military operation earn? How much commission does the Mexican "*Pantaleón*" get? Are the prostitutes the same for the officers and the troops? Does this "service" exist in all the garrisons of the campaign "in defense of the national sovereignty"?[5]

If the Mexican Federal Army exists to guarantee national sovereignty, shouldn't they have accompanied Ortiz to Washington, instead of persecuting Mexican indigenous dignity in Chiapas?[6]

P.S. that armor-plates its heart again to tell what follows. . . . The 8th of March, the inhabitants of Prado finish coming down from the mountains. Toñita's family was part of the last contingent. When they come to what was left of their little house, each Prado family's scene is repeated in Toñita's family: the men, impotent and enraged, look over the little that is left standing; the women cry and tear their hair, praying and repeating: "Oh my God, oh my God," while they pick up the torn clothes, the few broken pieces of furniture, the food, spilled and contaminated with excrement, the broken images of the Virgin of Guadalupe, their crucifixes trashed alongside "fast food" wrappers from the U.S. Army. This scene is now almost a ceremony among the inhabitants of Prado. They have repeated it 108 times in the last few days, once for each family. 108 times the impotence, the rage, the tears, the cries, the "Oh my God, oh my God . . ."

However, this time there is something different. There is a tiny little woman who doesn't cry. Toñita didn't say anything, she didn't cry, she didn't yell. She walked over the rubbish and went directly to a corner of the house, as if looking for something. There, in a forgotten corner, was a little teacup, broken, thrown away like a worn-out hope. That little cup was a gift someone had sent her so that someday Toñita-Alice could drink tea with the Mad Hatter and the March Hare. But this time it isn't a hare that Toñita finds in March. It is her house,

---

4 *Pantaleón y las visitadoras* (Barcelona: Editorial Seix Barral, 1973), a novel by Mario Vargas Llosa, examines the conflicts and contradictions that result from the enthusiasm of a junior officer dedicated to following orders in the Amazon jungle. It was published in English as *Captain Pantoja and the Special Service* (New York: Harper & Row, 1978).

5 The hospital in Guadalupe Tepeyac, originally funded by President Carlos Salinas de Gotari through the structural adjustment program *Solidaridad*, was turned into a brothel during the 1995 military offensive.

6 Guillermo Ortiz Martínez replaced Jaime Serra Puche as Mexico's Minister of Finance following the peso crisis and Serra's subsequent resignation in December 1994. Ortiz immediately traveled to the U.S. to reassure foreign investors and begin negotiating a bailout package for investors in the Mexican capital market.

destroyed on the orders of the one who claims to defend sovereignty and legality. Toñita doesn't cry, she doesn't shout, she doesn't say anything. She picks up the pieces of the little teacup and the little saucer that served as its base. Toñita leaves, walks again through the torn and dirty clothes on the ground, through the corn and beans strewn about the destruction, she passes by her mother, her aunts, and her sisters who weep, and cry out, and repeat "Oh my God, oh my God." Outside, near a guava tree, Toñita sits down on the ground and, with mud and a little saliva, starts to stick the pieces of the teacup together again. Toñita doesn't cry, but there is a cold and hard glimmer in her eyes.

Brutally, as has been the case for indigenous women for the last 500 years, Toñita is no longer a girl and becomes a woman. It is the 8th of March of 1995, International Women's Day, and Toñita is five years old, going on six. The cold and piercing glimmer in her eyes rescues, from the broken little teacup, sparkles that wound. Anyone would say that it is the sun that sharpens the rancor that betrayal has sown in these lands. . . . As if mending a broken heart, Toñita reconstructs, with mud and saliva, her broken little teacup. Someone, far off, forgets for the moment that he is a man. The salty drops that fall from his face don't manage to rust his leaden heart. . . .

P.S. that risks "the most valuable thing I own" (the account in dollars?): I read that now there is a "Subcomandante Elisa," a "Subcomandante Germán," a "Subcomandante Daniel," and a "Subcomandante Eduardo," so I have decided to make the following resolution: I'm warning the PGR that if they keep coming out with more "Subs," I will go on a total fast.[7] Furthermore, I demand that the PGR declare that there is only one "Sub" (fortunately, says My Other Self when he reads these lines), and that they clear me of all blame for the dollar's weakness against the Japanese yen and the German MARKS (note the narcissistic repetition).[8] (And don't send me to Warman—please!)[9]

---

7 Prior to President Zedillo's military offensive, the PGR Office of the Attorney General, claimed to have discovered the identities of several Zapatista leaders in cities throughout Mexico. The "total fast" is undoubtedly a reference to Carlos Salinas' one-day hunger strike on the previous March 3. He protested allegations that he was involved in a cover-up of the assassinations of PRI presidential candidate Luis Donaldo Colosio and PRI party official José Francisco Ruiz Massieu. Salinas also demanded exoneration from responsibility for the December 1994 peso crash, despite having repeatedly ignored his own economists' advice.

8 The government tried to blame the EZLN for the peso devaluation of 1994. In Spanish German Marks are "Marcos."

9 Once a left-leaning intellectual specializing in indigenous social movements, Arturo Warman was one of the architects of the revision of Article 27, allowing for the privatization of *ejidos* or communal lands. In 1995 he served the Zedillo administration as *Secretaría de Agricultura Ganadería y Desarrollo Rural* (Secretary of Agriculture).

P.S. that acknowledges receipt of promises attached to a sonnet and returns with . . .

When, in disgrace with fortune and men's eyes,
I all alone beweep my outcast state,
And trouble deaf heaven with my bootless cries,
And look upon myself and curse my fate,
Wishing me like to one more rich in hope,
Featur'd like him, like him with friends possess'd,
Desiring this man's art and that man's scope,
With what I most enjoy contented least;
Yet in these thoughts myself almost despising,
Haply I think on thee, and then my state,
Like to the lark at break of day arising
From sullen earth, sings hymns at heaven's gate;
For thy sweet love remember'd such wealth brings
That then I scorn to change my state with kings.
—William Shakespeare, Sonnet XXIX

P.S. that tells about what happened February 17 and 18 of 1995, the eighth and ninth days of the withdrawal. We were following the double point of a lunatic arrow. "Waxing quarter, horns to the East," I remembered, and repeated to myself as we came out into some pastures. We had to wait. Above, a military airplane rained down its purr of death. My Other Self starts to sing softly:

And we heard it strike ten and eleven,
twelve, one, two and three.
And hidden at dawn,
we were soaked by rain . . .

I give him a threatening sign to shut up. He defends himself: "My life is a song by Joaquín Sabina."[10]

"It sure must not be a love song," I tell him, forgetting my own prohibition on talking.

Camilo reports that the plane is gone. We go out into the pasture and keep walking in the middle of a field still damp from the rain. I move forward, looking upward, seeking on its dark side some answer to old questions.

"Watch out for the bull," I managed to hear Camilo warn me. But it was too late—lowering my gaze after a trip through the Milky Way, I met the eyes of a steer that, I think, was as frightened as I was because he ran just like me, but in the opposite direction. When I got to the fence, I managed to throw my pack over the barbed wire.

---

10 Joaquín Sabina is a Spanish singer and political activist.

I stretched out to drag myself under the fence. I did it with such good luck, that what I thought was mud was cow shit. Camilo was roaring with laughter. My Other Self even got the hiccups. The two, sitting there, and me, signaling them to shut up.

"Ssshhh, the soldiers are going to hear us!" But no, they keep laughing. I cut a bunch of star-grass to clean the shit off my shirt and pants as best I can. I put on my pack and go on walking. Camilo and My Other Self followed behind me. They weren't laughing anymore. When they got up, they realized that they had been sitting in shit. Attracting cows with such a seductive odor, we finished crossing the wide pasture that had a stream running through it. When we got to the wooded zone I looked at my watch. 0200. "Southeastern time," Tacho would say. With luck and without rain, we would arrive at the foot of the mountain before dawn. So it was. We went in by an old trail between big and well-spaced trees that announced the closeness of the jungle. The real jungle, where only wild animals, the dead and guerrillas live. There wasn't much need for a light; the moon still tore through the branches, like a white streamer, and the crickets hushed with each step on the dry leaves. We came to the great ceiba tree that marked the gate of entry; we rested a while and, now with the morning light, advanced for a couple hours more up the mountain.

The trail was lost at times, but despite the years gone by, I remembered the general direction. "Towards the east, 'til you hit a wall," we said eleven? years ago. We rested beside a little creek that surely wouldn't last in the dry season. We rested awhile. I was awakened by a cry from My Other Self. I took the safety off my weapon and aimed where the groan came from. Yes, it was My Other Self, grabbing his foot and complaining. I came near. He had tried to take off his sock without thinking and had pulled off a piece of skin.

"What an idiot," I told him, "you have to soak it first."

It was the ninth day with our boots on. Fabric and skin combine with dampness and mud, become one, and taking off your sock is like skinning yourself. I showed him how to do it. We stuck our feet in the water, and little by little, pulled back the fabric. Our feet smelled like dead dogs and the skin was a deformed and pale white mass. The disadvantages of sleeping with your boots on.

"You scared me. When I saw you grabbing your foot, I thought a snake had bitten you," I reproached him.

My Other Self paid no attention to me; he kept on soaking his feet with his eyes closed. As if he were invoking something. Camilo began to hit the ground with a stake.

"Now what?" I asked him.

"Snake," said Camilo while he threw stones, sticks, boots and everything he found at hand. At last, a heavy stick lands a blow to the head.

We approached fearfully.

"*Mococh*," says Camilo.

"*Nauyaca*," I say.

Limping, My Other Self comes close. He puts on a knowing look when he says, "It's the famous *Bac Ne'* or Four Noses."

"Its bite is fatal and its venom very poisonous," he adds, imitating the tone of a barker at a town fair. We skin it. Skinning the snake is like taking off its shirt. The belly is opened like a long *cierre relámpago*, or zipper, the guts are emptied and the skin comes off in one piece.[11] The meat is left, white and cartilaginous. It's pierced with a thin stick and put on the fire. It tastes like grilled fish, like *macabil*, like we used to catch in the *Sin Nombre* river, eleven? years ago.[12] We ate that and a little *pinole* with sugar that we had been given.[13] After a little rest, we wiped out our tracks and continued the march. Just like eleven? years ago, the jungle welcomed us as usual: raining. The rain in the jungle is something else. It starts to rain but the trees act as a big umbrella, few are the drops that escape from between the branches and leaves. Afterwards, the green roof begins to drip, and then, yes, you get wet. Like a big watering can, it keeps dripping, raining inside, although above it has stopped raining. The same thing happens with rain in the jungle as with war: you know when it starts, but not when it ends. I went along the way recognizing old friends: the *huapac'* with its modest coat of green moss; the capricious and hard rectitude of the *cante*; the limp horse, the mahogany, the cedar; the sharp and poisonous defense of the *chapaya*, the fan of the *watapil*; the disproportionate gigantism of the leaves of the *pij'* that look like green elephants' ears; the vertical rise to the sky of the *canolte'*, the hard heart of the *canolte'*; the threat of the *cheche'm* or "evil woman," that, as its name indicates, causes a very high fever, delirium, and severe pain. Trees and more trees. Nothing but brown and green filling the eyes, the hands, the steps, the soul anew . . .

Like eleven? years ago, when I arrived here the first time. And then I was climbing this damned hill and thinking that each step I took was the last one, and saying to myself, "one more step and I die," and I took a step and then another and I didn't die and I kept walking and it felt like the load weighed 100 kilos, and what a lie since I knew that I was carrying only 15 kilos and "it's just that you're a rookie," said the *compas*[14] who went to get me and they laughed with complicity, and I kept repeating to myself that now for real the next step would be the last and I cursed the hour when it occurred to me to become a guerrilla, and I had been doing so well as an organic intellectual, and the revolution has many tasks and all are important, and why did I have to get involved with this one, and for sure at the next rest I'll tell them here and no farther, and it would be better for me to help them there in the city, and I kept walking and kept falling and the next rest came and I didn't say a thing, partly out of shame and partly because I

---

11 *Cierre relámpago* is literally a "lightning-bolt closure."
12 *Sin Nombre* translates as "Without a Name."
13 *Pinole* is a toasted corn flour beverage.
14 *Compas* is the diminutive of *compadres*, which translates roughly as friends or comrades.

couldn't even speak, and gasping for air like a fish in a puddle that's too small, and I said to myself, all right, at the next rest I'll tell them, really, and the same thing happened and that's how I got through the 10 hours of that first trip on the trail in the jungle, and late in the afternoon, they said, we're going to stay here, and I let myself fall right there, and I said to myself, "I made it," and I repeated, "I made it," and we put up the hammocks and then they made a fire and then they made rice with sugar and we ate and ate and they asked me what I thought of the hill and how did I feel and if I was tired and I only repeated, "I made it," and they looked at each other and said, "He's only been here one day and he's already gone crazy."

The next day I found out that the trail I'd covered in 10 hours with a 15-kilo load, they could do in four hours and with 20 kilos. I didn't say anything. "Let's go," they said. I followed them, and with each step I took I asked myself, "Did I make it?"

Today, eleven? years later, history, tired of walking, repeats itself. We made it. Did we? The afternoon was a relief; a light, like that wheat that relieved me many early mornings, bathed the spot where we had decided to camp. We ate after Camilo ran across some (*cara de viejo* or *cabeza blanca*).[15] It turns out that there were seven. I told Camilo not to shoot; maybe they were some running deer and I thought that we'd come across them. Nothing, neither *Sac Jol* nor deer. We put up the tarps and the hammocks. After awhile, at night now, the *martruchas* came to bark at us, and afterward, the *woyo* or night monkey. I couldn't sleep. Everything hurt, even hope . . .

P.S. self-critique that shamefully disguises itself as a story for women who, at times, are girls, and for girls who, at times, are women. And, as history repeats itself once as comedy and again as tragedy, the story is called . . .

Durito II: Neoliberalism as seen from La Lacandona

It was the tenth day, with less pressure now. I distanced myself a little to put up my tarp and move in. I was going along, looking up, searching for a good pair of trees that didn't have a dead hanging branch above. So I was surprised when I heard, at my feet, a voice that shouted,

"Hey, watch out!"

I didn't see anything at first, but I stopped and waited. Almost immediately a little leaf began to move and, from under it, a beetle came out and began to protest:

"Why don't you watch where you put your big boots? You were about to squash me!" he yelled.

That protest seemed familiar to me.

"Durito?" I ventured.

---

15 *Cara de viejo* or *cabeza blanca* translates as "old man's face" or "white head."

"Nebuchadnezzar to you! Don't be an upstart, know your place!" answered the little beetle indignantly.

Now I had no room for doubt.

"Durito! Don't you remember me?"

Durito, I mean Nebuchadnezzar, just kept looking thoughtfully at me. He took out a little pipe from between his wings, filled it with tobacco, lit it, and after a big puff that brought on a cough that wasn't at all healthy, he said, "Hmmm, hmmm." And then he repeated, "Hmmm, hmmm."

I knew that this was going to take awhile, so I sat down. After several more occasions of "hmmm, hmmm," Nebuchadnezzar, or Durito, exclaimed,

"Captain?"

"The same!" I said, satisfied to see myself recognized.

Durito (I believe that after being recognized, I could call him that again) began a series of movements of feet and wings that, in the body language of beetles, is a kind of dance of joy and to me has always seemed like an epileptic seizure. After repeating several times, with different emphases, "Captain!" Durito finally stopped and fired the question I so feared:

"Got any tobacco?"

"Well, I . . ." I drew out the answer to give myself time to calculate my reserves.

Just then, Camilo arrived and asked me,

"Did you call me, Sup?"

"No, it's nothing . . . I was singing and . . . and don't worry, you can go," I responded nervously.

"Oh, good," Camilo said and walked away.

"Sup?" asked Durito, surprised.[16]

"Yes," I told him, "now I'm a Subcomandante."

"And is that better or worse than Captain?" Durito asked insistently.

"Worse," I told him and myself.

I changed the subject quickly and held the bag of tobacco out to him saying, "Here, I have a little."

To receive the tobacco, Durito performed his dance again, now repeating "Thank you!" over and over.

The tobacco euphoria over, we started the complicated ceremony of lighting our pipes. I leaned back on my pack and just looked at Durito.

"You look the same as ever," I told him.

"You, on the other hand, look pretty beat up," he responded.

"It's life," I said, playing it down.

Durito started with his "Hmmm, hmmm." After a while he said to me, "And what brings you here after so many years?"

"Well, I was thinking and since I had nothing better to do, I said to myself, why not take a stroll around the old haunts and say hello to old friends," I responded.

"Even old mountains still turn green!" Durito protested indignantly.

---

16 El Sup is a nickname for Subcomandante Marcos.

After that followed a long while of "hmmm, hmmm" and his inquisitive looks.

I couldn't take it any longer and confessed to him,

"The truth is that we are withdrawing because the government launched an offensive against us ..."

"You ran!" said Durito.

I tried to explain to him what a strategic withdrawal is, a tactical retreat, and whatever occurred to me in that moment.

"You ran," said Durito, this time with a sigh.

"Well, yes, I ran and so what?" I said, annoyed, more with myself than with him.

Durito didn't press. He stayed quiet a good while. Only the smoke of the two pipes formed a bridge between us. Minutes later he said,

"It seems like there's something more that's bothering you, not just the 'strategic retreat.'"

"'Withdrawal,' 'strategic withdrawal,'" I corrected him. Durito waited for me to go on:

"The truth is that it bothers me that we weren't prepared. And it was my fault we weren't prepared. I believed the government did want dialogue and so I gave the order that the consultations with the delegates should begin. When they attacked us we were discussing the conditions of the dialogue. They surprised us. They surprised me ..." I said with shame and anger.

Durito went on smoking, and waited for me to finish telling him everything that had happened in the last ten days. When I finished, Durito said,

"Wait here."

And he went under a little leaf. After a while he came out pushing his little desk. After that he went for a little chair, sat down, took out some papers, and began to look through them with a worried air.

"Hmmm, hmmm," he said with every few pages that he read. After a time he exclaimed,

"Here it is!"

"Here's what?" I asked, intrigued.

"Don't interrupt me!" Durito said seriously and solemnly. And added, "Pay attention. You have the same problem as many others. It refers to the economic and social doctrine known as 'neoliberalism' ..."

"Just what I needed now ... classes in political economy," I thought. It seems like Durito heard what I was thinking because he scolded me:

"Ssshh! This isn't just any class! This is a treatise of the highest order."

That bit about "a treatise of the highest order" seemed exaggerated to me, but I got ready to listen to it. Durito continued after some "hmmm, hmmms."

"It is a metatheoretical problem! Yes, you start from the idea that 'neoliberalism' is a doctrine. And by 'you,' I am referring to those who insist on frameworks that are rigid and square like your head. You think that 'neoliberalism' is a capitalist doctrine to confront the economic crises that capitalism itself attributes to 'populism.' Right?"

Durito doesn't let me answer.

"Of course right! Well, it turns out that 'neoliberalism' is not a theory to confront or explain the crisis. It is the crisis itself made theory and economic doctrine! That is, 'neoliberalism' hasn't the least coherence; it has no plans or historic perspective. In the end, pure theoretical shit."

"How strange . . . I've never heard or read that interpretation," I said with surprise.

"Of course! How could you, if it just occurred to me in this moment!" says Durito with pride.

"And what has that got to do with our running away, excuse me, with our withdrawal?" I asked, doubting such a novel theory.

"Ah! Ah! Elementary, my dear Watson Sup! There are no plans; there are no perspectives, only i-m-p-r-o-v-i-s-a-t-i-o-n. The government has no consistency: one day we're rich, another day we're poor, one day they want peace, another day they want war, one day fasting, another day stuffed, and so on. Do I make myself clear?" Durito inquires.

"Almost . . ." I hesitate and scratch my head.

"And so?" I ask, seeing that Durito isn't continuing with his discourse.

"It's going to explode. Boom! Like a balloon blown up too much. It has no future. We're going to win," says Durito as he puts his papers away.

"We?" I ask maliciously.

"Of course, 'we!' It's clear that you won't be able to without my help. No, don't try to raise objections. You need a super-advisor. I'm already learning French, for continuity's sake."

I stayed quiet. I don't know what is worse: discovering that we're governed by improvisation, or imagining Durito as a super-secretary in the cabinet of an improbable transitional government.

Durito attacks:

"I surprised you, eh? Well, don't feel bad. As long as you don't squash me with your big boots I will always be able to clarify for you the road to follow in the course of history, which, despite its ups and downs, will raise this country up, because united . . . because united . . . Now that I think of it, I haven't written to my old lady," Durito cracks up laughing.

"I thought you were serious!" I pretend to be annoyed and throw a little branch at him. Durito dodges it and keeps laughing.

Once calmed down, I ask him, "And where did you get those conclusions that neoliberalism is crisis made economic doctrine?"

"Ah! From this book that explains the 1988-1994 economic project of Carlos Salinas de Gortari," he answers and shows me a little book with the Solidarity logo.[17]

---

17 Begun in 1988, the National Solidarity Program, or PRONASOL (*Programa Nacional de Solidaridad*), was part of the economic reform strategy of President Salinas. It allowed the executive branch, through a network of "solidarity committees," to use social spending in urban and rural areas to strengthen its political power.

"But Salinas isn't president anymore . . . it seems," I say with a doubt that shakes me.

"I know that, but look who drew up the plan," says Durito and points out a name. I read,

"Ernesto Zedillo Ponce de León," I say surprised and add, "So there isn't any break in the chain?"

"What there is . . . is a den of thieves," says Durito, implacable.

"And so?" I ask with real interest.

"Nothing, just that the Mexican political system is like that dead tree branch hanging over your head," says Durito, and I jump and look up and see that, sure enough, there is a dead branch that is hanging threateningly over my hammock. I change places while Durito keeps talking:

"The Mexican political system is just barely attached to reality with pieces of very fragile branches. It will only take one good wind for it to come down. Of course, when it falls, it's going to take other branches with it, and watch out, anyone who's under its shade when it collapses!"

"And if there is no wind?" I ask, while I check whether the hammock is well tied.

"There will be . . . there will be," says Durito and looks thoughtful, as if he were looking at the future.

We both remained pensive. We lit our pipes again. The day began to get underway. Durito kept looking at my boots. Fearful, he asked,

"And how many are with you?"

"Two more, so don't worry about being stomped," I said to calm him. Durito practices methodical doubt as a discipline, so he continued with his "hmmm, hmmm," until he let out,

"But those coming after you, how many are they?"

"Ah! Those? Like about sixty . . ."

Durito didn't let me finish:

"Sixty! Sixty pairs of big boots on top of my head! 120 *Sedena* boots trying to crush me!"[18] He yelled hysterically.

"Wait, you didn't let me finish. They aren't sixty," I said. Durito interrupted again: "Ah! I knew so much misfortune wasn't possible. How many are they, then?"

Laconically, I answered, "Sixty thousand."

"Sixty thousand!" Durito managed to say before choking on his pipe smoke.

"Sixty thousand!" he repeated several times, wringing his little hands and feet together with anguish.

"Sixty thousand!" he said to himself with desperation.

I tried to console him. I told him that they weren't all coming together, that it was an offensive in stages, that they were coming from different directions, that they hadn't found us, that we had rubbed out our tracks so that they wouldn't follow us. In short, I told him everything that occurred to me.

After a while, Durito calmed down and started again with his "hmmm, hmmm." He

---

18 *Sedena* is the acronym for the *Secretaría de la Defensa Nacional* (Secretary for National Defense.)

took out some little papers that, I started to realize, looked like maps, and began questioning me about the location of enemy troops. I answered as best I could. With each answer, Durito made marks and notes on his little maps. He went on a good while after the interrogation, saying "hmmm, hmmm." A few minutes passed, and after complicated calculations (I say this as he used all his little hands and feet to do the figuring) he sighs, "What this means is that they're using 'the anvil and hammer,' 'the slipknot,' 'the rabbit hunt,' and the vertical maneuver. Elementary, it comes from the Ranger's Manual of the School of the Americas," he says to himself and to me.[19] And adds,

"But we have one chance to come out well from this."

"Ah, yes? And how?" I ask with skepticism.

"With a miracle," says Durito as he puts his papers away and lies back down.

The silence settled down between us, and we let the afternoon arrive between the branches and vines. Later, when night had finished detaching itself from the trees, and flying, covered the sky, Durito asked me: "Captain ... Captain ... Psst! Are you asleep?"

"No. ... What is it?" I answered.

Durito asks with pity, as if afraid to hurt me,

"And what do you intend to do?"

I keep smoking; I look at the silver curls of the moon hung from the branches. I let out a spiral of smoke and I answer him and answer myself:

"Win."

P.S. that tunes in to nostalgia in the quadrant.
On the little radio, someone lets loose in a blues rhythm, that song that goes, "All's gonna be right with a little help from my friends ..." [sic][20]

P.S. that now, really, says goodbye, waving a heart like a handkerchief.
So much rain
and not even a drop
to sate the yearning ...

Vale again. *Salud*, and be careful with that dry branch that hangs over your heads and that pretends, ingenuously, to shelter you with its shade.

El Sup, smoking ... and waiting.

---

19 The U.S. Army Rangers are elite combat units that can be rapidly deployed for infantry assaults and special operations. The U.S. Military School of the Americas (SOA) in Ft. Benning, Georgia trains Latin American military personnel in counterinsurgency, intelligence and anti-narcotic operations. Graduates of the SOA have been responsible for many of the most notorious human rights violations within Mexico and Latin America. Ft. Benning has been the target of massive civil disobedience organized by School of the Americas Watch, a coalition of clergy and laypersons founded in 1990 to work toward closing the school. On January 17, 2001 the U.S. Congress renamed the SOA The Western Hemisphere Institute for Security Cooperation (WHISC), a change both critics and supporters recognize to be purely cosmetic.

20 This passage appears in English in the original Spanish text. The [sic] is Marcos' notation.

The Cave of Desire

During the flight from the government's February 1995 military offensive, while avoiding guns, bombs, and in Durito's case, sixty thousand pairs of large boots, Marcos tells Durito the story of an ugly man and the Cave of Desire. During those weeks of withdrawal, widespread protests in Mexico opposed the Zedillo offensive. In massive demonstrations in Chiapas and Mexico City, hundreds of thousands marched with banners, costumes and masks. The crowds chanted slogans against the military attacks and in support of the Zapatistas. Such public actions in Mexico inspired demonstrations in over forty countries, often at Mexican embassies or consulates. As a result, an embarrassed Mexican government halted its offensive and returned to a new round of peace talks in San Andrés. Fully aware of these important solidarity actions, Marcos includes this story within a letter of thanks to international supporters.

First published in *La Jornada* March 22, 1995. Originally translated by Bonnie Schrack.

To the national weekly *Proceso*
To the national newspaper *El Financiero*
To the national newspaper *La Jornada*
To the local newspaper of San Cristóbal de las Casas, *Tiempo*
March 17, 1995

Ladies and Gentlemen:
Another thank-you letter going out, this time for those abroad. Let's see if Gurría manages to read it, since he's sending out nothing but lies all over Europe.[1] We aren't hiding from soldiers anymore, but now we're fleeing legislators. There's a helluva lot of them and they turn up where no one expects them. It looks like they took that part about "verification" seriously.[2] That might not be bad; it may be the first committee that does more than buy crafts in San Cristóbal. How are we doing in the Pan-American games? Too bad I couldn't attend. I'm sure I would have done very well in the "cross-country race." If only you could see how much training they've put me through since February 10th!

Vale. Salud, and may the spring in your blood be destined for someone.

From the mountains of the Mexican Southeast
Subcomandante Insurgente Marcos

P.S. that, in mourning, cries.
I was listening on the little tape player to that tune by Stephen Stills, from the album *Four Way Street*, that goes, "Find the cost of freedom, buried in the ground. Mother Earth will swallow you, lay your body down . . ." when My Other Self comes running and tells me, "It looks like you got what was coming to you . . ."[3]
"Don't tell me the PRI has already fallen?" I ask with hope.
"No man! They killed you!" says My Other Self.
"Me! When? Where?" I ask as I go through all my memories of where I've been and what I've done.
"Today, in a confrontation . . . but they don't say exactly where," he responds.
"Oh, good! . . . And did I end up badly hurt or really dead?" I insist.

---

1 José Ángel Gurría Treviño was Secretary of Foreign Affairs from December 2, 1994 to January 5, 1998 when a cabinet shake-up precipitated by the Acteal Massacre of December 1997 resulted in his transfer to Secretary of Housing and Public Finance.
2 As part of the Law for Dialogue, Reconciliation and Dignified Peace in Chiapas (see also note 1 in "Durito II"), a "Verification and Peace Commission" of federal legislators was created to mediate the peace talks in San Andrés. The EZLN strongly voiced its opposition to the Commission that put the Legislative branch in a position of mediating the conflict, stacking the balance of power in the dialogue with six delegates from the Federal Government to two from the EZLN. [*La Jornada*, March 6, 1995]
3 "Find the Cost of Freedom," Crosby, Stills, Nash and Young, *Four Way Street*, Atlantic Records, 1971.

"Really, really dead . . . that's what it says in the news," says My Other Self and leaves.

A narcissistic sob competes with the crickets.

"Why are you crying?" asks Durito while he lights his pipe.

"Because I can't attend my burial. I, who loved me so much . . ."

P.S. that tells what happened to El Sup and Durito during the twelfth day of the withdrawal, of the mysteries of the Cave of Desire, and of other unfortunate events that today make us laugh, but at that time took away even our hunger.

"And if they bomb us?" asked Durito in the early morning on the twelfth day of the withdrawal. ("That was no withdrawal! It was pure flight!" says Durito.) It's cold and a grey wind licks with its icy tongue the darkness of trees and earth.

I'm not sleeping; in solitude the cold hurts twice as much. Nevertheless I keep quiet. Durito comes out from under the leaf he's been using as a blanket and climbs up on top of mine. To wake me up, he starts tickling my nose. I sneeze with such emphasis that Durito ends up tumbling over himself onto my boots. He recovers and makes his way back to my face.

"What's happened?" I ask him before he tickles me again.

"And if they bomb us?" he insists.

"Yes . . . well . . . well . . . we'll look for a cave or something like that to hide ourselves in . . . or we'll climb in a little hole . . . or we'll see what to do," I say with annoyance, and look at my watch to insinuate that it isn't the hour to be worrying about bombings.

"I won't have any problems. I can fit anywhere. But you, with those big boots and that nose . . . I doubt that you'll find a safe place," says Durito as he covers himself again with a little huapac leaf.

"The psychology of terror," I think, with respect to the apparent indifference of Durito regarding our fate . . .

"Our fate? He's right! He won't have problems, but me . . ." I think. I get up and speak to Durito, "Psst . . . Psst . . . Durito!"

"I'm sleeping," he says from under his leaf.

I ignore his sleep and begin talking to him: "Yesterday I heard Camilo and My Other Self saying that there are a lot of caves around here. Camilo says he knows most of them. There are small ones, where an armadillo would barely fit. And there are some as big as churches. But he says there is one that no one dares to enter. He says there is an ugly story about that cave. 'The Cave of Desire,' he says they call it."

Durito seems to get interested; his passion for detective novels is his ruin.

"And what is the story of that cave?"

"Well . . . It's a very long story. I've heard it myself, but that was years ago now . . . I don't remember it well," I said, making it interesting.

"Fine, go on, tell it," says Durito, more and more interested.

I light my pipe. From amid the aromatic smoke comes the memory, and with it . . .

The Cave of Desire

"It happened many years ago. It is a story of a love that was not, that was left just like that. It is a sad story . . . and terrible," says El Sup sitting on one side, with his pipe between his lips. He lights it, and looking at the mountain, continues. "A man came from far away. He came, or he already was there. No one knows. It was back in other times long past and however that may be, in these lands people lived and died just the same, without hope and forgotten. No one knows if he was young or old, that man. Few saw him at first. They say that was because this man was extremely ugly. Just to see him produced dread in men and revulsion in women. What was it that made him so unpleasant? I don't know; the concepts of beauty and ugliness change so much from one age to another and from one culture to another. In this case, the people native to these lands avoided him, as did the foreigners who were the owners of land, men and destinies. The indigenous people called him the Jolmash or Monkey-face; the foreigners called him the Animal.

"The man went into the mountains, far from the gaze of all, and set to work there. He made himself a little house, next to one of the many caves that were found there. He made the land produce, planted corn and wheat, and hunting animals in the forest gave him enough to get by. Every so often he went down to a stream near the settlements. There he had arranged, with one of the older members of the community, to get salt, sugar, or whatever else he, the Jolmash, couldn't obtain in the mountains. The Jolmash exchanged corn and animal skins for what he needed. He would arrive at the stream at the time when evening began to darken and the shadows of the trees brought forth night onto the earth. The old man had a problem with his eyes and couldn't see well, so that, with the dusk and his illness, he couldn't make out the face of the man who caused so much revulsion in the clear light.

"One evening the old man didn't arrive. The Jolmash thought that maybe he had mistaken the hour and arrived when the old man had already gone home. To make no mistake, the next time he made sure to arrive earlier. The sun still had some fingers to go before it wrapped itself in the mountains, when the Jolmash came near the stream. A murmur of laughter and voices grew as he approached. The Jolmash slowed his steps and silently came nearer. Among the branches and vines he made out the pool formed by the waters of the stream. A group of women were bathing and washing clothes. They were laughing. The Jolmash watched and stayed quiet. His heart became his only gaze, his eyes his voice. It was a while since the women had gone and the Jolmash stayed on, watching. The stars were already raining down on the fields when he returned to the mountains.

"I don't know if it came from what he saw, or from what he thought he saw, whether the image that was engraved on his retina corresponded to reality or if it existed only in his desire, but the Jolmash fell in love or thought that he had fallen in love. And his love was not something idealized or platonic, it was quite earthy, and the call of the feelings that he bore was like a war drum, like lightning that becomes fierce rain. Passion took his hand and the Jolmash began to write letters, love letters, lettered delirium that filled his hands.

"And he wrote, for example, 'Oh, lady of the wet glimmer! Desire becomes a haughty colt. Sword of a thousand mirrors is the yearning of my appetites for thy body, and in vain its double edge rips the thousand gasps that fly on the wind. One grace, long sleeplessness! One grace I ask thee, lady, failed repose of my grey existence! Let me come to thy neck.

"'Allow that to thy ear climbs my clumsy longing. Let my desire tell thee, softly, very softly, that which my breast silences. Do not look, lady-so-far-from-mine, at the pitiful sight that adorns my face! Let thy ears become thy gaze; give up thine eyes to see the murmurs that walk within me, longing for thy within. Yes, I wish to enter. To walk with thee, with sighs, the path that hands and lips and sex desire. Thy wet mouth, and I, thirsting, to enter with a kiss. On the double hill of thy breast to softly brush lips and fingers, to awaken the cluster of moans that hide within. To march southward and to take prisoner thy waist in warm embrace, burning now the skin of the belly, brilliant sun announcing the night that below is born. To evade, diligently and skillfully, the shears on which thy grace goes and whose vertex promises and denies. To give thee a tremor of cold heat and arrive, whole, to the moist stirring of desire. To secure the warmth of my palms in the double warmth of flesh and movement. One slow first step, a light trot next. Then the runaway gallop of bodies and desire. To reach the sky, and then collapse.

"'One grace, promised weariness! One grace I ask thee, lady of the soft sigh!

"'Let me come to thy neck! In it I am saved, far off I die.'

"One stormy night, like the passion burning his hands, a bolt of lightning burnt down the little house of the Jolmash. Wet and shivering, he took refuge in the neighboring cave. With a torch he lit his way in and found there little figures of couples giving and receiving, the pleasure worked in stone and clay. There was a spring, and little boxes that when opened, spoke of terrors and marvels that had passed and would come to be. The Jolmash now could not or would not leave the cave. There, he felt the desire fill his hands once more and wrote, weaving bridges to nowhere ...

'A pirate am I now, lady of the longed-for port. Tomorrow, a soldier at war. Today, a pirate lost in trees and lands. The ship of desire unfolds its sails. A continual moaning, all tremor and wanting, leads the ship between monsters and storms. Lightning illuminates the flickering sea of desperation. A salty dampness takes the command and the helm. Pure wind, word alone, I navigate seeking thee, amidst gasps and sighs, seeking the precise place the body sends thee. Desire, lady of storms to come, is a knot hidden somewhere by thy skin. Find it I must, and muttering spells, untie it. Free then shall be thy longings, feminine swayings, and they will fill thine eyes and mouth, thy womb and deep within. Free one moment only, as my hands already come to make them prisoners, to lead them out to sea in my embrace and with my body. A ship shall I be and restless sea, so that thy body I enter. And there shall be no rest in so much storm, the bodies moved by so many capricious waves. One last and ferocious slap of salty desire hurls us to a beach where sleep arrives. A pirate am I now, lady of tender storm. Don't await my assault, come to it! Let the sea, the wind, and this stone-become-ship be witnesses! The Cave of Desire! The horizon clouds over with black wine, now we are arriving, now we go . . .'

"So it happened, they say. And they say that the Jolmash never again left the cave. No one knows whether the woman to whom he wrote the letters existed in truth or was a product of the cave, the Cave of Desire. What they say is that the Jolmash still lives in it, and whoever comes close becomes sick with desire . . ."

Durito has followed the whole story attentively. When he sees I have finished, he says,

"We have to go."

"Go?" I ask, surprised

"Of course!" says Durito, "I need literary advice to write to my old lady . . ."

"You're crazy!" I protest.

"Are you afraid?" asks Durito ironically.

I waver.

"Well . . . afraid, really afraid . . . no . . . but it's very cold . . . and it looks like it's going to rain . . . and . . . yes, I'm afraid."

"Bah! Don't worry. I'll go with you and I'll be telling you where to go. I think I know where the Cave of Desire is," says Durito with certainty.

"All right," I say, giving in. "You'll be in charge of the expedition."

"Great! My first order is that you march in the vanguard, in the center nobody, to disconcert the enemy, and I will go in the extreme rearguard," indicates Durito.

"I? In the vanguard? I protest!"

"Protest denied!" says Durito with firmness.

"OK, soldier to the end, I'll go along."

"Good, that's what I like. Attention! This is the plan of attack: first, if there are many, we run. Second, if there are a few, we hide. Third, if there isn't anyone, forward, for we were born to die!" dictates Durito while he prepares his little pack.

For a war plan it seemed too cautious for me, but Durito was the chief now, and given the circumstances, I had no reason to object to prudence marching in the vanguard.

Above, the stars were beginning to blur.

"It looks like it's going to rain," I say to Durito—excuse me—to the chief.

"Silence! Nothing will detain us!" shouts Durito with the voice of the sergeant in that Oliver Stone film Platoon.[4]

A gust of freezing wind and the first drops . . .

"Haaalt!" orders Durito.

The drops of rain start to multiply . . .

"I forgot to mention the fourth point of the plan of attack," says Durito with doubt.

"Oh yeah? And what is it?" I ask insidiously.

"If it starts to rain . . . strategic withdrawal!" The last words are said by Durito now in an all-out run back to camp.

I ran behind him. It was useless. We got soaked, and shivering, we reached the little plastic roof. It rained as if desire had, at last, been unleashed . . .

Vale again. *Salud*, and may the hunger for tomorrow be a desire to struggle . . . today.

El Sup, within, deep within, the Cave of Desire.

It's March, it's early morning, and for being a dead man, I feel veeery well.

* * *

---

4 Oliver Stone's *Platoon* (Orion Pictures, 1986), a film about the horrors of war, is set in the jungles of Viet Nam. A letter from Stone had just been published in *La Jornada* (March 3, 1995) in support of filmmakers Javier Elorriaga and Maria "Gloria" Benavides, who were among those arrested and accused of being Zapatista leaders. One year later, just prior to the First Continental Encounter, Stone returned to Chiapas as part of a human rights delegation. Stone's trip caused him to miss the Academy Awards, for which his film *Nixon* (Hollywood Pictures, 1995) had received several nominations. At their meeting Marcos handed him an old pipe with a broken stem, saying, "I'm afraid we can't give you an Oscar here, but I would like to give you this. Maybe you can get it fixed somewhere." ("Stone Meets With Mexico Rebels," Associated Press: March 25, 1996) The visit was very controversial: Stone criticized the government's "regime of terror," the Interior Ministry of Chiapas seized television reporters' footage of Stone in Chiapas, and *Nixon* was abruptly pulled from Mexican film theaters ("Oliver Stone Film Pulled in Mexico After Visit," Reuters: March 30, 1996).

Durito Names Marcos His Squire

Reflecting on the government's broken promises, Durito shows off his bullfighting moves as "Durito el Camborio," claiming that "bullfighting is like politics, although in politics the bulls can be really crafty and treacherous." The Zapatistas and the government continued to negotiate the logistics and agenda in preparation for the dialogue of San Andrés against the backdrop of an ongoing low-intensity war. The Mexican Congress later stated that if peace talks did not resume by April 10, the government could renew the February offensive. Assuming his role as knight-errant amidst these tensions, Don Durito names Marcos his squire, laments his misfortunes in love, recites poetry, and pokes fun at the ignorance of the government.

First published in *La Jornada*, April 8, 1995. Originally translated by Bonnie Schrack.

To the national weekly *Proceso*
To the national newspaper *El Financiero*
To the national newspaper *La Jornada*
To the local newspaper of San Cristóbal de Las Casas, Chiapas, *Tiempo*
April 4, 1995

Sirs:

Here goes a letter and a communiqué that confirm the anticipated meetings (I imagine that by the time you get this, they will be about to take place). Finally, the powers-that-be rejected our proposal of a more attractive site.[1] We are clear that, as befits good thinking, the ee-ze-el-en should show signs of flexibility and reason before the obstinacy of the government. That's why we presented a new proposal that, we were sure, would be to more than one person's liking:

A)   Date: April 10, 1995, in the afternoon hours.

B)   Place: Chinameca Hacienda, Morelos.

C)   Sole point on the agenda: Mexican History.[2]

We would have only placed three conditions on the meeting:

1.   That the government forces not shoot us in the face. This is because later it is a problem to identify the cadavers, and so that the obligatory photos do not present our country's image as one of barbarity and irrationality.[3] This last point is very important, especially now when one must read *Newsweek, The New York Times, The Washington Post,* and other well-known publications of wide national distribution (in the USA), to know what's happening with the Mexican government.

2.   That the order to fire be given by the legislators of the so-called "COMCOPA" (which, as everyone knows, means "Commission for Connivance and Paraphernalia"), so that their "peace-keeping" role is made clear.[4]

3.   That, when all is realized, the choreographer of the Chamber of Deputies, Roque Villanueva, delights the honorable members with that refined bodily expression that serves to convey the jubilation over popular and nationalist measures.[5]

I don't know for what reason the powers-that-be rejected the proposal. Wasn't it good?

---

1 Due to the increased military presence in Chiapas, the Zapatistas proposed that the peace talks be moved to Mexico City.

2 In addition to marking the date of the Mexican Congress' deadline to the Zapatistas, April 10 is the anniversary of General Emiliano Zapata's assassination in 1919 at Chinameca Hacienda.

3 Since Zapata was shot many times at close range, it was hard to identify his body and there are many popular rumors that the body exhibited in Cuautla, Morelos was in fact the cadaver of his close friend Jesús Delgado. Popular folklore later suggested that Zapata had survived.

4 COMCOPA: another acronym for COCOPA. See Introduction, page 6.

5 Roque Villanueva was the president of the PRI's Executive National Committee at the time this communiqué was written.

Vale. Salud, and a life preserver (for the holidays and for the crisis).[6]

From the mountains of the Mexican Southeast
Subcomandante Insurgente Marcos

P.S. that, determined, enters the bullring.
I still can't get down out of the ceiba. The moon is a bull in silver ornament and, with a pair of sharpened horns, it charges to the east. I think that if I were not a guerrilla, I would be a matador. I try then to take the night as a black cape, but it has so many holes resembling stars that I desist in my attempt. I take from my neck the faded bandanna, now more brown than red, and unfurl it with an elegance that Sánchez Mejías would envy.[7] Crickets and fireflies fill the shaded front rows, the sun seats are empty for obvious reasons. I head to the center of the bullring, which, as it's the center of the crown of the ceiba, is safer and a few steps away. I summon the moon, trying some half veronicas with the cape. The moon-bull stays far away. It's inexplicable that it doesn't notice such a gallant matador. I summon again. The public is impatient and a little weasel yawns with boredom. Nothing; only a firefly charges, zigzagging. A wave of the red cape, spread out at the waist, draws from the honorable members of the audience nothing more than the continuous sawing of the crickets. The lunatic bull continues forward without even turning. I sit down in a corner and sigh with sadness. My problem is that neither women nor moons pay any attention to me . . .

Durito too has climbed up to the top of the ceiba, wondering what's taking me so long. As soon as he gets comfortable, I quickly inform him of the situation. Durito thinks that it's easier to bullfight with comets; they come from where you least expect, and they're spirited like a Miura bull.[8] The moon always stays on course, and while this facilitates the final thrust, it doesn't allow the matador's suit to shine and the respectable aficionados tend to get terribly bored . . .

I admit he is right and give him the cape. Durito wants to show me some passes that, he says, Federico García Lorca taught him. To my question as to whether beetles also bullfight, Durito responds that one should know about everything and that bullfighting is like politics, although in politics the bulls can be really crafty and treacherous. "In fact, they called me 'Durito el Camborio' and what they didn't envy in others, they envied in me," he says.[9] We're going on

---

6 "Holidays" refers to the celebration of Holy Week, the week ending on Easter Sunday.

7 In the poem "Lament for Ignacio Sánchez Mejías," Federico García Lorca eulogized a matador who was killed in the bullring. Lorca, well known for his antifascist views and defense of the *gitanos*, or Spanish gypsies, was executed by General Francisco Franco's fascist troops in 1936 during the Spanish Civil War.

8 The Miura bull, named for Eduardo Miura (its original breeder), is renowned for its courage and spirit.

9 "Durito el Camborio" is a reference to Antonio Torres Heredia, who appears in two poems by Lorca. See Christopher Maurer, ed., *Federico Garcia Lorca: Selected Verse: A Bilingual Edition,* Vol. 3 (New York: Farrar, Straus and Giroux, 1996). The verse "What they didn't envy in others, they envied in me" appears in the poem "Muerte de Antoñito el Camborio."

like this when we hear voices at the foot of the ceiba.

"It's a *woyo*," says Camilo.

"No, it's a badger, 'the loner,'" says My Other Self.

"See if you can get it in your sights to shoot it," instructs Camilo to My Other Self while he loads the gun.

I stay still, smoking. My bullfighting moves will have to wait for better occasions and less belligerent audiences for their skill to be demonstrated. Durito sighs in a flamenco tone, as there are no offerings from the spectators in the arena. Below, they get bored and leave . . .

The moon finishes by charging the horizon, right into the dark cape of a mountain.

Out of the corner of its eye the moon watches El Sup. He is wiping his face with the cape. It couldn't tell if he had been crying . . .

P.S. that, although you don't realize it, contains a mystery (enchanting, like all mysteries):

This is the spot, oh heavens, I choose and hereby take in order to bewail the misfortune in which you yourselves have placed me! Here is where the flooding of my eyes will join the waters flowing in this tiny stream, and where, night and day, my deep and unbroken sighs will shake the leaves of these wild trees, in witness to and as symbol of the suffering experienced by my afflicted heart. Oh you, whoever you may be, you rustic gods that dwell in this uninhabitable place, hear the moans of this wretched lover, who by reason of a long absence and fancied jealousies has been brought to this harsh wilderness, here to lament and complain of that ungrateful beauty's cruel disposition, she who is the very end and finality of all human loveliness! Oh you, nymphs and dryads, who love to live in the thick shrubbery of these mountains, may the graceful, lecherous satyrs, who long for you, but always in vain, never ever disturb your sweet rest, so you can help me lament my misfortune, or at least not yourselves grow tired of hearing it! Oh Dulcinea de Toboso, day of my night, glory of my suffering, true north and compass of every path I take, guiding star of my fate, so too may Heaven grant you whatever boons you seek of it, and bring you to reflect upon the place and the condition to which your absence has brought me, and grant me as much delight as my faithfulness deserves! Oh lonely trees, from now on the only companions of my solitude, give me some sign, by the gentle movement of your branches, that my presence here is not disagreeable to you! And oh you, my squire, cheerful companion in both prosperity and adversity, never forget what you shall see me do, here, so you may tell and recite it to she who is the sole cause of it all![10]

---

10 Footnote by Marcos: "Chapter XXV. Dealing with the strange things that happened to the brave knight of la Mancha in the Sierra Morena, including his imitation of Beltenebros' penance." See Miguel Cervantes, *Don Quijote*, trans. Burton Raffel, ed. Diana de Armas Wilson (New York: W. W. Norton and Co., 1999), 153.

Durito recited it all by heart and with impressive intonation. Standing on a little stone, and raising in his right hand a twig that I later learned was a sword, Durito turned to look at me when he said that part about, "Oh you, my squire, cheerful companion, etc." I turn and look behind me to see if he's referring to someone else, but there isn't anyone there.

"Yes, you," says Durito pointing toward me with his twig. "You will be my squire."

"I?" I say, visibly surprised.

Durito pays no attention to my question and continues, "Furthermore, it isn't a twig . . . it's a sword . . . the only, the best . . . Excalibur!" he says, brandishing the twig.

"I think you are confusing the times and the novels," I tell him. "The beginning of your speech seems an awful lot like a part of *Don Quijote de la Mancha*, and Excalibur was King Arthur's sword," I ended up hesitating over this last part, trying to remember the video that Eva had called the *Sword in the Stone*.[11] Durito took advantage of my silence to attack:

"Silence, rogue! Knowest thou not nature imitates art? What difference does it make if it's Alonso Quijano or the page Arthur?[12] Now, it is . . . *Don Durito de la Lacandona*."

I laughed.

"At what do you laugh, oh vulgar and ignorant person?" reproaches and threatens Durito.

"At nothing," I say, in a conciliatory manner. "I was remembering that in the files of the PGR, where they charged those alleged to be Zapatistas, they put '*La Candona*.'"[13]

"Those ignoramuses of the PGR can't even find the jungle of Chiapas, much less the murderers of LDC, JFRM and Cardinal Posadas," says Durito with scorn.[14]

"All right, but how did you become a knight-errant?" I ask, sitting down and taking care not to get too close to "Excalibur." Durito sits down, too, lets out a quixotic sigh, and laments, "Oh, my ignorant squire, a woman is to blame for my raving, the wound in my side, the reason for my sleeplessness, the cause of my sorrow, and responsible for my misfortune."

---

11 *Sword in the Stone* (1963, directed by Wolfgang Reitherman, Walt Disney Home Studios)
12 Alonso Quijano is the country gentleman of La Mancha who takes on the noble identity of *Don Quijote*.
13 In their February 1995 arrest warrants for suspected Zapatista leaders, the Mexican Justice Department (PGR) incorrectly referred to the Lacandon region as "La Candona."
14 On March 23, 1994, while campaigning for the presidency, PRI candidate Luis Donaldo Colosio was assassinated in Tijuana, Mexico. In August 1994, President Salinas' brother, Raúl, was jailed for ordering the assassination of his brother-in-law José Francisco Ruiz Massieu. Cardinal Juan Jesús Posadas Ocampo was assassinated May 24, 1993, in Guadalajara.

Durito doesn't let me protest over the "ignorant" nor the "squire," and continues sadly to pour out his woes, "It is good that I tell you my tragedy so that your heart may learn to go with care and caution on the rugged road of love. See, it is not for pleasure that my steps have carried me to such distant places, where solitude cuts like a sharpened knife and silence oppresses men and the heavens. Know well, my wretched squire, that it is divine law that a gallant knight-errant must roam sadly through the world and through life, and die sighing for some absent Lady, who, adorable criminal, has robbed him, with only a glance, of all judgment. Oh, but what a glance! A lightning bolt in the April sun! A starburst at midday! A diamond that floats and kills! A sea all waves and coral! A desire that looking speaks! A mute plea of longing!"

I implore him to finish the story at once. "You had better hurry because we've gone on for several pages and there won't be a newspaper that will publish this. As it is, they say I only use the communiqués as a pretext to send whatever occurs to me . . ."

"By my faith, you are right and there is truth in your words. I am certain that there is neither newspaper nor book nor encyclopedia that could contain all the fortunes and misfortunes that, lovesick, I have suffered. Not even the library of 'Aguascalientes' would suffice for a love so great and aggrieved as pains my breast!" says Durito, his voice breaking.[15]

"Don't even worry about the library of 'Aguascalientes,' they have it at the PGR now," I say to console him.

"That sounds very good to me. That way those rogues and scoundrels will learn something of geography and spelling," says Durito, putting away his sword and walking toward his little leaf. Night has clouded over all corners and one of those rains that March splashes on April can be felt in the dampness of the wind.

Disconcerted, I ask, "Aren't you going to continue the story?"

"It's useless, there aren't enough words to contain so much pain and sorrow," says Durito as he covers himself with his little leaf. Before he covers himself completely he tells me, "Don't forget to have the mounts ready. Tomorrow we will leave at daybreak, as is the law for when knights-errant ride. At dawn, so the shine of our weapons puts the sun to shame when he dares to confront us and he may be, thus, less savage."

Durito heaves a last sigh and is silent. I stay seated, ready to watch over the sleep of my master, the valorous knight, "Don Durito de la Lacandona." I am determined to defend his noble sleep against any adversity. Monsters and giants will not dare disturb such noble repose. I have even found a branch that, with a little imagination, resembles a fearful lance. It begins to rain, and like any self-respecting squire, I abandon guard and master. I run and take refuge under my shelter. Now dawn begins to arrive with its cold embrace and the rain isn't stopping . . .

---

15 The library of Aguascalientes built for the 1994 CND was destroyed by the Mexican Army during their February 1995 military offensive.

I can't sleep. I haven't been able to figure out where the devil I'm going to find the mounts on which we're to ride out tomorrow . . .

P.S. that, hanging from a reddish fringe, murmurs apologies in the ear (since Baudelaire was taken prisoner by the PGR and hasn't been presented[16]) and offers, instead, that . . .

Poetry works with the sweetest
ideas, and becomes the sweetest,
the noblest, most sober and wise
Oh lady, delighting all eyes,
Accept my soul in these lines,
And by letting my earnest praise
enfold you, you earn yourself
Envy for the rest of your days,
And find your fortune raised
Higher than the moon in the skies.
　　　—Miguel de Cervantes Saavedra[17]

El Sup, in the middle of the bullring, waiting patiently for the clock to strike five in the afternoon . . .[18]

* * *

---

16 Charles Baudelaire (1821-1867) was a French poet whose work critiqued bourgeois society while searching for transcendence.
17 Cervantes, *Don Quijote*, 466.
18 Lorca's poem "Llanto por Ignacio Sánchez Mejías" contains the refrain "At five in the afternoon, at five in the afternoon"—the hour at which the gored Mejías died.

Durito III: The Story of Neoliberalism and the Labor Movement

During the period of the new peace talks between the government and the EZLN, Marcos and Durito discuss the relationship between neoliberalism and the labor movement. Intimidated by the rank and file agitation and massive public support for the Zapatistas, the government and its longtime labor boss Fidel Velázquez had called off, for the first time in 75 years, the traditional May Day celebrations and parade to Mexico City's Zócalo. Furious, with all the injured pride of a passionate knight-errant, Durito proposes traveling on his steed, a turtle named Pegasus, to Mexico City to challenge Velázquez to a duel.

To the weekly news magazine *Proceso*
To the national newspaper *El Financiero*
To the national newspaper *La Jornada*
To the local newspaper of San Cristóbal de Las Casas, Chiapas, *Tiempo*
April 15, 1995

First published in *La Jornada*, April 21, 1995. Originally translated by Cecilia Rodríguez.

Sirs:

Here is a communiqué for vespers. In this place, April plays at disguising itself like March, and May begins to flutter about some stray flowers, with their red color resplendent amidst so much green. I cannot stop keeping and losing hope among so many crickets. Meanwhile, I plan on founding the society of Tired Lungs Anonymous. I'm sure it would be quite successful in D.F.[1] But, by the time this happens, Holy Week will, once again, be an ordinary week. How much longer will the lie prevail?

Vale. Salud, and a mouthful of this fresh air that, they say, is breathed in the mountains and that some displaced people call "hope."

From the mountains of the Mexican Southeast
Subcomandante Insurgente Marcos

P.S. that continues righting wrongs at dawn and offers to a far-away maiden a little bouquet of red carnations hidden in a story called . . .

Durito III: Neoliberalism and the Labor Movement

The moon is a pale almond. Sheets of silver re-shape trees and plants. Zealous crickets nail on the tree trunks white leaves as irregular as the shadows of the night below. Gusts of gray wind agitate trees and uneasiness. Durito climbs up into my beard. The sneeze he provokes makes the armed knight tumble to the ground. Durito sits up with some difficulty. To the already imposing armor that is his body, Durito added half a *cololté* shell (which is a species of wild hazelnut found in La Lacandona) on his head and holds the top of a bottle of medicine like a shield. Excalibur is sheathed and a lance (that looks suspiciously like a straightened paper clip) completes his attire.

"Now what?" I ask as I try, in vain, to help Durito with my finger.

Durito rearranges his body, I mean, his armor. He unsheathes Excalibur, clears his throat a couple of times, and says in a presumptuous voice,

"Dawn, my battered squire! This is exactly the hour when night arranges its vestments to leave and day sharpens its thorny Apollo's mane to appear to the world! It is the hour when knights-errant ride off seeking adventures that elevate their prestige in the absent gaze of the lady that prevents them, even for an instant, from closing their eyes to seek oblivion or rest!"

I yawn and let my eyelids bring me oblivion or rest. Durito becomes irritated and raises his voice:

"We must go out to despoil maidens, take advantage of widows, come to the aid of bandits and incarcerate the penniless!"

---

1 Mexico's Distrito Federal (Federal District), its seat of government, has some of the worst air pollution in the world. The terms D.F. and Mexico City are used interchangeably, and it is also referred to as the "*Ciudad de Palacios*" ("City of Palaces").

"That menu sounds like a government program," I tell him with my eyes still closed.

Durito appears to have no intention of leaving without waking me fully:

"Wake up, scoundrel! I remind you of your duty to follow your Master wherever misfortunes or adventures may take him!"

I finally open my eyes and stare at him. Durito looks more like a broken-down army tank than a knight-errant.

To clear up my doubt I ask him, "And who are you supposed to be?"

"I am a knight-errant: not one of those whose names are never noted by Fame, to render them eternal in her memory, but rather one of those who, despite and in defiance of that same envy, and in the face of who knows how many Persian Magi, Indian Brahmans, or Ethiopian Gymnosophists, has carried his name straight into the temple of immortality, to serve as a model and example for all time to come, whereby knights-errant will see footsteps they have to walk in, if they long to attain the summit and highest honors that war and weaponry can bestow,"[2] Durito answers, assuming his most (according to him) gallant pose.

"It sounds to me . . . it sounds like . . . like . . ." I begin to say but Durito interrupts me:

"Silence, foolish plebeian! Thou wouldst want to disparage me by saying that I plagiarize my speeches from *The Ingenious Gentleman Don Quijote of La Mancha*. And certainly, since we are on this subject, I should tell you Sir, that you are wasting space in your epistles. That nonsense of footnotes! If you continue on that course you'll end up like Galio, citing six or seven authors in one paragraph in order to cover cynicism with erudition."[3]

I feel profoundly wounded by comments so close to home and I change the subject.

"That on your head . . . it looks like a *cololté* shell."

"It is a helmet, ignoramus," Durito says.

"Helmet? It looks like a shell with holes," I insist.

"*Cololté*. Helmet. Halo. That's the order, Sancho," Durito says as he arranges his helmet.[4]

"Sancho?" I stutter-say-ask-protest.

"Well, stop this nonsense and prepare to leave because many are the injustices that my indefatigable sword must remedy, and its blade is now impatient to test the necks of independent unions." As he says this, Durito brandishes his sword like the regent of a capital city.

---

2 Footnote by Marcos: "Book One: Chapter XLVII—all about Don Quijote de La Mancha's strange enchantment, along with other celebrated events." See Cervantes, *Don Quijote*, 324.

3 Galio is the protagonist of a novel that takes place during the "dirty war" carried out against guerrilla forces by the Mexican government during the 1970s. See Hector Aguilar Camín, *La Guerra de Galio* (México D.F.: Cal y Arena, 1991).

4 Sancho refers to Sancho Panza, Don Quijote's squire and companion.

"I think you've read too many papers recently. Be careful, or they'll have you committing suicide," I tell Durito while I try to delay as long as possible the moment I get up. Durito, for a moment, abandons his 16th-century language and explains, proudly, that he has secured a mount. Durito says it is as swift as lightning in August, silent as the wind in March, docile as the rain in September, and I don't remember what other marvels, but there was one for each month of the year. I appear incredulous, so Durito announces solemnly that he will do me the honor of showing me his mount. I agree, thinking that this way I can sleep a little.

Durito leaves and is so long in returning that, in fact, I fall asleep . . .

A voice awakens me, "Here I am!" It is Durito and he is mounted on the logical reason for his delay: a little turtle! At a pace that Durito was bent on calling an "elegant trot" and that to me looked more like a very prudent and drawn-out one, the turtle stopped in front of me. Mounted on his turtle (they call it "*pegasus*" in Tzeltal), Durito turns to look at me and asks, "So how do I look?"

I stare at him and maintain a respectful silence before this knight-errant that who knows what reasons brought to the solitude of La Lacandona. His appearance is "peculiar."

Durito baptized his turtle, excuse me, his horse with a name that seems more a delirium: *Pegasus*. So that there is no doubt, Durito has written on the shell of the turtle, with large and decisive letters, "*PEGASUS. Copyrights Reserved,*" and below that, "*Please fasten your seat belts.*" I just can't resist the temptation of making a comparison with the economic recuperation program when Durito turns his mount so I can see his other side. Pegasus takes his time, so that what Durito announced as a "vertiginous spin of his horse," is actually a slow turn. A movement that the turtle makes so carefully that anyone would say that he doesn't want to get dizzy. After a few minutes, I can read on Pegasus' left flank "*Smokers' Section,*" "*Union Charros not allowed.*"[5] "*Free advertising space.*" "*For information call Durito's Publishing.*" I believe, however, that there isn't much free space available because the ad covers all the left and rear flank of Pegasus.

After praising the ultra-mini-micro entrepreneurial vision of Durito, the only way to survive the wreckage of neoliberalism and NAFTA, I ask him, "So where does thy future lead thee, my lord?"

"Don't be a clown. That language only belongs to noblemen and lords and not to vagabonds and plebeians who, were it not for my infinite compassion, would continue in their hollow lives and would never be able even to dream about knowing the secrets and marvels of knight-erranthood," responds Durito while trying to restrain Pegasus, who for some strange reason seems impatient to leave.

It seems to me that, for it being two in the morning, I've already received enough scolding, so I tell Durito, "Wherever you go, you'll go alone. I don't plan to leave tonight. Yesterday Camilo found tiger tracks and he says it must still be close by."

---

5 The use of *charro* conveys both the national image of the middle–class, landed horseman popularized after the Mexican Revolution, and the popular moniker for bureaucrats.

I believe I've found a vulnerable flank of our brave knight, because his voice trembles when he asks, "Ti...ti...tiger?" And he adds, after swallowing saliva with audible difficulty, "And what do these tigers eat?"

"Everything. Guerrillas, soldiers, beetles . . . and turtles!" This last part I say observing the probable reaction from Pegasus. The little turtle must have really believed it is a horse, because it did not seem to be alarmed. Actually, I thought I heard a soft whinny.

"Bah! You say so just to frighten me, but you should know that this armed knight has defeated giants disguised as windmills that in turn disguised themselves as armed helicopters. He has conquered the most impregnable kingdoms, he has subdued the resistance of the most demure princesses, he has . . ."

I interrupt Durito. I know that he can take up pages and pages talking and then I'm the one who gets criticized by the editors, especially when the communiqués arrive so late at night.

"Fine, fine. But tell me, where are you going?"

"To Mexico City!" Durito says, brandishing his sword. It seems the trip's destination surprises Pegasus, because he gives sort of a start, which for a turtle is like a discreet sigh.

"Mexico City?" I ask incredulously.

"Sure! Do you think I would be deterred just because Comcopa didn't let you all go?"[6]

I wanted to warn Durito not to speak ill of Comcopa because the legislators are so sensitive and then they get mad during the negotiations, but Durito continued: "You should know I am a knight-errant, but more Mexican than the failure of the neoliberal economy. Therefore, I have the right to go to the so-called 'City of Palaces.' What do they want palaces for in Mexico City if not so that a knight-errant like myself, the most famous, the most gallant, the most respected by men, loved by women, and admired by children, should honor them by stepping foot inside?"

"It will be with your many legs—I remind you that besides being a knight-errant and a Mexican you are also a beetle," I correct him.

"Regardless of my foot or legs, a palace without knights-errant stopping by is like a child without a present on April 30th,[7] like a pipe without tobacco, like a book without words, like a song without music, like a knight-errant without a squire," and arriving at this last point Durito looks at me fixedly and asks: "Are you sure you don't want to follow me on this intriguing adventure?"

"It depends," I say, pretending to be very interested, and adding, "It depends what you mean by 'intriguing adventure.'"

"It means I'm going to the May Day parade," Durito says as if he were saying, "I'm going to the corner for some cigarettes."

"To the May Day parade! But what if there's not going to be a parade?! Fidel Velázquez, who has always worried about workers' pocketbooks, said there was no

---

6 COMCOPA, or COCOPA.

7 This day is celebrated in Mexico as the official "Day of the Child."

money for the parade.[8] Some rumor-mongers insinuated that he is afraid that the workers will get out of control and, instead of being grateful to the supreme one, will only curse him with those words that cartoonists dislike. But it's a lie, the Labor Secretary quickly said it was not out of fear, that it was just a 'veeery respectable' decision from the labor sector, and . . . ."

"Whoa, whoa, stop your parade float! I'm going to the May Day parade because I am going to challenge this Fidel Velázquez to a duel. He is, as everyone knows, a fierce ogre who oppresses poor people. I will challenge him to fight in the Azteca stadium to see if that way the attendance will improve, because ever since they fired Beenhaker (don't criticize me if it's misspelled, not even the directors of the Américas team can spell it, and they're the ones who wrote his checks), no one goes to the games anymore."[9] Durito is silent for a moment and looks pensively at *Pegasus*, who must have gone to sleep, because it has been a while since he moved. Suddenly Durito asks me, "Do you think Fidel Velázquez has a horse?"

I hesitate a bit. "Well, he's a *charro* so it's very likely that he has a horse."

"Magnificent," says Durito, and digs his spurs into Pegasus.

Pegasus may think he's a horse, but his body is still that of a turtle and he has the hard shell to prove it, so he doesn't even notice Durito's cowboy exhortations to get him going. After struggling a bit, Durito discovers that by hitting him on his nose with the paperclip, excuse me, the lance, he can make Pegasus stretch out into a full gallop. A "full gallop" for this horse-turtle is about 10 centimeters per hour, so one can see that it will take Durito a long time to reach D.F.

"At that rate, you will arrive when Fidel Velásquez is dead," I tell Durito as a parting thought.[10]

I should never have said it. Durito pulled back the reins and reared his horse like when Pancho Villa took Torreon. Well, it's a good literary image.[11] In reality what Pegasus did was to stop, which, at his rate was almost imperceptible. In contrast to Pegasus' calm, Durito is furious when he tells me:

"Your problem is the same as what happened to the advisors of the labor movement in the last decades! They recommended patience to the worker, and they sat down to wait for the *charro* to fall off his mount, and did nothing to knock him down."

"Well, not all of them sat down to wait. Some have struggled, and hard, to create a truly independent labor movement."

"Those are the ones I'm going to see. I'm going to join them so I can show all of them that we workers have dignity too," Durito says, who I recall once told me that

---

8 Fidel Velázquez dominated labor relations for 60 years, co-founding the Mexican Workers Confederation, or CTM (*Confederación de Trabajadores Mexicanos*) in 1936.

9 Leo Beenhaker managed the Américas soccer team from Mexico City.

10 Velázquez, popularly known as "the mummy" for his advanced age and tenure, was 95 at the time of this communiqué. He died in 1997.

11 The image of General Francisco Villa triumphantly entering the city of Torreon, Coahuila on April 3, 1914, marks a critical turning point in the Revolution, and is celebrated in photos and paintings.

he was a miner in the state of Hidalgo and an oil worker in Tabasco.

Durito leaves. He takes a few hours to disappear behind the bush that's a few meters from my plastic roof. I get up and notice that my right boot is loose. I shine my flashlight on it and discover that . . . the lace is missing! And it's then that I realize why Pegasus' reins looked familiar. Now I'll have to wait until Durito returns from Mexico. I look for a reed to tie my boot and I think that I forgot to recommend to Durito to visit that restaurant with the tiles.[12] I lie down again. It's almost dawn . . .

Above, the sky stretches out, and with reddish-blue eyes, contemplates, amazed that Mexico is still there, where it was yesterday. I light my pipe, I watch the last spirals of night detach themselves from the trees, and I tell myself that the struggle is very long and it is worth it . . .

P.S. that with the face of a full moon looks toward the jungle and wonders, who is this man that rides over a squalid shadow? Why does he not seek relief? Why does he endure new pain? Why so many journeys while standing still? Who is he? Where is he going? Why does he say goodbye with such a noisy silence?

P.S. to a CND that can't decide whether to fight against the party-state system or against itself.

I read somewhere that while the supreme government beats on both sides, the CND beats on itself. About that and other things, a few lines:

As the poet with the graying mustache who hides behind the piano writes,

Mexico is a joyful flower
That never sought a vase
A wild boar that brags
About its youth
A javelin at the heart of justice
The "x" camouflaged as a "j"

And so Manuel may be right when he says that the meetings of the "Collective Centers of Civilian Support" are like meetings of "Alcoholics Anonymous" or "Weight Watchers." Maybe there is more to learn from these meetings than from party assemblies.

After all, the CND was born with the idea of unity, not to enter into the market of party clientelism. A plan that includes the greatest possible number and quality of civic will was and is necessary. The CND had that plan. It shouldn't be the political arm of the Ee-Ze, or a new party, or a new white elephant of the inconsistent Mexican left. It must be the space where the imaginations and proposals for democratic change meet. And about these imaginations and proposals, the freshest, the most audacious, come from civil society, not from political society, that is, not from political organizations. Its

---

12 The Sanborns restaurant, located near the Zócalo, was the site of the famous meeting between Zapata and Villa.

flag is national, that's what it is, the one that rises above parties and armies. From that space of encounter can come proposals to impose, with imagination, on the government, on the parties, on the Zapatista army, and on itself. That ship does not want to arrive at the port of power. In that sense, it does not comply with the pragmatic and cynical premises of Galio–Machiavelli, but it does want to arrive at the port of a country with no return to the shadows, a country with democracy, liberty, and justice. Is there dead weight? Throw them overboard! Will only a few remain aboard? Imagination will replace quantity with quality! Civil society has much to learn from itself, and very little to learn from political society (with its full spectrum of colors, flavors, and cynicisms). It is not a space for those against the party, but it could be for those without a party. This civil society will manage, in the midst of the threats of the dirty war (although there isn't, I believe, a war that can be called clean), to make the Angel of Independence rappel off its column and begin to chat with Juárez, Columbus, and old grandfather Cuahtémoc, with the kind Diana hunting stars, and a stray palm tree drunk with smog.[13] This civil society will turn its non-proposals into realities; civil dialogues in the middle of tanks, machine guns and cannons; campaigns of humanitarian aid, in the middle of a profound crisis and a generalized inflation, meant to relieve its most vulnerable and impoverished flank, the indigenous. If the CND is not an ample space for this and other initiatives, the shapeless but effective irreverence of civil society will escape from that straitjacket. And then? Correct, it will build its own meeting spaces. The CND will become another acronym, added to the inefficiency of existing acronyms. There's still a lot to learn. This country has a lot to learn from itself.

P.S. To Whom It May Concern in the supreme government:
There is a type of lens cut so that it has many surfaces, like a multifaceted prism. This lens is mounted on a small wooden viewfinder, like an eyepiece. Looking through this lens, the light becomes many. When it is turned or moved, it offers many new configurations. Is it the same light broken into many lights? Are there many lights imprisoned in the eyepiece? Is it just confirmation that there is no singularity even in the most apparent unity? Is it only one light or many that one must be able to distinguish, recognize, and appreciate? And, finally, thinking about the tiny eyepiece, is it a light with many *marcos* [frames] or a single *marco* [frame] for many lights?

Vale, once again. *Salud*, and only by arriving in hell will we know the answer.

El Sub with a red carnation in his lapel, playing at being a crystal and a mirror.

---

13 These refer to landmark statues on Reforma Boulevard in Mexico City: Benito Juárez (first Mexican President of the 19th century); Cuahtémoc (the last *Tlatoani*, emperor of the Aztec Empire); Diana is the Roman goddess of the hunt and the moon, and sister to the sun god Apollo. The Angel of Independence was built to commemorate 100 years of Mexican independence and has become a symbol of Mexico City.

Durito's May Day Postcard

After traveling to Mexico City to find Fidel Velázquez, Durito participated, with hundreds of thousands of workers, in the May Day protests that went on despite government opposition. While the dominant theme of the protests was clearly opposition to the neoliberal austerity programs put in place in the wake of the Peso Crisis and the $50 billion investor bailout engineered by the International Monetary Fund, President Bill Clinton, and President Ernesto Zedillo, there was also tremendous support expressed for the Zapatistas in their struggle with the government. This communiqué recounts a postcard Durito sent back from Mexico City telling of the demonstrations.

To the national weekly *Proceso*
To the national newspaper *El Financiero*
To the national newspaper *La Jornada*
To the local newspaper of San Cristóbal de Las Casas, Chiapas, *Tiempo*
May 5, 1995

Sirs:
Here go letters for the indicated recipients. I would appreciate your addition of some special stamps and elegant envelopes. Today's celebration promises to be bloody.[1] The absence of Durito and the continuing heavy rain promise skirmishes instead of a formal battle. The problem is getting worse because no one wants to be the French. It is obvious that this is another *sexenio*.[2]

Vale. Salud, and congratulations for May 10th to all those who still have a mother.[3]

From the mountains of the Mexican Southeast
Subcomandante Insurgente Marcos

P.S. that gives an account of Durito's travels and advice.
Durito has sent me a postcard. It contains a photo of him, with Pegasus on his left and the Monument of the Revolution on his right. The caption reads, "Which is slower? The left or the right?" Durito writes, in the postcard, that he failed to find Fidel Velázquez, but that he took part in the May Day march. He

---

First published in *La Jornada*, May 11, 1995. Originally translated for this volume by Harry Cleaver and Marco Iñiguez.

1 The Mexican defeat of the French at the Battle of Puebla in 1862 is celebrated on May 5th.
2 The *sexenio* is the six-year term of office of the Mexican Presidency.
3 Mother's Day is celebrated in Mexico on May 10th.

recounts the following: that when he passed in front of the American Embassy he cried out, "Dodgers *Sí*, Yankees No!" (Durito didn't know that Valenzuela is now with the San Diego Padres);[4] that he doesn't remember when he entered the Zócalo or when he left;[5] that a man, after observing him for a long time, approached him and said, "Excuse me, I don't mean to offend, but I cannot resist the temptation to say that you look remarkably like a scarab"; and that there were a whole lot of people there. "EVERYBODY was there," said Durito, and added, with his eternal tendency to state the obvious, "The only thing missing was a revolution."

P.S. that explains the delay in consultations within Zapatista communities.

We are confused with respect to the government proposal: we are not sure what is meant by the declaration of Gurría, this agent of foreign sales, who brags about his duties as Secretary of Foreign Relations, while he demands the regrouping of Zapatista "insurgents." Insofar as he thinks that the conflict in Chiapas is a "war of ink," does he refer only to those Zapatistas who know how to read and write?[6] If this is the case, then the three locations where they want the Zapatistas to concentrate are far too many and it will be much cheaper for the government to care only for the literate.[7] If you don't believe me, ask the ever-pleasing Del Valle, who laughs at the way our representatives speak Spanish.[8]

* * *

---

4 Fernando Valenzuela, a famous baseball player from Mexico, played for the Los Angeles Dodgers, sparking an enthusiasm among many Mexican fans known as "Fernandomania."

5 The Zócalo is the large plaza facing the Presidential Palace in Mexico City.

6 Speaking to 150 businessmen at the World Trade Center in New York, José Angel Gurría said, "The shooting lasted ten days, and ever since the war has been a war of ink, of the written word and a war on the Internet." See, "Chiapas es Guerra de Tinta e Internet," *La Reforma*, April 26, 1995.

7 The government proposal made at the end of the first new round of talks on April 23, 1995 included a demand that all Zapatista forces be concentrated in three locations. In return, the government offered to provide food, housing, healthcare and a partial pullback of its troops. The EZLN returned from their communities to the second round of talks with a firm rejection of the proposal. Instead, they demanded that the Mexican government withdraw its troops to where they had been before the February 1995 offensive.

8 José Del Valle was one of the Mexican government representatives at the negotiations. During the negotiations, he and government representatives were often insulting and disdainful of their indigenous counterparts. See Marcos' letter to the press published in *La Jornada* on February 10, 1996, and included in this volume as "The Riddle." See also "The Story of the Hot Foot and the Cold Foot."

On Bullfighting,
Détente and Rock

In this communiqué, consisting almost entirely of postscripts, Marcos begins where they left off before Durito's trip to Mexico City, recounting how he and Durito el Camborio get down from the ceiba—with Durito continuing his display of matador moves. Other postscripts include an outline of 13 government actions undermining peace negotiations and Durito's praise of Mexican rock music in the light of his participation in a recent rock concert.

First published in *La Jornada*, May 30, 1995. Source: *EZLN Documentos y communicados* 2: 15 de Agosto de 1995/29 de septiembre de 1995 (México, D. F.: Ediciones Era, 1995), 306-309. Originally translated by irlandesa for this collection.

To the national weekly *Proceso*
To the national newspaper *El Financiero*
To the national newspaper *La Jornada*
To the local newspaper of San Cristóbal de Las Casas, Chiapas, *Tiempo*
May 24, 1995

Ladies and Gentlemen,
Here goes a self-explanatory letter. The May 10 fiesta at this camp was
embarrassing. It is rumored that we have no ancestors, or their equivalent.
Camilo, who is the best situated in this regard, has very few.

Vale. Salud, and may the "shipment" of hope travel a long distance.

From the mountains of the Mexican Southeast
Subcomandante Insurgente Marcos

P.S. that explains how, prior to Durito's trip, we got down from the ceiba.[1]
When Durito finished teaching the matador's moves, he discovered that he
did not know how to get down from the ceiba either. As we always do when we
don't know what to do, we lit our pipes. Durito began to hear a buzzing at one
side of the ceiba, and he started imagining that a new adventure was drawing
near.
"The sixth bull! The time and place to write a brilliant page in this uppity
bullring!" Durito said, while walking to the center of the plaza. I picked up the
carnation that sweet girl with the Guadalajara eyes had thrown to me at the
beginning of the bullfight ("bullflight," Durito will then say). (I already know the
carnation was sent on April 19, and I didn't receive it until the 23rd, but I can use
the carnation however I wish. After all, it is my postscript).
"Ah, squire! Think about whistling a *pasodoble,*[2] and prepare your eyes and
your pen, for what you are about to see merits a bullfighting chronicle like those
that are at least as festive as the marvels which inspire them," Durito ordered me.
"Pay attention to what you are doing, they could be wasps," I warned him.
But Durito was inciting the improbable bull. Nothing. The snub made him
bolder, and he began hurling little branches at the tree across from him. The
buzzing grew. Expectation was mounting among the spectators. I was not able
to describe the magnificent image. Clumsy squire and worse chronicler, I could
write nothing about the solitary and ungainly figure of Durito, who had abandoned his cape and secured two little branches that, he shouted to me, were

---

1 'Durito's trip' to Mexico City for the May Day parade was detailed in "Durito III," and in
"Durito's May Day Postcard." Prior to that trip, Marcos and Durito were up in a ceiba discussing
bullfighting and Spanish poet Federico García Lorca.
2 A *pasodoble* is a two-step march played prior to the release of the first bull at the beginning of a
bullfight.

banderillas.[3] The Moon, amazed, had stopped to observe the denouement. A milky "Road to Santiago," full of sandy light, parts the expectant night.[4] Unable to stand the tension, a star lets itself fall in a faint, and traces a weak ray of light across the dark, nocturnal face. Durito begins running around and changes his pace; he raises two of his little hands, the *banderillas* glittering on high. The buzzing comes together, the zoom-zoom becomes ordered, consolidates and approaches. The drum rolls out a prophecy. Almost an instant . . .

Durito suddenly veers from his headlong rush, and, in a hurried and unattractive fashion, turns half-around and runs towards me with a shout:

"Bees!"

I had managed to write: "The bugle sounded the retreat," when Durito arrives and is hanging from a braid that the moon left forgotten at one side of the ceiba. When I realized what had happened, I threw the bullfight chronicle and the pen down and leapt behind Durito. Killer bees were attacking. No *el muletazos* or anything else could stop them.[5] They left my face with elephantiasis, and, most certainly, Camilo and My Other Self will not be running to Guatemala.

Durito consoled me (he was untouched):

"Let's get down! No? I wish you had taken care to have brought the chronicle, without having to go up and get it."

The pain I felt kept me from insulting him . . .

Section of postscripts in which a knight-errant (suspiciously resembling a beetle) gives, to a squire of legendary nose and imprudence, council and thoughts of the type that expand the spirit and strengthen one's path.

P.S. that continues to speak of the postcard received.[6]

Durito says goodbye, warning me to be careful with the capitulators, former opponents, former leftists, former revolutionaries, former guerrillas, former progressives, and those formerly in solidarity with the foreign revolution. "They make a religion of cynicism and end up serving the system they were criticizing yesterday. They fight rebellion with the ferocity of those who see in a mirror exactly what they are: thinking and prudent capitulators. They want to break the mirror, not for what it means, but because it shows them the uselessness of having become 'crazy persons' again."

---

3 *Banderillas* are the two flagged sticks with barbed darts that are placed into the bull's neck.
4 The "road to Santiago," or "St. James Way," is the pilgrimage path through Europe to Santiago de Compostella in Galicia, Spain. The road was called the "Milky Way" by pilgrims who saw their earthly road mirrored in the sky. In Mexico, the Church's influence led to the celestial Milky Way—called the White Road in Mayan mythology—itself being called the "road to Santiago." See *Popul Vuh: The Mayan Book of the Dawn of Life*, trans. Dennis Tedlock, 2nd ed. (New York: Touchstone, 1996).
5 *Muleta* literally means "crutch." A matador uses a *muleta*, a large red flannel cape supported by a stick, for the final period of a bullfight in which he dispatches the bull. *Muletazos* are especially graceful and well-executed passes with the *muleta*.
6 See "Durito's May Day Postcard."

"Watch out," Durito continues, "for people like that, you can find them everywhere. Excuse the paternal tone of these lines, but you are too ingenuous, Sancho."

I remained, seeing the ending and thinking, "Sancho?"

I wanted to answer Durito, but my time had been given to correcting the errors of spelling, punctuation, and conceptual clarity in the text of the *El Supremo*'s "détente proposal."[7] I had been thinking of sending *El Supremo* his delegation's text with spelling corrections. I hope the government appreciates this détente measure; I am going to charge absolutely nothing for the spelling consultation. Although I doubt it's true, the government delegates appear to be busier with their "heroic" fight against the CONAI than they are in analyzing real détente measures.

Incidentally, I'm tempted to respond to *El Supremo*'s argument that "a great moment" for détente was . . . the ceasefire of January 12, 1994! It would appear they have not been informed that Salinas de Gortari is no longer president. Why do they claim as theirs a measure taken by another government? Will it be necessary to go on a hunger strike in order for the current government to not appropriate the good moves of the previous one, or to foist on them the errors of the present one?[8] One could, for example, enumerate 13 government measures that have gone against the détente process and that have put the country on the edge of war. For example:

a) Backing the imposition of Robledo Rincón on Chiapas[9]
b) Madrazo's imposition in Tabasco[10]
c) Harassment of the *avendañista* movement[11]
d) Displaced persons[12]
e) The re-arming and sponsoring of the White Guards[13]
f) The February 9 betrayal
g) The attacks against civilians in the military campaign

---

7 *El Supremo* refers to President Ernesto Zedillo. The "détente proposal" was the proposal made by the government at the second round of peace talks at San Andrés Sacamach'en de los Pobres, May 12-15, 1995.

8 This is undoubtedly a reference to Salinas de Gortari's hunger strike. See note in "Durito II."

9 Eduardo Robledo Rincón, PRI governor of Chiapas, took office in 1994 over widespread protests of election fraud.

10 Opposition to the corrupt regime and fraudulent election of Roberto Madrazo, the PRI governor of Tabasco, led to a protest march to Mexico City under the banner of "Exodus for Dignity."

11 The *avendañista* movement emerged in support of Amado Avendaño's formation of a "Transitional Government in Rebellion" in protest to the fraudulent election of Robledo.

12 Zapatista communities were forced to flee in order to escape the brutality of the federal Army, judicial police and the paramilitaries. The day this communiqué was written, the National Commission for Human Rights, or CNDH (*Comisión Nacional de Derechos Humanos*), denounced the collaboration of the police and paramilitaries in the violent expulsion of people from their communities. See *La Jornada*, May 24, 1995.

13 The White Guards are paramilitaries hired by ranchers to control local peasant labor forces.

h) The slander against the CONAI

i) Harassment and threats against journalists

j) The lies in the media

k) The lack of seriousness within the government delegation

l) The racism and authoritarianism

m) The taking of dozens of communities and thousands of indigenous as hostages

I could do so, but they say the number 13 is bad luck, so I better not . . .

P.S. that explains the relationship between good sense, rock, festivals, and life.

"Everyone raved about my slam dancing," Durito boasts, while shining his shell, after having attended the "Serpiente 12" festival.[14]

"There is nothing more foolish in all of Mexico today than being indigenous or young or a rocker or a knight-errant or a beetle," Durito says. "And so the most foolish of all Mexicans is your servant, because I am all five things, and a few more that have nothing to do with the postscript."

"Mexican rock is an irreverent and reckless critique. Their songs have the sharp edge of those who cannot help but cut tracks. But, in addition, their songs, their work, their music-making find a reflection in, and of, the indigenous rebellion in the Southeast. Through that complicated play of mirrors that is Mexican life outside the circle of Power, the ski mask and a re-named peace come together in young people who have nothing in common other than their exasperation at immobility and their longing to be better. All the groups and solo acts that performed were foolish," Durito says, who holds firmly to the thesis that good sense is like ties: an elegant garrote that changes with fashion. He explains that good sense turns love, music and life ("Yes, in that order," Durito warns) into an instruction manual with abundant footnotes and produces loss of sexual appetite. "In addition to other sorrows we suffer, Sancho."

P.S. that asserts, boldly, that a mirror can reflect everything, except itself.

"We are not all Marcos. It is obvious that Marcos, at least, is not Marcos," writes Durito, who, as can be seen, studied dialectical materialism in the polyester manual.[15]

P.S. that responds to Lozano's and de Alamilla's threats:[16]

Now look here, you vulgar, lowborn wretches! [. . .] Tell me: what illiterate peasant signed an arrest warrant against a knight like me? What kind of ignoramus is

14 The Serpiente 12 Festival was one of a number of concerts organized by a Mexico City band for the benefit of the Zapatista communities.

15 A popular slogan at pro-Zapatista rallies has been "*Todos somos Marcos,*" "We are all Marcos."

16 Antonio Lozano Gracia was the spokesperson for the PGR when it issued arrest warrants against the EZLN in February 1995. Genaro Alamilla Arteaga was bishop emeritus of Papantla who spoke out in support of the actions by the PGR and the Army.

he, unaware that knights-errant are exempt from the application of all laws and statutes, that for them law is their sword, statutes are their spirit, and edicts and proclamations are their will and desire? Tell me, I say, who was the idiot who had no idea that, on the day a man's dubbed a knight-errant and devotes himself to his rigorous profession, he acquires privileges and exemptions surpassing anything granted by charters of nobility? What knight-errant has ever paid taxes—rent-tax, king's wedding-tax, land-tax—or paid a highway toll or a ship toll? When did a tailor ever charge for making a knight's clothes? What warden, giving him lodging in his castle, ever charged a knight for his bed? What king ever denied him a seat at his table? What lovely maiden could keep herself from loving him and humbly surrendering herself to his will and his desire? And, finally, what knight-errant has there ever been or will there ever be, in all the world, without the spirit to deliver 400 blows, single-handed, against 400 policemen, if they happen to get in his way?"[17]

Vale once more. *Salud*, and remember that "virtue is more persecuted by the wicked than it is loved by the good."[18]

* * *

---

17 Footnote by Marcos: "Chapter XLV — in which the investigation into the helmet and the saddlebag is concluded, along with other events of an equally veracious nature." See Cervantes, *Don Quijote*, 314. In the quoted passage, Don Quijote is threatened with arrest for having stolen a barber's basin that he believed was an enchanted helmet.
18 Footnote by Marcos: "Chapter XLVII — all about *Don Quijote* de la Mancha's strange enchantment, along with other celebrated events." See Cervantes, *Don Quijote*, 324.

Durito IV: Neoliberalism and the Party-State System

Derrida

While accompanying the Exodus for Dignity and National Sovereignty, a 41-day protest march against electoral fraud from Tabasco to Mexico City, Durito writes a letter to a fictional professor at the UNAM on the current crisis of the Mexican political system and the question of a transition from PRIista one-party rule to democracy. The Tabasco marchers were accompanied by Manuel López Obrador, the PRD candidate whose bid for governor was thwarted by fraud and violence, and they were greeted in the Zócalo by Cuauhtémoc Cárdenas, former presidential candidate for the PRD. Durito explains why the Zapatistas have refused to participate, and by doing so legitimize the political realm of formal electoral politics. Instead, as he explains, the Zapatistas have called for a diversity of forms of political struggle, with their own being but one among many. Durito IV and V are part of *The Book of Mirrors*, a pivotal document discussing the representation of reality, history, politics and culture. Durito IV is the fourth chapter of the first section, and its beginning references the first chapters.

First published in *La Jornada*, June 11, 1995. Originally translated by Cecilia Rodríguez.

Open your eyes and look into the mirror. No, don't look at your reflection. Direct your gaze below, to the left. There? Fine, pay attention and in a few moments another image will appear. Yes, it's a march: men, women, children, and old people that come from the Southeast. Yes, it's one of the highways that lead to Mexico City. Do you see what's walking on the left side of the caravan? Where? There below, on the ground! Yes, that very small and black thing! What *is* it you ask? A beetle! Now pay attention, because that beetle is . . .

Durito trying to keep up. These folks from Tabasco, even after so many days of walking and physical hardship, don't seem tired. They walk as though they had only begun this Exodus for Dignity and National Sovereignty this morning. Once again, as before in the voice of the Zapatistas, a call to the entire Nation comes from the Mexican Southeast. It is the same desire: democracy, liberty and justice. In the heroic delirium of the Mexican Southeast, hope implies a name: *Tachicam*, the unity of longing for a better future.[1] The dream of a place where the right to dance is guaranteed by the Constitution.

Durito takes advantage of a break in the march, and overcome by the heat, he seeks refuge under a small bush. After awhile, and having caught his breath, he takes out paper and pencil. On a rock replacing the tiny desk he left in the jungle, Durito writes a letter. Go on! Don't be afraid! Look over Durito's shoulder and read:

Zapatista Army of National Liberation
Mexico, May 1995
To: Mister So and So
Professor and Researcher
National Autonomous University of Mexico
Mexico, D.F.
From: Don Durito de la Lacandona,
Knight-errant for whom Sup Marcos is squire
Zapatista Army of National Liberation
Mexico

Sir:
It may seem strange to you that I, a beetle that carries out the obligations of the noble profession of knight-errant, write to you. Do not be perturbed or seek out a psychoanalyst, because I will quickly and promptly explain everything to you . It turns out that you proposed that El Sup write an article for a book (or something like that) about The Transition to Democracy. The book (or whatever it is) would be edited by the UNAM (which just about guarantees that no one will read it; espe-

---

1 *Tachicam*, a utopian project for a new autonomous region comprised of the states of Chiapas, Tabasco and Campeche, was promoted during this time by a network of small political groups that were disillusioned with electoral politics.

cially if the crisis in the publishing industry and the increase in the cost of paper are taken into account). The agreement was that the exorbitant amount of $N 1,000 (one thousand new pesos) that UNAM pays for the written "collaboration" would be delivered in its equivalent dollars or Italian liras to the workers of Fiat in Turin. We have learned as well that the Italian workers in the COBAS have already received this amount from the Zapatistas in solidarity with the struggles of European workers.[2] You have complied, the Fiat workers have complied, and the only one here who has failed to do so is El Sup, because I remember the deadline well and El Sup has not written anything. January of 1995 arrived, and El Sup was naively going on about the government being, in fact, inclined to the dialogue, and that is why he did not write the assignment. The betrayal of February snapped him out of it and made him (El Sup) run until he arrived at my side. Recovered from the disillusionment, he told me about his commitment to write the article and asked me to help him as he was in such a grave predicament. I, dear sir, am a knight-errant, and we knights-errant cannot refuse to help the needy, no matter how large-nosed or delinquent the helpless soul in question is. So I willingly agreed to grant the help that was demanded of me and that is why I am writing to you and not El Sup. Surely, you must wonder why, if I received the task in February, I am writing to you in May. Just remember, as a journalist pointed out, this is the "rebellion of the hanged."[3]

I should also warn you that I write veeery seriously and veeery formally, so do not expect to find my writing style full of jokes and irreverence like El Sup's, that so scandalizes the government delegates. That is why I am late. Do not be irritated, it could have been worse, you could have had to wait for El Sup to write to you one day. But it is not worth the risk to wait for such an improbable publication, so here I send you this long boring essay that has the theme I proposed, and that, if memory serves me, is entitled . . .

The Transition To Democracy According To The Zapatistas

Some would prefer to say, "According to the Neo-Zapatistas," but as Old Antonio already explained in "The History of the Questions," here the Zapatistas of 1994 and those of 1910 are the same.[4]

---

2 *Comitati di base*, or COBAS, are militant rank-and-file worker organizations active in a variety of sectors that have challenged the established trade unions and the austerity measures of the Italian government since the early 1980s.

3 "Rebellion of the hanged" refers to the 1954 film *La Rebelión de Los Colgados* (*Rebellion of the Hanged*), directed by Alfredo B. Crevenna and starring Pedro Armendáriz. Based on the novel by B. Traven, who also wrote *The Treasure of the Sierra Madre*, the film depicts a rebellion of loggers deep in the jungle of Chiapas working in semi-slave conditions. See B. Traven, *The Rebellion of the Hanged* (New York: Hill and Wang, 1972).

4 "The History of the Questions" appeared in a communiqué published in *La Jornada* December 13, 1994. See EZLN, *Documentos y comunicados 2:15 de agosto de 1994 / 29 de septiembre de 1995* (México, D.F.: Ediciones Era, 1995), 153–165.

I will proceed to explain how we view the current political situation, democracy, and the transition from one to the other.

"The Current Political Situation: The Party-State System, Principal Obstacle to a Transition to Democracy in Mexico"

In present-day Mexico we are faced with a structural deformation that cuts across the spectrum of Mexican society, as much in what are called the social classes, as in its economic and political aspects, including its urban and rural geographic "organization." This "deformation," in reality a consequence of the savage capitalism at the end of the 20th Century, masks itself in what is called "NEOLIBERALISM" and bases all its development on the permanence and intensification of said deformation. Any effort to "balance" this deformation by Power itself is impossible and never goes beyond cheap demagoguery (Procampo) or the most complete attempt at fascist control at the national level: The National Solidarity Program (Pronosol). We mean by this that the social "imbalance" in Mexico is not a product of excess or a problem of budgetary adjustment. It is the very essence of the system of domination; it is what makes it possible. Without this imbalance, the entire system would collapse.

We will not refer to economic and social "deformations," but only to the political ones in a very hurried manner: the political system of Mexico has its historical basis, its present crisis, and its mortal future, in that deformation called "the Party-State System." This is not just about the marriage of the government and the Party-State (The Institutional Revolutionary Party) but of an entire system of political, economic and social relations that invade even the oppositional political organizations and what is called "civil society."

Even in the best of cases, any attempt at equilibrium by political forces within this system does not go beyond a good intention that encourages the democratizing sectors within the PRI and some members of the opposition. The only way this political system has survived until now is by maintaining a brutal imbalance. On one side is all the force of the state apparatus: the repressive system, the mass media, big capital, and the reactionary clergy under the banner of the PRI. On the other is a fragmented opposition that is challenged primarily from within. In the middle, or better yet, on the margins of these extremes, are the vast majorities, the Mexican people. Both forces, the Party-State system and the organized opposition, bet on that third actor which is the Mexican people, on their absence or presence, on their apathy or mobilization. To immobilize it, all the system's mechanisms are put into motion; to mobilize it, the opposition's political proposals (legal or illegal, open or clandestine) are engaged.

Any attempt to equalize the imbalance within the system is impossible. Equilibrium means the death of the Mexican political system consolidated for more

90

than 60 years. Within the "rules of the game" of the system it is not even possible to concede to a new, more just model of social organization, or to a party system. Just as the dream of free play between supply and demand cannot become reality in an economic system increasingly dominated by monopolies, the free play of party politics cannot become reality in a system based on the monopoly of politics: the Party-State system.

Permit me to leave this point as noted (that is, as a problem and not a solution). Permit me to postpone, for an improbable moon, further explanation. For a more profound characterization of the Party-State system you can refer to more brilliant and forceful analyses (said without sarcasm) by excellent analysts. We are only pointing out one difference with respect to other positions that, in all likelihood, will be presented in this book you are preparing; namely, that any attempt to "reform" or "balance" this deformation is impossible FROM WITHIN THE PARTY-STATE SYSTEM. There is no "change without rupture." A profound and radical change of all social relations is necessary in today's Mexico. A REVOLUTION IS NECESSARY, a new revolution. This revolution is possible only from outside the Party-State system.

"Democracy, Liberty and Justice: Foundation for a New Political System in Mexico"

The triptych of Democracy-Liberty-Justice is the foundation of the EZLN's demands, included within its primarily indigenous base. One is not possible without the others. It is not about which comes first (an ideological trap whispers in our ear, "Let's postpone democracy, justice first"). It is more about the emphases or the hierarchy of expression, about the dominance of one of these elements in different historical eras (somewhat precipitated in the year 1994 and in what we have seen of 1995).

I will refer now to this thing about a REVOLUTION that we pointed out in a letter to the media on January 20, 1994, when government forces tightened their grip on our troops and our leadership was "hunted" by commando units of the Federal Army:

"We believe that revolutionary change in Mexico will not be the product of only one type of action. That is, it will not be, in a strict sense, an armed revolution or a peaceful revolution. It will be, primarily, a revolution resulting from struggle on various social fronts, with many methods, under different social forms, with varying degrees of commitment and participation. And its result will not be that of a triumphant party, organization or alliance of organizations with its specific social proposal, but rather a chance for a democratic space for resolving the confrontation among diverse political proposals. This democratic space for resolution will have three fundamental premises that are now historically inseparable: democracy, in order to decide upon the dominant social proposal; the freedom to subscribe to one

91

or another proposal; and justice, to which all proposals should conform."[5] (January 20, 1994)

Three points in a single paragraph, three points as dense as bitter *pozol*.[6] El Sup's style: conceptual obscurity, and ideas that are difficult to understand and harder to digest. But, I will allow myself to develop what he barely outlined. It addresses then, three points that contain an entire conception of revolution (in lowercase letters, in order to avoid polemics with the multiple vanguards and guardians of "THE REVOLUTION"):

The first point refers to the nature of revolutionary change, of this revolutionary change. It is about a nature that incorporates different methods, diverse fronts, various forms and distinct levels of commitment and participation. This means that all methods have their place, that all fronts of struggle are necessary, and that all levels of participation are important. It is about, then, an inclusive conception that is anti-vanguard and collective. The problem with revolution (note the lowercase letters) is no longer a problem of THE organization, THE method, THE *caudillo*[7] (note the uppercase letters), it becomes rather a problem that concerns all those who see revolution as necessary and possible, and in its realization, everyone is important.

The second point refers to the objective and the result of that revolution. It is not about seizing Power or the introduction (by peaceful or violent means) of a new social system, but about something that precedes both. It is about successfully constructing the antechamber of the new world, a space where, with equal rights and responsibilities, the different political forces "fight for" the support of the majority of society. Does this confirm the hypothesis that the Zapatistas are "armed reformists?" We do not think so. We are only pointing out that an imposed revolution, without the endorsement of the majority, ends up turning against itself. I know that this is a theme worthy of pages, but since this is only a letter, I am only making points to be developed on other occasions or to provoke debate and discussion (which seems to be the Zapatistas' "specialty of the house.")

The third point is about the characteristics, not of the revolution, but of its

---

5 The Clandestine Revolutionary Indigenous Committee-General Command of the Zapatista National Liberation Army (CCRI-CG) of the EZLN issued four communiqués on January 20, 1994 that were published in *La Jornada*, January 25, 1994. The communiqué addressed to Mexican and international civil society outlines the Zapatista demands and forms of struggle. See EZLN, *Documentos y comunicados 1 de enero / 8 de agosto de 1994* (México, D.F.: Ediciones Era, 1994), 95-106.

6 *Pozol* is a fermented corn drink that Mayan peoples have developed and used over generations for its nutritional and medicinal benefits, particularly with intestinal ailments. It is also one of the new Chiapan resources targeted for exploitation. In 1999, the Dutch corporation Quest International and the University of Minnesota jointly obtained US patent #5919695—not for the *pozol* itself, but rather an active component that the drink contains, thereby violating indigenous rights to the knowledge used to develop *pozol*. See "Biopiracy: A New Threat to Indigenous Rights and Culture" (San Francisco: Global Exchange, 2000).

7 *Caudillo* translates as "chief" or "leader" and often refers to a military leader who exercises political power.

92

results. The resulting space, the new political relationships, should fulfill three conditions: democracy, liberty and justice.

In summary, we are not proposing an orthodox revolution, but something much more difficult: a revolution that makes revolution possible ...

A Broad Opposition Front? *Focault (Binary Justice)*

The fragmentation of the forces opposing it allows the Party-State system to not only resist attacks, but also to co-opt and weaken the opposition. The principal concern of the Party-State system is not the radicalism of the forces that oppose it, but their eventual unity. The division of political forces against the regime allows the Party-State System to negotiate or "fight" to conquer the political "islands" that form in opposition. They apply a law of war, the "economy of forces": a diffuse enemy of small nuclei that is beaten by concentrating forces against each nucleus, isolating it from the others. These opposing nuclei do not consider themselves as confronting ONE enemy but MANY enemies, that is, they emphasize what makes them different (their political proposals) and not what makes them similar (the enemy that they confront: the Party-State system). Of course, we are referring here to the real opposition, not to the puppets. This dispersion of opposing forces allows the system to concentrate its forces to besiege and conquer (or annul) each "island."

The unity of these "islands" would be a serious problem for the Party-State system, but it alone (unity) would not be enough to see the regime defeated. Still missing would be the presence and action of the "third element," the Mexican people. Yes, that is in lowercase, avoiding its definition and sanctification. Does this third element have a definitive characteristic as a social class? Yes, but not the one that jumps out at first. What prevails is its skepticism and mistrust of politics, that is, of political organizations. In saying "Mexican people," we point out a problem and not a solution. A problem, yes, and a reality that presents itself with an obstinacy that overcomes all theoretical schema on one side, and corporate controls on the other.

The unity of these "islands" faces many obstacles. One of them, not the only one but an important one, is the difference in the character of that unity. A unity of exploited classes, or of organizations of exploited classes, versus a multi-class unity. This is where the subdivisions emerge.

Is a parallel construction of both fronts possible or does one counter the other? We believe it *is* possible, that they do not counter one another. But in any case, it is best to ask the third mirror, the one to be "liberated" or "redeemed." Ask, respond. Speak, listen. A dialogue, then. A national dialogue ...

(End of the article, commitment fulfilled).

93

That is all, sir. I'm sure my literary style deserves to be printed under the slogan "Through my people, rock music shall speak," and not like that of my shield-bearer who, although he is loyal and honest, tends to view life as if it were a game of glass and mirrors ...[8]

Vale. Salud, and courage! The looking glass is just over there. All we have to do is find it ...

From who-knows-what kilometer on who-knows-what highway, but, we are, indeed, in Mexico.

Don Durito de la Lacandona

* * *

---

8 This is a play on the UNAM motto introduced by José Vasconcelos in 1921: "*Por mi raza hablará el espíritu*" (Through my people the spirit shall speak).

Durito V: Durito in Mexico City

In this second section of the *Book of Mirrors*, Durito wanders Mexico City after the "Exodus for Dignity" protest march and writes to Marcos about his disillusionment with the loneliness and fear of the city. He then narrates his encounter with a ballerina in a storefront window, and of the liberating effects of music.

The Day to Come:
The Looking Glass to See from the Other Side

Scratched on the other side, a mirror stops being a mirror and becomes a piece of glass. Mirrors are for seeing on this side, and glass is for seeing what's on the other side.
Mirrors are for scratching.
Glass is for shattering . . . and crossing to the other side . . .

From the mountains of the Mexican Southeast
Subcomandante Insurgente Marcos

P.S. that, image of the real and imaginary, seeks, among so many mirrors, a piece of glass to shatter.

Dawn. Mexico City. Durito wanders through the streets bordering the Zócalo. With a tiny trench coat and a hat cocked like Humphrey Bogart in *Casablanca*, Durito tries to pass unnoticed. Neither his outfit nor his slow crawl is necessary, as Durito sticks to the shadows that escape from the bright store windows. Shadow of the shadows, silent walk, cocked hat, dragging trench coat. Durito walks through the Federal District dawn. No one notices him. They don't see him, and not because he is well disguised or because that little, tiny Quixote dressed as a 50's detective is barely distinguishable from the mounds of garbage. Durito walks alongside papers dragged by someone's feet or by a gust of one of those unpredictable winds of the Mexico City dawn. No one sees Durito for the simple reason that, in this city, no one sees anyone.

"This city is sick," Durito writes to me. "It is sick of loneliness and fear. It is a great collection of lonelinesses. It is many cities, one for each inhabitant. It's not about a sum of anguish (do you know of any loneliness that isn't full of anguish?), but about a potentiality. The number of lonely people that surrounds it multiplies each experience of loneliness. It is as if the loneliness of each one were to enter one of those 'House of Mirrors' that you find at the local carnivals. Each loneliness is a mirror that reflects other loneliness, that like a mirror, repels loneliness."

Durito has begun to realize that he is in foreign territory, that the city is not his place. In his heart and in this dawn, Durito packs his bags. He takes this route as if it were an inventory, a last caress, like the one a lover gives when he knows it is farewell. At times, the number of people passing by diminishes while the ululation of the patrol car sirens increases, startling outsiders. And Durito is one of those outsiders, so he ducks into a corner each time the flashing red and blue lights pass through the street. Durito takes advantage of the complicity of a doorway in order to light his pipe with guerrilla technique: barely a spark, a deep breath, and the smoke enveloping gaze and face. Durito stops. He looks and watches. In front of him, a store window is still lit. Durito looks at the large glass and what is offered behind it: mirrors of all shapes and sizes, porcelain and glass

96

figurines, cut crystal, tiny music boxes. "There are no little talking boxes," Durito says to himself without forgetting the long years spent in the jungle of the Mexican Southeast.

Durito has come to say goodbye to Mexico City and he has decided to give a gift to this city that everyone detests and no one abandons. A gift. This is Durito, a beetle of the Lacandona in the middle of Mexico City.

Durito says goodbye with a gift.

He makes an elegant magician's gesture. Everything stops, the lights go out just like candles do when a gentle wind licks their face. Another gesture, and a streetlight becomes a spotlight illuminating one of the music boxes in the store window. A ballerina with a fine lilac costume keeps a perpetual position with her hands intertwined above her, her legs together as she balances on point. Durito tries to imitate the position, but it doesn't take long for him to become entangled with all the arms he has. Another magical gesture and a piano the size of a pack of cigarettes appears. Durito sits in front of the piano and puts on it a mug of beer that he got who knows where, but it must have been a while ago because it's already half-empty. Durito cracks his knuckles and does some of those digital gymnastics like barroom piano players do in the movies. Durito turns toward the ballerina and nods his head. The ballerina comes to life and bows. Durito hums an unknown tune, begins to tap a beat with his little legs, closes his eyes and starts to sway. The first notes begin. Durito plays the piano with four hands. From the other side of the glass, the ballerina begins a turn and slowly raises her right leg. Durito leans over the keyboard and attacks with fury. The ballerina executes the best steps that the prison of the little music box will permit her. The city vanishes. There is nothing, only Durito at his piano and the ballerina on her little music box. Durito plays and the ballerina dances. The city is surprised, its cheeks redden like when one receives an unexpected gift, a pleasant surprise, some good news. Durito gives the best of his gifts: an unbreakable and eternal mirror, a good-bye that doesn't hurt, that heals, that cleanses. The performance lasts only a few moments, the last notes fade off just as the cities that populate this city take shape. The ballerina returns to her uncomfortable immobility, Durito turns up the collar of the trench coat and takes a gentle bow towards the store window.

"Will you always be on the other side of the glass?" Durito asks her and wonders. "Will you always be on the other side of my here and will I always be on the other side of your there?

"*Salud*, and until forever, my beloved troublemaker. Happiness is like a gift, it lasts as long as a flash and it's worth it."

Durito crosses the street, arranges his hat and continues to walk. Before turning the corner, he turns towards the store window. A star-shaped hole adorns the glass. Alarms are ringing uselessly. Behind the window the ballerina on the little music box is no longer there . . .

"This city is sick. When its illness becomes a crisis, it will be cured. This collective loneliness, multiplied by millions and realized, will end by finding itself and finding the reason for its impotence. Then, and only then, this city will lose the gray that it wears and will adorn itself with the brightly colored ribbons that are abundant in the countryside.

"This city lives a cruel game of mirrors, but the game of mirrors is useless and sterile if there is not a clear glass as a goal. It is enough to understand it, and as I-don't-know-who said, struggle and begin to be happy . . .

"I'm coming back, prepare the tobacco and your insomnia. There's a lot to tell you, Sancho," Durito ends the letter.

It's morning. A few piano notes accompany the coming day and Durito who is on the road. To the west, the sun is like a rock shattering the clear glass of the morning . . .

Vale once again. *Salud,* and leave surrender for empty mirrors.

El Sup getting up from the piano and looking, confused by so many mirrors, for the exit . . . or the entrance?

* * *

Mirrors
Glass
Break on Through

We look at our world and receive its reflection of ____. Once you see through the barrier as glass, you realize the mirror does not reflect depict the present on the other side but hides it through a trick upon vision.

"Its Not the Mirror but you" that is a lie.

Durito's Return

Returning from Mexico City, Durito tries to tell a story about how the magician Merlin appeared to him, but Marcos protests that he already knows the story from *Don Quijote*. Durito and Marcos, along with Camilo and Marcos' "Other Self," form a study group on politics and culture beginning with a session on criticism and self-criticism. This communiqué follows the EZLN's call for a *consulta*, a national and international plebiscite on Zapatista politics and coincides with the meeting of the National Citizens' Consultation (June 30- July 1), in which over 800 non–governmental organizations proposed a national dialogue regarding economic, political and social reforms of the state.

First published in *La Jornada*, June 30, 1995. Originally translated by Cecilia Rodríguez.

To the national weekly *Proceso*
To the national newspaper *El Financiero*
To the national newspaper *La Jornada*
To the local daily of San Cristóbal de Las Casas, *Tiempo*

June 30, 1995

Sirs:
Here are a communiqué and letters to their respective addressees. June left us after pretending it was turning May when it was turning July. In fact, according to the "efficient" PGR, this June would be my birthday, and according to the complicated computers of the PGR, I would turn 38 years old.[1] I solemnly declare that I have not received (yet) a single gold coin of the 38 to which I am entitled. Camilo laughs and says "What-38-you're-more-like-83." Well then, it should be 83 gold coins or their equivalent in UDI.[2]

Vale. Salud, and I say what is needed to solve that puzzle is . . . shame.

From the mountains of the Mexican Southeast
Subcomandante Insurgente Marcos

P.S. that tells of Durito's return and of other unhappy (for me) events.
"No, no and no," I answer Durito who has started a story with an account of how Merlin appeared to him with a skull's face and a bony body, to reveal the secret of the enchantment of Dulcinea de la Lacandona.[3]
"Why do you say 'no' if you still don't know what I'm going to ask you?" says Durito.
"Because I already know that story from Part 2 of the *Ingenious Hidalgo Don Quijote de La Mancha*, where Merlin tells Sancho Panza that he should give himself 3,600 lashes on his buttocks."[4]
And then I remember not Sancho's donkey nor the winged "Clavileño [little peg] the Fleet" (which is a suitable name because it's made of wood, it has a peg in its forehead, and it goes fast, so as far as names go it can certainly compare with your famous "Rocinante," upon which the noble knight defeated the giant and bewitching Malambruno), but rather the mounts he must have suffered with on previous paths: *El Salvaje,* who was as his name indicates inclined to take off into

1 In February 1995, the PGR claimed to have identified Marcos as Rafael Sebastián Vicente Guillén, as a pretext for their military offensive.
2 UDI or *unidad de inversión* is an accounting unit fixed daily in Mexico and designed to index loans against inflation. "*Udis*" reflect the changes in the price level against loan principal.
3 Dulcinea del Toboso was the noble name bestowed by Don Quijote on the peasant girl Aldonza Lorenzo converting her into a princess and lady for whom he could perform heroic deeds.
4 Actually, Merlin calls for 3,300 lashes. See Cervantes, *Don Quijote* (Chapter 33, p. 549)

dense woods when he wanted to be free of his rider, or who would throw himself on the ground and escape saddle and burden whenever both annoyed him.[5]

El Puma, famished horse, as skinny as a hat-rack who barely served to keep others company and who, so they tell, died of melancholy in a pasture. *El Choco*, who, if seniority were worth military rank, would be a commander. Old and noble horse that with a blind right eye managed with his left to clear steep banks and quagmires, which were so abundant on the roads back then. *El Viajero*, a high-stepping and spirited burro. *El Tractor*, a brilliant black stallion with an elegant and obliging step, a gentleman on the hills of sloping smooth stones and slippery and broken promises.

P.S. that tells how criticism and self-criticism. . . take shape?

A lazy cloud reclines among the trees and the moon pierces it with thousands of white pins. A fire beetle that forgot that it's already June, serpentines dubiously between the campfire and the red-gray of the cigarettes. An ordinary dawn, an ordinary mountain, some ordinary men and . . . a beetle?

"You have a beetle on your shoulder," Camilo tells me. I'm not surprised and respond,

"And you have a tick on your neck, and My Other Self, a spider on the ear, and I don't say anything. Besides, it's not a beetle; it's a little parrot that speaks in French . . ." Durito looks at me, surprised, but he is not intimidated and consequently begins to recite:

Ma pauvre muse, helas! Qu'as-tu donc ce matin!
Tes yeux creux son peuplés de visions nocturnes,
Et je vois tour à tour réfléchies sur ton teint
La folie et l'horreur, froides et taciturnes.[6]

And then he adds, forcibly:

We are not ten, nor are we a hundred,
we are about three,
count us well!

---

5 See Cervantes, *Don Quijote*, p. 568. Don Quijote called his horse Rocinante because the name "struck him as a truly lofty name, resonant, and also meaningful, because an old horse [rocin] was exactly what it had been, before [ante], while now it had risen to be first and foremost among all the old horses in the world" (p. 15). Malambruno, a giant and evil magician, appears in Volume II, chapters 39-41.

6 From the poem "*La Muse Malade*" (The Sick Muse) in Charles Baudelaire, *Les Fleurs du Mal* (The Flowers of Evil) (1855) (Paris: Editions Garnier Freres, 1959), 16-17. This first stanza of a poem that juxtaposes the insanity and horror of modernity to healthier and lustier antiquity reads, "My poor muse, alas! what's wrong with you this morning? / Your empty eyes are full of nocturnal visions / And I see reflected in your countenance, one after another, / madness and horror, cold and taciturn."

Life imitating Art
creative space for democratic space

The "cell" of three is meeting and Durito has decided to contribute his nonsense about life imitating art and so he joins in the session.

"Weren't there four three musketeers?" Durito asks me when I object to his attending the meeting of the cell. I agreed and Durito takes the affirmation as approval and here we are . . . The three of us who are four.

The first point on the agenda is to name our cell of political study and cultural activities. In honor of Ettore Scola we call ourselves the "dirty, ugly and bad."[7] But there were protests. Camilo said that we might be dirty and ugly, but that part about being bad was a simplistic and Manichaean vision. Camilo proposed changing "bad" for "rude" and it came out the "dirty, ugly, bad, and rude." Criticism and self-criticism usually provoke a profound silence that reveals complicity.

But today there are a lot of mosquitoes, a sign of rain, and no one wants to leave the fire or the smoke, so My Other Self begins a session that promises to be like a dialogue between the ee-zee-el-en and the supreme government: "I criticize myself for gathering firewood when it was El Sup's turn and in this way I have encouraged his laziness and his playing the fool with his stories about beetles and knight-errantry." I remain calm and respond with a conciliatory: "I criticize myself for always picking up after My Other Self and thus promoting his carelessness, laziness, and screwing-up." Camilo doesn't criticize or self-criticize; he only enjoys hearing how My Other Self and yours truly exchange criticisms disguised as self-criticisms. We would have spent all night like that if it had not begun to rain. The wood gets wet, the fire goes out . . .

The appointment of a secretary of the cell remained pending because Durito, that is, the parrot, argued that the electoral registry had to be purged.

P.S. that declares, I acknowledge receipt of a notebook (that they say was sent back in April), with a reproduction on the cover of Pablo Picasso's oil painting, entitled *Consulta* on the cover.

On the first page it reads, "For sonnets and other things. Take good care of yourself." I christened the notebook with the following: "If I knew how to write sonnets I would not have taken up arms, and if I took good care of myself I would not be here. Signed, El Sup." And I went on to use the notebook for "other things."

Vale once again. *Salud*, and if our eyes shine, what does it matter if night suffocates us?

---

7 The film *Brutti sporchi e cattivi* (1976) also known as *Ugly, Dirty and Bad* or *Down and Dirty*, written and directed by Ettore Scola, portrays a family struggling in a Roman shantytown while each dreams of ways to eliminate the others.

El Sup blowing out the little candles on the cake, just to show he still can ...
(Durito says that blowing out candles with sneezes doesn't count. I told him that
making mud pies just to thicken the pee-gee-ar's soup doesn't count).

* * *

Durito VI: Neoliberalism, Chaotic Theory of Economic Chaos

In this communiqué Durito continues his reflections on neoliberalism. Taking on the role of Sherlock Holmes' hitherto unknown mentor, Durito tells *El Sup* that he has discovered that the government cabinet is secretly directed by "an invisible element" whom he identifies as character X or "stupid improvisation." This improvisation or "neoliberalism made political doctrine" is faithfully carried out by "junior politicians," who have been trained abroad and who have successfully created a "virtual reality" hiding poverty and repression in Mexico. This communiqué follows the fourth round of negotiations between the government and the Zapatista delegates that ended on July 6, 1995.

To the national weekly *Proceso*
To the national newspaper *El Financiero*
To the national newspaper *La Jornada*
To the local newspaper of San Cristóbal de las Casas, Chiapas, *Tiempo*

First published in *La Jornada*, July 20, 1995. Originally translated by Peter Haney.

July 17, 1995
Ladies and gentlemen:

This is Durito writing you because *El Sup* isn't here right now. He climbed up the highest hill and is there, watching the horizon. He hopes the presents that are going to arrive for his birthday will be so numerous they'll need "the Grandmother of all Caravans" to reach the mountains of the Mexican Southeast. He says we'll be able to best appreciate the long line of trucks from afar. Poor guy! He doesn't realize that everyone already knows his birthday is the 30th of February.

Well, here go the communiqués and a postscript that I found thrown away here.

Finally we can breathe easily! The government has now declared that within two years, we will all be veeery happy. Now the only thing left to figure out is who can endure the 730 days that separate us from Paradise.

Vale then. *Salud*, and I hope they don't put Mejía Barón on the government team for the dialogue in San Andrés.[1]

From the mountains of the Mexican Southeast,
Don Durito de la Lacandona

P.S. that salutes the wheat that, like a flag, flutters in the wind of an ordinary dawn.

To the west, the moon drops down between the open legs of two hills and rests its cheeks at the vertex, where the river stirs up its sex, dripping a serpentine murmur. Some clouds, excited, rub their wetness against the trees. To the east, there are lightening bolts and tremors, the crickets sound their alarms, and now only a few scattered stars will be surprised by the storm that is announced to the south. The vigilant airplane purrs its threat and becomes distant.

Another dawn of waiting and tobacco. Everything is calm. An excellent occasion for the uninvited (as usual) appearance of...

Durito VI! (Neoliberalism: The Catastrophic Political Management of Catastrophe)

A firefly glows on Durito's shoulder. A stack of newspaper clippings serves as a bed-chair-desk-office for my master, the illustrious Don Durito of the Lacandon Jungle, greatest representative of the noblest profession that any human being has

---

1 Following two defeats to the United States, in both the U.S. Cup and the World Cup, the Mexican Soccer Federation (FMF) fired Mejia Barón, Mexico's head soccer coach, in July of 1995.

ever practiced: knight-errantry. Through the pipe smoke, I observe and guard the last and greatest righter of wrongs, the renowned knight for whose safety I lose sleep, and for whom I keep myself alert and ready in case... y-a-a-a-awn.

"Yawning again, knave!" Durito's voice interrupts a blink that, he says, lasted for hours.

"I wasn't asleep!" I defend myself, "I was thinking..." I look at my watch and I notice that...

"It's three o'clock in the morning! Durito, can't we go to sleep?"

"Sleep! You think only of sleep! How can you aspire to achieve the highest level of knight-errantry if you spend the most opportune hours sleeping?"

"Right now, I only aspire to sleep," I say as I yawn and make myself comfortable again on the backpack that serves as my pillow.

"Do so, then. Until Apollo shreds night's skirt with his golden knives, I will devote myself to thoughts of the highest and most dignified lady that any knight has ever chosen for his flag and desire, the one and only, the best, the one without equal, the... are you listening to me!?" I hear Durito shout.

"Hmmm," I respond, knowing that I don't need to open my eyes to notice that Durito must be standing on the stack of newspaper clippings, with Excalibur in his right hand and his left on his heart, and the other right on his waist, and the other adjusting his armor and the other... I don't remember how many arms Durito has anymore, but they're more than enough for the gestures he needs to make.

"And what keeps you up, my lazy squire?" Durito asks with obvious intentions of keeping me awake.

"Me? Nothing, if not for your midnight speeches and studies... Seriously, what is it you were studying?"

"The government cabinet," Durito responds, returning to his papers.

"The government cabinet?" I ask with surprise, doing what I didn't want to do, that is, open my eyes.

"Of course! I have discovered why the members of the cabinet contradict each other, each one pulls in his own direction and, apparently, forgets that the boss is..."

"Zedillo," I say, losing interest in the talk.

"Wrong! It isn't Zedillo," says Durito with satisfaction.

"No?" I ask at the same time that I look for the little radio in my backpack so I can listen to the news. "Did he resign? Did they get rid of him?"

"Negative," says Durito, enjoying my sudden activity. "There it is, just where we left it yesterday."

"So?" I ask, now completely awake.

"The head of the government cabinet is a character who, for the sake of convenience and discretion, I will now call, 'Character X.'"

"Character X?" I ask, remembering Durito's enjoyment of detective novels. "And how did you discover him?"

"Elementary, my dear Watson."

"Watson?" I manage to stammer upon seeing that Durito has turned around the *cololté* shell that he uses as a helmet, and I see that it now looks like a rapper's cap (although he insists that it's a detective's hat). With a tiny magnifying glass, Durito examines his papers. If I didn't know him so well, I'd say he isn't Durito, but rather...

"Sherlock Holmes was an Englishman who learned from me how to gather apparently inconsequential details, unite them into a hypothesis, and look for new details that would confirm or refute it. It's a simple exercise of deduction like those that I practiced with my pupil Sherlock Holmes when we would go out carousing through the slums of London. He would have learned more from me, but he went off with some Conan Doyle who promised to make him famous. I never found out what became of him." [2]

"He became famous," I say with sarcasm.

"I don't suppose he became a knight-errant?" asks Durito with some interest.

"Negative, my dear Sherlock, he turned into a fictional character and became famous."

"You are mistaken, my dear and big-nosed Watson, fame can only be reached through knight-errantry."

"All right, let's leave this and get back to the subject of the government cabinet and the mysterious 'Character X.' What about that?"

Durito begins to review his newspaper and magazine clippings.

"Hmmm... Hmmm... Hmmm!" exclaims Durito.

"What? Did you find something?" I ask on account of the last admiring "hmmm."

"Yes, a photo of Jane Fonda in *Barbarella*," says Durito with a look of ecstasy.[3]

"Jane Fonda?" I ask-get up-fidget-quiver.

"Yes, and *au naturel*," he says with a prolonged sigh.

A photo of Jane Fonda "*au naturel*" is enough to wake up anyone with a little self-respect, and I've always respected myself, so I get up and ask Durito for the clipping, who refuses to give it to me until I swear that I will listen to him attentively. I swore and swore again. What else could I do?

"Fine. Now give me your attention!" says Durito with the same emphasis with which he chews on his pipe. He puts one of his many pairs of hands behind his back and begins to pace up and down in a straight line as he speaks:

"Let's say that we have an ordinary country whose name is accented on the antepenultimate syllable and that is located, by chance, beneath the empire of stripes and turbulent stars. And when I say, "beneath," I mean just that, "beneath." Let's say that this country is struck by a terrible plague. Ebola? AIDS? Cholera? No! Something more lethal and more destructive... neoliberalism! Fine, I've already told you before about this sickness, so I won't stop to repeat myself. Let's suppose now that a young genera-

---

2 Arthur Conan Doyle (1859–1930) earned a medical degree from the University of Edinburgh in 1885, but, like his character Dr. Watson, was not fully taken with the medical profession and took to writing novels, including the famous series highlighting the brilliant detective work of Sherlock Holmes.

3 Jane Fonda, model, actress, and political activist, starred in the science fiction classic *Barbarella: Queen of the Galaxy* (1968; Roger Vadim, director).

tion of 'junior politicians' has studied abroad the way to 'save' this country in the only way that it conceives of its salvation, that is to say, without knowing its history and hitching it to the caboose of the fast train of brutality and human imbecility: capitalism. Let's suppose that we manage to get access to the notebooks of these students without a country. What do we find? Nothing! Absolutely nothing! Does this mean they're bad students? By no means! They're good and quick students. But it happens that they've learned one and only one lesson in each subject that they studied. The lesson is always the same: 'Act like you know what you're doing.' 'This is the fundamental axiom of power politics under neoliberalism,' their teacher has told them. They asked, 'And what is neoliberalism, dear teacher?' The teacher doesn't respond, but I can deduce from his perplexed expression, his red eyes, the drool that drips from the corners of his mouth, and the evident wear on the sole of his right shoe, that the teacher doesn't dare tell the truth to his students. And the truth is that, as I discovered, neoliberalism is the chaotic theory of economic chaos, the stupid exaltation of social stupidity, and the catastrophic political management of catastrophe."

I take advantage of Durito stopping to re-light his pipe to ask,

"And how did you deduce all of that from the teacher's face, drool, eyes, and shoe-sole?"

But Durito doesn't hear me, his eyes are shining, and I don't know if it's from the lighter or from what he says next:

"Fine. Let's move on. The aforementioned students return to their country, or to what remains of it. They arrive with a messianic message that nobody understands. While the respectable decipher it, they make off with their booty, which is to say, power. Once they have that, they start to apply the only lesson they ever learned: "act like you know what you're doing," and they use the mass media to acquire that image. They obtain consummate levels of pretense, to the point of constructing a virtual reality in which everything works to perfection. But the "other" reality, the real reality, followed its course, and something had to be done. Then, they started to do whatever occurred to them: this way one day, that way the next. And then..." Durito stops, examines his pipe and looks at me in silence...

"And then what?" I urge him on.

"And then... the tobacco ran out. Do you have more?" he answers me. I don't want to stop to warn him that the strategic reserve is about to run out, and I throw him the little bag I have at hand. Durito refills his pipe, lights it, and continues.

"Then it happens that they lose their understanding of the real reality and they start to believe that the virtual reality that they created with lies and pretense is the "real" reality. But this schizophrenia isn't the only problem. It turns out that each student started to create his own virtual "reality" and to live according to it. That's why each one dictates measures that contradict those of the others."

"That explanation is pretty... hmmm... let's say... bold."

Durito doesn't stop and continues with his explanation.

"But there's something that gives coherency to all that governmental incoherence. I've been analyzing several clues. I read all of the cabinet's declarations, I clas-

108

sified all of its actions and omissions, I contrasted their political histories, I requested and obtained even their least important acts, and I arrived at a very important conclusion."

Durito stops, takes in air to give himself importance and lengthens the pause so I will ask...

"And what is that conclusion?"

"Elementary, my dear Watson! There's an invisible element in the cabinet, a character that, without making itself known, gives coherence to and makes systemic all the braying of the government team. A boss to whose command everyone submits. Zedillo included. That is to say, 'X' exists, the real governor of the country in question..."

"But who is the mysterious 'Character X?'" I ask, unable to hide the shiver that runs up my spine as I imagine that it might be...

"Salinas?"

"Something worse..." says Durito, arranging his papers.

"Worse than Salinas? Who is he?"

"Negative. It's not a 'he'; it's a 'she,'" says Durito, puffing on his pipe.

"A 'she'?"

"Correct. Her first name is Stupid and her last name is Improvisation.[4] And take note that I say, 'Stupid Improvisation.' Because you should know, my dear Watson, that there are intelligent improvisations, but this isn't the case here. 'Ms. X' is the stupid improvisation of neoliberalism in politics, neoliberalism made political doctrine; that is to say, stupid improvisation administering the destinies of this country... and of others... Argentina and Peru, for example.

"So you're insinuating that Menem and Fujimori are the same as...?"[5]

"I'm not insinuating anything. I'm affirming it. Just ask the Argentine and Peruvian workers. I was analyzing Yeltsin when my tobacco ran out."[6]

"Yeltsin? But wasn't it the Mexican government cabinet you were analyzing?"

"No, not only the Mexican one. Neoliberalism, as you should know, my dear Watson, is a plague that afflicts all of humanity. Like AIDS. Of course, the Mexican political system has an enchanting stupidity that is difficult to resist. But nevertheless, all of these governments that are ravaging the world have something in common: all of their success is based on a lie, and therefore, its base is only as solid as the bench you're sitting on."

I get up instinctively, examine the bench of logs and reeds we've constructed and make sure it's solid and firm. Now more relieved, I tell Durito,

"But let's suppose, my dear Sherlock, that the bad guys are able to maintain their lie for an indefinite period of time, that that false base remains solid and they keep

---

4 The noun is feminine in the original.

5 In 1995, Carlos Menem, a member of Argentina's Peronist Party, was president of Argentina. Alberto Fujimori had been president of Peru since July 28, 1990.

6 Boris Yeltsin, as president of the Russian Federation since 1991, led the implementation of IMF-designed neoliberal policies.

harvesting successes." Durito doesn't let me continue. He interrupts me with an...

"Impossible! The foundation of neoliberalism is a contradiction: in order to maintain itself it must devour itself and, therefore, destroy itself. That's why there are political assassinations, underhanded blows, contradictions between the acts and the statements of public functionaries at every level, battles between 'interest groups,' and everything else that keeps stockbrokers up at night..."

"It used to keep them up at night. I think now they're getting used to it, because the stock market is on the rise," I say with some skepticism.

"It's a bubble. It will burst before too long. Mark my words," says Durito as he smiles with a know-it-all air and continues:

"What keeps the system going is what will bring it down. It's elementary. All you have to do is read G. K. Chesterton's 'The Three Horsemen of the Apocalypse' to understand it. It's a detective story but, as is well known, life ends up imitating art.[7]

"Sounds to me like your theory is pure fant-..." I hadn't finished speaking; as I sat down on the log bench, it collapsed with the muffled sound of my bones hitting the ground and the not so muffled curse I uttered. Durito laughs as if he's about to choke. When he calms down a bit, he says,

"You were going to say that my theory is pure fantasy? Fine, as you can appreciate from your current lowly position, life proves me right. History and the people will also give their two cents worth."

Durito considers his talk over and lies back against the newspaper clippings. I don't even try to get up. I pull my backpack over and get comfortable again. We stay silent, watching how to the east, as honey and wheat pour through between the legs of the mountain. We sigh. What else could we do?

Vale. Salud, and may neither history nor the people take too long.

El Sup with a tender pain in his side.

---

7 This story by Chesterton refers to a paradox related by a government official named Mr. Pond. In this riddle about obedience and contempt, Pond recounts the fate of Prussian Marshal Von Grock, who sends an aide to prevent the release and bring about the execution of a celebrated Polish poet, Paul Petrowski. Upon learning of the poet's imminent death, a Prussian prince and admirer of Petrowski orders the swiftest rider of the White Hussars to overtake Grock's aide and stop him. Grock, learning of this intervention and determined to eliminate the Polish nationalist, sends a second rider to prevent the Prince's orders from reaching the executioner. Grock's first rider, discovering the Hussar upon him, turns, fires, and kills the Prince's messenger. Grock's second rider, unaware of these events and mistaking Grock's first rider for the Prince's Hussar, shoots and kills him, thus bringing about the downfall of Grock's own plans. Through the obedience of both aides the Pole survived and was released. G. K. Chesterton, "The Three Horsemen of the Apocalypse," in *The Paradoxes of Mr. Pond* (New York: Dodd, Mean, and Company, 1937), 3-27.

Durito, Chibo the Killer Tarantula, and the Plebiscite

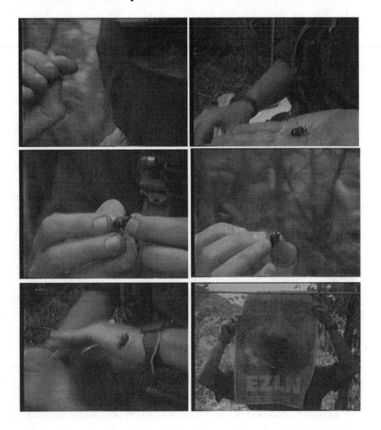

In this transcript of a "Durito Productions" video entitled "The National Plebiscite for Peace, Democracy and National Dialogue," Durito stars with El Sup and Chibo, a killer tarantula who represents the Mexican party-state system. Together, they introduce the Plebiscite, or Consulta to national and international audiences, outlining its purposes, the questions it poses, and the people and organizations involved with its execution. The production was aired on "Zapatista Television," that is, via videotape screenings in public spaces throughout Mexico and abroad.

Performative

disruption

Well now, we're going to introduce the stars of this exciting episode of the National Plebiscite for Peace and Democracy. As leading man we have Durito. In the role of El Sup we have El Sup himself. And in the role of Chibo, the killer tarantula, who for the moment will represent the party-state system (note its beautiful figure and spontaneous congeniality). Be careful, "camera," because if Chibo decides to strike, then there'll be no video, or anything else. Over and out.

Well, we're going to begin this explanatory program with a series of questions and themes that Durito has suggested to help with the realization of the plebiscite. He proposes (for those who don't normally listen to or understand beetle language), he proposes that, well, an important point to reference is the relationship that exists between the EZLN and civil society, and the entire national situation. In order to explain the National Plebiscite, we issued the Second Declaration of La Lacandona when we realized, or reflected on the role civil society has had in stopping the war and that it has also had in a process of democratization, a process that has not yet begun to concretize, a process that has not yet ceased. In one of the points of the Second Declaration of La Lacandona, we said that it would be necessary to open—that we would open—a national dialogue with civil society, and so as a first step we proposed a National Plebiscite in Aguascalientes, Chiapas. Today, August 8, 1995, marks one year since the time when there was that rain that washed clean many things in Aguascalientes, Chiapas near the community of Guadalupe Tepeyac, which is today occupied by the federal army.[2]

So as part of this national dialogue, we also thought it important to describe this National Plebiscite that we are convening, where we ask a series of questions that try to make more explicit the significance of each of them. But a series that tries, above all, to find out—or to listen to—what civil society thinks about our banners, our struggle, and above all, about the steps that we must follow or that we must take now. Since we cannot listen to or personally meet with each and every one of the people who have something to say to Mexican civil society and international civil society, we thought that this was one of the forms we could try out to see if it would be effective or would allow for a serious dialogue on some

---

1 The publication date is taken from the text. Translated for this volume by the AZ Editorial Collective. The text is an extract from the transcript of Marcos' remarks in the video "*La Consulta nacional por la paz y la democracia y el diálogo nacional.*" The full transcripts were done by *Revista Inprecor para América Latina.* Since the video is nearly 90 minutes in length, with a transcript of more than 10,000 words, it has been edited to include only those passages that feature Durito. A half-hour version of the video was shown in the plaza of the Cathedral of San Cristóbal de las Casas, as part of the commemoration of the first anniversary of the CND. A full-length version was shown in the Opera Movie Theatre in Mexico City where the celebration ceremony was double: the first anniversary of the CND and the 18th anniversary of the Eureka Committee, a support group for political prisoners headed by Rosario Ibarra de Piedra.
2 In August 1994, a torrent of rain brought the CND to a close.

questions that are very concrete, very simple, and very defined in respect to whether one is in agreement or not, or whether one can say yes or no in regards to what is being asked.

[Continued reflection on the purposes and processes of the plebiscite.]

Durito has insisted that it is necessary to situate the plebiscite in a national context. He's adamant that it's a desperate maneuver of the EZLN—that we've been corralled, and that this is just about the last card we can play against war since breaking off dialogue with the government. We think the situation is more complex—that it's not possible to discuss the struggles of the EZLN concretely, or particularly, or in isolation (and what the government wants to do is isolate us), without referring to, or situating ourselves in respect to the problems facing democratic forces at a national level.

[Elaboration of the Mexican national situation with President Zedillo carrying on Salinas' legacy of political control and repression of opposition, particularly as seen in Guerrero and Tabasco.]

We had long ago perceived this national context . . . and called for the formation of a national liberation movement. In reality, what is needed is an internal dialogue among the opposition forces. I'm not referring just to political opposition forces. There is a strong citizens' movement, which is much respected, that is opposed not to the regime, but to anti-democratic ways of doing politics; and it must be recognized, say what they will, that in this sense an organization like Alianza Cívica has earned everyone's respect, although it's been accused of being an arm of one political party, or that it's been infiltrated by another. But in the end, it has demonstrated that a citizens' group can organize themselves to be vigilant of power. Its record is beyond reproach.

Durito would like me to touch on our relationship with Alianza Cívica, because he tells me that there have been rumors of tension among Alianza Cívica, the Convention, and the EZLN. Since we first solicited their participation in the organization of the plebiscite, our relationship with Alianza Cívica has always been very respectful. They've made their observations known to us, and the differences they had with what we've proposed. Together we've come to an agreement, and the questions and the organization of the plebiscite were made by mutual accord. There was never any trouble of any kind, and they did not in any way impose on us their decisions or point of view. They have always been very clear that they were ready to subject themselves to what we expressed. But we could not be blind to the series of proposals they made, to their need to maintain their neutrality, nor to the fact that the credibility of this plebiscite would lie with that neutrality.

So we've laid out the national context, which Durito once defined as: improvisation at a national political level.[3] When Power improvises, it has to pull

---

3 See "Durito II."

out all the arms it has on hand. On the one hand it has the mass communications media, above all the electronic media—I mean to say, the lie—and on the other hand, it has the army and the police. If you improvise or you cannot plan, then you work with the things you have on hand. So, in this sense, the question is not "if we're going to dialogue with the government;" it's "if we're going to dialogue amongst ourselves." And because of that I want to insist that the plebiscite is not the endpoint of anything, nor is it a watershed after which everything will change. We think it is a process. We don't want the same mistake that was made with the National Democratic Convention (CND), which we conceived from the beginning as a process that had to proceed advancing or proceed receding as any process, but which people thought would have immediate and spectacular results. The grand initiation of August 8 later seemed to become a battleground for infighting. We also want to say that the National Plebiscite needs to be part of a broad movement, including a process of referendums or a series of plebiscites that will be and that are necessary. Among these there is the need to put forth serious questions with respect to Mr. Salinas' successor in power, to point out that Mr. Zedillo is there as the figurehead, but that the power is still held by Mr. Carlos Salinas.

And so, in an effort to conclude this theme, Durito tells me that he wants to clarify a mirror that is making itself known in the national movement for democracy, which is the issue of whether to speak with the "*duros*" or the "*blandos*" within the government.[4] We think, well, let's look at Chibo the killer tarantula. Here, I'm going to tell you a story: Chibo is a tarantula who is also named *Hierba*,[5] her bite is fatal and her venom is venomous—as they say at the carnival. If Chibo encounters another of her type she will kill it. It is only during the time of heat or during the time of the elections that two of her kind will get along, but the rest of the time they spend fighting so that they alone survive. In this case, she survived because she killed her *compañera*. That's why she thinks she's made-to-order for the role of the party-state system in this interesting film that the Zapatista Army of National Liberation is making for the appreciation of young and old alike. Therefore, I insist that the option is not to speak with the government, but that the option this country needs to move forward is to "speak amongst ourselves" (and by "amongst ourselves" I mean to say the democratic forces, not just those who suppose and self-proclaim themselves revolutionaries, but all the forces that want a transition to democracy, that want a better country).

In other words, we could speak and dialogue amongst ourselves and we could bring ourselves to agreement or we could carry on separately, each one for his own cause, opposing one another, thus allowing this government double-speak—lie-repression ... lie-repression ...—as they govern, or act like they govern, the country. The economic crisis is not just a result of this form of

---

4 Playing on the different strategies undertaken by repressive regimes, "dura" connoting hard and "blanda" meaning soft, i.e., iron fist and velvet glove.
5 *Hierba* translates literally as "weed," figuratively as "troublemaker."

government; the political crisis IS the form of government, it's what's governing this country. Maintain the crisis: that is what paralyzes democratic forces, you keep them fighting each other. As for how they're going to take advantage of this crisis, or how they're going to go forward, we say: let's move the discussion from this terrain, this terrain that has no more future than the future of division, co-optation, isolation or self-annihilation. And in reality, the position of the government in relation to the EZLN is just that: "either we co-opt them or we annihilate them, pick one." We think that we need to move the discussion from this terrain; the transition to democracy will not be decided with the government; the transition to democracy will be decided amongst the democratic forces and so we are proposing a way, in this case the plebiscite.

[Here Marcos addresses each of the questions on the plebiscite.[6]]

This is what we want to say for now about the plebiscite. Some day, if we ever get the chance, we could prepare another video and send it to you, but I think that you'll be bored enough with this one, which must run about an hour, hour and a half. But I think we've touched on the most important points. We want to send, of course, greetings to all the conventioneers out there; it doesn't matter which political group they're with or which convention it is, (they say there are already two conventions). We want to congratulate you on your birthday, the celebration of your first year today on August 8th, and we want to wish that, well, that you understand Zapatismo's way of viewing things: that no successful process is fast or has a smooth path, but it has difficulties, costs, and takes time. Durito has told me to get him when I get to this part, because he wants to invite the Mexican people, and everyone possible, to participate in the organiza-

---

6 The plebiscite read: "1) Do you agree with the principal demands of the Mexican people and the EZLN for: land, housing, jobs, food, health, education, culture, information, independence, democracy, liberty, justice and peace? 2) Should the different democratizing forces [in Mexico] unite in a broad-based opposition front to struggle for the 13 principal demands? 3) Should a profound political reform be made [in Mexico] in terms which guarantee: equity, citizen participation, including non-partisan and non-governmental organizations, respect for the vote, reliable voter registration of all the national political, regional and local forces? 4) Should the EZLN be converted to a new and independent political force? 5) Should the EZLN unite with other forces and organizations and form a new political organization? 6) Should women be guaranteed equal representation and participation at all levels of civil and governmental responsibilities? These questions can be answered 'yes,' 'no,' or "I don't know.' Add other comments if you wish." Over 1.2 million Mexicans, and more than 100,000 people from outside of Mexico participated in this plebiscite with the following results: 97.5% of national voters expressed agreement with the principal demands of the EZLN; 92.7% agreed that all the democratic forces in the country should unite in a broad social and political opposition front in order to fight for those demands; 94.5% approved of a "profound political reform" in order to guarantee democracy; 52.6% suggested that the EZLN should convert itself into a new and independent political force; 48.7% suggested this should be done through a unification process with pre-existing organizations; and 93.1% agreed that women should be guaranteed equal representation and participation at all levels of civil and governmental responsibilities.

tion of the plebiscite with Alianza Cívica and in the promotion of the plebiscite with the National Democratic Convention and other forces that want to gather. Though they may not be conventioneers, nor from Alianza Cívica, it seems that those who want to promote the plebiscite should do it. So for the pleasure of his admirers, Durito is going to say this with his own words. [Beetle language is heard here.]

And I, for my part, well, I want to encourage all those who are listening to participate. You have nothing to lose and you have much to win. And your support, your participation—whether it be in the promotion of the plebiscite, in its organization, or in the marking of the ballot—is participation in the new national history of this country, that is being made despite the government. In other words, despite the stupidity, reason will begin to seek its own pathways.

From the mountains of the Mexican Southeast, for Zapatista Television, El Sup.

* * *

The Story of the Little Mouse and the Little Cat

In this letter to a gathering of European Zapatista supporters in Brescia, Italy, Durito tells a story about a mouse who got fed up with a cat that continually blocked his efforts to satisfy his desires. The letter was written at the beginning of the National Plebiscite in which over 1.2 million Mexicans and nearly 100,000 people outside of Mexico participated. In another letter, written the same day and addressed to a National Peace Conference, the CCRI denounced the Mexican government's continuing blockage of real negotiations.

First published in *La Jornada*, September 4, 1995. Originally translated by Eduardo Vera.

August 27, 1995

To the men and women in solidarity with Chiapas, Mexico, meeting in Brescia, Italy

To the peoples of the world

Brothers and Sisters:

Don Durito de la Lacandona, knight-errant, righter of wrongs, the restless dream of women, the aspiration of men, the last and greatest example of this race that made humanity great with such colossal and selfless feats, beetle and warrior of the moon, writes to all of you.

I have ordered my loyal squire, the one you call "Sup Marcos," to send you a greeting in writing with all the requirements demanded by today's diplomacy, excluding the forces of intervention, economic programs and the flight of capital.

Nevertheless, I have wanted to write some prose with the single goal of contributing to the enrichment of your spirit, to be of one mind with good and noble thoughts. That is why I send you the following story that is certainly full of rich and various feats. The story forms part of the collection *Stories for a Suffocating Night* (of improbably near publication) and it's called:

The Story of the Little Mouse and the Little Cat

There once was a little mouse who was very hungry and wanted to eat a little bit of cheese that was in the little kitchen of the little house. And so the little mouse went very decidedly to the little kitchen to grab the little bit of cheese, but it happens that a little cat blocked his way and the little mouse became very frightened and ran away and he couldn't get the little cheese from the little kitchen. So the little mouse was thinking of how to get the little cheese from the little kitchen and said to himself,

"I know, I'll put a little dish with a little bit of milk and then the little cat is going to start drinking the little bit of milk because little cats like a little bit of milk very much. And then, when the little cat is drinking the little bit of milk and is not paying attention, I'll go to the little kitchen to grab the little bit of cheese and I'll eat it. Veeery good idea."

And so he went to look for the little bit of milk but it turns out that the little bit of milk was in the little kitchen and when the little mouse tried to go to the little kitchen the little cat blocked his way and the little mouse was very frightened and ran away and he couldn't get the little bit of milk. So the little mouse was thinking of how to get the little bit of milk in the little kitchen and he said to himself,

"I know, I'm going to throw a little fish very far away and then the little cat is going to run to eat the little fish because little cats like little fish a lot. And then, when the little cat is eating his little fish and is not paying attention, I'm going to go to the little kitchen to grab the little bit of milk to put in a little dish and then when the little cat is drinking his little bit of milk and is not paying attention, I'll go to the little kitchen to grab the little bit of cheese and I'll eat it. Veeery good idea."

And so he went to look for the little fish but it happened that the little fish was in the little kitchen and when the little mouse tried to go to the little kitchen, the little cat blocked his way and the little mouse became very frightened, and ran away and he couldn't get the little fish.

And then the little mouse saw that the little bit of cheese, the little bit of milk and the little fish, everything that he wanted was in the little kitchen and he couldn't get there because the little cat impeded his way. And then the little mouse said "Enough!" and he grabbed a machine gun and riddled the little cat with bullets and he went to the little kitchen and he saw that the little fish, the little bit of milk and the little bit of cheese had already gone bad and could not be eaten, and so he returned to where the little cat was and cut him into pieces and then he made a great roast and invited all his friends and they had a party and ate the roasted little cat, and they sang and danced and lived very happily. And history began . . .

This is the end of the story and the end of this letter. I remind you that the divisions between countries only serve to create the crime of "smuggling" and to justify wars. It's clear that at least two things exist that are above borders: one is the crime that, disguised as modernity, distributes misery on a global scale; the other is the hope that shame exists only when one fumbles a dance step and not every time we look in the mirror. To do away with the first and to make the second flourish we need only to struggle and to be better. The rest follows on its own and is what usually fills libraries and museums.

It is not necessary to conquer the world, it is enough to build it anew . . .

Vale. Salud, and know that for love, a bed is only a pretext; for dance, a tune is only an adornment; and for struggle, nationality is merely a circumstantial accident.

From the mountains of the Mexican Southeast
Don Durito de la Lacandona

P.S. Excuse the paucity of these letters. It happens that I must hurry to prepare an expedition to invade Europe this winter. How do you feel about a landing by next January 1st?[1]

* * *

---

1 The plan to invade Europe is elaborated in "Durito to Conquer Europe."

Of Trees, Transgressors, and Odontology

Durito has given Marcos a copy of *The Rituals of Chaos* written by cultural critic Carlos Monsiváis.[1] The gift of the book and the subsequent correspondence with Monsiváis led Durito and El Sup to examine the role of intellectuals in Mexican politics, both those who play the game under the banner of "efficiency" and those who seem to seek alternatives to current one-party rule. Against Machiavellian strategies in which apparent change (of the party in power) hides the essential continuity of Power, Marcos introduces the Zapatista political program, highlighting the necessity of a political space for the construction of entirely new political relationships, including a new political morality as in the Zapatista maxim *"mandar obedeciendo"* ("lead by obeying").

First published in *La Jornada*, January 14th, 1996. Originally translated by Cecilia Rodríguez.

1 Carlos Monsiváis, *Los rituales del caos* (México: Procuraduría Federal del Consumidor, 1995).

September–November of 1995
To: Carlos Monsiváis,
Mexico, D.F.
From: Subcomandante Insurgente Marcos
Mountains of the Mexican Southeast
Chiapas, Mexico

Maestro:
Sir, I send (you)[2] a greeting and acknowledge receipt of the book *The Rituals of Chaos*. I read it quickly at one of those impasses that the Supreme Government calls the Dialogues of San Andrés.[3]

Vale. Salud, and let's see if by following Alice you will manage to find the Red Queen and solve the enigma that the last postscript invites you to do.

From the mountains of the Mexican Southeast,
Subcomandante Insurgente Marcos

P.S. that recalls, a little late, the principal reason behind this chaotic epistle and is first entitled

Rorrim Eht Dna Otirud
(Politics, Odontology, and Morality)
In that instant I saw the Apocalypse face to face. And I understood that the holy terror about the Final Judgment lies in the demonic intuition: one will not live to see it. And I looked over my shoulder at the Beast with seven heads and ten horns, and among its horns ten diadems, and on each head a blasphemous name. And the people applauded it and took pictures and videos, and recorded its exclusive declarations, while, with a clarity, which would become a painful burden, I had the belated realization: the most horrible nightmare is the one that excludes us definitively.
—Carlos Monsiváis, *The Rituals of Chaos*, p. 250.[4]

The period is the hinge that binds two mirrors that, face to face, spread out to the sides like wings to fly over an era of chaos. A hinge; that is the point.
"Look on page 250," Durito says, as he unpacks his bags.
And I look hurriedly and murmur,

---

2 Throughout the original text, Marcos plays with the formal "you" (*usted*) and informal "you" (*tú*) with the pronoun in parentheses. This translation uses "sir" and "you" to distinguish between the formal and informal.
3 The Dialogues began in April 1995 in San Andrés Larráinzar, renamed San Andrés Sacamach'en de los Pobres by the Zapatistas. These discussions resulted in a series of agreements between the government and the EZLN known as the San Andrés Accords, which were signed by both parties on February 16, 1996.
4 This reference appears in the original text. See Monsiváis, 1995.

"Page . . . 250 . . . hmmm . . . yes, here it is," I say with satisfaction.

"Or the one which includes us momentarily," I think, while Durito insists on hauling his little piano on top of his even smaller desk to show me how the small sustains the large, in history and in nature. The argument collapses with the piano and Durito tumbles down, landing after this spectacular feat with the piano and the desk on top of his shell. I finish reading that part of the book and look for my pipe, my tobacco, and Durito (in that order). Durito has no intention of coming out from under the catastrophe that he has on top of him, and a small column of smoke announces two things: the first is the location of my tobacco, and the second is that Durito is alive.

Lighting a pipe and remembering are the same thing. Something about the book's passage takes me back many years. It was a sweet and simple time. All we had to worry about was food. The books were few but good, and re-reading them was like finding new books within old ones. And this is relevant because Durito has brought me this book as a gift, and has pointed out a passage on page 250 to tell me something that will have to wait until later because there are more important things to point out now; for example, that books are made of leaves, and leaves, attached to some branches and roots, make trees and shrubbery. Trees, as everyone knows, are for guarding the night that by day is idle. Among branches and leaves, the night shares her fullness the same way in which a woman shares her curves inside moist and breathless embraces. Trees, notwithstanding this sensual mission, make time for other things. For example, they often house the most varied kinds of mammals, birds, insects and other creatures found in nursery rhymes. Sometimes, trees also house masked men. This refers to, so there is no doubt, delinquents and transgressors. Their concealed faces and the fact that they camp in trees leaves no room to doubt their character as persecuted beings. Such men live together with the night, by day, in the trees. That is the reason for their passion and drive to love the branch. It's also true that beetles often rest in trees like . . .

Durito interrupts me from the depths of—he now makes clear to me—the modern sculpture made by his piano and desk on top of his head.

"Do you have a lighter?"

"That sculpture should be called something like 'Chaos on a Smoking Beetle,'" I tell him as I throw him the lighter.

"Your gibes don't offend me. They only prove your ignorance. It's clear you've read Umberto Eco on artistic work in progress.[5] This lovely sculpture is the best example of modern and revolutionary art, and it shows how the artist so commits himself to his work that he becomes a part of it."

"And what's it called?"

"That's the tricky part. The audience must title it. That is why it is a work 'in progress.' As you know my dear 'Watson,' 'a work in progress' is not finished but

5 Durito may be referring to Umberto Eco, *Open Work* (Cambridge: Harvard University Press, 1989).

becomes 'complete' within the process of circulation and consumption in the artistic market. Elementary. In this way the spectator ceases to be so and becomes a 'co-author' of the work. Zedillo, for example, can title this work something like *My Government Program* and put it in Los Pinos;[6] Salinas de Gortari could title it *My Economic and Political Legacy* and house it at Almoloya;[7] and the neoliberals could call it *Our Proposal for a New World Order*. And you . . . what would you call it?" Durito asks me.

I analyze it with a critical eye and answer, "Hmmm . . . something like *Beetle Entombed Beneath a Little Piano and a Desk*."

"Bah! That's too descriptive," Durito reproaches.

As we talk, the rituals of the night unfold slowly: the sound of the airplane, the pipe smoke, the solitude, the discreet gossiping of crickets, the intermittent and luminous blinking of fireflies, the heaviness of the heart, and above, the stars made dust along the Road to Santiago.[8]

Maybe it'll rain. The past months have been as inconsistent as the rain; even the calendar seems disoriented and can't quite find itself amid such unstable events. Durito asks me for the name of the book's author.

"Monsiváis," I answer.

"Oh, Carlos!" Durito says with a familiarity that surprises me. I ask if he knows him.

"Of course! The historical essay is a genre we share . . . but it's better if you keep writing. I have other things to do," Durito answers.

I pause, because in beginning this letter, I've suddenly remembered that I haven't yet resolved the dilemma of the informal 'you' and the formal 'you,' that is to say how I should address you (sir). Durito firmly maintains an axiom, a pillar of his conception of the world: there is no problem so big that you can't ponder it for a while. And so with that philosophic *corpus*, I've decided, once again, to leave the solution of this dilemma pending and continue with the gentle pendulum that takes us from *you* to *sir*.

And then I decide. I chew on my pipe with determination. I take on the look of a Southeastern-governor-willing-to-defend-the-popular-will-at-all-costs-who-sees-how-things-are-and-it-just-so-happens-that-I-am-the-popular-will, and undertake the rigorous task of writing to you (sir).

What a sight I must be! Too bad I have no witnesses (Durito is already snoring beneath the ruins of his exhibit), too bad I sent off all the mirrors in that document called something like *Mirrors: Mexico Between the Nights of Day and the Crystal of the Moon*.[9] What? That wasn't the title? Oh well, no matter. The thing

6 Los Pinos is the Presidential Palace of Mexico.

7 Almoloya de Juárez is a maximum-security federal prison.

8 For a discussion of the "Road to Santiago," also known as "St. James Way" or "The Milky Way," see, "On Bullfighting, Détente and Rock."

9 This document first appeared as a series in *La Jornada* (June 9, 10, 11, 1995) titled *"México: La Luna entre los espejos de la noche y el cristal del día."* See also *EZLN Documentos y comunicados 2* (Mexico City: Ediciones Era, 1995), 367-385.

is I need a mirror right now to check if I have that delirious glow of a genius getting ready to abort his best idea. What? A self-defeating goal? Why? Because of the "abort?" But no! You (sir) must agree with me that the best ideas are those that are never expressed. The moment they enter the prison of language, ideas are materialized, they become letters, words, phrases, paragraphs, pages . . . even books if you're careless and let them loose. And once there, ideas become quantifiable, they can be weighed, measured, compared. Then they become really boring, in addition to turning independent and not following orders of any kind. I understand that to you (sir) it is unbelievable that orders are not carried out, but for military bigwigs like yours truly it is a real toothache. Teeth, as all scientists with PhDs know, are pieces of bone that serve to give jobs to dentists, so that the toothpaste industry flourishes, and so that the profession of shameful torturer exists: odontology. The word "odontology" is an idea made language and become measurable and classifiable: it has ten letters, carries its stress on the third syllable, and is as heavy as the bill that must be paid after you leave the office . . .

"Definitely," says Durito.

"What?" is the only thing I can think of saying after Durito's sudden interruption.

"There's no doubt. This plebiscite excludes beetles," Durito continues, who apparently was not asleep and continues reviewing papers even under the chaos that overwhelms him.

"This plebiscite excluded us beetles and that is a form of racism and apartheid. I shall take my protests to the appropriate international organizations."

It's useless to try to give Durito explanations. He insists that what he calls "the Seventh Question" was missing, the wording of which was more or less: "Are you in agreement that knight-errantry should be added to the National Registry of Professions?"

I explain to him that I sent various postscripts making discreet insinuations to the CND and the Civic Alliance, but no one took the hint.

"It's infuriating that that question is missing. It's a matter of aesthetics. Whose idea is it to have a plebiscite with six questions? Even numbers are not aesthetically pleasing. Odd numbers, on the other hand, have the charm of asymmetry. It surprises me that someone as asymmetrical as you, my large-nosed squire, should not have noticed that detail before."

I pretend to be offended and keep silent. An atrocious noise is heard from the north. Lightning rips the dark curtain that dilutes the distance between mountains and sky.

Durito tries to console me by telling me a story (it's difficult to understand him beneath the modern sculpture) about how he once had a practice that specialized in the big toe of the left foot. I don't fail to appreciate the subtle insinuation which Durito offers in order to help me concentrate on the subject of this letter, which was something like "Ethics and Political Parties," or "Politics and Morality," or "The New Left, New Morality and New Politics," or "We are all

Prigione"[10] or . . . A lightning bolt just struck that rivals the apocalypse, and Durito says that it serves me right for picking on the papal nuncio, and I tell him that I'm not picking on the nuncio, I'm just looking for a re-e-e-ally good title for this epistle, so good that even some ambassador will copy it.

"How about this one . . . 'The Lovely Lie and the Lost Cause . . . '"

Durito says that what I've lost is my mind, that he'd rather go back to sleep, and that I should wake him when civil society arrives to rescue him from the ruins. I realize then that I now have all the necessary elements for the epistle: title, characters (political parties, the ambassador, the papal nuncio, the political spectrum and civil society), a polemic (the one about the relationship between morality and politics) in which to stick my nose, of which I have more than enough. Now I only need a subject to justify the stationery, the stamps, the request to Juan Villoro of the *La Journada Semanal* to be the host of such a "lovely" story, and the pretext to renew that amiable epistolary exchange which we began on the eve of the Convention a year ago.[11] Do you remember (sir)?

My Other Self comes near and says that if I'm going to enter into polemics, I should be serious about it, because one shouldn't play with nuncios and Machiavellians. "And if you don't believe me just ask Castillo Peraza, whose political ethics demonstrated his effectiveness in Yucatan," says My Other Self as he leaves to check on the beans.[12]

Every polemic is a nightmare, not only for the polemicists, but above all for the readers. That's why it occurs to me that it's not worth it, especially when I remember that prophecy of a certain Salinista intellectual (who now has amnesia) in December of 1993, who augured great successes for Salinas in 1994, since he had "all the marbles" in the bag.

But it occurs to me that I cannot remain a spectator and that I should take sides. So I take sides, in this case, for those who do not have a side, and with Durito we make a "wave" and don't think it's a pitiful "wave"; with all Durito's pairs of hands and feet it almost looks like a "wave" of Mexican fans during the penalty kicks at the World Cup.

But Durito must be dreaming about Brigitte Bardot because he's let out a sigh that sounds like his last, so I can't count on him and it would be better to concentrate on the discussion at hand. And in this discussion, the most important thing is the relationship between morality and politics, or better yet, between morality and political parties, or even better, between politics and power.

10 Archbishop Girolamo Prigione was *papal nuncio*, the diplomatic and ecclesiastical representative of the Pope in Mexico.

11 Juan Villoro has published a number of short story collections, translated such authors as Graham Greene and written for publications such as *Nexos, Proceso, Uno Más Uno* and *La Jornada*.

12 Carlos Castillo Peraza, president of the PAN, challenged the May 1995 election of PRI candidate Victor Cervera Pacheco over Luis Correa Mena for governor of Yucatan. Earlier in March, the PAN refused to allow the peace talks as part of the Law for Dialogue, Reconciliation and Dignified Peace to be convened in Mexico City. See *La Jornada*, March 3, 1995.

However, there is reasoning that goes beyond this, and the problem of the relationship between morality and politics is hidden (or displaced) by the problem of the relationship between politics and "success," and between politics and "efficiency." Machiavelli is revived by the argument that, in politics, the "superior" morality is "efficiency," and efficiency is measured in shares of power, that is, in the access to power. From here, one leaps over the previous juggling of Machiavellian rhetoric, to define democratic change as if the political opposition were to govern. The National Action Party is the example, they say, of this political "success," this political morality. *[handwritten:] N A P*

But then it is adjusted and given color: the accumulation of power, they say, serves to contain the antagonism that pluralistic societies keep within themselves. Power is exerted to defend society from itself!

Fine, let's leave this new referent for measuring political efficiency for later, and return to the original. Not to argue with those who measure "success" and political "efficiency" by the number of governorships, mayor's offices, and congressional seats, but rather, to reclaim that sign of "success" that has so many followers on the current government team, that is, on Carlos Salinas de Gortari's team.

Is political "success" defined in terms of efficiency? Is a politics more successful the more efficient it appears? In such a case, Carlos Salinas de Gortari deserves a monument and not a police investigation for his alleged complicity in the magnacides of J. F. Ruiz Massieu and Luis D. Colosio.[13] His politics were "efficient" to the point that he kept the entire country living in a virtual reality that was, of course, shattered by real reality. Knowledge of reality was acquired through the media. A great "success," to be sure. The political and economic "efficiency" of Carlos Salinas de Gortari won him the applause of National Action and of intellectuals now orphaned; and not just from them; powerful businessmen and high-ranking clergymen now complain of having been deceived. Together they delighted in having "all the marbles." The consequences of the Salinista "success" are suffered today by all Mexicans, and not just the poorest ones.

After all, isn't "political efficiency" as perennial in Mexico as a presidential term? Sometimes it doesn't last as long. The government of Ernesto Zedillo is an excellent example of "successes" as durable as the pages of a calendar without photos. *[handwritten:] → and Neoliberalism*

The other stated problem, the one of sharing power, was to point out that the efficiency of democratic change lies in the alternation of power. The alternation of power is not synonymous with democratic change, or its "efficiency," but

---

13 José Francisco Ruiz Massieu, former PRI party leader, was murdered on September 28, 1994. On February 28, 1995, Attorney General Antonio Lozano García arrested Raúl Salinas de Gortari on charges of ordering the murder of the PRI official. Luis Donaldo Colosio, anointed as President Salinas' successor, was assassinated on March 24, 1994, while campaigning for the presidency in Tijuana, Mexico.

with bribes and divorces in the planning stages. The politics followed by National Action in Baja California, Jalisco, and Chihuahua, are far from being "another" way of practical politics, and they are sufficiently authoritarian so as to try to regulate the length of skirts (Guadalajara) and the uncovering of the human body (Monterrey).

The alternation of power is a separate problem and is perhaps on the rebound from the polemics of the maestro Tomás Segovia with one Matías Vegoso: "Well, the bipartisan government ideal is tied to this position, perhaps not just because bipartisanship is its only essential manifestation, but because at least until now it is the clearest concrete manifestation of not an 'ideological' but a 'technical' government. [14] The first thing I have to say (and perhaps it's not the most important) is that this position confirms most clearly the continuation of ideologies and surely not their end. The conviction that a 'technical government' is better than an 'ideological' one is in itself an ideology, or a belief that conditions and distorts the image of reality, in exactly the same way that the conviction that 'positive' truth is better than 'metaphysical' truth, is in itself a metaphysical conviction."

(Certainly, I interject, now there is talk of "tripartisanship" but the problem remains.) Tomás Segovia continues:

"In the same way, I give you this friendly advice in order to defend neoliberalism: don't forget that it is an ideology and nothing more than an ideology. Don't you understand that this is the most astute trap of ideology? There is nothing more ideological than to say: 'Everyone else is ideological; I am lucid.'"

Here I could cite in my favor those arguments of the maestro Tomás Segovia opposing Matías Vegoso, but in addition to not having Tomás Segovia's authorization to do so, that argument leads me to another problem: the morality of immorality (or should I say "amorality?"). *Mutatis Mutandis*: the ideology of no ideology. And from here we can jump to the problem of knowledge, and intellectuals who produce and distribute that knowledge.

The process followed by some intellectuals is typical: from the critique of power to critique from a position of power.

With Salinas they showed that knowledge is ready to serve power. Then they collaborated to give him theoretical substance. Their logic, no matter how you looked at it, arrived at the same result: power is not mistaken in analyzing reality, and if it is mistaken then it is a problem with reality and not power.

It is a painful truth, it's true, but inevitable; power has not only managed to surround itself with a group of "brilliant" intellectuals; it has also produced a corps of analysts capable of theorizing, from now on, the future solidification of power (be they images of the PRI or the PAN reflected in the mirror of power).

---

14 Celebrated for his poetry, Tomás Segovia is known for his work as a literary editor, translator, professor and columnist for *La Jornada*.

Machiavelli is now the head of a group of intellectuals who seek to give the-oretical–ideological support to the repression to come (Porfirio Díaz's grandson and *Rebellion of the Pipeline* have enlisted in their cause).[15] This is the fundamental contribution of its elite; it has succeeded in evolving from the justification of a stupid system to the theorization of the imbecility yet to come. Not to mention that they are the new kind of organic intellectuals in power. They are capable of seeing beyond power. They represent the image of what the organic intellectual of neoliberalism aspires to be. They will drop out of school . . .

I stop here in order to reload my pipe and rest my back. Now a gray haze adds a new curtain to the heavy backdrop of night. There are noises from beneath Durito's "work in progress," evidence that he is not asleep and is still working. A small column of smoke rises from between the drawers of the desk and the piano keys. Somewhere beneath that jumble that aspires to be a sculpture, Durito is reading or writing.

In the fire, the dance of colors goes out and little by little turns black. On the mountain, sounds and colors continually change. And what to say about the inevitable turning of day into afternoon, of afternoon into night, of night into day . . .

I've got to get back to writing and that's what I do. Machiavelli is revisited and converted not into a guide but into an elegant garment that disguises cynicism as intellectualism. Now there is an ethic of "political efficiency" that justifies whatever means are necessary to obtain "results" (that is, shares of power). This political ethic should distance itself from "personal ethics" whose "efficiency" is zero since it is measured by loyalty to principles.

Once again, efficiency and its "results," in addition to the subject of political morality, are restricted to "personal ethics," to the ideology of the "salvation of the soul." In opposition to the "moralists," Machiavelli and his contemporary equivalent propose their "science," their "technique": efficacy. One must abide by efficiency.

This "non-ideological" doctrine has followers and "practitioners." I mean, besides the Salinista and neopanista intellectuals. Before the applause of the intellectuals who have no memory, the ambassador unfurls with all its details, the doctrine of cynicism and efficiency:

If I strike him, he speaks;
if I speak to him, he strikes me.

The ambassador does not represent himself, I mean, not only himself. He represents a political position, a way of doing politics that already characterizes this undefined path that is the first eleven months of the Salinas administration without Salinas. The ambassador is part of the neocorpus of presidential "advi-

---

15 Carlos Tello Díaz, *La rebelión de las cañadas* (México, D.F.: Cal y Arena, 1995). Marcos has changed the title from *cañadas* to *cañerías* or pipeline.

sors" who recommend to Zedillo to strike in order to speak. The price he pays, they say, can be covered up with an adequate manipulation of the media.

I don't remember the name of the movie (maybe the maestro Barbachano remembers it), but I do remember that one of the main actors was Peter Fonda.[16] I do remember the plot clearly. It was, more or less, about a group of brilliant Harvard students who raped a girl. She accused them in court and they countered that she was a prostitute. Their lawyer defends them by citing their brilliant grades and good families. They are acquitted. The girl commits suicide. As adults, the "juniors" look for "stronger emotions" and they dedicate themselves to "hunting" couples on weekend vacations. The "hunt" is not figurative; after the obligatory rape, the "juniors" set the couple free in the country, and then hunt them down with shotguns.[17]

I don't remember the ending, but it's one of those where justice is done, where Hollywood tries to resolve onscreen what goes unpunished in reality.

Now, the modern "juniors" have found that they have a country with which to play. One of them is at Los Pinos and the other was in Bucareli.[18] They get bored with Nintendo so they try hunting down "the bad guys" in a game of real war. They give their prey time to escape, and move their "pieces" to pen them in and make the game more interesting. But it turns out that the country is not ready for games and mobilizes in protest. The "juniors" find themselves in a quandary because the game grows longer and they can't catch the "bad guy." Then the ambassador appears to get them out of (?) their predicament: "It was all planned," he tells us, "the dead are not dead, the war is not war, the displaced are not displaced, we always tried to talk and we only sent tens of thousands of soldiers so that we could tell the 'bad guy' that we wanted to talk." A pathetic argument for the aforementioned government.

Meanwhile, reality looms . . . and the media tries to dominate reality. Lapses of memory begin to multiply within government discourse; the stock market crash is forgotten, the devaluation, the "negotiations" of San Andrés as a showcase to flaunt the true indigenous politics of neoliberalism, instability, mistrust and suspicion, ungovernability and uncertainty. They forget what is primary, according to Machiavelli; they've had no results, they haven't been "efficient."

They forget that they defend a lost cause, and the ambassador knows that but he forgets it when it's time for exclusive interviews. The latest declarations of the government are clear; they forget reality, that is, they forget that each time there are fewer who believe in lovely lies and who are ready to bet on lost causes . . .

---

16 Miguel Barbachano Ponce has published numerous essays, plays, and novels. He has also contributed as drama and film critic to a number of journals including *La Jornada*.

17 The film referred to here is *Los Cazadores* also known as *Open Season* (1974), directed by Peter Collinson.

18 Bucareli is the location of the Palacio de Cobian, the residence of the Secretaría de Gobernación or Interior Ministry.

Meanwhile, the modern Machiavellians complain about our little morality and they prescribe that in politics there are no good or bad guys, and, therefore, the issue cannot be settled with the classification of factions.

And here they hit the mark, but only in reference to the relationship between ethics and politics, that it is not an issue easy to resolve with the definition of factions: bad guys vs. good guys. That is, "if the Machiavelli of Salinista intellectual nostalgia is bad, then we, who do not agree with him, are good." It remains tempting to take the polemic in that direction, but I think that when you (sir) pointed out that "if efficiency in the neoliberal manner has brought us to the present tragic situations, the cult of doctrinaire purity, without such costly results, has not taken us very far either" (Carlos Monsiváis, *Proceso*, number 966).[19] You (sir) pointed out a new problem that is worth pursuing.

From the Left, the alternative to Machiavelli is not very attractive, that's true. But that's not the problem; it's not "doctrinaire purity," or not only that. It's also something else: the complicity of a mirror that is offered as an alternative and simplifies all its political relationships (and human ones as well, but that's another matter) into an inversion. This is the ethical foundation of "revolutionary" science: "scientific" knowledge produces a morality inverse to capitalism. It proposes impartiality against egoism; collectivity against privatization; the social being against individualism.

But this mirrored knowledge, like moral fundamentalism, doesn't contribute anything new. The inversion of the image is not a new image, but an inverted image. The alternative political (and moral) proposal is a mirrored reflection: where the right is dominant, now the left will be; where it's white, black; where the one from above, the one from below; where the bourgeoisie, the proletariat; and so on. The same, only inverted. And this ethic was (or is) the one that was engraved (or is engraved) in the full spectrum of the left.

I agree. The modern Machiavellians say, and say well, that we offer nothing better than they do: cynicism and effectiveness. That we criticize them with a new "morality" that is as criminal as theirs (well, they don't say that theirs is a criminal morality, they only say that ours is) and that we try to reduce politics to a struggle between black and white, forgetting that there are many shades of gray. It's true, but our critique is not only that the morality of the resurrected Machiavelli is cynical and criminal, we also point out that it is not efficient . . .

Durito interrupts again to recommend prudence to me when discussing morality.

"Your immorality is common knowledge," Durito says, trying to justify his indescribable failure in bringing me some videos that I asked him to bring, ones with a lot of X's, from the capital.

"We're not talking about 'that' kind of morality. And stop preaching to me as if you were a Panista mayor," I defend myself.

---

19 Carlos Monsiváis, "*Sobre la cacería de lectores indeseables* . . ." *Proceso*, 966 (May 8, 1995), 48.

"I'd never. But it's my duty to reproach you for your warped cinematic preferences. Instead of those immoral videos, here, I brought you something more edifying. They're pictures of my trip to the D.F."

This said, Durito tosses me an envelope. In it there are pictures of different sizes and subjects. One of them is of Durito at Chapultepec Park.[20]

"You don't look too happy in this picture at the zoo," I tell him.

Durito answers from under the desk and he tells me that the picture was taken after he was detained by a zoo guard. It turns out that the man mistook Durito for a miniature rhinoceros and was determined to take him back to a cage. Durito tried diverse and varied defenses dealing with botany, zoology, mammals, insects, knight-errantry, and I don't know what else, but he ended up in the rhino pit. He escaped somehow, the moment the guard took his break.

He was so happy to be free he decided to take this picture where he looks like a white rhinoceros. He was that pale. From fear, he says.

And then there were several pictures with Durito in various poses and in typical urban settings.

For example, there was a picture of Durito among many feet. He made me take note that none of the feet wore boots, and that's something that Durito applauded. I told him not to be so enthusiastic, that back then, Espinosa had not yet shown his hooves.

After that one, there was a picture with a lot of people. Durito explains to me that he took that one just so I wouldn't feel so lonely.

The next one was of Durito and another beetle. In the background you could see what looked like the "islands" of the Ciudad Universitaria.[21] I asked him who the other guy was.

"It's not a he, it's a she," he answered with a drawn-out sigh.

There were no more photos. Durito was silent and all you could hear were sighs emanating from the sculpture. I return to Machiavelli's indignation at our critique of his efficiency.

Does this critique mean, in light of that morality, that we offer an alternative? Is this the blasphemy that terrifies the adopted and adapted Machiavellians? A new morality? A better morality? More successful? More efficient? Is that what we offer? Negative. At least not to what refers to us Zapatistas. We believe that it is necessary to construct a new political relationship, that the new relationship will not only have one source (neozapatismo, in this case), and that the new relationship will produce effects in and of itself. So new that it will not only define a new politics, but new politicians as well. A new way to define the political arena and those who do well in it.

I won't insist much on why the new political morality cannot be born from neozapatismo; suffice it to say that our reason is also the old one. We have resort-

---

20 Chapultepec Park is a four square-kilometer open-air park, containing the National Museum of History, the Museum of Anthropology, and Chapultepec Castle.
21 Ciudad Universitaria (University City) is the UNAM campus and surrounding area.

ed to the argument of weapons (no matter how much J. Castañeda, for the sake of rescuing his book from a publishing disaster, denies them and claims that we are an army in name only), and with them, the argument of force.[22] The fact that the weapons are few or old or that they've hardly been used changes the situation only a little if at all. The fact is that we were, and are, willing to use them. We are willing to die for our ideas, it's true. But we are also willing to kill. That is why a new political morality, or better yet, a political morality superior to the one that weighs us down today and the better part of tonight, can not emerge from a "maimed" army, no matter how revolutionary, heroic, etc. it may be. She, the night, still holds some surprises, and I'm sure that many more brains will be racked trying to understand that . . .

"Things are not that simple," Durito says. "It may be that I didn't bring you the videos you wanted and that's why you want to lay on my noble shoulders the weight of a blame much heavier than this piano and desk. But I should say in my own defense that instead I brought some things for the Zapatistas: bracelets, headbands, earrings, barrettes . . . I worked ten nights straight to get all of that . . ."

Speaking of nights, this night displays the sharp horns of a moon-bull that, new, returns from the west. Her clouds are absent now, and without a cape to help her, the night fights the bull alone and in silence. Her spirit is not daunted by the storm announced to the east, and among her resources she wears as many sequins as the suit of the best matador.

And there I was, seeing if I would rise to her defense, even though there was no wheat in the stands, when I was held back by the wide smile that, drawn between her horns, the moon offered me. Ten times I begged her pardon, and ten times the stars demanded that I continue to take up the task.

Then I tossed my writing aside and moved towards the center of the nocturnal bullring, asking Durito first to play a *pasodoble*. He said I should return to finish the letter because I'd already taken too much time to write it, and he, Durito, wasn't thinking of helping me. There was nothing more to say, the bullfight was left for later and I returned to my writing and the problem of political morality. The thousand heads that the light made visible through the night's wall began to stir slightly . . .

Where did I leave off? Oh yes! By our critique I am not implying that, contrary to Machiavelli, we are better, more acceptable, or superior. But we do say that it is necessary to be better. The problem is not which political morality is better or more efficient, but what is necessary for a new political morality.

In any case, it's not the nuanced cynicism of those intellectuals anxious for a theoretical support of chaos that will produce a better or more efficient political

---

22 Immediately following the January 1994 rebellion, Mexican intellectual Jorge Castañeda dismissed the Zapatistas as "armed reformists." See Jorge G. Castañeda, "The Chiapas Uprising," *Los Angeles Times* (January 3, 1994). See also Jorge G. Castañeda, *Utopia Unarmed: The Latin American Left After the Cold War* (New York: Vintage Books, 1994). In 2000, Castañeda went on to become Secretary of State under the Fox administration.

morality. In terms of political parties, Machiavelli runs a complicated scale of compensation: once formalized as alternatives to power, all of their pettiness (secrets, negotiations, opportunism, pragmatism, and betrayals) do not weigh enough to shift the balance of real power in their favor.

But it turns out that the nature of that "pettiness" doesn't take long to exact its historical dues. And the higher the position reached with all that "little and great political savvy," the more dues history demands. Once again, Carlos Salinas de Gortari is the model-made-history lesson (that, it seems, no one in the political class wants to learn).

Is it a better world that we offer? Negative: we do not offer a new world. Machiavelli does, and he says that it is not possible for it to be better, that we should resign ourselves to the fact that the grays that inhabit Mexican politics do not become so antagonistic, and that they fade into new shades of gray, more diluted, that is, more gray. We disagree, and not just because of the sad perspective that the mediocrity of "neither one or the other" offers, but because it is a lie, it has no future, and sooner or later, reality sets in, with the stupidity that reality often assumes, and it begins to ruin the halftones and sharpens the most neutral grays . . .

"Seven questions. That would be the right thing to do," Durito says, who, as is evident, hasn't forgotten his disagreement with the National Plebiscite. I try to distract him and ask him about Pegasus. Durito's voice cracks when he answers me.

"What happened to Pegasus is part of that daily tragedy that lives and dies in the D.F. Pegasus was an amiable and intelligent beast, but too patient for the traffic of Mexico City. I had disguised him as a compact car after he refused to disguise himself as a subway car because of all that skidding in the rain. Things were going well, but it turns out "Pegasus" was a "Pegasa" and she fell in love with a Ruta 100 bus. The last time I saw her she was panhandling for the resistance fund.[23] But I don't regret it, I'm sure she will learn good things there. She said she'd write, but she won't know where to send the letter."

Thunder shakes the sky. Out of the corner of my eye I look over at Durito. Silence and a cloud of smoke surround the sculpture. I try to cheer up Durito

---

23 Ruta 100 is the bus line that serves many of the impoverished communities in the outskirts of Mexico City and functions as part of SUTAUR, *Sindicato Único de Trabajadores del Autotransporte Urbano*, an independent urban transportation union. The union resisted the government's efforts to privatize transportation in Mexico as well as attacks on its leadership for their support of the Zapatistas. On April 8, 1995, in an effort to destroy SUTAUR, the government declared Ruta 100 bankrupt due to corruption and mismanagement, and arrested six top leaders. On April 10, Luis Miguel Moreno Gómez, chief of Ruta 100, was found murdered in his office with two gunshot wounds. Many refused to believe the government claim that he committed suicide. The Zapatistas directly addressed Ruta 100 in a communiqué in which they explained their initial silence and their unequivocal support for their struggles. See "Al Sindicato de Ruta-100," *La Jornada*, August 9, 1995. See also *EZLN 2, Documentos y comunicados 15 de agosto/29 de septiembre de 1995* (México, D.F.: Ediciones Era, 1995), 427.

and ask him to tell me more about his trip to the capital.

"What can I tell you? I saw what is seen in any city, large or small; injustice and anger, arrogance and rebellion, great wealth in the hands of a few and a poverty that each day swallows up more people. It was worth seeing. For many, fear is no more; for others it disguises itself as prudence. Some say it could always be worse; for others the situation will never be so desperate. There is no unanimity, unless it is in the repudiation of everything which is government."

Durito lights his pipe and continues:

"One early morning I was about to fall asleep in one of the few trees on the Alameda.[24] It was another city then, different from the one that lives by day. From high in the tree I saw a squad car patrolling slowly. It stopped in front of a woman, and one of the officers stepped out of the car. His demonic look gave him away. My intuition never fails: I knew instantly what was going to happen. The woman didn't move and waited for the officer as if she already knew him. Silently, she gave him a roll of bills and he put it away looking from side to side. He said goodbye, trying to pinch the woman's cheeks but she brushed his hand away brusquely. He returned to the vehicle. In an instant the squad car pulled away . . ."

Durito is quiet for a long time. I suppose he finished and has returned to his paperwork, and I should return to mine: instead of arguing which political morality is better or more "efficient" we could talk and argue about the necessity of fighting for the creation of a space in which a new political morality can be born. And here the problem resides in the following:

Should political morality always be defined in opposition to the problem of power? Alright, but it's not the same as saying "in opposition to the taking of power." Perhaps the new political morality is constructed in a new space that is not the taking or retaining of power, but serves as the counterweight and opposition that contains it and obliges it to, for example, "lead by obeying."

Of course, to "lead by obeying" is not among the concepts of "political science" and it is scorned by the morality of "efficiency" that rules the political acts from which we suffer. But in the end, confronted by the judgment of history, the "efficiency" of the morality of cynicism and "success" remains naked unto itself. Once it looks itself in the mirror of its "accomplishments," the fear it inspires in its enemies (who will always be in the majority) turns against itself.

On the other side, the side of the "pure," the saint is discovered to be a demon, and the inverse image of cynicism discovers that it has made intolerance change direction and religion into exchange rate and political project. The puritanism of National Action, for example, is part of a sign that it remains unexhausted in the Mexican Right.

---

24 One of Mexico's finest parks, the Alameda sits between Avenida Hidalgo, Avenida Juárez, Calle Ángela Peralta, and Calle de Doctor Mora. Located amidst its renowned sculptures, fountains, and monuments is the Diego Rivera Mural Museum.

Well, dawn is approaching, and with it, the time for goodbyes. Maybe I didn't understand the argument/controversy/polemic that the resurrection of Machiavelli invited, and I see now that I presented (and did not resolve) more polemical lines than the original. And I don't think that's bad; it probably is, in any case, not too "efficient."

Surely the debate may continue, but it's unlikely to happen face-to-face given ski masks, persecution and military siege . . . In the words of Muñoz-Ledo, "I don't believe that he, Marcos, is someone who will remain on the country's political scene." Did he already have a "pact" with Chuayffet? A "disappearance," like the ones ordered from the Ministry of Government of Chiapas, by that other great PRD member, Eraclio Zepeda?[25]

In the meantime, Power will continue to promise us the Apocalypse as an equivalent to change. He deduces that it is better to avoid it and resign ourselves to it. Others adduce, by their silence, that the Apocalypse is eternal and that chaos is not about to come, but that it is already a reality . . .

I don't know how to finish this, so I turn to Durito for help. The spectacle of his sculpture silhouetted against the storm's lightning bolts is astonishing. The sudden bursts of light make the darkness that covers it more contrasting. Maybe that's why I didn't see Durito come out from behind the ruins, and for a moment I thought something extraordinary had happened. Durito was now smoking, sitting on top of the little piano.

"But, how did you get out from under there?"

"It was very simple. I was never down there. I moved to one side when the piano started wobbling. In an instant, I decided that no work of art deserves to be on top of my body. Besides, I am a knight-errant, and for that you need to be a soulful artist and there are few of those. Alright, what troubles you, my dear 'Watson'?"

"I don't know how to end this letter," I say with embarrassment.

"That's an easy problem to solve. Finish the way you started."

"How did I start? With a period?"

"Yes. It's elementary my dear 'Watson,' it's in any book of mathematical logic."

"Mathematical logic? And what does mathematical logic have to do with political morality?"

"More than you think. For example, in mathematical logic (not to be confused with algebra) the period represents a conjunction, an and. The period is the same as an and. To say A and B, or A plus B, you write A.B. The period is not the end; it is a sign of unity, of something that increases. It only defines the X num-

---

25 Emilio Chuayffet resigned as *Secretaría de Gobernación* (Mexican Interior Minister) on January 3, 1998, as a result of political pressure following the massacre of 45 people in the town of Acteal on December 22, 1997. He was replaced by Francisco Labastida Ochoa. Porfirio Muñoz-Ledo was elected president of the PRD on July 1993 and held office until July 1996 when he was replaced by Mario Saucedo Pérez. Eraclio Zepeda was appointed *Secretaría de Gobierno de Chiapas* (Secretary of State of Chiapas) in 1994.

ber of paragraphs between one period and another, where X is a number that the mirror does not alter and reflects faithfully," Durito says as he arranges his papers. To the west, the sun uncovers clouds and seizes the sky.

And things as they are, I end this postscript with a period and, according to Durito, I don't end but I continue.

Vale, well: and . . .

P.S. that invites you to solve the enigma that contains its central theme:

Instructions:

First. *Through the Looking Glass (and what Alice found there)*, Lewis Carroll, Chapter II, "The Garden of the Live Flowers."
Second. Each period marks the end of a paragraph.
Third. Punctuation marks don't count.
Fourth. Numerical chaos in the logic of the number in the mirror:
1-111. 14-110. 9-109. 247-107.
11-104. 25-103. 47-97. 37-96. 3-95.
14-94. 3-89. 24-87. 22-86. 6-85.
10-84. 48-82. 21-81. 43-79. 55-78.
10-77. 49-76. 83-72. 21-71. 42-64.
6-63. 27-62. 52-61. 63-59. 13-58.
11-57. 3-56. 6-54. 101-53. 141-51.
79-50. 35-49. 32-49. 51-46. 11-45.
88-44. 12-43. 12-42. 31-41. 3-40.
24-39. 15-38. 20-37. 18-37. 17-36.
27-35. 22-33. 111-32. 7-32. 115-31.
20-31. 12-31. 5-31. 68-30. 46-30.
31-30. 12-30. 9-30. 54-29. 45-29.
12-29. 49-28. 20-28. 9-28. 40-27.
15-27. 42-22. 111-21. 91-21. 29-21.
3-21. 34-20. 6-20. 81-19. 66-19.
44-19. 36-19. 18-19. 11-19. 123-18.
90-18. 80-18. 76-18. 65-18. 43-17.
4-17. 51-15. 48-15. 28-15. 16-15.
47-14. 20-14. 8-14. 39-13. 12-13.
55-12. 54-12. 53-12. 18-11. 43-10.
25-10. 41-8. 9-6. 6-4. 1-1.

Fifth. In the mirror, chaos is a reflection of logical order and logical order is a reflection of chaos.
Sixth. A.A=?
Seventh. There are seven mirrors: the first is the first. The second and third open

the mystery of the chaos that is ordered in the fourth. The fourth is constructed with the fifth and the sixth. The seventh is the last one.

Vale, once again. *Salud*, and as you can see (given trees, transgressors and odontology), it's not so easy.

love the branch[26]
Subcomandante Marcos
EZLN
Mountains of the Mexican Southeast

* * *

---

26 The original Spanish, *amar a la rama*, is a palindrome.

The Story of the Hot Foot and the Cold Foot

During a Zapatista Red Alert issued in the wake of the government's arrest of Fernando Yáñez Muñoz on October 21 and in response to conflicts between the EZLN and the PRD over elections, Durito tells Marcos a story about how those who fight each other may be defeated by a common enemy. Then, in response to a newspaper article complaining about his frequent appearance in Marcos' communiqués, Durito furiously demands a National, International and Interplanetary plebiscite on his popularity. As it happened, on the day this letter was written, the government dropped charges against Yáñez and the day it was published the EZLN called off the Red Alert.

First published in *La Jornada*, October 20, 1995. Originally translated by Eduardo Vera.

October 27, 1995
To the National and International Press

Sirs,
Here goes a communiqué. We're not going to run anymore. It's our custom to flee only once a year and for 1995 we did that in February. With regards to the judicial police, they deserve the national agronomy prize for their ability to "plant" evidence. Whatever the case, the key question is: Who gave the orders for the arrest? And this question begs others, for example: Who benefits from the failure of the dialogue process in Chiapas? Send the answers (if anybody has them) to the Secretary of State, where they are already known . . . they just need confirmation. Anyway, they've already ruined the World Series for me, although in baseball (as in politics) the best does not always win. If you don't believe me, ask Castillo Peraza. No, better not ask him anything. He's liable to think you're flirting with him. That's what illiteracy gets you![1]

Vale. Salud, and may you always walk with a notary public at your side to certify that you're not carrying more arms than God gave you.

From the mountains of the Mexican Southeast
Subcomandante Insurgente Marcos
Mexico, October 1995

P.S. that accepts all scoldings that don't come from the mediocre arrogance that reigns in certain political parties.

The dawn is just beginning to appear. Cold and darkness blanket the watch of a gallant knight-errant and the sorrow of his wretched squire. There is no one to greet the moon and a bolt of lightning is followed by thunder. Mud is renewed with rain and wheat with a kiss. Durito reviews the newspaper, chews on his pipe, and directs a look of reproach my way.

"So thou hast provoked a scandal of historical proportions!" he says, putting down the newspaper.

"Me?" I say, pretending that I am veeery busy with my torn boot.

"Surely! Who else? You have demonstrated once more that your speech has the same quality as a stampede of elephants inside a china shop. And not only

---

1 After the PAN won the mayoralty of Tuxtla Gutierrez, the capital of Chiapas, Marcos took an indirect shot at the PRD, commenting in a press conference that, "The PAN is Power's only real option to offer an alternative to the PRI in this country," and, "This is not desirable, I repeat, but it is the only organized force of opposition that can succeed to power and it's Power's only alternative, but not the nation's." PAN leader Carlos Castillo Peraza responded that Marcos' comments were in recognition of the serious political work of the PANistas, but that he wouldn't accept flattery from someone who was so fickle in their compliments. See Guadalupe Irízar, "PAN, Only Option to Power," *Reforma* (October 18, 1995), 1.

139

that, your clumsiness has allowed an avalanche of mediocre people to declare one-and-a-half stupidities about the half-stupidity that you said . . ."

"I . . . I was misunderstood! I did not want to say what I said, but to say what I did not say, and that is why I did not say what I wanted to say and said what I did not want to say . . ." I defend myself while hiding my shame in the hole in my boot, the left one of course.

"Nonsense! This reasoning has the same logic as that of a PRI representative explaining his vote against the reduction of sales tax."[2]

I remain quiet and start to draw spirals and little circles on the ground with a short stick. Durito feels sorry for me and pats my shoulder. To do this, Durito must climb on my arm and loosen his chinstrap. He sits next to my shirt collar, and says,

"Oh my dear and clumsy squire, speaking is slippery and problematic. In reality, it's only worth the trouble to speak to a woman—the only being with whom it is gratifying to be slippery and get into trouble. And to speak to a woman one must whisper in her ear. That way, what matters is not so much what one says, but the warmth of coming close to her neck. In politics, words hold a thousand traps and tangles, and not only those that are spoken to us, but also the ones that we speak. And now that we are speaking of politics, I'm reminded of a story that might be good for that book you are preparing, which is entitled, if I remember correctly, *Stories for a Suffocating Night*.

I sigh, resigned to tolerating another of Durito's stories, but he thinks that it's because of the shame of my declarations against Don Porfirio, so he continues.[3] He clears his throat and orders me to take paper and pencil, and I write while he dictates the story that is called . . .

---

2 The Mexican national sales tax was raised from 10% to 15% during March 1995, as part of the national recovery Program to Strengthen the Unity Agreement to Overcome the Economic Emergency, or PARAUSEE (Programa de Acción para Reforzar el Acuerda de Unidad para Superar la Emergencia Económica). The program also included the removal of price controls and subsidies for basic foodstuffs such as milk, tortillas, and beans, as well as gradual price hikes on energy (natural gas, oil, etc.). In the December 1997 budget debates, the PRD proposed returning the tax to 10%, arguing that the measure was intended to be temporary and that a tax on consumption is fundamentally regressive, but the PAN sided with the PRI and killed the proposal.
3 PRD leader Porfirio Muñoz Ledo criticized the Zapatista call to abstain from the elections. He claimed that this move hurt the PRD more than any other party and that as many as 20 municipalities may have been lost because of it. In response, Marcos stated that "the difficult conditions of militarization, harassment and persecution in the state forced our organization not to participate or to call on people to participate in this process . . . Muñoz Ledo also forgets that the EZLN did not take up arms so that the PRD could assume power . . . I remind him and the rest of the country that our arms are not in the service of any political party. He's making a fool of himself treating us as if we were the armed faction of the PRD, as if we had an obligation that we have never had." See Guadalupe Irízar, "Marcos Lashes out at Muñoz Leda" *Reforma* (October 18, 1995), 1.

The Story of the Cold Foot and the Hot Foot

"There once were two feet together. They were together, but not united. One foot was cold and the other was hot. And then the cold foot said to the hot foot, 'You are very hot.' And the hot foot said to the cold foot, 'You are very cold.' And that's what they were doing, that is, fighting each other, when Hernán Cortés arrived and burned them both." [4]

"Is it over?" I ask, incredulously.

"Of course! It's a story—not one of your press conferences," he answers.

I just look at him with reproach. He says, "Okay, okay, you're right. Let me think . . . Hmmm, Hmmm, I know! Below that write: And Hernán Cortes lived happily ever after. And that's the end—except this story's not over."

"No?" I ask while I put the paper in my pocket.

"Of course not! There are still many cold and hot feet, so Hernán Cortés could end up having a veeery disagreeable surprise."

"Speaking of disagreeable things," I interrupt, "they're complaining about you in some newspaper."

"About me? Who dares complain about the knight-errant longed for by countless damsels of all ages, dreamt of by children big and small, and respected and admired by all the noble men that have ever lived?"

"Well, they don't exactly complain about you. All they say is enough already with Durito. Durito over here, Durito over there. Anyway, they suggest that I leave you out of my letters and that . . ." Durito does not allow me to continue and shouts in my ear:

"Shut up insolent rogue! It could only occur to a good-for-nothing like you that respectable people would not enjoy and find relaxing solace and noble lessons in stories of my great feats, my undeniable charm, and the profound wisdom that is abundant in my discourse."

"But Durito! It is not I who has thought of such absurdity! Consider that there could exist—it's just a hypothesis—someone in whom you don't generate the same enthusiasm as . . ."

Durito interrupts again, "Well, I concede that it is possible that some being exists that may not be interested in me or my marvels. So we should do something to determine the rating that you have, insolent yokel, and the one that I have, a high knight-errant."

"I agree with the 'errant,' but allow me to doubt the 'high.'"

"I'm referring to the height of my ideals, cretin."

---

4 The conquistador Hernán Cortés invaded Mexico in 1519. By 1521, he was able to form alliances with indigenous groups, primarily the Tlaxcaltecans, to capture the imperial city of Tenochtitlan. Cuauhtémoc, nephew of Moctezuma and a successor to the throne, was captured and tortured in order to reveal the whereabouts of Moctezuma's treasure. When he refused to submit, Cortez applied boiling oil to his feet.

"Well, what do you propose?"

"A plebiscite."

"A plebiscite? But Durito . . . they're going to say it's a joke . . ."

"Not another word! A plebiscite it will be. National, International and Interplanetary. And these will be the questions: First: should El Sup eliminate Durito's stories from his letters? Second: should the despicable being who dared to demand the disappearance of Durito's stories die in the flames of an inferno that would make Dante's look like an icebox? These two questions are to be answered: 'Yes,' 'No,' or 'I don't know.'"

"And where should the ones who want to respond send their answers?" I ask skeptically.

"To my office: 'Don Durito de la Lacandona, Little Huapac Hole Number 69. Mountains of the Mexican Southeast, Chiapas, Mexico.'"

I see that Durito is very determined, so I suggest that he clarify some matters.

"And what are the minimum and maximum age limits for participating in this 'consultation'?"

"The minimum is six months old. The maximum is a minute before taking your last breath."

"But Durito, do you think that at six months somebody could answer these questions?"

"Of course! At six months I was already composing some of those sonnets that make a moist and feminine womb provoke tempests and—paradoxically— offer tranquility."

"But you are a beetle!"

"Even more in my favor! No more discussion! Elaborate the convocation and add that all females may adorn their ballot with their best sigh . . . Although, on second thought . . . no—better not mention sighs . . . because surely so many would arrive that they'd turn into a hurricane that would leave Roxanne in the category of 'inopportune breezes.'[5] Better for them to send red carnations. Maybe we can start a business exporting them . . . Well, what do you think?"

"I think you're delirious; that you've gone mad," I tell him.

"My dear and scraggly squire! It takes a certain dose of delirium and madness for the dawn to break," Durito says while he returns to his place and covers himself again with his little huapac leaf, but not before drawing a huge "69" on top of it.

"Let me know when the answers start arriving. Hell! I won't even be able to sleep because of the sweet anticipation . . ." Durito says seconds before starting to snore as if he were a chainsaw with no muffler.

I remain quiet. I light my pipe and slowly inhale a memory. Above, dawn dis-

---

5 Tropical Storm Roxanne struck southeastern Mexico for two weeks in mid-October. With winds up to 115 mph, the storm reached hurricane levels twice, killing fourteen and leaving as many as 300,000 people displaced.

solves its last gloomy grays, far away day takes a bite of the horizon and the cold turns tepid here . . . in the mountains of the Mexican Southeast . . .

Vale again. *Salud*, and may the madness and the delirium multiply.

El Sup yearning for the flower with which October decorated the ceiba.

* * *

On Love

A few days before the second anniversary of the EZLN uprising, Durito reflects on Toñita's statement on the nature of Love. We first met Toñita, a five-year-old girl from the community of Prado Pacayal, in "Durito II" where Marcos related how she had found her teacup broken amidst the debris of her home left by the Army offensive of February. Here Toñita uses the breaking and repair of teacups as a metaphor for the anxieties of love. Durito, for his part, prefers the metaphor of a scale. Marcos' account of these reflections is attached to two communiqués by the CCRI: the first on the upcoming celebrations inaugurating four new centers of resistance or Aguascalientes in the communities of Oventic, La Garrucha, Morelia and La Realidad, and the second on the government's response: increased military pressure.

First published in *La Jornada*, December 26, 1995. Originally translated by Cecilia Rodríguez.

December 23, 1995
To the National and International Press

Sirs:

Here go a couple of communiqués. I know well that you have had a lot of work chasing after ex-presidents and their cohorts.[1] It was to be expected. The only thing that is surprising is the amnesia of the zealots of the First World, modernity and other lies. On the other hand, it is paradoxical that he who denounced us for using masks has now become the most popular mask for sale on the Mexican streets.

They tell me that there are now piñatas.[2] Could you send one for the post-*posadas*?[3] (It turns out that with these tanks, planes and indigenous time, the *posadas* are going to be held around February.)[4]

Vale, salud and hope that in January they don't make a piñata out of the people.[5]

From the mountains of the Mexican Southeast
Subcomandante Insurgente Marcos
Mexico, December 1995

P.S. that speaks of love, indifference and other foolishness.

Toñita comes to brag about her new teacup. Without mercy, she lets me have it . . .

"Love is like a teacup that each day we drop on the floor and it breaks into pieces, at dawn the pieces are back together and with a little moisture and warmth, they stick together and the teacup is like new again. The person who is in love spends his life fearing the arrival of the terrible day when the little cup will be so broken that it will no longer be possible to put it back together."

---

1 After his failed hunger strike (see note in "Durito II") former president Carlos Salinas disappeared into self-imposed exile. He was sighted by reporters in the Bahamas, Switzerland, Cuba, the United States, and Ireland.

2 Street vendors in Mexico City hawked *piñatas* or paper maché dolls of ex-president Salinas, often in prison uniform.

3 *Posada* literally means "inn" or "small hotel." In this context, the term *posadas* refers to the annual fiestas around the re-enactment of the night that Mary and Joseph searched for lodging in Bethlehem.

4 On December 23, 1995, the CCRI-CG released a communiqué that detailed the intensification of Mexican military mobilizations. Military patrols included tanks, artillery jeeps, combat planes, and artillery helicopters. The communiqué denounced the government for these actions, highlighting the army's harassment of Oventic, La Garrucha, Morelia, and La Realidad, all sites of the new Aguascalientes. See *La Jornada*, December 26, 1995.

5 There were rumors that the Mexican government would launch an official offensive against the Zapatistas on January 1, 1996. See communiqué issued by the CCRI-CG, published in *La Jornada*, December 26, 1995

She leaves the way she came, reiterating her denial of a kiss that, now more than ever, "burns a lot."

"Love is no more than a complex scale," says Durito. "On one side you put the good things and on the other the bad ones. Love endures as long as the good outweighs the bad. The one who loves spends his life accumulating weights and concerns on the good side. He pays so much attention to that weight that he forgets about the bad side. He will never understand how a weight, that was barely the whisper of a feather, shifted the balance in favor of indifference, in a categorical, definitive, irremediable manner . . .

I was left thinking and smoking. The moon was a pearly fingernail, a sail swollen with light on the evening boat. A naked edge appeared along the mountain's peak and then it was launched with such force that its path mistreated not a few stars.

Vale again. Happy New Year; I hope that now it will really be new.

Sup Marcos

El Sup preparing a gift for Durito whom, as almost no one knows, this December celebrates years of confounding and criticizing me. What if I give him some scotch tape to cover his mouth? I don't know about him, but I would sleep veeery well . . .

* * *

The Story of Dreams

Marcos vividly describes Durito and his role in helping the EZLN cope with the difficulties of war. Written on Christmas Day, this communiqué reflects growing tensions the Zapatistas faced in the aftermath of the first two rounds of the San Andrés negotiations on indigenous rights and culture, and as the Mexican Army sought to intimidate them during the inauguration of four new "Aguascalientes." He closes with a story told to him by Old Antonio about the importance of dignity and dreaming.

First published January 2, 1996. Originally translated by irlandesa for this volume. See *EZLN Documentos y comunicados 3: 2 de octubre de 1995 / 24 de enero de 1997* (México, D. F.: Ediciones Era, 1997), 72–75.

December 25, 1995

In the oppressive solitude of the first years of the Zapatista war, an odd character presented himself in our camps. A little beetle, a pipe-smoker, a good reader and even better teller of tales, set himself to the task of easing the cold dawns of a combatant, El Sup.

With the legal name of "Nebuchadnezzar," the little beetle chose the *nom de guerre* of "Durito" because of the hardness of his skin. Durito, like all children, has thick skin. And in the same way, Durito chose as his first interlocutor the child we have within, whom we have forgotten, along with our principles.

One dawn, ten years later, almost at the end of the military retreat which had been forced upon us by the betrayal of February, Durito found us once again, and once again he inspired the best that human beings possess: their capacity for wonder, their tenderness, their aspiration to be better . . . as well as other qualities.

At times a detective, at times a political analyst, at times a knight-errant, and at others a writer of letters, Durito speaks to us, offering us a mirror of the future that shows us what we can be. The *Tales for a Suffocating Night* are begun in order to lighten hearts made heavy by the unknown. Through them, Durito opens a wound in our chest, a wound that hurts and that relieves, a painful wound, but one that allows us to breathe better.

Self-proclaimed knight-errant, with the new title of "Don Durito de la Lacandona," this little beetle resolves to travel the paths of the world in order to right wrongs, to rescue damsels, to relieve suffering, to support the weak, to instruct the ignorant, to humiliate the powerful, to raise up the humble. Always full of vitality, Don Durito de la Lacandona is the greatest knight-errant who has ever lived. He lives, astonishing the stars that discover him in the forest dawns. News of his deeds have now gone round the world, and millions of women sigh for him, thousands of men speak his name with respect, and hundreds of thousands of children revere him.

Don Durito de la Lacandona describes some of his adventures and thoughts to us, and tells us disconcerting tales that have a thousand-and-one interpretations, that teach and that relieve the innumerable nights of suffocation in the mountains of the Mexican Southeast.

Durito will be ten years old in this month of December, 1995. He only awaits the results of the Intergalactic Plebiscite that he called in order to know if he will continue to astonish us with his wonders or if he will be lost again among numerous paths that cross the mountains of the Mexican Southeast.[1]

Today, December 25, 1995, I salute the greatest and the best practitioner of knight-errantry, Don Durito.

From the mountains of the Mexican Southeast
Subcomandante Insurgente Marcos

---

1 For the genesis of that plebiscite, see "The Story of the Hot Foot and Cold Foot."

148

P.S. that teaches one to dream or, that which is the same, to struggle.

Old Antonio was sharpening his machete and smoking in the doorway of his hut. I was dozing by his side, covered by the buzzing of crickets and weariness. Just like ten years before and ten years after, the smoke of Old Antonio's cigarette rose in the still air. The sky was a nocturnal sea, so large that one could see neither beginning nor end. The moon had floated into view a few minutes earlier. A cloud of light marked the point of the hill that would be a balcony for a silvery flirtation, a springboard for a clean dive, a platform for a new flight. A golden sliver subtly winked the glen that awaited it into being. Afterwards, there was the change from gold to silver, and from there to pearly white. With swollen and mended sails, night launched itself and sailed on. Below, silence and nostalgia waited.

December 1975, 1985, 1995. Always, the sea opens to the East. It was not raining, but the cold dampened the clothes and the restless dreams of the light sleep of slow suffocation. Old Antonio confirmed out of the corner of his eye that I was awake, and he asked me:

"What did you dream?"

"Nothing," I told him as I looked for my pipe and tobacco in my cartridge belt.

"Bad, then. One dreams and one learns. Dreaming, one knows," Old Antonio replied as he returned to the slow caress of the file across the tongue-shaped blade of his machete.

"Bad? Why?" I asked, now lighting my pipe.

Old Antonio stopped his sharpening and, after testing the edge, put the machete to one side. With his hands and his lips he lit a cigarette and began a story.

The Story of Dreams

"The story I'm going to tell you was not told to me by anyone. Well, my grandfather told it to me, but he warned me that I would only understand it when I dreamed it. So I'm telling you the story that I dreamt and not the one my grandfather told me." Old Antonio stretches his legs and rubs his tired knees. He releases a puff of smoke that clouds the reflection of the moon in the length of steel resting across his legs, and he continues . . .

"In every furrow of the skin that is borne on the faces of great grandparents, our gods are kept and they live. It is a faraway time that comes to us. The truth of our ancestors travels through time. The great gods speak through the oldest of the old and we listen. When the clouds settle over the land, barely grasping the hills with their little hands, then the first gods come down to play with the men and women; they teach them true things. The first gods reveal little with their faces of night and cloud. Dreams are what we dream in order to be better.

"Through dreams, the first gods speak to us and teach us. The man who does not know how to dream himself remains very alone and he hides his ignorance in

149

fear. So that they could speak, so that they could know and be known, the first gods taught the men and women of the corn to dream, and they gave them *nahuales* so they could walk through life.[2]

"The *nahuales* of the true men and women are the jaguar, the eagle and the coyote. The jaguar in order to fight, the eagle so that dreams fly, the coyote in order to think and to pay no attention to the tricks of the powerful.

"In the world of the first gods, those who formed the world, everything is a dream. The earth on which we live and die is a great mirror of the dream in which the gods live. The great gods live all together. They are equals. Not one is above or below the other. It is injustice, which makes itself government that splits the world and puts a few above and many below. It's not like that in the world. The true world, the great mirror of the dream of the first gods, those who created the world, is very large and everyone fits equally. It is not like the world of today that they make too small so that a few stay above and many remain below. The world of the present is not complete; it is not a good mirror reflecting the world of dreams where the first gods live.

"That's why the gods gave the people of the corn a mirror that is called dignity. In it, men see themselves as equals, and they become rebels if they are not equal. That is how the rebellion of our first grandparents began, those who now die in us so we might live.

"The mirror of dignity serves to defeat the demons that spread darkness. Seen in the mirror, the man of darkness sees himself reflected as the void that forms him. As if he were nothing, the man of darkness, the de-equalizer of the world, becomes undone in front of the mirror of dignity.

"The gods set out four points so that the world could lie down. Not because it was tired, but so men and women would walk as equals, so that all would fit, so that no one would put themselves above the other. The gods set out two points in order to fly and to be able to stand on the earth. The gods set out one point so that true men and women could walk. Seven are the points that give meaning to the world and work to true men and women: front and back, one side and the other, above and below, and the seventh is the path we dream, the destiny of the men and women of the corn, the true ones.

"The gods gave mothers a moon in each breast so they could nurture new men and women with dreams. History and memory come with them; without them, death and neglect eat up everything. The earth, our great mother, has two breasts so that men and women may learn how to dream. Learning to dream, they learn how to become great; to become dignified, they learn to fight. That is why when true men and women say, 'we are going to dream,' they are saying, and they are saying to each other, 'we are going to fight.'"

---

2 According to Mayan tradition, the Gods made human beings out of corn. See Part Four of *Popul Vuh: The Mayan Book of the Dawn of Life,* trans. Dennis Tedlock, 2nd ed. (New York: Touchstone, 1996). *Nahuales* are guiding animal spirits that embody abilities and wisdom accessible only to those who understand them.

Old Antonio fell silent. He fell silent or I remained asleep. I am dreaming that I dream, I am dreaming that I know, I am dreaming that I understand . . .

Above, the bosom of the moon offers milk on the road to Santiago.[3] The dawn was queen and everything was ready for doing, for dreaming, and for struggling.

El Sup, packing memories and bullets.

* * *

---

3 "Road to Santiago" refers to the Milky Way. See note in "On Bullfighting, Détente and Rock."

The Story of the Bay Horse

From January 1-8, 1996 the National Indigenous Forum was held in San Cristóbal de las Casas. The Forum, called by the EZLN and its advisors, was designed to receive the opinions and thoughts from indigenous peoples throughout Mexico whose decisions and proposals were to be taken up by the EZLN in the San Andrés talks. The Forum was attended by 24 comandantes of the EZLN, and nearly 500 representatives of more than 30 indigenous groups. Attending in disguise, Durito tells Marcos a story of a bay horse who changes the rules of the game. In his Closing Address to the Forum, Marcos explains Durito's recent silence while waiting for the results of the plebiscite on his popularity.

First published in *La Jornada*, January 10, 1996. Original translator unknown.

San Cristóbal de Las Casas
January 9, 1996
Through my voice speaks the voice of the Zapatista Army of National Liberation

Brothers and Sisters:
We want to say a few words to those present at this National Indigenous Forum.

I. Advisors
During the first days of January, there exists, in many of our indigenous communities in Mexico, the custom of reading how the months of the coming year will be. This knowledge tells when to prepare the earth, when to plant the seed and when to harvest. Among the most ancient Mayans, this practice was known as *Xoc-kin* or "the counting of the days."

And there were, as today there are among us, the most knowledgeable men and women: the *h-men*, "those who know."[1] These *h-men* had great knowledge that they had learned in their dreams. Through dreams the gods taught the *h-men* the knowledge of the world. In this way, they could find things that were lost, cure sickness with their herbs and their prayers, and see the future by reading their sacred stones or counting grains of corn. But their main responsibility and concern was to help ensure, with their guidance, a good harvest.

Today we have our *h-men*, those men and women of knowledge who make up the body of counselors of the EZLN in the search for a peace with dignity. These men and women are the ones who organized this forum that allowed us to find one another and build the bridge of the seventh rainbow.[2] They dreamed together of the great gods, the ones who gave birth to the world, the very first ones, and from them they learned their great words and their best thoughts. These men and women have been able to find things that were lost, like words, like reason, like unselfishness, like dignity. They have been able to cure that most mortal illness that exists, oblivion. These men and women can read the future by reading what their hearts say and counting grains of corn, which in today's world are called hearts.

But, just like our ancient *h-men*, their principal responsibility and concern is to help us with their guidance to ensure a good harvest. Therefore we want to ask you, the attendees of this National Indigenous Forum, to join us in this salute that we give to our advisors and that, together, we ask that with their wisdom they help bring about a good harvest in the sowing of words and understanding

---

1 "H-men" is an indigenous word, pronounced "achemen."
2 "The Story of the Seven Rainbows" was told by Marcos two days earlier at the Forum's plenary session on January 7, 1996, and published in *La Jornada* (January 8, 1996). See also EZLN, *Documentos y comunicados 3, 2 de octubre de 1995 / 24 de enero de 1997* (México, D.F.: Ediciones Era, 1997), 94-98.

of dignity that we fulfill today. We ask that they calculate the *Xoc-kin* well, that they calculate well the counting of the days so that our harvest may be good and the hearts of the brown men and women who first lived on these lands may never lose hope.

Some of our advisors are not here today; they have not been able to accompany us on this bridge that begins today for different reasons. But there is one group of our *h-men* that is not here because they are imprisoned.

They are accused of the crime of belonging to an organization with which the government dialogues under the protection of the law. By keeping them imprisoned, the government violates the law that obliges it to talk and not to fight. That is why these men and women who are our advisors, our counselors, are not here with us on this good road. We, the Zapatistas, want to ask all of you to send, together with us, a salute to these, our imprisoned advisors. And we ask that we all greet them, as is the custom in our indigenous communities, with applause.

II. Participants

The task of planting the seeds of the words that we have gathered in these days falls to us, the participants of this National Indigenous Forum. Here, in the Valley of Jovel, where today reign the intolerance, racism and stupidity that exclude, we have come together to speak and get to know one another.[3] We have gathered up the seed. We must prepare what we are planting: the future. Today we must live in a country that is not like the one of our ancestors. Today we live in a country with a government that wants to deliver us to foreign lands, sold as though we were animals, things. We, the indigenous people, are bad merchandise, they say. The great Power of money does not want to buy merchandise that does not produce good profits. And we indigenous people do not produce good profits. We are a bad investment. That is why the government shopkeeper gives us oblivion and repression for free, because he can't get a good price if he sells it to us. Today the shopkeeper said he was going to modernize his store and he has to eliminate all of the merchandise that is unattractive and we, with our dark skin and this desire to stay close to the earth, which makes us pretty short, are not attractive.

They want to forget us. But it is not only the indigenous who are threatened by this forgetfulness, there are also many other Mexican men and women who are unattractive because they can't be priced in dollars. They who are not indigenous, and we who are, have been condemned to oblivion. They sell our entire house and with it, our history. If we want to save ourselves from oblivion, we must do it together, united. Today the hope of this homeland that hurts us has an indigenous heart; it is up to its brown skin to start to save it from oblivion. It is no longer enough to die, this we have learned for five centuries. Now it is necessary to live for ourselves and to do so together with the others who are also us.

---

3 San Cristóbal de las Casas, the colonial capital of Chiapas, is located in the Valley of Jovel.

The past is the key to the future. In our past we have thoughts that can serve to construct a future, where we fit without getting squeezed as much as those who live above us squeeze us today. We will find the future of the homeland by looking to the past, to those who first sheltered us, to those who first thought of us, to those who first made us.

We have to prepare for the planting. We must become rain, we have to be like the *Chaacob* or gods of rain who came out of the cenotes and met in the sky to travel from there by horse, each one with his sacred gourd full of water, watering the earth from one side to the other so that all might have life-giving rain.

If the rain doesn't come, then we will have to squat down like our ancestors and sing like frogs do before it rains and shake branches as if a stormy wind were beating them and someone will play the role of *Kunu-Chaac*, the principal god of rain, with his lightning rod and sacred gourd.

We have to sow and cultivate ourselves. Gone are the days when stones were soft and could be moved with a whistle, when it wasn't necessary to labor to plow the cornfield, and one grain of corn was enough to feed a whole family. Since the chief was defeated by a foreigner at Chichen Itza, the good times have ended and the bad times have begun. The ancient chief entered a tunnel that led east from Tulum descending below the sea, and then the foreigner, the *Dzul,* took power. Now we have to return so that reason can reign again in our lands.[4] We will do this by sowing our word.

We are our earth. We understand well how the earth and we are one. In olden times, four spirits protected the planting field, what we call the *milpa,* and there were another four that cared for the village, there was one for each of the crosses planted at the corners of the village. The *macehuales,* our most ancient ones, had seven directions; the first four were the corners of the *milpa* or the village, the fifth was the center and each community was accustomed to marking it with a cross and, generally, a ceiba tree. The sixth and seventh directions were up above and down below. In addition to the four guardians of their field and the four of their village, each person had their individual guardian. To represent the five points, the four corners plus the center, our ancestors used a cross. As time passed the fifth point was lifted, and the four corners became five and then it was the five-pointed star that represented the guardian of the people and the planting season.

Guardian and heart of the people, Votán-Zapata, is also the guardian and heart of the word.[5] He, the man, the five-pointed star represents the human being, he. Now that we have spoken and listened, he is happy, the happy heart of Votán-Zapata, the guardian and heart of the people.

4 Chichen Itza was a Mayan city-state of the post-classic period, located in the northern Yucatan Peninsula. Tulum, also known as The Fortress (El Castillo), is a Mayan site dating from the late post-classic period, situated on the coast of the Yucatan Peninsula, near the present-day resort town of Cancun.

5 Votán-Zapata is the syncretism of Votán, the Mayan God known as the guardian of the people, and Emiliano Zapata, who rose up to fight for all Mexicans during the Mexican Revolution. See the communiqué that first appeared in *La Jornada* on April 10, 1995.

Brothers and Sisters:

Each of us has our own *milpa*, our piece of land, but we all belong to the same people, although sometimes we speak different languages and we wear different clothes. We invite each of you to plant in your own place and in your own way. We invite you to make of this Forum a good planter and we will see to it that the seed reaches everyone and that all the earth is well prepared.

Here we have listened to wise people and good planters such as our *Mixe* brothers and sisters whose position on autonomy has been a bridge between brothers and thoughts. With great truth our *Totonaco* and *Huichol* brothers have also spoken. From the states of Guerrero, Veracruz and Oaxaca, brown and dignified voices reach us speaking the word that is persecuted by Power and yet, still wise. Our *Chinanteco* brothers speak through the wisdom of the woman representing them. The *Mazatecos*, *Mixtecos* and *Zapotecos* have opened the eyes and ears that our heart possesses but sometimes forgets. The *Chatinos*, *Chochos*, *Chontales*, *Cuicatecos*, *Mayans*, *Nahuatl*, *Nanhu*, *Otomíes*, *Popoluca*, *Puréhpechas*, *Chocholtecos*, *Tarahumaras* and the *Tepehuas* are also light and color with their word. Our *Zapoteco* brothers from the United States also have given us the benefit of their thought. All who are seven, you, we, the brothers and sisters that we are.

All of them, you have undergone great suffering to get here, to speak with each other and, with us, to listen to each other and listen to us. We know it, but many others don't. You all came without our material help; your communities supported you so you could come here. And you always knew that you weren't coming to receive any land, money or promises. You always knew that you wouldn't leave here with anything material for you and your community. You always knew that you were coming to give your word and your example. And knowing all this, you made it here. And my *compañeros-jefes*, the commanders of the CCRI-CG of the EZLN, have ordered me to thank you in their name and in mine for all that is known and for all that is unknown. We want to thank you for having made it here, for having spoken and having listened, for reaching the good agreement that guides our path.

We have nothing material to give you; all we have is our greeting, which we ask that you accept as all greetings should be accepted, that is, as a gift.

III. Guests and Observers, CICR, Mexican Red Cross and Cordons of Peace[6]

As an observer at this National Indigenous Forum, a character has been present, who, timid as he is, slips away from the room at this moment. I refer to the very great and much loved Don Durito de la Lacandona, knight-errant and noble lord who rides the mountains of the Mexican Southeast. The highest and most dignified representative of the lofty and gallant profession of knight-

---

6 CICR is the Spanish acronym for the International Committee of the Red Cross. Peace observers organized to protect the EZLN leaders formed one of three different walls of people around the building where the peace talks took place; the other two were made up by the Red Cross and the Military Police.

errantry, the always lively Don Durito de la Lacandona has asked me, being as I am his squire and companion, to say a few words to you in his name. Due to one of those promises that knights-errant should make and fulfill, Durito has had to keep silent for some time, awaiting the results of the intergalactic plebiscite that he convened.[7] I should say, taking advantage of his absence and that he won't hear me, that his silence was pretty strident and he never gave me a dawn's rest, which, I believe all valiant squires deserve.

It happens that early this morning I was smoking and trying to think of how to tell you all that we thank you for coming, when suddenly I see that beneath the door something that looks extraordinarily like a beetle enters. It took me a moment but then I recognized . . . Durito!

Dressed in an old and torn coat, with a hat down to his eyes that in my estimation was too big for him, and a cane in his hand, Durito quickly told me that he was incognito to avoid his many admirers and he made it clear that it wasn't a cane he was carrying, but Excalibur, his righteous sword, camouflaged as a cane.

"The ones you need to avoid are the agents of the national security, the PGR, military intelligence, the CIA, the FBI and the etceteras who usually show up to these types of events," I told him, alarmed, as I watched him swipe a bag of tobacco.

"Quickly," he tells me, "Write down what I'm about to dictate because I have to leave!"

And without giving me a chance to ask the reason for his haste, Durito dictated to me the story called . . .

The Story of the Bay Horse

There once was a bay horse that was brown like a bay bean, and the bay horse lived in the house of a very poor *campesino* and the poor *campesino* had a very poor wife and they had a very skinny chicken and a lame little pig. And so, one day the very poor wife of the very poor *campesino* said: "We have nothing more to eat because we are very poor so we should eat the skinny chicken." And so they killed the skinny chicken and they made a skinny chicken soup and ate it. And so for a while they were fine but the hunger returned and the very poor *campesino* told his very poor wife: "We have nothing more to eat because we are very poor so we should eat the lame little pig." And so the lame little pig's turn came and they killed it and they made a lame soup out of the little lame pig and ate it.

And then it was the bay horse's turn. But the bay horse didn't wait for this story to end; and he fled and left for another story.

"Is that the end of the story?" I ask Durito, unable to hide my discomfort.

"Of course not. Didn't you hear that the bay horse left to go to another story?" says Durito as he prepares to leave.

---

7 The plebiscite was demanded by Durito in the "Story of the Hot Foot and Cold Foot."

"And so?" I ask exasperated.

"And so nothing, you have to go look for the bay horse in another story!" he says adjusting his hat.

"But Durito!" I say, attempting a protest that I know will be useless.

"Not one more word! You tell the story the way I told it to you. I can't because I have to leave on a secret mission."

"Secret? And what's it about?" I ask lowering my voice.

"Insolent knave! Don't you understand that if I tell you what it's about it stops being secret . . . Durito manages to say as he slips away under the door.

Durito already knows the results of the intergalactic consultation that ended with the year of 1995. He already knows that his victory was resounding and indisputable and that I have been condemned to narrating his great feats and marvels. That is why Don Durito de la Lacandona has already left to right wrongs and to astound the entire world with his achievements. The greatest thief of feminine sighs, the aspiration of men, admired by children, the great Don Durito de la Lacandona now returns to us. I know well that many of you rejoice at his return, but as for me, it doesn't please me at all to have to be the writer of such absurd and marvelous stories like these . . . *Stories for a Suffocating Night*.

IV. The Press

Finally, we want to thank the press that has also sacrificed to cover this Forum. And we want to make it clear that we are referring to the true press and not the police who hide behind a press badge. We know that we've been somewhat inattentive and discourteous; some of you have even said this is the press politics of the EZLN. But today we repeat what we told you almost two years ago here in San Cristóbal at the Cathedral talks: the press has had an important role in holding back the war and opening a path for dialogue and peace.

The press acted like a great mirror so that this country that is still called Mexico could see its true image reflected in a war against oblivion. We know that you are doing your job and that you do it with interest, professionalism and pride. We also know that, many times what is made public is not what you produced but only what suits Power and money.

Some of you complained yesterday that there were no political declarations that were newsworthy. You complained that El Sup only came to write literature with the stories of Old Antonio. So now we want to make a very clear political declaration, as are all the political declarations of the EZLN. And, in view of the audiovisual media present here, the declaration will come in the following, as a rough draft of a video script . . .

P.S. disguised as a video-clip.

First, a distorted image and a long and bothersome screech in the audio. Afterward, the image comes into focus and in the background you can hear that song "*Cartas Marcadas.*"[8] The images pile up: Power laughing approvingly, hastening its historic and definitive triumph in the last minutes of 1993. An army of shadows creeps in amid the cold and dampness. Power looks in the mirror and finds itself eternal and omnipotent. The great wise ones predict for him great triumphs, praise and robust statues throughout the land. A killjoy has promised him, "You will rule until the jungle walks toward your palace." A handful of shadows multiplied in the mountains. Power knows that it is impossible for the jungle to walk and its confidence and euphoria are confirmed. The great wise ones are at his side and pick up the crumbs of the feast. With wooden guns walks the collective shadow in the dawn of the beginning. In the dawn of 1994, the indigenous people come down from the mountains. They go to the palace of Power to claim death and oblivion. In their rifles made of wood walk the trees of the jungle. Power trembles and begins to die. A stick rifle has wounded it mortally. The end and the beginning.

And if this video-clip too closely resembles William Shakespeare's *Macbeth*, it's not my fault. Perhaps it belongs to the great gods who during these times are restless in Chiapas and choose to travel in other worlds and in another time; because that's how playful and mischievous these gods are, the greatest, the ones who bore the world, the first ones.

Thank you very much.

From the mountains of the Mexican Southeast
Subcomandante Insurgente Marcos
Mexico, January 1996

* * *

---

8 "*Cartas Marcadas*" ("Marked Cards") is a popular song from the movie of the same title starring Pedro Infante (1948), directed by René Cardona.

Durito to Conquer Europe

In a letter to the Fifth European Encounter in Solidarity with the Zapatistas, which took place in Paris on January 26-28, 1996, Marcos warns NATO that Durito is still thinking about embarking on the conquest of Europe. His letter also contains the First Declaration of La Realidad calling for Continental Encounters in the spring of 1996 and then an Intercontinental Encounter against Neoliberalism and for Humanity in the summer to take place in the Zapatista autonomous communities. This letter was sent during the EZLN consultation with Zapatista base communities regarding the agreements reached at the San Andrés negotiations on Indigenous Rights and Culture.

To the Comité de Solidarité avec les Peuples de Chiapas en Lutte
To those attending the Fifth European Encounter of Solidarity with the Zapatista Rebellion, Paris, France

This sounded nonsense to Alice so she said nothing, but set off at once towards the Red Queen. To her surprise, she lost sight of her in a moment, and found herself walking in at the front door again.

First published January 30, 1996. Originally translated by irlandesa. Source: *EZLN Documentos y comunicados 3 (2 de octubre de 1995 / 24 de enero de 1997)* (México, D.F.: Ediciones Era, 1997), 129-131.

A little provoked, she drew back and, after looking everywhere for the Queen (whom she spied out at last, a long way off), she thought she would try the plan, this time, of walking in the opposite direction.

It succeeded beautifully. She had not been walking a minute before she found herself face to face with the Red Queen, and full in sight of the hill she had been so long aiming at.

"Where do you come from?" said the Red Queen. "And where are you going? Look up, speak nicely, and don't twiddle your fingers all the time."

Alice attended to all these directions, and explained, as well as she could, that she had lost her way.

"I don't know what you mean by *your* way," said the Queen; "all the ways about here belong to *me*..."

—Lewis Carroll[1]

Brothers and Sisters:

In the name of my *compañeros*, the men, women, children and elders who make up the Zapatista Army of National Liberation, I am writing you to greet you and to welcome the celebration of this Fifth European Encounter of Solidarity with the Zapatista Rebellion.

You should know that we have not been able to send any of our Zapatista *compañeros*, and no one will be representing the EZLN at this Fifth Encuentro. Currently we find ourselves in the process of internal consultation in the Zapatista indigenous communities in order to respond to the proposals of the accords reached at the dialogue at San Andrés Sacamach'en de los Pobres. That's why it has been impossible for us to attend your Fifth Encounter. Nor have we been able to ask anyone (nor will we) to carry our voice to you. That is why we will again use the epistolary medium so that you can hear us.

Attached to this greeting you will find what's known as the *First Declaration of La Realidad* that calls for the celebration of the First Intercontinental Encuentro for Humanity and Against Neoliberalism. We wish to ask you to read it and, if you are in agreement, to sign it, next to the EZLN, so that, united, we summon the people to this encounter to find humanity and each other.[2]

We know that you have many issues to deal with at your encounter, but we implore you to take some time for this matter of the encounter that Durito calls "intergalactic."

Concerning this point, we wish to tell you the following:

We propose that the Organizing Assembly for the Intercontinental Encuentro for Humanity and against Neoliberalism of the European Continent

---

1 Lewis Carroll, *Through the Looking Glass*, ed. Donald Grey (New York: W.W. Norton & Co., 1992), chapter 2: "The Garden of Live Flowers," 123–124.
2 The First Intercontinental Encounter, held in Chiapas at the end of July 1996, was attended by over 3,000 activists from more than 40 countries.

be held the first week of April 1996 in Berlin, Germany.[3]

We also say to you that this is just a proposal, and, of course, we will accept if you choose another venue. In any case, be it in Berlin or some other place, we ask you to support the host group. We must begin to instill a new political culture where unity produces effects. And what better demonstration of that new politics than having that assembly (and those of the other continents) be the result of an international effort, and not just that of the host country. Is it not an attempt to form an international of hope? Well then, let us also smash the borders in another sense.

I would like to explain why we are proposing that the venue for the European organizing assembly be in Berlin. I could say that I plan to get the CCRI to send me as a delegate, or that I have always wanted to visit Germany, or that it is a narcissistic strategy for self-promotion (because of the *deutsche 'marks'*).[4] This is all true, but it is not the fundamental reason.

As the First Declaration of La Realidad says, the powers have sold us a lie as a truth, the lie of our defeat. Without much caring about defeating us in fact, the powers have devoted themselves to making us believe that we are defeated. Who? We, you, all of us who believe that a world is possible and necessary where democracy, liberty and justice would leave their comfortable utopias and libraries, and would come to live (and to struggle, which is a splendid way of living) with us.

On top of the lie of our defeat, the powers have constructed the lie of their victory. And the powers have chosen the Berlin Wall as the symbol of their omnipotence and immortality. Upon the ruins of the Berlin Wall, the powers built a larger and stronger wall: the wall of despair.

The wall continues there, it is part of history, but it does not mean the defeat of hope, or the victory of cynicism. In Berlin there is a fragment of the broken looking glass that we inherit as history.

As Alice discovers, that in order to reach the Red Queen she must walk backwards, so too we must turn to the past in order to move forward and to be better. In the past we can find the paths to the future. And we, you, have no greater aspiration than the future. That is why the past is important. If something new is born, it is because something old is dying. But, in the new the old can extend itself and it can consume the future if we do not contain it, become familiar with it, speak to it, listen to it, in sum, if we cease to fear it.

A symbol? Yes, a symbol. Why not pull something up from the remains of the old? What do we have to lose? Nothing, other than fear, shame, regrets . . . and nightmares.

---

3 The proposed meeting became the First European Continental Encounter that, along with similar meetings in America and Asia, prepared the way for the Intercontinental Encounter later that summer.

4 This is a play on words; in Spanish, German marks are called *marcos*.

Why not begin with a symbol? Why not begin to walk once more there, in the symbol that the powers maintain as the end of history and the eternity of their mandate?[5] Why not take that broken piece of the mirror in our hands? Perhaps we shall hurt our hands, but perhaps we shall manage to see, through one of the cracks in its reflection, the window that we seek, the one that we long for, the one that we deserve . . .

Berlin. The first week of April in the year 1996. Seven years later. Seven times seven walking to seven. Berlin. Why not?

Good, I repeat our greetings and wishes that everything goes well at your Fifth European Encounter in Solidarity with the Zapatista Rebellion.

Vale. Salud, and may we, together, encounter the Red Queen.

From the mountains of the Mexican Southeast
Subcomandante Insurgente Marcos

P.S. that alerts NATO.

Durito has not abandoned his idea of landing and beginning the conquest of Europe. He has invited me, but I have many reservations. The vessel he is preparing looks too much like a can of sardines. And besides, I'm afraid he wants to take me so that I can serve as oarsman, and, for me, any dampness that is not feminine makes me seasick . . .

* * *

---

5 Francis Fukuyama, a political science professor and senior researcher at the Rand Corporation, popularized the notion that with the fall of Soviet Communism humanity has arrived at the "end of history." See Frances Fukuyama, "The End of History?" *National Interest* 16 (1989), 3-18.

To Lady Civil Society

Citing chivalric code, Durito argues with El Sup on how to properly address a "Lady," in this case a character called: Lady Civil Society. Marcos, commemorating the first year anniversary of Zedillo's treacherous military invasion of indigenous communities in La Lacandona, salutes civil society's important role while condemning the imprisonment of civilians alleged to be Zapatistas. In closing, Marcos offers Lady Civil Society a red flower that Durito proposes be a carnation.

February 1996
To National and International Civil Society

Brothers and Sisters:

I write to you in the name of my Zapatista *compañeros*. I write to you so that, together, we remember that we have memory to remember that we must remember . . .

A year ago, maybe some will remember, government officials (including the so-called president of the republic) trampled over each other to make declarations against the "bad guys" of the movement (that is, against the Zapatistas), the military chiefs trampled over each other to make declarations about their "overwhelming" military victories (such as the destruction of libraries, hospitals and dance halls), and we trampled over each other in our withdrawal into the moun-

First published in *La Jornada*, February 10, 1996. Originally translated by Monique J. Lemaitre.

tains which we had already rehearsed in 1989. Among all the traffic and trampling, there was an "actor" (that's how they now call someone who takes action) with no particular name or distinctive face. An EZLN "transgressor"? No, something else, something better. It was a character that now receives the disdain of big politicians and "intellectuals" (those who used to trample over each other to pay honor to Carlos Salinas de Gortari and who now trample over each other to ask that public opinion not lead to "political and moral lynchings" of their illustrious former heads of state . . . and of their not so illustrious "intellectuals"). The character who is spared existence and efficiency is a bothersome and disconcerting character because there is no schema that locates him (which is a more subtle way of saying: "that co-opts him"), nor a definition that suits him. The most heroic character at the end of this century in this country whose rulers are determined to make disappear: lady civil society. Already Durito and My Other Self are on top of me (the first on top of my right shoulder and the second climbing on top of my left shoulder) criticizing me for the "lady" civil society . . .

"Don't masquerade as a feminist," My Other Self says. "Your machismo is public knowledge."

Durito doesn't question making her a woman, but rather my use of lower-case letters.

"You ought to know, my large-nosed squire, that knights-errant never refer to any female with a rank as high as "Lady" without the capital letter to introduce her, and this is so not only because one must proceed cautiously with women (especially if they are formidable), but because the supreme profession of knight-errant has no higher calling than to turn every young maiden into a lady. So amend that letter and mend your conscience because the lady, if she is indeed a lady, will choose to pardon you . . ." Durito continues reading a detective novel that Manuel Vázquez Montalbán sent for his review.[1]

So be it. Like a good squire I abide by what Durito said and I hope for a benevolent judgment for what was said by My Other Self. Where were we?

Oh, yes! In that Lady Civil Society (Durito leans over again and tells me that capitalizing the "L" of "Lady" is enough and that there's no need to exaggerate), well, in that Lady civil society didn't join (a year ago) the generalized trampling. Instead of staying at home, or at least on the sidewalk, civil society took to the streets and organized the streets (is there any mayor or city regent who can boast the same?) and turned them into first a brook and then a river and, if they're not

---

1 A Catalonian leftist, Manuel Vásquez Montalbán is one of Spain's best-known mystery writers. His main character, gourmet private eye Pepe Carvalho, roams the mean streets of Barcelona observing and critiquing the venality and corruption of Spanish business, politics and sports. The Carvalho novels include: *The Angst-Ridden Executive* (1977), *Southern Seas* (1979), *Murder in the Central Committee* (1981), *Offside* (1988) and *An Olympic Death* (1992). He published a book-length interview with Subcomandante Marcos, *El Señor de los Espejos*, in 1999 and a collection of his writings concerning Chiapas and the Zapatistas appears on the Montalbán website: www.vespito.net/mvm/chiapas.html.

careful, she wasn't far from turning them into a sea, complete with its sirens (for fog and the other kind as well). With civil society sailing upon itself (or does anyone award himself the honor of having organized it: I mean, aside from Muñoz Ledo?), the government stopped trampling over itself in its declarations and returned to its routine of contradicting itself.[2] The military stopped trampling over themselves in the destruction of libraries ("because there were none left," say the generals). And we Zapatistas stopped trampling over ourselves in our retreat ("because there was no where else to go," says Camilo). The dialogue returned, but this time along a longer and more tiring road. The "feat" of February 1995 (which is the one Mr. Limón Rojas wants to avoid when he says that Chiapas won't appear in textbooks.[3] "Because we are going to make Chiapas disappear," insists the smiling Del Valle, "and all that will be left of the Zapatistas will be their *zapatos*—that is why we have to abbreviate their name and situate those that we recognize as interlocutors in the future we're planning for them"). They will be left, along with thousands of indigenous people without houses or lands, a bunch of civilians imprisoned in the jails that the government has been building for *zapatos* and Zapatistas, since the time of Venustiano Carranza.[4]

The alleged Zapatista prisoners, imprisoned because they are "alleged" and because they are Zapatistas. Imprisoned are those who want a free, just and democratic country. Free are the presumptuous corrupt ones, free to be corrupt and to be presumptuous. Free are those who sold a Nation's freedom, those who mocked justice, those who defined democracy as "that's bullshit . . ."

The alleged Zapatista prisoners, imprisoned by Mexican soldiers. By Mexican soldiers who decorate their service records with the expulsion of the inhabitants of Guadalupe Tepeyac, with the destruction of Prado, with the demolition of the library of "Aguascalientes."[5] By Mexican soldiers like those who spend their salary on the prostitutes that their superiors "administer." By Mexican soldiers who do not understand why when the children of Guadalupe Tepeyac insult each other, they call their offenders "soldiers". By Mexican soldiers like those in the crews of the three helicopters that "disappeared" in January 1996 without a trace. By Mexican soldiers like . . .

Mexican soldiers who form the ranks of the Federal Army realize they were deceived. For years they were taught that their duty was to defend the homeland and now they find themselves pursuing indigenous people (like themselves) in Chiapas, Tabasco, Guerrero, Veracruz, Oaxaca, Hidalgo, Chihuahua, Michoacan, Campeche, Yucatán, Jalisco, Nayarit and in any state of the federation suspected of being a place where poor Mexicans reside.

---

2 Muñoz Ledo's reaction to the February 1995 military offensive is described in "The Story of the Hot Foot and the Cold Foot."
3 Miguel Limón Rojas was Secretary of Public Education when this communiqué was issued.
4 Venustiano Carranza became First Chief during the Mexican Revolution and in 1917 the first Constitutional President of Mexico.
5 See "Durito II" regarding military attacks on Prado Pacayal during the February 1995 offensive.

But didn't the politicians tell them that it was a question of only one group of "transgressors of the law" whose strength was limited to four municipalities? Didn't they teach them that one they called "General"—last name Cárdenas, first name Lázaro—returned to Mexico what belonged to it?[6] From the news, the Mexican soldiers find out that the oil wells they are taking in Tabasco will not be for Mexicans, but for a client with a different flag than the one with the eagle devouring a serpent;[7] from the news they find out that the oil profits that are the goal of Operation Rainbow in La Lacandona already have a destination and that the future owner speaks a language foreign to this history and these soils;[8] from the news, they learn that the U.S. government is militarizing the border with Mexico while they, the Mexican soldiers are ordered to militarize the borders of Mexico with Mexico; from the news, they learn that their "Commander-in-Chief," "Mr. President," is getting the highest homage that Europe bestows upon . . . a salesman![9] Mexican soldiers begin to question what they are doing persecuting Mexicans. Where did the homeland and its history go, where did honor and shame go . . .

But we weren't talking about soldiers. At least we weren't talking about soldiers armed with guns (or "with sticks," says Durito, who insists that the boots are the problem).[10] We were talking about Lady civil society, and of how, when no one knew what to do (I'm talking about politicians and members of the military regardless of their leanings or uniform), she knew what to do, and—surprise, she did it! When the time and smell of gunpowder and blood, salty like sweat, had passed, and after we sent those letters to national and international civil society, someone wrote to me and, among other things, asked me why we insisted so much in addressing civil society, since it was an entity that didn't exist ("for those in power, what cannot be accounted for doesn't exist," says My Other Self, who has a flair for axioms and skepticism), and that we were naive to hope for something from civil society that it could never achieve: the transition to democracy. Well, I told myself (because I didn't even answer the letter in writing), we have never hoped that civil society will achieve the transition to democracy.

---

6 Following a labor dispute with foreign companies in 1938, former President Lázaro Cárdenas nationalized all petroleum holdings.

7 The Zedillo administration used revenues from petroleum to cover its debt as part of the agreement for the $50 billion investor bailout provided by the U.S. in response to the peso crisis.

8 The Rainbow Task Force is the name for an elite counter-insurgency force developed to combat guerrilla forces as part of a strategy of low-intensity war. It operated in conjunction with other elite units, including the Aztec 7 Task Force designed to battle the "drug war" and the South Gulf Force organized to protect PEMEX oil wells and hydroelectric installations.

9 In late January 1996, Zedillo traveled to London and Madrid, where he was granted audiences with heads of state and representatives of the European Union, to lobby for trade agreements with Mexico.

10 Although the EZLN is a community that has taken up arms, not all members are able to carry guns. Remarkably, many Zapatista insurgents used pieces of wood carved to look like weapons during the January 1, 1994 offensive.

What we have hoped for, and still hope for, is that civil society may achieve something somewhat more complicated and as indefinable as herself—a new world. The difference between now and then is that now we want to participate along with her in that dream that may deliver us from the nightmare. We don't seek to direct her, but neither to follow her. We want to go with her, march by her side. Are we hopelessly naïve? Maybe, but against "realist" cynicism, naïveté may produce, for example, a January 1st, and just look at the heap of dreams brought about by one January 1st. So, we have nothing to lose: Lady civil society and the Zapatistas share the contempt the big politicians have for us, we share an indefinable face and diffuse name; why not share a dream? Believe me, no matter what happens when we awake, it will always be better, infinitely better than the nightmare we are now suffering . . .

Well then, allow me to salute through these letters, those men and women who are Zapatista political prisoners; allow me to salute their determination and their dignity. Allow me to salute the indigenous people of Chiapas, those men and women who have preferred a dignified example to a comfortable surrender.

But, above all, allow me to salute Lady civil society, the men and women who do not exist, who have no name, who are without a face. Allow me to thank them for existing, for having a little-known name, and having a face like any other. Allow me to give them a present, not a promise nor an intention, a flower, yes. A red flower. Red, not for blood or for ideas. Red just because, because I didn't find any other. Red because it's the color the moon turns when she blushes, full-faced, if she looks at herself in the mountain's mirror, and the mountain gives her back, as well, the best image of herself. A red flower that, carefully considered, is also a promise and an intention . . .

Vale. Salud, and may that red flower never lack water or hope . . .

From the mountains of the Mexican Southeast
Subcomandante Insurgente Marcos

P.S. that polemicizes. Durito has shown enthusiasm about the red flower. He proposes a carnation that goes well with knight-errantry, in addition to bullfighting. My Other Self is more traditional and leans towards roses. I say that there is no rose or carnation that can equal that moon that blooms up above, nor a gift bigger than the one that, without possessing it, we already have . . .

* * *

168

The Riddle

Durito appears in the postscript of this communiqué to give another clue to solve the riddle that first appears in "Of Trees, Criminals and Odontology" and continues in "Durito on Cartoonists." This clue comes while the Zapatistas are consulting with their base communities of support regarding the first table of the San Andrés Accords on Indigenous Rights and Culture.

First published in *La Jornada* on February 10, 1996. Original translator unknown.

February 1996
To the National and International Press

Ladies and Gentlemen:
I am sending this letter along with a communiqué to a familiar addressee.

I hope you will know how to interpret my lamentable and long absence from the epistolary medium. With such companions as were present, abstention was best. Now that, it seems, they have calmed down a bit, it is possible to relapse into so amiable a vehicle of expression. I am sure that you have already solved the riddle of the postscript "RORRIM EHT DNA OTIRUD" and that, of course, you will not tell me. For those who are still struggling, here is another clue (the previous one was in the letter-salutation to the Fifth European Gathering in Solidarity with the Zapatista Rebellion): there are seven times seven the seven mirrors. Simple, no? The governmental protests against the U.S. militarization of the northern border "forget" the national protests against the governmental militarization of the entire country. Why do they militarize Chiapas, Tabasco, Guerrero, Veracruz, Puebla and Oaxaca? To cover the backs of the governors in league with Salinas? Well, then soldiers need to be sent to Tamaulipas, Nuevo León, Chihuahua (yes, I know that it is dominated by the PAN, but for that very reason), and, "but of course," the well-promoted (in Europe) Aguascalientes.

Vale. Salud, and please! tell the PRI not to assassinate any of its high officials before the Zapatistas finish consulting with their communities.[1]

From the mountains of the Mexican Southeast
Subcomandante Insurgente Marcos
Mexico, February 1996

P.S. that the early bird gets.
Durito says that in the next episode he will solve the riddle. There's nothing to it, with all his hands and feet calculations are a breeze. To whomsoever solves it on their own, we'll give, at no cost whatsoever, a two-hour long talking session with the ex-leftist, ex-GCI, ex-Trotskyite, ex-ultra, ex-MAP, ex-"forty-niner," ex-*Punto Crítico*, and ex-smiley face, Jorge Del Valle.[2]

* * *

---

1 On February 16, 1996, after consulting with their communities, the EZLN, represented by 17 *comandantes*, signed the Accords of Indigenous Rights and Culture, which the government would later refuse to honor. Regarding assassinations, see note in "Durito Names Marcos Squire."
2 As a faculty member at the UNAM, Del Valle participated in the 1968 student uprisings and was also a member of the Internationalist Communist Group or GCI (Grupo Internacional Comunista) and other leftist groups.

Durito on Cartoonists

As the second round of the San Andrés negotiations on Democracy and Justice begin between the EZLN and the government, Durito and Marcos discuss cartoonists. Unfortunately, the topic becomes all too appropriate as the government negotiators refuse to discuss any of the EZLN's proposals and remain almost completely mute, turning the meetings into a caricature of negotiations. At the same time, in moves that revealed the government's hypocrisy in even pretending to negotiate, the police launched large-scale attacks against peasant squatters, killing three, while the military intensified its harassment in the villages.

March 21, 1996
To the National and International Press

Ladies and gentlemen
Yes, a communiqué. I also wanted to remind you that, exactly one year ago, I wrote to ask who was the author of "There are days when spring invades us through the smallest wound," and to date you haven't answered me. And, while

First published March 22, 1996. Originally translated by irlandesa. Source: *EZLN Documentos y comunicados 3: 2 de octubre de 1995/24 de enero de 1997* (México, D. F.: Ediciones Era, 1997), 198-201.

you are busy with falling helicopters and falling governors and placing bets on whether or not I will respond to Peace, the former confirms what Galeano wrote and says, I believe, "It was not pain, but it was painful. It was not death, but it killed."[1] You may pay no attention to me, but it is my duty to warn you that there is no analgesic or coffin for that pain.

Vale. Salud, and may "forever" be synonymous with "new."

From the mountains of the Mexican Southeast
Subcomandante Insurgente Marcos

P.S. that reiterates his poetic mediocrity. I was going to write, "The moon was a milky tooth in the nocturnal mouth of the jungle, a silver scarf fluttering alone, a diadem of light for those black and star-studded tresses." I was going to write that "A cloud flung the moon from the night like a dirty rag." I was going to write any one of these things, but it occurred to me that you had surely seen them already at the movies and so I am only going to write, "First quarter moon, relative humidity of so many millibars, partly cloudy with moderate winds from the south to the north . . ."

I was mending my boots and my heart when Durito arrived and told me that he had his contribution for *El Chamuco* ready.[2]

"So?" I asked him, without even turning around to look at him so as not to be distracted because when you have a needle in your hands, it's like having a sigh on your skin, that is, it can hurt.

"What do you mean, 'So'? Don't you know that I now dedicate myself to artistic cartoons? Besides, what are you complaining about? Wasn't it you who told that cartoonist named Wolinski that the world would be better off if it were governed by cartoonists?"[3]

"I not only said it, but I reaffirm it. Here in Mexico it's preferable to be governed by a cartoonist than by a cartoon."

---

1 Uruguayan writer Eduardo Galeano, an outspoken critic of the dehumanizing effects of globalization, is the author of numerous works and a regular contributor to *La Jornada*.

2 *El Chamuco* is a popular Mexican magazine of political cartoons, lampoon, and satire.

3 On December 15, 1995, near the Zapatista community of La Realidad, Marcos gave an interview to Francoise Escarpit, a writer for the French left-wing newspaper *l'Humanité*, as well as George Wolinski and Cyrán, cartoonist and editor, respectively, of the French humor magazine *Charlie Hebdo*. In the course of the interview, Marcos remarked that cartoonists "are the only ones who can laugh at themselves in the mirror. Politicians, when they see themselves in a mirror, see someone who listens to them: like [French President] Chirac who, seeing himself in a mirror, sees a man who accepts his arguments in favor of the bomb. When a woman sees herself in a mirror she smiles or she begins to cry . . . . When children see themselves in a mirror, they look for what is behind it . . . . Only cartoonists laugh . . . The World would be better if it were governed by cartoonists!" This passage, along with other excerpts from the French interviews, was subsequently published in *El Chamuco*, 1:2 (March 10, 1996), 15–20.

"You are right about that, and that makes me even more right."

"But," I interrupt him, "it's one thing to be governed by a cartoonist, and quite another to be governed by a cartoonist beetle. Let's just say, like my grandmother used to say, that's all we need!"

"What you need is a brain and a good sense of humor," Durito says, offended, but not enough to withdraw and let me finish the last (for now) patch. I keep quiet and pay veeery close attention to the final stitches.

Durito does not surrender (a true Zapatista beetle), and charges ahead:

"That stuff about your having a sense of humor is a myth lacking ingenuity. No wonder they say that you're in your twilight," Durito says, rather cuttingly.

"It would be 'We are in our twilight' because, may I remind you, we are in this together. If we rise, we rise together, and if we fall, we fall together," I respond, while I make the last knot (for now).

"Alright already, the only thing left for you to say is 'Till death do us part.' Besides, may I remind you that the intellectuals are repeating their criticism of your pretentiousness, and that's even without any mention or postscript about spring, and that reiteration has occurred to you in March for two years in a row," Durito says, while settling himself at his desk.

"Is that an attempt at censorship?" I say, standing up and stomping the ground with my boot, to see if the patches held and to remind Durito that the war, that is, the nightmare of boots, has not ended. Durito doesn't even notice, spreads a long parchment out on his desk and looks at it through the smoke from his pipe. After a bit, he says to me,

"Ah, my pale and haggard squire! You don't understand anything! It's not a question of censorship, but of good taste. Understand that you shouldn't confuse them: the wall that separates the pretentious from the sublime is thinner than the web of that spider that you have on your cap." The spider had already, in effect, woven an irreverent hammock between the faded, yet respectable, stars on my cap. I put up with it for a bit, but when it wanted to extend its domain to my nose, I said my "*Ya basta!*" and with a sublime sneeze, I sent it flying. Durito laughs.

"And, besides reading intellectuals, how am I going to know whether I write pretentiously or sublime things?" I asked, between repeated sneezes.

"It's veeery simple. When you write, you write pretentiously. And when I write, I write sublimely. If you write 'love,' you accompany it with a pennant from Irapuato.[4] And if I, the great and sublime Don Durito de la Lacandona, write 'love,' I accompany it with one of those lightning bolts that announce storms and shipwrecks. It's elemental; it's in all the treatises on aesthetics," Durito says, while scribbling on the parchment.

---

4 Irapuato, a city and municipality in the Mexican state of Guanajuato, is sometimes seen as a symbol of Mexican provincialism.

I sneeze in response and hide the little piece of paper where I had written, "It is not to mark the beginning of the hips of the moon, or to promise the wheat that your womb announces, nor to swell up soon with the life to come. Your waist exists only because of and for my embrace . . ."

Above, the rain purrs . . .

P.S. that fulfills the promise.

Durito sent a cartoon to Naranjo and another to Monsiváis.[5] And the parchment? I found it a little later. In it could be read the . . .

Preliminary, provisional, dispensable, predictable preconceived and premature instructions for solving the riddle of "Durito and the Mirror":

First. Take the pages of *La Jornada Semanal*, where that delirium of anarchy appears which the Sup disguised as a letter to Carlos Monsiváis, and spread it out on the floor, being careful that the four corners are turned towards the four cardinal points, according to the following instructions: the top right pointing to the South, the lower left corner pointing towards the North, the top left corner pointing towards the East, the bottom right corner pointing to the West.

Second. Take off your shoes (that is if the crisis hasn't already removed them for you), and, barefoot, stand right in the middle and on top of the spread-out newspaper.

Third. Now, dance, whistling that tango that says, "In my tumble downhill, illusions of the past, etcetera." (No, it doesn't matter if you have a bad voice. We're solving a riddle, not doing an audition to play a well-known ex-president.)

Fourth. That done, and if the newspaper hasn't been torn, make a little paper boat or a little airplane out of the same material.

Fifth. If you made a little paper boat, then take a pill for seasickness, and embark through the dampness of your choice.

Sixth. If you made a little paper airplane, then close your eyes to avoid getting vertigo, and hang from that odor which your dampness of choice tends to have.

Seventh. Now, turn on your computer and start to play the game that you most enjoy. (Note: if you don't have a computer, you can replace it with an abacus.) Yes, I know that the riddle won't be solved this way but, instead, you'll have some fun for a while.

Good, that's all for now. Don't forget to send your solutions to our address for intergalactic correspondence: Little Huapac Leaf #69, Mountains of the Mexican Southeast, Chiapas, Mexico.

---

5 Naranjo, a prominent Mexican political cartoonist regularly published in *Proceso* and *La Jornada*. He is also mentioned in Marcos' letter to Monsiváis included in this collection as "Of Trees, Transgressors, and Odontology."

Last minute note. Due to the tumult of protests we received at the prospect of having to listen to the ex-gentleman Del Valle's "witticisms," we have changed the prize for solving the riddle.[6] Now the reward is a voucher for a drink and a sandwich (so that Mr. Zedillo no longer fails you in economy), which can also be cashed in if you mention that the PAN, the PRI and the PRD will succeed in becoming "centrist" parties, and that you, my dear reader and permanent candidate to take an unusual exam, realize that you are at the very . . . bottom.

Who would say that '97 is being decided in the spring of '96? Quirks of the calendar, I believe.

* * *

---

6 See note in "Durito's May Day Postcard."

Durito IX: Neoliberalism, History as a Tale ... Badly Told

Durito helps Marcos write his presentation to the First Continental Encounter against Neoliberalism and for Humanity, held in Chiapas in April 1996. Here, Durito points out how neoliberalism reduces history to a poorly written tale that glorifies the powerful and ignores everyone else. In the tale of neoliberalism, he argues, only money counts and dignity is bought and converted into a commodity. After a brief digression on Mexican rock bands and a display of his personal style of dance, Durito finally hands El Sup his own, one-sentence paper on neoliberalism, and introduces the notion of "Duritismo."

First published in *La Jornada*, April 10, 1996. Originally translated by Esther Rodríguez and Robin Yeamans. "Tale" is a translation of *historieta*—a comic book or simplified storybook with illustrations.

Zapatista Army of National Liberation
Mexico, April 6, 1996
La Realidad, America[1]

I saw that the moon was slowly beginning to deflate, like those old balloons that get tired of holding air and shrink, little by little, like the spirit shrinks when goodbyes draw near. I was thinking that, perhaps, the night was walking so much that the edges of the moon were being worn away by its grinding feet and that the stars are nothing more than the dust left behind. I was thinking of those things and, of course, nothing occurred to me about what to say on neoliberalism at one of the tables of the continental encounter, and I knew well that we had already committed ourselves, and anyway I wasn't thinking about that, but instead I was looking at the moon, trying to guess what she could be announcing or what was hiding that deformity that made her shrink. I was surely in what one might call a state of "lunatic irresponsibility," when a black, shiny object fell on my nose. It bounced and landed on my feet, it began to climb up my pants and it wasn't until it reached my right knee that I was able to make out a figure very similar to a beetle. And yes, it could well be considered a beetle if it were not for the unfolded paper clip that he carried in one right hand, the little lid of a flask that he carried in another right, the small twig that was bound to his belt, and the *cololté* shell that he wore on his head. I should say that the single horn that jutted out in the middle of his face could well cause one to confuse this being with a unicorn, but no, it was clear as the moon that will keep us awake tonight that this was not a unicorn. I declared myself firmly disconcerted and, as always when I find myself firmly disconcerted, I devoted myself to sneezing with that vivacious and frolicsome style that has caused the joy and delight of small and big ... pharmacists. One of the sneezes fully reached the figure that had already managed to climb two inches above my knee. He went down to the ground, and again began the ascent, but this time up the left leg. I pretended not to notice and I amused myself looking at how the moon, worn away and all, was flinging clouds to one side and another. Suddenly I heard a voice telling me,

"It's common knowledge that going by way of the right one always ends up falling down. Going by way of the left usually takes work, but at least one gets there."

I thought that it was the voice of some of the presenters in this Continental Encounter, and that the wind had been able to catch in a ripple a fragment of what was said and that it had allowed it to fall right above me when I was occupied with moons and astral erosion. I would have been satisfied with this veeery logical explanation if it were not for something pricking me in the neck and I could see, on my left shoulder ...

---

1 *La Realidad* literally means "reality," but it is also the name of a Zapatista community in the Highlands of Chiapas. Marcos' use of the term "America" designates both American continents together, not just the United States.

DURITO IX
(Neoliberalism: History as a Tale . . . Badly Told)

"I am speaking to you, brainless simpleton," says Durito while he reiterates his pricks with the paper clip against my neck.

"And it is not a paper clip, ignorant plebeian, it is a knight-errant's lance," says Durito while he finally leaves his paper clip, I mean his lance, to one side and takes out his pipe and lights it. I take advantage of the pause to tell him,

"Durito, it's a good thing you've come. Listen, I have a big problem . . ."

"Just a moment!" says an indignant Durito. "Since when are squires here allowed the sacrilege of directing themselves to their masters and sires, the knights-errant, in such disrespectful and inappropriately equal terms? Have you forgotten, pale and big-nosed rogue, what I have taught you of the sacred laws of knight-errantry?"

The "pale" and the "rogue" offended me. As for the "big-nosed," I was not offended because one should not hold a grudge against nature. I began to protest . . .

"But, Durito . . ."

"No 'but' nor any 'Durito'! I am the great and sublime Don Durito de la Lacandona, the highest example of knight-errantry, the supreme righter of wrongs, the dark object of desire of all women who consider themselves so, the superior status to which all honest males aspire to rise, the hero of children, the comfort of old men, the best and only one!" says Durito while he unsheaths his twig, pardon, his sword "Excalibur," sucks in his chest and sticks out his belly, pardon, I meant the other way around, although the truth is that with Durito, it is very difficult to make out which one is his chest and which his belly. Well, in any case, Durito looks truly indignant, so I had better opt for a conciliatory attitude.

"And should I address you, pardon me, address THEE, with all those qualifiers?"

"That you should, but this morning I arose magnanimous and generous, so you can call me "Don Durito" or simply "Sir."

"Okay, Don Durito or simply Sir, I was telling your grace that I have a serious problem that distresses my soul and clouds my vision with anxiety," I said, and I accompanied my words with a bow, because of that business about the relationship between plebeians and noblemen.

"Well, that's better," says Durito, now seated on the edge of my shirt collar, sufficiently close to leave my line of sight, and to manage to wound me with the lance if the circumstances and his mood deem it necessary.

"And what is the problem that brings so much anguish to a soul as simple as yours? Are you, perhaps, lovesick?"

"No," I responded decisively. "Well, not only that," I continued doubtfully. "Well, I mean, that is, you see, well, it really is something else," I ended, firmly emphasizing my indecision.

"Well, stop stammering and spit it out.[2] Durito becomes impatient.

"Well, it turns out that I have to write a paper for the American continental encounter for humanity and against neoliberalism. That's one thing, but the problem is that I have not thought of a topic to develop. I have here some drafts that I made ...," I say while I take out a file of papers.

Durito snatches them from me immediately and begins to review them with impatience.

"Hmmm, hmmm, hmmm," murmurs Durito while he chews on his pipe. I already know what those "hmmms" mean, so I sneeze to urge Durito to hurry. Durito just takes out a little umbrella, and continues his reading. After awhile, he remains silent, and he looks fixedly at me.

"And well?" I ask him, impatiently.

"Rather you should ask, 'And bad?'" says Durito and continues, "Your prose, my illiterate squire, is lamentable. Your resemblance to my colleague Cyrano de Bergerac is limited to the exaggerated promontory that you wear as a nasal appendage.[3] Although one must duly recognize that, in size, yours notably surpasses that of Bergerac."

"Well, it's best we not speak of promontories, my illustrious gentleman," I say as I sneeze with such emphasis that the storm of a while ago is forgotten.

"Fine, it is common knowledge that it is neither the time nor the way to speak about mirrors, so I'll continue," says Durito, putting away the little umbrella and putting on an asbestos suit.

"Hmmm. This part about the economy is too political, this one about culture is very economical, the political one is very cultural, and the social one has everything except society. So, what we have ... it's useless!"[4]

"I already know that. The question is, how do we solve the problem?" I reiterate my impatience to him.

"Not to worry. You have before you the greatest and most wonderful righter of wrongs the world has ever seen. I will see you through this predicament, into which your proverbial inexperience has put you," says Durito while he throws my papers into the latrine nearest to his heart.

With bitterness and pain upon seeing how my papers flounder in the simile of neoliberalism, I tell him,

"And how do you plan to solve the dilemma, my lord?"

"Veeery easy. I have with me a magic potion that a great sorcerer of the Amazons gave me. It has wonderful properties, and it can make miracles happen," says Durito while he extracts from his shell a tiny bottle of sherry.

---

2 The original Spanish suggests a pun on *chiclés*, "gum," and *chicles*, "rubbish."
3 Cyrano de Bergerac, the central character in Edmond Rostand's 19th-century novel by that name, not only had a huge nose, but was a skilled writer whose words won the heart of a woman he loved—for another.
4 At the suggestion of the EZLN, discussions at the first continental and intercontinental encounters were organized around the "social," "political," "economic," and "cultural" dimensions of, and struggles against, neoliberalism.

I ask, "And if one drinks that liquid, can he understand neoliberalism and construct an intelligent alternative?"

"Of course not! This liquid works wonders on the luster of any type of shell. It has given me a 'look' that has caused a furor among the respectable," says Durito while he throws the liquid on his back and rubs it in with my bandana, well, with what remains of it.

"But, Durito . . . what does the shine of your shell have to do with neoliberalism?" I say, forgetting all the protocol of knight-errantry.

"Quiet! Attention everyone! Quick! Pen and paper! Take note for I am about to speak!" says Durito, going to a pasture that, if not for fifteen million ticks and four cows, was vacant of any listeners.

Durito clears his throat and puts on some eyeglasses that I had not seen on him before. One of the bullets that he carried in the chinstrap of his helmet is his improvised pulpit and, without any paper, he begins to speak, directing himself to the mirror that we all are:

"In neoliberalism, my squalid squire, history becomes an obstacle because of what it represents of memory, graduate students are promoted into forgetfulness and the meticulous statistics of the trivialities of Power become the object of study and of great and profound dissertations. Power converts history into a badly told tale, and their social scientists construct ridiculous apologies with, indeed, a theoretical scaffolding so complex that they are able to disguise stupidity and servility as intelligence and objectivity. In the tale of neoliberalism, the powerful are heroes because they are powerful, and the villains to be eliminated are the 'expendables,' that is to say, Blacks, Asians, Chicanos, Latinos, the indigenous, women, the young, prisoners, migrants, the ones who have been screwed over, homosexuals, lesbians, the marginalized, the elderly, and, very especially, rebels. In the tale as told by Power, the happening that is worth something is the one that can be recorded on a spreadsheet that contains respectable indices of profit. Everything else is completely dispensable, especially if that everything else reduces profit.

"In the tale as told by Power everything is foreseen and determined ahead of time: the bad can be bad, but only to contrast with the power of good. The ethical balance between good and evil transforms into the amoral balance between Power and the rebel. For Power, money carries weight; for the rebel, dignity carries weight. In its tale Power imagines a world not without contradictions, one with all the contradictions under control, administrable as escape valves that let off the social pressures that Power provokes. In its tale Power constructs a virtual reality where dignity is unintelligible and not measurable. How can something have value and carry weight that is not understood and that doesn't change? Ergo, dignity will be defeated, irremediably, by money. So 'no problem,' there can be dignity because money will already take charge of buying it and converting it into merchandise that circulates according to the laws of the market . . . of Power. But, it turns out that the tale as told by Power is just that, a tale, a tale that disdains Reality and, therefore, a badly told tale. Dignity continues escaping from the laws of the market and begins to have weight and value in the place that matters, that is to say, in the heart . . ."

Durito takes a deep bow. The crickets applaud loud and long, figuratively speaking. I venture a,

"Well, it's dense . . ."

"Silence! Don't ruin art with your trivialities and addendums!" protests Durito while he puts away his glasses. Then he continues:

"I hope that you have taken note of everything and that this brilliant dissertation helps you out of your jam."

"Actually, I believe that it has confused me more," I say, trying to hide the fact that I didn't write a single letter.

"You're hopeless. Your reasoning is as limited as your nose is limitless. Better we leave that matter in peace, and inform me of the latest happenings," says Durito with resignation.

I take out my notebook, stand at attention and report,

"'El Serpiente Motorizado' has said that they propose La Realidad be electrified and that its first installation will be . . . an electric chair that will be at the disposal of all those who perform the 'slam.'"[5]

"Ah! *Cosas veredes* Sancho!" muses Don Durito.[6]

"Moreover, everyone says that the best musician in El Serpiente Desvielada is La Flama and the only thing that *he* plays is the horn," I say while I load a round, just in case anyone wants to kill me.

"What that 'Serpiente de Hoy No Circula' needs is for I, the great Head-Banger Durito, to incorporate myself as artistic director."

"Will they learn to play like that?" I ask while I prepare the hard rock version of "Cartas Marcadas" in case we have to do a "number."

"Don't even think about it, however, I'm sure that our concerts will be filled to capacity with those who come to admire my style of *baile*, which I call 'Durito's Dance.' *Wacha bato*—look at this *beautiful* move!" says Durito as he begins a kind of epileptic seizure.[7]

I remind the great and never prudent Don Durito de la Lacandona that it is not the time go twisting things around and that we have to solve the problem of the paper for humanity and against neoliberalism. The reminder takes me many

---

5 Throughout this story Marcos and Durito are garbling words, and using hybrid slang terms. *El Serpiente Motorizado* ("The Motorized Snake") is the name of a musical group that attempted to raise money for Zapatista communities. The group is referred to as *El Serpiente de Hoy No Circula* ("The Snake that doesn't drive today") a play on Mexico City pollution-control campaigns that rotate driving privileges, and as *El Serpiente Desvielada* ("The Broken Down Snake"). The English "slam" in the Spanish original is presumably a reference to slam-dancing. Marcos has often said that "Cartas Marcadas" ("Marked Cards") is his favorite song. See note in "The Story of the Bay Horse" These items are referenced in: *Desde las montañas del sureste mexicano* (Mexico: Plaza y Janés, 1999), 20-21.

6 "*Cosas veredes*," a phrase connoting archaic Spanish and popularly attributed to Don Quijote, translates literally as "the things you will see."

7 "*Wacha bato*" is Caló for "Check it out, man!"

sneezes because Durito mistakes the first ones for applause.

"Ahem, ahem," says Durito while he readjusts his helmet and again sheaths "Excalibur," which had simultaneously played the roles of guitar, piano, drums and electronic synthesizer. The paper clip stops being a stand-up microphone and is once again the fierce lance of the knight-errant.

"You are right. It is necessary to return to the prosaic things of this world. I have foreseen your incompetence . . ." This said, Durito takes some papers out from I don't know where.

"Here is my paper. Make five million copies and distribute them throughout *La Realidad*," says Durito while he tosses the pages to me.

"If you speak of the community La Realidad, that will be too many copies, and if you speak of *the* real *reality* that'll be too few," I say while I thumb through his writing. The title is:

"Promissory Elements For An Initial Analysis As The First Basis Of An Original Approach To The First-Born Fundamental Considerations Concerning The Supra-historical And Supercalifragilisticespiralidocious Foundation Of Neoliberalism In The Decisive Juncture Of April 6, 1994 At 01:30 Hours On-The-Dot, Southeastern Time, With A Moon That Tends To Empty Itself As If It Were The Pocket Of A Worker At The Peak Of Privatization, Monetary Adjustments And Other Economic Measures So Effective That They Provoke Encounters Such As That Of *La Realidad* (First Of 17,987 Parts)."

The paper is quite concise. In fact, it is composed of a single sentence that goes like this:

"The problem with globalization under neoliberalism is that bubbles have a tendency to burst."[8]

I scratch my head after reading. Durito becomes restless:

"Well? What do you think?"

"Well, what can I tell you," I respond carefully. "At least let us recognize that the workshop coordinators will not have to struggle with the synthesis."

"Come on. Don't be stingy with your praise! And do not fear, my modesty is proverbial. You can say that it is clear, overwhelming, illuminating, clarifying, undebatable, definitive and defining. You can add that it's at the forefront of a new scientific paradigm, that it's no longer a secret who will win the Nobel prize in economy, that a new science is born, that 'Duritismo' will revolutionize all research and all economic models, that world history will from now on be organized as 'before Durito' and 'after Durito.'"

"No," I say hurriedly, "let's not exaggerate."

---

8 At the beginning and end of this article Marcos makes a play on the double-meaning of the Spanish "*globos*," which translates literally as both balloons and globes, and evokes speculative financial bubbles.

"Well," says Durito sliding down one of my guns, "I have to leave because there is going to be a concert, and it is known that a serpent on wheels, without me, will end up with flat tires."

Durito leaves. The moon takes overhead a cloud of petticoats and its blush stains the edges. Underneath there are men and women dreaming, wheat celebrates existence, and I sigh as if ending, as if continuing, as if beginning . . .

Vale. Salud, and do not be sad. The moon and hope always return. And do they give up? Never!

From the mountains of the Mexican Southeast
Subcomandante Insurgente Marcos

P.S. In La Realidad, during the Continental American Encuentro for Humanity and Against Neoliberalism, Old Antonio discovered that all those who had boarded the boat were the same ones who had been excluded, forever, from all the boats.

And that is why they boarded, Old Antonio told Subcomandante Marcos, because those men and women—young people, some prisoners, most of them indigenous—"no longer wanted to follow orders, but to participate, whether as captains or sailors" and to make the boat move forward, towards a greater future, with seriousness and joy, meeting as full human beings.

But indeed, warned Old Antonio, between cigarettes, there will be many shadows, and it will take much work to find the midnight sun, "that which joins word and desire about itself. That is why I wanted to tell them not to go, that, if they remained, they would also see the moon turn itself into drum and beat desire with the wind. And they would see that the crickets are nothing more than lazy stars who are constantly complaining about having fallen down, that the fireflies paint teardrops and that the light can be perceived in even the darkest corners of the night."

* * *

Durito on Liberty

Appealing for support from civil society, Marcos offers "definitions" of three words: *Liberty*, which Durito compares to daybreak; *Struggle*, which Old Antonio's likens to a circle and *History*, which Marcos describes as scribbles in the sands of time. This communiqué was written during increasing repression against the EZLN and Zapatista communities in conjunction with the government's sabotage of the March negotiations at San Andrés on Democracy and Justice. It also follows the EZLN's convening of the First Continental Encounter in La Realidad in April.

To National and International Civil Society
May 18, 1996

Wherever You May Be Found:
Excuse me, Lady Civil Society, for distracting you from your numerous activities and countless anxieties. I am only writing to tell you that we are here, that we continue to be ourselves, that resistance is still our flag and that we still believe in you. Whatever may happen, we shall continue to believe. Because hope, my lady of many faces and great name, is now an addiction for us.

First published May 20, 1996. Originally translated by irlandesa. Source: *EZLN: Documentos y comunicados*, 3: 2 de octubre de 1995 / 24 de enero de 1997 (México D.F.: Ediciones Era, 1997).

Thy grace will now know that the horizon is becoming overcast, with a gray fading to black with the same alacrity with which our history is being sold. Nonetheless, know that liberty is still there, ahead, that it continues to be necessary to struggle, and that history still waits for the one who shall complete the plans. That is how things are. Fearing that we shall not see you again, accept these three straightforward, simple definitions, which very much suit days as tragic as those which are awaiting us:

Liberty. Durito says liberty is like the morning. There are those who wait for it to arrive while sleeping, but there are also those who stay awake and walk throughout the night to reach it. I say that we Zapatistas are addicts of the insomnia of which history despairs.

Struggle. Old Antonio said struggle is like a circle. One can begin at any point, but never end.

History. History is no more than the scribbling that men and women write in the sands of time. The powers write their scribbles, they praise them as sublime scripture, and they worship them as the only truth. The mediocre are limited to merely reading the scribbles. He who struggles smudges the pages as he passes. The excluded do not know how to write ... yet.

Accept, my lady, these three flowers. The other four will arrive later ... if they arrive at all.

Vale. Salud, and remember that wisdom consists in the art of discovering hope behind the pain.

From the mountains of the Mexican Southeast
Subcomandante Insurgente Marcos

P.S. I forgot to warn you, my lady, to not be deceived by officials, columnists and etceteras that infinitely echo the lie. Nothing is resolved; everything is shattered. And there are, essentially, two gambits: theirs, that of war, which bets on your continuing to remain indifferent; and ours, that of peace, which bets on your dancing up a storm, which will make everything tremble, exactly as love trembles, when it is true.

P.S. that translates:
The translators in Paris are asking if, in the American Continental Encounter, I said, "zapatismo is an institution." I said "zapatismo is an intuition," but, if zapatismo ends up being an institution, then it is a bad intuition. The "*focador,*" *mon cherie,* comes from "*foco*" or flashlight, and not from "*foca*" or seal, whose wetness I shall not speak of, or else I will be in trouble with the feminists. Onward, then.

* * *

Durito's Comment on Hunger

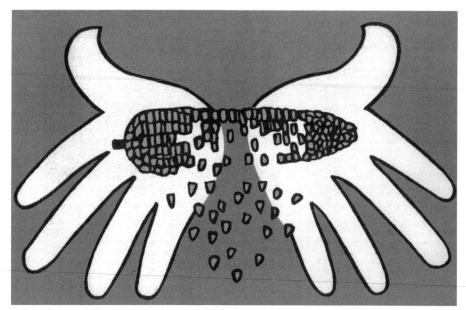

Writing to the National Campaign for Peace and Against Hunger, Marcos takes the opportunity to reaffirm the Zapatista commitment to struggle for peace and against the violence of the federal government. He also shares a brief dialogue with Old Antonio about hunger and hope. Durito appears at the end of this communiqué lightening the mood with a demand for a Campaign for Pecan Ice Cream for My Beetle.

June 1996

To: The National Campaign for Peace and Against Hunger, Grain for My Brother[1]

Brothers and Sisters:

We want to take advantage of your meeting to send you greetings and our appreciation of the concerns around which you have organized and gathered together.

First published in *La Jornada*, June 9, 1996. Originally translated by irlandesa.

1 The Caravan, "*Un grano para mi hermano*" (Grain for My Brother), left Mexico City's Zócalo with food and supplies for the communities of Chiapas on July 10, 1996.

A few weeks ago, in response to the government campaign that was hiding its interest in resuming the fighting—behind a so-called campaign against drug trafficking—our Indigenous leaders of the CCRI-CG of the EZLN decided to respond with the campaign "For Indigenous Peoples: No to Soldiers and War, Yes to Corn and Peace." Since 1994, the EZLN has responded with peace initiatives to each war initiative made by the government. You are familiar with them. Time and again the Zapatista communities have declared themselves to be for a dignified peace; the government's peace is synonymous with death or surrender. That is why we cannot reach an agreement. We rebel indigenous people have decided to resist, to not make war, but also not to surrender. We believe that our position is understood by many Mexicans and honest people in other countries. We also know that we are not the only ones who are resisting and who are rebels. Throughout the territory of the Mexican nation, points of resistance and rebellion exist that do not acquiesce to the Opposition, but long to build something new and better. Here, in the mountains of the Mexican southeast, thousands of Tzeltal, Chol, Tzotzil, Tojolabal, Zoque and Mam families resist, as they have resisted for hundreds of years, with patience and hope. You, through your efforts, make it possible that both patience and hope become strong and are healing.

Here there is a race between time and life. "This is the time of hunger. And, through hunger, time tries to kill man. Only hope relieves man from time's wound," Old Antonio said when, on an early morning in June ten years ago, he saw the corn barely rising up in the field. "There is no corn in the huts or in the fields. It is a time of hunger, of waiting. Look how the corn is beginning to paint the fields green, look how the rain is beginning to relieve the dryness and the hardness. The two, corn and rain, are telling us that we must wait, that one must resist, that one doesn't have to die. The time will soon come when the corn reaches the huts and the tables of the true men and women, the time will come when the rains wash away the sorrow from the hard ground. But while the time of time is arriving, many will die because hunger and sorrow defeat them." Old Antonio had just buried one of his children. "She didn't make it," Old Antonio said, after putting up the cross, bound with reeds that marked a little girl's grave, the child whom Doña Juanita and he, Old Antonio, had brought to life.

"Hunger and man, man and hunger. That's what those two opposites were named, that's what the very first gods called them, those who gave birth to the world, to death and to life, *hunger* was called death, *life* was called man. There must be some reason . . .," Old Antonio said after seeing, with despair, how the corn was just a few centimeters above the ground. He lit his pipe and, now walking towards the hill, he invited me to accompany him to seek the edible roots used to distract death.

Yes, I know this memory of Old Antonio has nothing to do with your meeting, but it came to me when, on the hill facing me, I saw a newly sown cornfield and three helicopters staining the horizon. Those helicopters carry soldiers; they don't carry corn. They promise hunger and death, they drive away peace and life.

187

For Peace and Against Hunger: Isn't that what your campaign is called?"

"That's what it's called," Old Antonio tells me (who is a good distance ahead of me now, since my clumsy way of climbing hills is now legendary in the mountains of the Mexican southeast). "Or what is the same thing: For Man and Against Death," Old Antonio says while he waits for me, as usual, that is, smoking. And, as everybody knows, no one can beat Old Antonio when it comes to translating struggles and hopes . . .

Yes, I know I wandered off the topic and I should limit myself to just thanking you and telling you that we are waiting here for you, but now you see how, rain, suffocation, sleeplessness . . . and Old Antonio appear in the dawn of June. Well then, here it is:

Thank you brothers and sisters. We are waiting for you here.

Vale. Salud, and may those who should win in the struggle against hunger, win, that is, the children.

From the mountains of the Mexican Southeast
Subcomandante Insurgente Marcos

P.S. Durito wants to know when someone will think of having a campaign called "Pecan Ice Cream for My Beetle." I told him it doesn't rhyme, but Durito said that when faced with pecan ice cream, meter is allowed certain poetic license.[2] I gave him some tobacco. "It doesn't taste the same," Durito objects, but he refills and lights his pipe, and he continues writing. "What are you writing?" I ask him. "Ah! A surprise," he says as he shelters himself from the rain under a little leaf.

* * *

---

2 "*Un helado de nuez para mi escarabajo*" is the original Spanish version of the slogan.

Big Sharks and Little Fishes

Once again, the great Don Durito de la Lacandona helps Marcos prepare a presentation. This time it is on "Culture and Media in the Transition to Democracy" for the First Intercontinental Encounter that was hosted in five different Zapatista communities at the end of July 1996. Durito recounts a story he claims to have dictated to Bertolt Brecht back in the 1940s about what would happen if "sharks were people." He then goes on to elaborate that story on his little microcomputer, adding revolt to a parable of divided communities. This elaboration was written during a period in which state funding and the provision of arms and training was expanding the presence of paramilitary forces such as Los Chinchulines and Paz y Justicia as part of a counterinsurgency strategy aimed at splitting local communities and terrorizing Zapatista supporters.

July 1996

July reaps the humid legacy of the June night and, nonetheless, allows a bit of sun to slip into the gray day. The moon offers, as consolation for its absence, the nostalgia of ceiba trees and jungle mud. A failed military intelligence satellite grows bored and yawns ostentatiously. Down below, it makes out men and women talking and listening, walking, tripping and walking once more, seeking. They are seeking many things, for example, they are seeking to find what they are seeking. They seem happy in this search. Nothing special is seen in them, they seem to be ordinary men and women. Well, it seems that one of them is particularly large of nose, but, aside from those details, everything seems normal. Yes, we could say that Power can rest easy. No important danger is detected; there are no weapons, or anything like that, only words. Good, I believe today will be a normal day, a day and a night with men and women talking.

Just a minute! What is that sneaking through the crack of the door of the one who is called El Sup? Is it a cockroach? No. The satellite's powerful electronic machinery begins to analyze all the data: size, specific weight, texture, form, velocity, rhythm and all the etceteras which this complicated software has incorporated in order to justify its elevated price. In a matter of seconds, the space computer finishes confirming the data, and it begins its correlation with the gigantic file that contains all the data of all the proven probable enemies of Power and of their daily habits. Suddenly the alarms sound, and the colored bulbs light up. One would think it was a Christmas tree, if it were not for the fact that one can read, clearly, on the screen: "Supreme danger!" The comput-

---

First published in *La Jornada*, July 5, 1996. Originally translated by irlandesa.

er seems to be cybernetically terrified. In the great capitols, the arrogant activate their super-defense plans. The financial centers register the worst catastrophe in their histories. Heavily armed military units take up nervous positions at all the borders. What is happening? The answer appears on all the screens.

"Supreme danger! Durito. Supreme danger! Durito."

Read "D" for "Don and for Durito, Righter of wrongs," "E" for "Exceptional Beetle" and for "Emergency." "A" for "Active Knight-errantry" and for . . . "Alert, maximum alert!"

"That satellite is an imbecile," Durito tells me, taking off his raincoat and leaving a tiny puddle of water on the floor. "Look at them, confusing me with a cockroach . . ."

"What are you reading?" Durito asks, sitting now upon one of my shoulders and lighting his tiny pipe. I do not respond, showing him the title page of the book, which reads:

"Bertolt Brecht. *Tales from the Calendar*. 19/5. 19. Wednesday."[1]

"Ah! My colleague, Bertolt . . ." Durito sighs, while he starts going through my pack.

"And might I know what you're looking for?" I ask, closing the book.

"Tobacco," Durito responds laconically.

"I don't have any," I lie, but it's useless now. Durito found a black tobacco pouch and prepares to fill his knapsacks.

"And might I know how you came to be here?" Durito begins to transform himself as his lecture progresses.

"I am the great Don Durito de la Lacandona. *El Mío Cid* reborn, he who took up the sword at just the right moment. I am the lord and gentleman of the unutterable and passionate dreams of women of all ages. He for whom, when he passes by, men take off their hats and recognize their own imperfections. The hero who renders all superficial neoliberals inconsequential in children's imaginations. I am the fortunate one, he whose sword exceeds the exploits of Don Rodrigo Díaz de Vivar, of Minaya, of Martín Antolínez, of Pedro Bermúdez and Muñoz Gustioc.[2] I am he whom the villain in Ireland fears, the nightmare of the thief hiding in Manhattan.[3] I am the one who was born at just the right moment. I am the last and first hope of all the poor wretches and large-nosed swordsmen who wander about without destiny or reason. I am . . ."

---

1 Eugen Berthold Friedrich Brecht, the German Marxist poet and dramatist, fled Nazi Germany in 1933, arriving in the US in 1941 only to become a target of McCarthyism. In 1949 he returned to Berlin and founded his own theatre company. *Tales from the Calendar* (*Kalendergeschichten*), a collection of stories and poems written during his exile, evokes the tradition of popular almanacs. *Tales from the Calendar*, English translation by Yvonne Kapp and Michael Hamburger (London: Methuen, 1961).

2 Rodrigo Díaz de Vivar, a great medieval folk hero of Spain, was born near Burgos about 1040 and died in 1099. Known by the honorific title *El Cid*, his exploits are recounted in the epic *The Song of El Cid (El Cantar de Mío Cid)* (1150). Minaya Alvar Fanez, Martín Antolínez of Burgos, Pedro Bermúdez and Muñoz Gustioz were knights who followed El Cid to battle.

190

"A beetle who can be confused with a cockroach," I say, resentfully. Durito stops his speech and turns around to look at me, taken aback.

"What's going on with you?" he asks, after a puff. I feel ashamed and tell him:

"It's that I have to give a presentation at the Table on Culture and Media in the Transition to Democracy, and I don't have anything ready."[4]

"Ah! I knew it! You find yourself in a serious predicament, and your anachronistic pride prevents you from turning to the best and supreme paradigm of the sublime art of knight-errantry. And tell me, my elephantine squire, why do you allow anguish to weigh you down? Are you not aware, perhaps, that it is precisely to come to the aid of the helpless, that wise destiny has chosen well among human beings: those who combine ingenuity, valor, a gallant presence, goodness of heart, intelligence, boldness and . . ."

"A hard shell?" I interrupt, because I well know that Durito can spend entire hours talking about the virtues that knight-errantry requires and demands, but everyone knows that the time period for appearing at the tables is limited to a few minutes. Durito stops and falls into my trap.

"Well, a hard and shining armor is needed by every knight-errant. Everyone knows that, and I do not see why nature in her wisdom did not take that into account. But, where was I?"

"You, Sir, were going to help me with the presentation for the Table on Culture and Mass Media," I hurry him.

"Yes?" Durito hesitates. "Alright, so it shall be. I do not believe that an ignorant squire would dare deceive his master."

"Never, my lord," I say, with deep reverence.

"Good, let me consult and see what I can find to help you with such a ridiculous theme." Durito gets down from my shoulder and onto the table. Durito takes a teeny-tiny, mini-microcomputer out of his knapsack. I cannot help but be surprised and say:

"Don't tell me you have a computer?"

"Of course, you rogue! We knights-errant must always be modernizing ourselves in order to better carry out our work. But do not interrupt me . . ." Durito begins typing and typing. Someone later wrote that the moon was full that night. A bit later I woke up from a nightmare I was having. In it, Zedillo was re-elected by a wide margin in the year 2000, after an intelligent election campaign focused on the well-being of the family, social peace and fighting corruption. Startled, I looked all around me. Durito was still typing at the small table. Between yawns, I asked him,

---

3 The "villain in Ireland" is undoubtedly Carlos Salinas de Gortari, who fled Mexico amidst public outrage. The "thief in Manhattan" is likely his brother Raúl Salinas de Gortari, who was charged with involvement in the narcotics industry and with shipping millions of dollars of payoff money to Switzerland. Seized by US officials and extradited to Mexico in 1999, he was found guilty and sentenced to 50 years in prison.

4 The first Intercontinental Encounter was organized around a series of *mesas* or "tables" that functioned as workshops.

"Did you find something for the presentation yet?"

"Presentation? What presentation?" Durito asks, without taking his eyes off the mini-microcomputer screen. Desperately I tell him,

"What do you mean, what presentation? The one on Culture and Media! What, you weren't looking for it in your computer?"

"Looking in the computer?" Durito says, not asks, mimicking Olivio. He continues, without turning around to look at me, and says,

"Of course not! What I'm doing on the computer is playing. They just gave me a program where the beetles defeat the boots . . ."

I begin to whine:

"But, Durito, if you don't get me a presentation for this table, they are going to tear me to bits at the coordinators' meeting. They already have it in for me . . . sniff . . . sniff . . . sniff."

"Now, now," Durito consoles me, putting his little palms on my shoulder. "Don't worry. I will know how to rescue you from such a grave predicament . . ."

"You'll make me a written presentation?" I ask him, hopefully.

"No, no way! I will give you a written excuse so that the coordinators will not hit you so hard. Especially since all of us are into strengthening the path of peace . . ." I sigh in resignation. Durito looks at me for a bit, and then says,

"Alright, don't be like that. Here is the presentation." Durito picks up some written pages and shows them to me. With ill-disguised anxiety, I take them, and, babbling, try to express my gratitude:

"Thank you, Durito! You don't know how much . . . just a minute! What's this about the presentation being signed by Don Durito de la Lacandona and Bertolt Brecht?"

"What's so odd about that?" Durito says, lighting his pipe again. "You've never heard of joint presentations? Well, this is one of them . . ."

"But, Durito, Bertolt Brecht died many years ago . . ." I reproach him.

"Forty, to be exact. I know, we had begun the presentation at the end of World War II, and then we couldn't finish it. But I should warn you that Brecht only transcribed what I was dictating to him. Something very similar to what you are doing right now. But do not make that detail public. It would not be fair, during the homage to the 98th anniversary of his birth, for it to be known that some of Bertolt's texts are, in fact, mine."

"Durito . . ." I say to him, with incredulity and reprobation. He doesn't take the hint.

"No, say nothing. Do not insist on making public the debt that universal culture owes me. We knights-errant must be modest, so do not let it be known that the presentation is mine alone. I wrote here that it is from both. In addition, in order to lend credibility to the collective work, I will separate the text that was published in 1949 and, in another part, what I added these last few hours. And now, if you will pardon me, I must retire because during these cold and helpless nights, I must see if some damsel requires the aid of my strong arm."

Durito would not listen to my protestations. He scurries underneath the door and once more sets World Powers trembling. I anxiously review the presentation. The title is convincing:

Joint presentation by Bertolt and Durito, in which it is explained why wisdom consists not in knowing the world, but in intuiting the paths which must be followed in order to be better.

Dedicated to the children, Dalia and Martina,
of Tlaxcala and to the prisoners accused of being Zapatistas.

Part I
Where Bertolt responds to the question:
What would happen if sharks were people?[5]

"If sharks were people," the landlady's little daughter asked Mr. K, "would they be nicer to the little fishes?"

"Certainly," he said. "If sharks were people, they would build enormous boxes built in the sea for the little fishes, with all sorts of things to eat in them, plants as well as animal matter. They would see to it that the boxes always had fresh water and, in general, would take hygienic measures of all kinds. For instance, if a little fish injured one of its fins, it would be bandaged at once, so that the sharks should not be deprived of it by an untimely death. To prevent the little fishes from growing depressed there would be big water festivals from time to time, for happy little fishes taste better than miserable ones. Of course, there would also be schools in the big boxes. In these schools, the little fishes would learn how to swim into the sharks' jaws. They would need geography, for example, so that when the big sharks were lazing about somewhere they could find them. The main thing, of course, would be the moral education of the little fishes. They would be taught that the greatest and finest thing is for a little fish to sacrifice its life gladly, and that they must all believe in the sharks, particularly when they promise a splendid future. They would impress upon the little fishes that this future could only be assured if they learned obedience. The little fishes would have to guard against all base, materialistic, egotistical and Marxist tendencies, reporting at once to the sharks if any of their number manifested such tendencies. If sharks were people they would also, naturally, wage war among themselves, to conquer foreign fish boxes and little foreign fishes.

---

5 The following passage reproduces "If Sharks Were People," one of the "Anecdotes of Mr. Keuner" that make up the last story in *Tales from the Calendar*. In Marcos' communiqué, the Spanish translation of the German word *Menschen* is given as *hombres*, usually translated into English as *men*. Yvonne Kapp's translation of *Menschen* as "people" is more accurate and we have used her translation of the Brecht text. The original can be found in Bertolt Brecht, *Werke: Vol. 18, Prosa 3* (Ertste Auflage: Suhrkamp Verlag, 1995), 446–448.

They would let their own little fishes fight these wars. They would teach the little fishes that there was a vast difference between themselves and the little fishes of other sharks. Little fishes, they would proclaim, are well known to be dumb, but they are silent in quite different languages and therefore cannot possibly understand each other. Each little fish that killed a few other little fishes in war—little enemy fishes, dumb in a different language—would have a little seaweed medal pinned on it and be awarded the title of Hero. If sharks were people, they would also have art, naturally. There would be lovely pictures representing sharks' teeth in glorious colors, their jaws as positive pleasure grounds in which it would be a joy to gambol. The sea-bed theaters would show heroic little fishes swimming rapturously into sharks' jaws, and the music would be so beautiful that to its strains the little fishes, headed by the band, would pour dreamily into the sharks' jaws. There would also be a religion, if sharks were people. It would teach that little fishes only really start to live inside the bellies of sharks. Moreover, if sharks were people, not all little fishes would be equal any more than they are now. Some of them would be given positions and be set over the others. The slightly bigger ones would even be allowed to gobble up the smaller ones. That would give nothing but pleasure to the sharks, since they would more often get larger morsels for themselves. And the bigger little fishes, those holding positions, would be responsible for keeping order among the little fishes, become teachers, officers, box-building, engineers and so on. In short, the sea would only start being civilized if sharks were people."

Here the text published in 1949 ends, which the history of literature attributes to Bertolt Brecht. Durito added the following in 1996:

Part II
Wherein Durito tries to demonstrate that flags can offer refuge and a new world to a bay horse, and tells of other marvels that the wheat would understand.

But there would be, most certainly, among all the little fishes, some who would leave behind the meager "I" that the sharks had taught them, and who would raise, quite high, the flag of "we" that would grant the yearning for freedom and for being better beings. And the mere fact of raising that flag in such a watery medium would itself be something that would make them better. And so great was their joy that they would discover themselves made even better, and they would try to talk and the first word they would speak would be "liberty." And they would use the flagstaff, but not to lead a rebellion that would destroy the sharks and supplant their power with that of the little fishes. No, they would use the flagstaff as a battering ram, and they would break apart all the boxes of the sea, and everything in the sea would be emptied and there would be neither sharks nor little fishes, rather crabs and sailors and relatives of beetles, and those who know that the best way to advance is to go backwards. In a word, there would finally be a struggle in the sea for a new culture, a culture that would do without sharks and little fishes and would remake everything anew, without fisheries or jails. A culture that would not always have to imagine people in a condition other than human in order to suppose them good and better, always. A culture which has room for the lost bay horse who rides, still, seeking a story where he can be horse and bay without anyone demanding that he stop being so or that he change his color.

End of the Joint Proposal which Bertolt Brecht and Don Durito de la Lacandona made for the Table on Culture and Media in the Transition to Democracy. Berlin-San Cristóbal, 1949-1996.

I am getting nervous. I don't know which is worse: not submitting any presentation at all, or submitting the presentation by the Bertolt-Durito duo. Then I decide to resolve the dilemma through a scientific method that my brother taught me. I take a coin out of my wallet and flip it up in the air. How did it fall? I paid no attention. When I came back to this table, the money had not yet fallen. On the other hand, I also believe Durito's presentation in this forum will have unexpected repercussions. Tomorrow the newspapers will carry the news of a profound financial crisis, and of the obvious nervousness in all the armies of the world. No one will be able to know that the cause was a smoking and talkative beetle, knight-errant and astute critic of neoliberalism, who, righting wrongs, aiding damsels in distress and winning the loves of moons, wanders through the mountains of the Mexican southeast, still believing that there is no better enterprise than fighting injustice, nor any prize greater than the feminine smile which this hopeful bridge has tried to evoke.

Vale. Salud, and may the sea that is multiplied in the mountains have moon and skin.

From the mountains of the Mexican Southeast
Subcomandante Insurgente Marcos

Presentation in Seven Voices
Seven: Politics and *"Bolsas"* (Theirs and Ours)

In the opening address at the First Intercontinental Encounter, Marcos presents a paper he found in a bottle. The paper is dedicated to the prisoners accused of being Zapatistas and to all the prisoners of the world. Later, Durito explains the relationship between neoliberalism, slippers, combs, toothbrushes and *bolsas*. In Spanish the word *bolsa* refers to money or goods such as stocks and bonds, but can also refer to flexible containers such as bags, backpacks, sacks, and purses. He claims that *bolsas* can be classified into two types, "theirs" and "ours." Also included in this communiqué are the stories of Olivio and Old Antonio as well as musings on the writings of Julio Cortázar.

First published by Monique J. Lemaitre online at Chiapas–L 9/14/96. Original translator unknown.

July 31, 1996

Prologue

This presentation is to be delivered at Table 1 of the Intercontinental Encounter for Humanity and against Neoliberalism. Everyone knows that the so-called Table 1 ("table" is a euphemism with which stubborn *Zapatudos* hope to amuse the conference guests at the Encounter and to make the tender quagmire of La Realidad seem more friendly) is named "Of Combs, Toothbrushes, Slippers and other concepts of a New Political Science" . . .[1]

What? That's not what it's called?

What is it called then? "What politics do we have and what politics do we need?"

Really? Well, it's obvious that this thing about *Zapatones* having a lot of imagination is another myth, I mean, another myth besides that nose which thinks it's so great. Well, let's leave that for later. This is a prologue and should do what all prologues do, that is, try to convince the reader or listener that what follows is worth the trouble (or to console him, in case he becomes disillusioned when he realizes that what follows the prologue isn't worth it); its contributions to the political debate are indisputable and overflow with wisdom, conviction and other spices. The way in which this presentation comes to this Encounter and to this table is something that certainly merits another intergalactic encounter. But that will have to wait until we all recover from this intercontinental delirium that some dreamer calls "encounter." While that happens, I will give you a brief account:

This writing was found inside an empty liquor bottle, discovered in the middle of one of those storms that lashes the embrace the *julio* of the mountain gives us. The other Julio who continues to give us embraces, Julio Cortázar, held his own interplanetary Encounter all in one day, and moreover, gave himself the luxury of teaching us to travel *Around the Day in Eighty Worlds.*[2]

In one of those worlds, Julio sent us his own presentation, which he called: "Personal Coda."

For this, Madam, I told you that many would not comprehend this chameleon's promenade over the multicolored carpet, and that my preferred color and orientation can only be perceived if you look closely: anyone would know that I live on the left, on the red. But I will never speak explicitly of these preferences—or then again, maybe I will. I don't promise anything nor do I negate anything. I believe that I do

---

1 Throughout the communiqué, Marcos plays with the word Zapatistas. The Spanish suffixes -*udo* and *-on* are used to express an abundant or excessive quality of the root word. *Zapatero* refers literally to those who make and repair shoes.

2 Argentine expatriate Julio Cortázar's experimental prose such as *Around the Day in Eighty Worlds* (*La vuelta al día en ochenta mundos*, Siglo XXI Editores: Mexico, 1967), juxtaposed fantasy and reality with a commitment to social activism. The proper name *Julio* is juxtaposed with the word julio, Spanish for July.

something which is better, and that many understand—even a few police chiefs—
because nobody is irredeemably lost, and because many poets continue writing
with chalk on the jail walls of the north and of the south, of the east and of the
west, of this horrible, lovely earth.[3]

Things being the way they are, there's no harm in commemorating that Julio
this July, and with two Julios, remembering all the prisoners in all the police stations
all over the world. I know that a prologue is not the place to dedicate a piece of
writing, but it seems that the two Julios have conspired to disrupt the pleasant routine of the mountains of the Mexican Southeast with a message in a bottle. If a bottle with a message can be found in the middle of a storm in the mountains, then
surely a dedication can be found in the middle of a prologue. Therefore, and given
the messages, bottles, Julios and police stations, this presentation is dedicated . . .

To those prisoners accused of being Zapatistas and,
through them,
To all the political prisoners of the world.

To all the disappeared Zapatistas and,
through them,
To all the politically disappeared of the world.

Fine, let's continue with the writing that we found in a bottle and that is presented today at Table 1 of the First International Encounter for Humanity and
Against Neoliberalism. And since we're already talking about encounters, someone would be doing a lot for humanity if they were to tell the *Zapateros* not to
use such long names to refer to their acts of madness. The name of this
encounter is so long that when you get to the part that says, "against
Neoliberalism" you are so tired that, believe me, it's enough to make you want to
do anything except confront something.

Where was I?

Oh, yes! The presentation we found inside a bottle. Well then, although the
text has no date, computerized scientific studies have determined that it could
have been written on any day, in any part of the world, and by any of the human
beings that are or have ever been in the world. Nevertheless, the most important
thing has not yet been clarified. The greatest centers of repute and ill repute have
been consulted, but all to no avail. It has not been possible to determine who
emptied, to the last drop, the contents of that bottle or what strange dance provoked in this improbable being the joy that he was able to find in the liquid, and,
everyone knows, actually, that human beings already carry joy where it should
be, that is, in their feet . . .

---

3 The translation here is by irlandesa. See *Around the Day in Eighty Worlds*, trans. by Thomas
Christensen (San Francisco: North Point Press, 1986), 189

Chapter I
Where Olivio explains why there's no need to fear airplanes, helicopters and other terrors with which Power intends to punish the rebel dignity of the indigenous Zapatista people

A few days ago, in one of the American corners of the world, a group of persons held a meeting. A friend of mine was there. I had received notice via email that a group of dignitaries would meet to toast and salute Zapatista rebelliousness. I didn't know whether to be thankful or regretful about the toasting, but either way I took advantage of it to return the greeting with a letter, and to ask for a cup of coffee from the kitchen. It wasn't because I went for a cup of coffee, I only wanted a friendly pretext to refuse the toast, in case they would offer me a drink. Yes, I know you can't drink a toast by email, but with the advances in technology you never know. They say that in Mexico there is a guerrilla movement that used a fax to declare war against the supreme government, and utilizes the Internet and satellite communication to make its declarations known. "*Cosas veredes* Sancho," Durito would say, who fortunately is not in this, but another chapter.[4]

Now through this mud, pardon me, I meant through this land, walks the friend in question. I'm not trying to impress you, but the friend has been a friend of mine for many years. Of course, he didn't know that he was my friend. He arrived a long time ago. He arrived like good friends do, that is, through letters. The friend, whom I will call "my friend," taking advantage of his being trapped now in the mud and unable to protest, says that in the world, words of resistance are numerous and sound like the dense rain now falling on the roofs of the Zapatista indigenous people, on the roofs now shared by thousands of dignified men and women from around the world. The friend is one of those who look for rain in the world. He walks along, like others walk, gathering little drops of the rain of resistance that falls in America. In Africa, in Asia, in Oceania, in Europe, there are other seekers of rain, of stories of resistance that find no place in the history full of omissions, written by the dry power of Arrogance. I believe that all the seekers of rain who have come here realize that we have all gathered to rain on ourselves, and that we realize that the rain can be friendly if the word that gets us wet is our sister. So we can say that this is an encounter of rainmakers, a wet way of saying that it is an encounter of brothers and sisters.

Once, I wrote to my friend, telling him about Olivio. I told him that:

Olivio is a Tojolabal child. He is not yet five years old, still threatened by the high infant mortality rate that annihilates thousands of indigenous children in these lands. The risk that Olivio will die from a curable disease before the age of five is the highest in this country called Mexico. But Olivio is still alive. Olivio presumes to be a friend of the "Zup" and to play soccer with Major Moisés. Well, to say he plays soccer is arrogant. Actually, the Major limits himself to kicking the ball just far enough to

---

4 See note in "Durito IX".

free himself from an Olivio who thinks, as any child would, that the most important job of a Zapatista officer is to play with children.

I observe from a distance. Olivio kicks the ball with a determination that chills you to the bone, especially if you imagine that your own ankle could be the target of that kick. But no, the target of Olivio's kick is a little plastic ball. Well, this is also a figure of speech. In reality, half of the kick and its force end up in the mud of Chiapas' reality, and only part of it sends the ball on its erratic and short trajectory. The Major then gives a powerful kick and the ball passes by me and goes a long way. Olivio runs after the sphere with resolve (this, and what follows, should be read with the voice of a sports announcer.) He nimbly dodges a tree-trunk and a not-so-hidden root, prancing and dribbling past two *chuchitos* ("puppies" for the people of Chiapas) who were fleeing in terror on their own before the implacable, determined and lightning advance of Olivio. The defense had stayed behind (well, "Yeniperr" and Jorge are sitting down and playing in the mud, but what I mean is there is no enemy in front of him) and the opposing goal post is unarmed before an Olivio who grits the few teeth he has and lines up the ball like a derailed locomotive. An expectant hush falls over the crowd in the stands . . . Olivio catches up—finally!—to the ball, and just when the whole galaxy is expecting a huge kick that will rip through the net (well, the truth is that behind the supposed enemy goal posts there is only a sunflower with branches, thorns and reeds, but they serve as a net), and just when the cry of "*goooal!*" begins to rise from the gut up to the throat, and everything is ready for the world to demonstrate that it is worthy of itself, just then Olivio decides that he had run after the ball long enough and that a big black bird flapping around overhead can't do so with impunity, and suddenly Olivio changes direction and profession and heads for his slingshot to kill, he says, the black bird and bring something to the kitchen and to his belly. It was something, how can I describe it? . . . something anti-climatic ("very Zapatista," my brother would say), so very incomplete, so very unfinished, as if a kiss were left hanging on the lips without anyone doing us the favor of collecting it.

I am a discreet, serious and analytical fan, who goes over the percentages and records of teams and players, and who can explain perfectly the logic behind a tie, a triumph, or a defeat, no matter which it is. In effect, one of those fans who afterwards explains to himself that there's no need to be sad about the defeat of their favorite team, that it was to be expected, that they'll turn it around in the next game and other etceteras that deceive the heart with the useless work of the brain. But in that moment I lost my head, and like a fan who sees the supreme values of the human race betrayed (that is, those that have to do with soccer), I jumped from the stands (actually, I had been sitting on a log bench) and, furious, I headed straight for Olivio, to protest his lack of honor, professionalism and sportsmanship, and his ignorance of the sacred law that demands that soccer players owe everything to the fans. Olivio sees me coming and smiles. I stop myself dead in my tracks, frozen, petrified, immobile. But don't believe for a moment, my friend, that I stop out of tenderness.

200

It isn't Olivio's tender smile that paralyzes me.

It's the slingshot that he has in his hands . . .

Well yes, friend. I already know that it's quite evident that I'm trying to create a simile for you of the tender fury that makes us soldiers today so that, tomorrow, military uniforms will only be good for costume parties, and so that, if someone had to put on a uniform, it would be the kind used for playing, for example, soccer . . ."

That was the 8th of this wet *julio*, and as the other Julio says, nature imitates art. So it was that a few days later, today, I found Olivio using his shoes the way they should be used, that is, to kick a ball. Olivio was running after the ball just as a Special Forces military plane was passing over La Realidad. Olivio tripped over a rock and fell. Olivio fulfilled his duty with complete integrity, that is, he began to cry with a dedication worthy of admiration. That's where we were, that is, the plane searching for transgressors of La Realidad, Olivio crying, and me smoking under a tree, when the incredible took place: Olivio stopped crying and began to laugh.

Yes, it turns out that Olivio was taking a breath in order to renew his screaming when he lifted his head and he stayed watching the military plane. He then suspended his inhalation and stopped it short with a smile. I made a face that said: "I always told you I thought that kid would end up going crazy." But don't think that I have a heart of stone. Immediately, I ordered a red alert and sent an intermediary to the UN to request a child psychiatrist. I wasn't about to leave Olivio alone with his madness; I thought it would be good if he had company. But because the UN acts rapidly only when authorizing the deployment of multinational armed forces, I thought it best to carefully approach Olivio in order to discover the irrationality of his delirium. At a prudent distance I stopped and very tactfully asked him:

"How come you were crying a while ago but now you are laughing?"

Olivio smiled and got up, telling me:

"I looked at the soldier's plane. If I fall down, well, I cry and then I get back up. But that airplane, if it falls, it won't cry or get back up."

Olivio went after the ball. I ran back, canceled the red alert and the intermediary to the UN, and I sent a war report to the CCRI to inform them that we were going to win, and that they should prepare for the promotion of Olivio to, at least, Division General.

Olivio doesn't seem excited about his imminent promotion. On the contrary, later he is pestering me, trying to convince me that, as he says, we should make a big, big ladder so we can climb up to the night and play ball with the moon . . .

Chapter II
Where the rain, julio and Old Antonio announce the present, but 10 years before

It rained lying down. I mean that the rain almost laid down when the wind took her by the waist. Old Antonio and I had gone out hunting that night. Old Antonio wanted to kill a badger that was stealing the corn that had begun to appear in the *milpa*. We waited for the badger to come, but in his place came a wind and a rain that obliged us to take refuge in the almost empty barn. Old Antonio made himself comfortable in a corner further inside, and I sat down in the doorway. We were both smoking. He snoozed and I watched how the rain was leaning from one side to another, following the steps marked for it by the dance of a wind more capricious than usual. The dance ended, or it moved to another spot. Soon, nothing was left of the rain except the deafening competition between the crickets and frogs. I went out, trying not to make any noise so as not to wake Old Antonio. The air remained humid and hot, as it must remain when desire ends the dance of bodies.

"Look," Old Antonio tells me, and stretches out his hand towards a star that barely peers out from behind the curtains made by the clouds in the west. I look at the star and feel I-don't-know-what kind of sorrow in my chest. Something like a sad and bitter solitude. Nevertheless, I smile and before Old Antonio can ask me, I clarify:

"I was remembering a proverb that goes more or less like this: 'When a finger points out the sun, the fool looks at the finger.'" Old Antonio laughs wholeheartedly and says:

"He would be even more foolish if he looked at the sun. He would end up blind." The overwhelming logic of Old Antonio leaves me stuttering the explanation of what I suppose the proverb means. Old Antonio keeps on laughing, I don't know if at me, at my explanation, or at the fool who looks at the sun when a finger points it out. Old Antonio sits down, lays his gun to one side and forms a cigarette with something like a roller that he took from the old barn. I understand that it is time to be quiet and listen. I sit at his side and light my pipe. Old Antonio takes a few puffs on his cigarette and begins to rain words with only the smoke to soften their fall.

"A while ago I wasn't pointing out the star to you with my hand. I was thinking about how far I would have to walk so that my hand could touch that star up there. I was going to ask you to calculate the distance between my hand and the star, but you came out with that stuff about the finger and the sun. I wasn't showing you my hand, nor the star. The fool that your proverb talks about doesn't have an intelligent alternative: if he looks at the sun and doesn't go blind then he will stumble a lot from looking up; and if he looks at the finger he won't find his own path, he'll either remain standing in one place or following the finger. In the end, both are fools: the one who looks at the sun and the one who looks at the finger. Walking, well, living, is not done with great truths that, if you measure them, turn out to be pretty small. The night will come when we will begin to walk through it to reach the day. If we

202

only look at what is near, then we will only end up walking a short distance. If we only look at what is very far off, then we will stumble a lot and lose our way." Old Antonio rests his word. I ask:

"And how will we know to look far and near?"

Old Antonio relights his cigarette and his voice:

"Speaking and listening. Speaking and listening to those who are near. Speaking and listening to those who are far away."

Old Antonio stretches out his hand again towards the star. He looks at his hand and says:

"When you dream you have to see the star up there, but when you fight you have to see the hand that points out the star. That is living. A continuous lifting and lowering of your sights."

We returned to Old Antonio's village. Dawn was just beginning to clothe herself with morning when we parted. Old Antonio came out and accompanied me as far as the gate to the pasture. When I was already on the other side of the barbed wire I turned to him and told him:

"Old Antonio. When you stretched out your hand towards the star I didn't see your hand or the star . . ." Old Antonio interrupts me:

"Oh! Very good, then you saw the space between the one and the other."

"No," I told him. "I didn't see the space between one and the other either."

"What, then?"

I smiled and began to move away when I shouted:

"I was looking at a badger that was between your hand and the star . . ."

Old Antonio looked at the ground for something to throw at me. I don't know if he couldn't find something or if I was already too far away for him to hit me. Anyway, I was lucky he wasn't still carrying his gun.

I went walking along, trying to look near and far. Above and below, the light brought night and day together, the rain linked July with August, and the mud and the stumbles hurt a little less. Ten years later we would begin to speak and listen to those whom we believed to be far away. All of you . . .

Chapter III
Where the illustrious and noble Don Durito de la Lacandona explains the strange relation between combs, slippers, toothbrushes, bolsas (theirs and ours) and the Intercontinental Encounter for Humanity and Against Neoliberalism

It is gray up here. As if the night and the day were lazy, one to leave and the other to arrive. A dawn gone on too long, so much time without night or day. There below, close to that young ceiba tree with the big canopy, weapons and dreams keep vigil. However, everything around here seems normal. There's mud, wandering lights, and skillful shadows. Only around the ceiba tree can one make out some movement. A powerful lens permits one to distinguish a seated man who is speaking and gesturing. It seems he's alone, and yes, a little crazy. But . . . just a moment! What's that at his side? A suit of armor from a museum of miniatures? A broken-down little war tank? An armored and mobile mini-bunker? A tiny warship run aground on reality? A . . . A . . . A beetle?

"Veeery funny, veeery funny," says Durito as he looks up defiantly. I lift my eyes upwards and see only the gray above the dark green of the ceiba's canopy.

"To whom are you speaking?" I ask, after listening to more complaints and challenges from Durito.

"It's that impertinent satellite that doesn't even know how to distinguish between a war tank and a brave and valiant knight-errant." Durito makes an obscene gesture towards the satellite and then turns to me and asks: "Where were we, my down-trodden squire?"

"You were about to tell me . . . how to get out of the problem I'm in."

"Oh! That . . . I understand that an impoverished heart like the one you carry in your battered chest is incapable of understanding the goodness that destiny confers upon you, placing you at the side of a knight-errant like myself. Thou must understand, miserable and foolish mortal, that the great gods have forged the destinies of humanity with threads of steel, and that evil sorcerers, besides speculating in the stock markets, have made terrible knots with those threads, so as to oppose the natural kindness of great do-gooders and to delight in the suffering of little people like thyself. Well, I mean little, not counting thy nose. But the powers of good have not abandoned their children to the perverse will of those wizards. No, to cut those terrible knots of pain and misfortune, to weave history with honesty, to right wrongs, to aid the destitute, to teach the ignorant, in sum, so that humanity does not shame itself, *that's* why knights-errant are here. If thou wouldst understand this thou wouldst doubt not the wonder of my arm, the wisdom of my word, the light in my eyes . . ."

" . . .and the big problems you get me into," I interrupt Durito. He hesitates and I take advantage of it to practice the old and dear sport of the reproach: "because it is my duty to remind thee, my illustrious knight-errant, that it was the wonder of thy arm, the wisdom of thy word, and the light in thine eyes, which set thy hand and seal to the letter of convocation and invitation to the Intercontinental Encounter in that absurd part about slippers, combs and toothbrushes. Besides, they all say that it is a cheap plagiarism of Cortázar's *cronopios* . . ." [5]

Durito doesn't ignore the criticism and counter-attacks: "They lie! How can they say that, if it was I, the great Don Durito de la Lacandona, who showed Julio the richness that beetles embody?"

Now it is I who interrupts: "No, that would be the *cronopios* . . ."

---

5 Cortázar's *Historias de cronopios y famas* (Barcelona: Bolsillo, 1970) is a collection of surreal vignettes and drawings. See Cortázar, *Cronopios and famas*, Paul Blackburn, translator (New York: Pantheon Press, 1969).

"Cronopios or beetles! 'Tis the same! Tell me quickly, who is the scoundrel that dares insinuate that my brilliant writing owes something to another," Durito draws his sword.

I try to collect on some outstanding debts and tell him:

"He's not a scoundrel. What's more, it's not a he; it's a she. And she doesn't insinuate that there was plagiarism. She declares it, and signs her name to it with no shame whatsoever."

Durito remains pensive for a while:

"A she?" Well, maidens may say whatever they want without fearing the fury of my Excalibur. It must be the malevolence of some perverse sorcerer who has worked evil magic on her, and has put evil thoughts where, surely, only kind thoughts for my person had previously been cherished. Yes, that must be it, because everyone knows that womankind cannot but sigh with admiration and secret desire when they hear the name of the greatest knight, that is, me. So there's nothing to do but wait for the effects of the dark brew that the sorcerer must have administered to wear off, or for me to find him and then, yes, the force and justice that empower my arm will cause him to withdraw the sorcery, and the problem will be solved. So why don't we leave that *Julio* fellow in peace, maybe he'll get this julio not to drown us with so much rain."

Durito sheaths his twig, or his sword, depending on the imagination of the satellite that, he says, is spying on him. I don't give up. I change my strategy:

"So be it, my lord and guide. May that wretch who has spoken ill against you be promptly freed of the sorcery, and once again surrender adoration to you. And if not, then may a terrible punishment fall upon her, may she obtain work as a spokesperson for one of the neoliberal governments that pummels the world, may they give her the post of psychiatrist for the powerful criminals who believe they govern the planet, may . . ."

"All right! All right! All right! That's too much punishment for that beauty!" Durito becomes magnanimous. I continue:

"As for my problem, lord of wisdom, I beg you to save me because the Encounter is already a reality in La Realidad and everyone is waiting for a satisfactory explanation of the requirement for slippers, combs and toothbrushes . . ."

"An explanation?" Durito looks at me with (it's worth being redundant) hardness.

"Yes. The invitation says that all the gullible ones, pardon me, all the guests at the Encounter, will find here the reason for that strangeness." I say trying to calm him down.

"Fine. If it is written, written it is. And it is the rule that we comply with what is written. So write down what I am about to dictate. You should do it meticulously because it is a contribution that will revolutionize political science, and moreover, will serve to distract the attention somewhat from accusations of plagiarism and other sorceries."

I immediately took out a ballpoint pen that, of course, had no ink. Durito noticed at once, and took out from who-knows-where an elegant ostrich quill and an inkwell.

"And this?" I asked, looking alternately at the quill and the inkwell.

"Ah! A gift from an African beetle," said Durito putting on airs.

"African?"

"Yes. You don't think that you're the only ones holding an Intercontinental Encounter? We beetles are meeting as well," says Durito.

I didn't try to find out more. I don't even know if there are beetles in Africa. What worried me was resolving the enigma of the slippers, combs and toothbrushes, so without further delay, I wrote down what Durito dictated to me, which is entitled:

Durito The-Next-Number (Neoliberalism, Slippers, Combs, Toothbrushes and Bolsas)

"*Bolsas*?" I asked, "But the invitation didn't say anything about *bolsas* . . ."

"No? Well, there's the problem. I believe I forgot to put in *bolsas*. I'm sure that, with the *bolsas*, everyone would have understood that part perfectly. Fine, fine, don't interrupt me again. Write, write!" Durito hurries me. I had doubts but I continued writing down what follows below:

a) Slippers are an alternative to boots. If you had paid attention to me, you wouldn't have brought all those different types of big boots with which you try, in vain, to defend yourselves from the mud. Boots or slippers get full of mud just the same, and they slip with the same enthusiasm. Right? Boots are useless, and moreover, dangerous. So you should have brought some slippers and that way, at least, you would have had a good excuse for spending so much time on the ground and being so muddy.[6]

b) In addition, one should argue that slippers can be taken off with complete ease, comfort and speed. Lovers and children will agree that I'm right, among other things, because the only beings that can understand the profundity of this message are children and lovers. Besides, winter is approaching and we need to keep warm. With slippers, we will make an overcoat that will cause a furor in the world of fashion. Ergo, there should be an Intercontinental Encounter for Slippers and Against Boots. That name is just as long as the other and, believe me, more definitive.

c) Combs are very useful in events of this kind, where nostalgia is a contagious disease. Using a little piece of paper and blowing just right, you have a musical instrument. With music you can make the heart and feet happy. There's nothing like slippers for this thing called dancing. With happy hearts and feet you can dance. And dancing is a happy type of encounter and, let's not forget, this is an encounter.

d) Ergo, combs are indispensable for all Intercontinental Encounters for Humanity and Against Neoliberalism. Oh! They're also good for combing hair. Toothbrushes are an invaluable aid in scratching your back. They come in many col-

---

6 It rained continually during the five days of the Encuentro.

ors, shapes and sizes. Although they're different, they all fulfill the function of a toothbrush, which, as everyone knows, is to scratch one's back. Everyone will agree, and I propose as an item of resolution for the final plenary session, that scratching is a pleasure. Ergo, toothbrushes are rather necessary for Intercontinental Encounters for Humanity and Against Neoliberalism. Slippers demonstrate that logic and boots are of no use when it comes to dreaming and dancing. Combs demonstrate that everything is a pretext for music and love. Toothbrushes demonstrate that one can be different and equal.

e)   Dance, music, pleasure, and being conscious of the other: these are the banners for humanity and against neoliberalism. Anyone who doesn't understand this surely must have cardboard for a soul.

f)   *Bolsas* can be classified into two types: their *bolsas* and our *bolsas*.

1) Their *bolsas* are known as "stock markets" and, paradoxically, distinguish themselves because they lack value. Usually they are full of holes, to speculators' advantage, and they have the sole virtue of provoking the insomnia and nightmares of our government officials.

2) Our *bolsas* are known as bolsas and as the word indicates, they're good for holding things. They usually have holes caused by neglect, but they are mended with hope and embarrassment. They have the enormous virtue of holding toothbrushes, combs and slippers.

g) *Finale fortisimo*: A *bolsa* that can't hold a toothbrush, a comb and slippers, is a *bolsa* that isn't worth having.

Here are the seven defining and definitive points for humanity and against neoliberalism. *Tan-tan*. It's finished.

Chapter IV
Where the famous knight-errant converses with his large-nosed squire, bags are packed and other marvelous or terrible things are announced

Durito has finished putting the saddle on Pegasus who, for a turtle, is quite restless. Durito has not stopped talking. At times it seems he's talking to Pegasus, at times it seems he's talking to me, and other times it seems like he is talking to himself. Is Durito convincing us that it's time to leave, or is he convincing himself?

"Not so fast, for now there are no more birds in last autumn's nest. I was mad and I continue to be . . ." Durito, as can be seen, adapts literary history as suits him best.[7]

---

7 This is a play on *Don Quijote's* dying words to Sancho Panza: "Not so fast, for now there are no more birds in last autumn's nest. I was mad and now I am sane. I was Don Quijote de la Mancha, and now, as I have said, I am Alonso Quijano the Good." The passage is from "Chapter LXXIV (74)—how Don Quijote fell sick, and the will he made, and his death." Cervantes, *Don Quijote*, 744.

Durito comes and goes with a bustle that, if it were not for his seriousness, would look like a complicated dance. I have become sad because at the hour of packing I've noticed that what I have is very little. However, I have some wheat, and that is enough. Durito, on the other hand, has made several trips for books, from his little leaf to *Pegasus'* back.

"Can it be known where we're going?" I ask Durito, taking advantage of his having stopped to rest. Durito hasn't caught his breath yet, so he makes an indefinite gesture, pointing in no particular direction.

"And is that very far?" I ask.

Durito is finally able to speak and says:

"The duty of a knight-errant is to travel the world until there no longer exists a corner with unpunished injustice. The duty remains in all parts and in none. It is always near and can never be reached. Knight-errantry rides on until it reaches tomorrow. Then it rests. But soon it resumes the march, because morning has continued on ahead and is already a good stretch ahead of it."

"And what must we bring with us?" I ask, now a little more serious.

"Hope . . ." Durito answers me and points to the *bolsa* that he carries in his chest. As he mounts *Pegasus* he adds:

"We don't need anything else. That's enough . . ."

Chapter V
Where the moon rehearses a dance that has a lot of copulation and joy

Full again, the moon tries to reveal her coquetry from behind the high bar of the eastern mountains. With care, she gathers up her large and full skirt, puts her little foot forward and climbs the back of the mountain like a staircase. When she reaches the top, she extends her white petticoat and spins around. Her own light bounces off the mountain's mirror and gives the gift of lilac and blue colors. Always spinning, a wind caresses her face and lifts her up high. With blind and useless eyes, the wind tries in vain to make out her belly that the rain has moistened. And the moon does not look at the wind, but not because she's blind. She only looks at herself, at the reflection that a little puddle of rain offers her from the reality below. Finally, the moon yields her hand and waist to the wind. Now they spin together. They spend the night together. Dancing. Wet and happy. But the nocturnal dance floor is now leaving and the moon tires after a few hours. Until he lays her on the eastern mountain, the wind carries her, always by the waist. Always blind, the wind tries to give her a goodbye kiss on the cheek, but he makes a mistake and it is her lips that he brushes against. He makes a mistake? The moon forgives him but she should hurry. Before letting herself slip to the west, the moon sees two figures, one small and round, the other tall and awkward. The moon doesn't know if the figures are coming or going, but she knows they're walking. That's why she gives them the touch that, just before she hides, makes one think for an instant that the two characters are going upwards, to the moon . . .

Chapter VI
Where the narrator digresses, rain and moon in the middle, on the sorrows, pains and the etceteras that weigh down the soul of the humans who walk there, himself included.

The moon barely appeared, perhaps to renew a promise disguised as a flower. But, jealous as she is, the rain brought her behind clouds and mist. That was a dawn for which solitude would ache. The narrator is alone, so he feels he has the right to stop narrating what is happening or what is dictated to him, and he decides to extract, with a sharp corkscrew of letters, a sorrow that clouds his vision and step. The narrator speaks. No, it's more like a whisper:

How I wish to have the air as my homeland and tomorrow as my flag! So many people and so many colors! So many words with which to speak of hope!

Would this be the moment to speak of death? Because there are those who have died a fighting death so that I could think of the many people, the many colors, the many hopes.

Is this the place to speak of our dead ones? No?

Who will tell them, then, that there was live blood that died dreaming, that one day some of the best men and women that this century has borne would arrive here? Who will ask a souvenir of all those people, a "forget-me-not" for those Zapatistas fallen in combat for humanity and against neoliberalism? Where are the chairs so that they, our dead, can sit down with us? The presentation of their blood in the streets and in the mountains—at which conference table is it registered? Who is the moderator in the silences of those deaths? How can you put a price on the blood of those dead who gave us a voice, a face, a name and a tomorrow?

Can I speak? Can I speak about our dead at this celebration? After all, they made it possible. It can be said that we are here because they are not. Can't it?

I have a dead brother. Is there anyone who doesn't have a dead brother? I have a dead brother. A bullet to the head killed him. It was at dawn on the 1st of January 1994. That bullet was up very early. The death that kissed the forehead of my brother was up at dawn. My brother used to laugh a lot but now he doesn't laugh any more. I couldn't keep my brother in my pocket, but I kept the bullet that killed him. On another day at dawn, I asked the bullet where it came from. It said: "From the rifle of a soldier of the government of a powerful person who serves another powerful person, who serves another powerful person, who serves another all around the world." The bullet that killed my brother has no homeland.

The fight that must be fought to keep our brothers, and not bullets, in our pockets has no homeland either. That's why the Zapatistas have many and big pockets in their uniforms. Not for keeping bullets. For keeping brothers.[8] That's what all *bolsas* should be for.

---

8 This passage was read by Mumia Abu Jamal in *Zapatista!*, a documentary by Big Noise Films (1996).

The mountain is also a *bolsa* for keeping brothers. Sometimes the mountain seems like the sea. Sometimes the night seems like the morning. *El mar. La mar. El mañana. La mañana.* The sea and the morning have no sex. Maybe that's why we fear them, or maybe that's why we desire them.

How painful it is to leave! What sorrow to stay!

I'm leaving now. I just wanted to tell you one thing:

The heart is a *bolsa* where the sea and the morning fit. And the problem is not in how to put the sea and the morning in your chest, but in understanding that the heart is just that, a *bolsa* for keeping the sea and the morning...

The narrator leaves. Together with the night he leaves. Together with the rain he leaves. Together with *julio* he leaves. The other Julio remains to organize the mission to be carried out in *Around the Day in Eighty Worlds*. Julio prepares for a trip:

The trip to a country of cronopios:

Of course, the traveling Cronopio visits another country and one day, when he returns to his own, he will write the memories of his trip on little pieces of different-colored paper, and he will distribute them at the corner of his house so that everyone can read them. To the Famas he'll give little pieces of blue paper, because he knows that when the Famas read them they will turn green, and nobody can ignore that a Cronopio likes the combination of these two colors very much. As for the Esperanzas, those who blush a lot upon receiving a gift, the Cronopio will give them little pieces of white paper, and that way hopes will be able to shield their cheeks, and the Cronopio, from the corner of his house, will see diverse and pleasant colors that will disperse in all directions, taking with them the memories of his trip.

Epilogue
Where it is explained why the accounts don't add up and it is demonstrated that addition and subtraction only work if they're for adding hopes and subtracting cynicisms

Yes, I know that the title of this is "Presentation in Seven Voices Seven," and there are only six voices and it can't be that it's already over because the title is very clear, and it even repeats seven times that there are seven voices seven. But my master and lord, the knight-errant who is a wizard in love and a sorcerer in combat, Don Durito de la Lacandona, tells me that we're leaving, that we should leave, that the seventh voice is the one that's worth it and counts, and that one, the seventh word, belongs to each and every one of you.

So goodbye, and I hope that someone writes to tell us how all this turned out.

Vale. Salud, and know that if the thieves ask us for our *bolsas* or our lives, they'll have to take our lives.

From the mountains of the Mexican Southeast,
El Sup Marcos
Planet Earth, July 1996

P.S. Durito has already left on his spirited Pegasus. Pegasus is a turtle that suffers vertigo at velocities greater than 50 centimeters per hour, which means that it will take some time to reach the exit. So I have time to tell you that you are welcome to the mountains of the Mexican Southeast, the place where the *bolsas* that are truly of value are ours, yours, and everyone who we are . . .

Salud, once again. *Salud*, and may you have much hope and the humility to repair your baggage, pockets and sleeping bags.

El Sup, disconcerted because he forgot which is the entrance and which is the exit.

* * *

STORIES FOR A
SLEEPLESS SOLITUDE

Love and the Calendar

Writing from the top of the ceiba, Marcos finds a bottle containing a letter from Durito. The letter includes a story composed for the latter's forthcoming book, *Stories for a Sleepless Solitude*, which tells how a man who was always late missed his own death. Durito's letter ends with a postscript warning that "fierce storms are coming." The previous June, the Popular Revolutionary Army, or EPR (*Ejercito Popular Revolucionario*), had emerged in Guerrero and carried out attacks in seven Mexican states just prior to the September 1st Presidential State of the Nation Address. On September 2nd, the EZLN suspended peace talks acting "on orders from their base communities," who doubted the government's sincerity in the negotiations and demanded respect for Zapatista delegates. In the coming weeks, they reported increased harassment of the communities, and military advances towards the EZLN's mountain camps.

First published in La Jornada, September 20,1996. Originally translated by Susana Saravia.

Morning voyage aboard communiqués
To the National and International Press
September 18, 1996

Ladies and Gentleman:
I am still on top of the ceiba. I made a paper airplane out of the communiqués and I launched it with great force. Almost immediately it started to rain. "You should have made a paper boat!" My Other Self yelled at me from a schooner. In the distance, daybreak amicably ceded its place to a lazy dawn.

Vale. Salud, and who can predict tomorrow's flower from today's bare ground?

From the mountains of Numancia[1]
Subcomandante Insurgente Marcos

The Recurrent Postscript:
The ceiba is the mast of unstable sailing.

I was at the highest point of the mast (yes, I know it's a ceiba branch, but the two look alike), checking the horizon, when there in the distance was a fleeting spout, alight in the lightning that gave it life. The night was a dark storm and, yet, the moon could just barely be seen charging towards the east. A reflection reached the sea so that a small bank of white sand could be seen. It's true that the sea at night holds surprises, but to spot a white sandbank is extremely rare. What I mean is that it's not unusual to spot data banks, financial banks or even blood banks, but never a white sandbank.[2] I reached for the telescope and aimed for the ship's bow, where the moon had illuminated the beach, but there was nothing, only the black yawn of a nocturnal rain. A lightning bolt again made visible that foamy spout but now on the port side. I turned in that direction and was able to distinguish a large white mass. Wait a minute! Now the watery spout is again portside! Is this a pirate ship or a merry-go-round? Hmmm . . . everything indi-

---

1 The citizens of Numancia, an ancient city in what is now Northern Spain, committed mass suicide rather than be overrun by the Romans in 134 B.C. In a communiqué dated September 7, 1996, Marcos quotes Miguel Cervante's *The Encirclement of Numancia:* "The right of the strongest is the violation of the essence of the right. The power (Rome) is the enemy of morality and of liberty (Numancia). Numancia speaks to the condemned of the Earth not to drive them to suicide, but to resistance and the final victory."
2 Marcos revives a metaphor used in "The Long Journey from Despair to Hope," which speaks of "neoliberal chants of 24 mermaids, of reefs of gold, of grounding on sand banks of depression and of other dangers that threaten the pirates on high seas," originally published in the Anniversary Supplement of *La Jornada* (September 22, 1994).

216

cates that the sandbank moves. Hmmm . . . I aim my one eye on the telescope and, focusing, say to myself that, if it's not a white sandbank that's moving, then, it could very well be a whale. Yes, a white whale like Moby Dick! Yes, it is he! Who else would present himself with such impunity—Córdoba Montoya?[3] No, it's not one of those pirates we talk about. Yes, it's Moby Dick. And here I am, all alone. That last sailor was drowned by a hurricane. Well, actually, it was a woman, but in this case it's the same thing. I chased Moby Dick away with that saying by Pavese that goes:

There is no voice that breaks the silence of the water
under the dawn.
And nothing that makes it shiver
under the heavens. Only a tepidity that dilutes the stars.[4]

The ceiba tree is a coin-toss.

I was on top of the ceiba tree, thinking about how to get down in a way that my pride and my backside would both come out unscathed, when My Other Self arrived and, without much ado, blurted out, "Everyone's saying . . . they're saying that the supreme one says that the coin has been tossed, and that it came up tails—and that now they're going to beat yours because your 'Ha!' hurt him more than the 'Ya basta!' of 94."[5] I didn't even flinch, I just started trying to figure out where in the ceiba tree there was room for a tomb. It was no use. "I have to get down," I tell My Other Self. He looks at me with irony and asks, "Are you afraid?" "Never ever," I respond, "but over there" (I point to the horizon) "it looks like better times are coming. If I stay up here I'll miss the best part . . ."

---

3 Córdoba Montoya, Former Chief of Staff to Carlos Salinas, wielded an exceptional amount of power for the office. Suspected of involvement in the Colosio assassination, narcotics trafficking and other crimes associated with the administration, he was questioned by the Mexican Congress the day this communiqué appeared in *La Jornada*.

4 Cesare Pavese, the Italian poet and author, also translated English and American literature including the work of Melville. In 1935, on charges of "anti-fascist activities," he was confined for three years in the isolated village of Brancaleone. There he completed his best-known work, *Lavorare Stanca*, a moving critique of fascist Italy first published in 1936. See *Hard Labor*, William Arrowsmith, trans. (New York: Grossman Publishers, 1976). The quoted text is from the poem *Creazione* (1935).

5 This "Ha!" appears to be a reference to Marcos' letter to President Zedillo published in *La Jornada* on September 3, 1995. Responding to the illegitimacy of the "*Segundo Informe de Gobierno*" ("Second Government Report") on the peace talks, Marcos states that the Zapatistas hopelessly await indications of the government's will to bring about peace, claiming that they "seem to have created a climate of terror" and "seem to think they have enough public opinion on their side that they can now attack the Zapatistas." "If that is the case," he concludes, "then we'll see you in hell!"

A ceiba tree is an island aspiring to fly.

A bottle arrived floating on the crest of a cloud and got stuck in one of the branches of the ceiba. I carefully moved closer—a fall from this height would be as hard as when the system crashed in 1988—and grabbed it.[6] As one would suppose, the bottle had a message inside. I took it out and found the following letter from Durito:

My dearest Cyrano in decadence:
I have learned that once again you find yourself prisoner on top of the ceiba tree. This happens when you get carried away with your nonsense about mirrors and falling upwards. At the moment, it is impossible for me to come rescue you. I am veeery busy with the writing of the second volume of *Stories for a Suffocating Night*. As of now, they will be titled *Stories for a Sleepless Solitude*. Herein I send you a sample so that you can retain an editor.

Love and the Calendar
There was once a man who was always late for everything. And it was not because he was lazy or slow, or that his watch was behind, or that it was a bad habit. It was because this man was living in another time, before time. Not much, really, but always a little. For example, when the calendar marked the month of September, this man was walking in an April morning. For that reason, his spring never coincided with its opposite. Death, however, continued to be obedient to the passing of time and went about delivering absences as the allotment of people's days and nights would run out. But since this man was never on time, well, he always arrived late to the hour of his death and could never meet up with her, because Death had to follow the calendar. Death knew that she was leaving that one pending—that this man should already be dead and yet, owing to his tardiness, was still alive. The man got tired of living and walking, which in this case is the same, and set out to look for Death so that he could die. And so time and untimeliness pass each other, Death, hoping for the man to arrive so that she can take him, and the man, hoping to meet Death so that he can die. There is no day on the calendar for those two wishes to meet. *Tan-tan.*

What do you think? No, leave your praises for later. Well, I give you my leave. I will write you later, my decadent and large-nosed squire.
Don Durito de la Lacandona

---

6 The 1988 Presidential elections were marked by widespread fraud in a multitude of forms. Most notably, the federal electoral commission reported a computer "system crash" while votes were being tallied. The system remained down for a week, during which time it appeared that opposition votes were destroyed. Although PRI candidate Carlos Salinas was pronounced the winner, PRD candidate Cuauhtémoc Cardenas is believed to have won 39% of the popular vote to Salinas' 37%. Ten days after the official results were announced, more than a half-million people protested the election fraud in Mexico City's Zócalo.

P.S. Don't forget to hold the rudder firm; they say fierce storms are coming.

End of the letter from Durito. No comment.

* * *

The Story of the Magical Chocolate Bunnies

In homage to *The Good, the Bad and the Ugly*, Durito writes Marcos a fable alluding to the government's spin on the EPR and the EZLN. The government's attempt to dismiss both groups prompted Marcos to state that the Zapatistas would not play the "good" rebels to the EPR's "bad" rebels. The communiqué stresses the terror of the continued low-intensity warfare, and the contradictions of the government's expressed desires for peace while it continued to build up the military presence in the region and sent disingenuous representatives to the peace negotiations. Refusing to be boxed in, the EZLN announced that it would walk out on the peace talks. It also announced plans to send representatives to Mexico City to participate in the first National Indigenous Congress convened by the EZLN and other indigenous groups to discuss the San Andrés Accords on Indigenous Rights and Culture that had been signed on February 16th. The government reacted to the announcement by threatening to arrest any Zapatistas who left Chiapas.

First published in *La Jornada*, October 3, 1996. Originally translated by Cecilia Rodríguez.

To the National and International Press
September 29, 1996

Ladies and Gentlemen:
We would greatly appreciate your attention to the attached communiqués.[1] Long live the unintentional humor of the Chiapas PRIista! The indigenous people of the PRI of the *ejido* San Caralampio in the Ravine of Río Perlas told the COCOPA very seriously, when they were visited, that, yes, they did receive help from the government: solar cells (which power four light bulbs and a tape recorder) and a sheep farm. In one of the poorest states of the country, with a large indigenous population and natural resources far beyond any country of Central America, the Mexican government renews its aspirations: for the producers of electricity, solar cells as alms; for those who rose up in arms for dignity, sheep as future promises. "Wish they were all like that," sighs Mr. Ruiz Ferro, a thief among thieves, who today dispatches messages from the governor's palace of Chiapas and dreams about providing for the indigenous people like animals.[2] "Wish they were all like that," sigh the two policemen, Eraclio Zepeda and Uriel Jarquim.[3] "But, they're not all like that," counters Comandante Rolando, an indigenous Tzeltal rebel who sharpens his machete and is sure that what runs through his veins is not the blood of a sheep, but of a human being.

Vale. Salud, and as Benedetti says, "He/who/hugs/his/bosom/hugs/ insanity."[4]

From under one of the beds at Numancia[5] (hiding, of course)
Subcomandante Insurgente Marcos
Mexico, September 1996

---

1 Attached were two communiqués: a thirteen-point document announcing the reasons for a Zapatista walkout of the peace talks; and another very brief missive, where Marcos responds to arrest threats by stating that the government was continuing to try to annihilate the Zapatistas, and concludes, "This is our response. First and only: UUUUY!!!!"(Ouch!)

2 Ruiz Ferro was Governor of Chiapas at the time.

3 Chiapas state officials Eraclio Zepeda and Uriel Jarquim presided over numerous violent police actions in which over 100 people were killed and many others were wounded or displaced. Zepeda, who had been a well-known poet, left-wing activist and prominent opposition figure, was appointed to the position of Government Secretary in 1994 by then-Governor Eduardo Robledo Rincón.

4 Uruguayan author and journalist Mario Benedetti, a well-known intellectual involved in the resistance to his country's right-wing dictatorship during the 1970s spent more than a decade in exile throughout South America and Europe. This poem, "*Intensidad*" (Intensity), is from *El Amor, Las Mujeres y La Vida* (Buenos Aires: Compañía Editora Espasa Calpe, 1995) The Spanish reads: "*quien/pecho/abarca/loco/aprieta,*" a play on the idiomatic expression "*quien/mucho/abarca/poco/aprieta*" (one should not bite off more than one can chew).

5 See note in "Love and the Calendar."

P.S. that sneaks a glance at El Sup's log:

September 27, 1996. It is the 1000th dawn of the war. The moon barely started to be full. An eclipse tried, in vain, to hide it. It was stained a faint red. For a moment the moon appeared to be a sun, the sun of midnight. We have in these 1000 days opened spaces in the country, on the continent, and in the world. The challenge we launched was not a small one; now we cannot hold ourselves back.

September 28, 1996. The 1001st dawn of the war. From the top of the ceiba a great distance can be seen. There are lights in the west. A city? Apparently. It begins to rain. At first the rain hurts the face. Later of course it heals, but at first it hurts. I was smoking nostalgias and trying to remember a poem, when . . .

"What you're thinking of doing is not wise," says My Other Self.

"Really?' I answer him, as I finally recall my Pavese and say, "The streets are like women, when mature they are firm." I don't know if I had already said, "When the rain begins, it hurts the face. The same as the night."[6]

P.S. that gets dizzy.
I read that a marina is a port that cloaks and protects one from hurricanes. That is what I need now. A marina.

P.S. that jumps ahead of itself.
Headline of the major regional and national dailies: "Civil Society Demands that Bernal and Del Valle Declare Themselves Policemen or Negotiators."[7]

The Recurring Postscript

The ceiba is a mailbox.

Correct. Another cloud, another bottle, and another letter from Durito:

My beloved, persecuted and harassed Cyrano,
It is my duty to tell you that your time is coming to an end. That ceiba is an excellent target for mortars, grenade launchers, snipers, cannons and machine guns—not to mention satellites. At the end of this letter you will find an infallible recipe for climbing out of ceiba trees. Follow it to the letter and soon you will find yourself on the ground.

---

6 "*Le strade sono come le donne, maturano ferme,*" is from the poem *Grappa a settembre*, published in the collection *Lavorare stanca* (*Hard Labor*, 1936). For more on Pavese see note in "Love and the Calendar."

7 Marco Antonio Bernal Gutiérrez and Jorge Del Valle were two of the primary negotiators representing the Zedillo administration at the San Andrés Peace Talks. During an interview on Televisa (Mexico's dominant television network) shortly before the appearance of this communiqué, Bernal threatened to arrest any Zapatistas who would leave Chiapas .

With the understanding that you will not last much longer and all that (let's just say you're not a very appealing client for life insurance agencies), I recommend that you speed up the contacts for the publication of my next book *Stories for a Sleepless Solitude*. Seeing as time is coming to an end, I send you now another story, which is part of a special section called "Stories for Getting Pregnant." It speaks for itself; one has only to read it. Here goes then:

The Story of the Magical Chocolate Bunnies Neoliberalism, Rabbit Libidos, and Children (Durito's homage to the Western: Remember "The Good, the Bad, and the Ugly"?)[8]

There were once three children: one was good, one was bad, and the other was El Sup. Walking from different directions, they all met up at a house and went in together. Inside the house there was only a table. On that table were three white plastic containers (like they use for ice cream or sorbet), one for each child. Inside each white plastic container (note: no trademark or logo) there were two chocolate bunnies and a piece of paper. The paper said,

Instructions for the use of the two chocolate bunnies:

After 24 hours, this pair of chocolate bunnies will reproduce themselves and will have a new pair of bunnies. Every 24 hours, the pairs of chocolate bunnies inside this white plastic container will multiply into another pair. That way the owner will always have chocolate bunnies to eat inside this magic plastic container (the kind used for ice cream or sorbet). The only condition is that there must be at all times a pair of chocolate bunnies inside this plastic container, like the ones used for ice cream or sorbet.

Each child took his white plastic container—you know, the kind used for ice cream or sorbet.

The bad child could not wait for 24 hours and ate his two chocolate bunnies. He enjoyed the moment, but he had no more chocolate bunnies. Now he has nothing to eat, but the memory and nostalgia of the chocolate bunnies remain.

The good child waited for 24 hours and was rewarded with four chocolate bunnies. After another 24 hours he had eight chocolate bunnies. As the months passed, the good child opened a chain of chocolate bunny stores. After a year, he had branches all over the country; he associated with foreign capital and went into the export business. He was eventually named "Man of the Year" and became immensely rich and powerful. He sold the chocolate bunny industry to foreign investors, and became an executive of the company. He never tasted the chocolate

---

8 Directed by Sergio Leone and starring Clint Eastwood, *The Good, the Bad and the Ugly* (1966) is the third of Leone's famed trilogy of "Spaghetti Westerns."

bunnies, in order to not diminish his profits. He no longer owns the magic white plastic container. He doesn't know the flavor of chocolate bunnies.

The *Sup* child took out the chocolate bunnies and put some nut ice cream in the white plastic container, the kind used to hold ice cream or sorbet. Changing the premise of the story, he packed half a liter of nut ice cream in his backpack and ruined the moral of the story of the chocolate bunnies by deducing that all final options are a trap.

Neo-moral: The ice cream with nuts has dangerous potentialities against neoliberalism.

Questions for reading comprehension:
Which of these children will become president of the republic?
Which of these children will belong to an opposition party?
Which of these children should be killed for violating the law for dialogue, reconciliation, and a peace with dignity in Chiapas?
If you are a woman, which child would you prefer to give birth to if you were pregnant?
Send your answers to 'Huapac Hole #69' with copies to the Interior Ministry and the COCOPA. *Tan-tan.* The End.

Well? What do you think? Oh, come on now. Do not refrain from saying it is marvelous! I look forward to you getting me a good editor, one of those who organizes readings with Carlos Monsiváis and etcetera. Over and out.

Don Durito de la Lacandona

P.S. Oh! I almost forgot about the recipe for getting down from the ceiba. It's simple, just follow the "Instructions for Getting Down from the Top of a Ceiba." Are you sure you want to get down? Walk to the edge with your eyes closed. Do not fear (although a parachute certainly wouldn't be a bad idea right now). You will soon arrive at your destination (?).

End of Durito's letter. Nothing to add.
From the ceiba to the ground there is the same distance as that between despair and hope.
I fell down. I don't know why they accuse us of violating the law. It's clear that among others, the law of gravity is rigorously observed by our stubborn flight.

P.S. that worries.
I think that little gray man who barks so much about arresting us if we leave really has something to worry about now. Look at the postmark on Durito's let-

ter. It comes from Mexico City along with a postcard from the Templo Mayor.[9] It's postmarked September 16th and it wouldn't surprise me if, among so many war tanks, Durito went unnoticed.[10]

P.S. for political columns:
According to confidential reports, Mr. Bernal will soon leave his position with the government delegation in San Andrés. Upset because now it is impossible for him to become a PRI candidate for the governorship of Tamaulipas (given that the statutes changed), Bernal aspires to replace Chuayffet. (Bernal is the one who writes the communiqués of the Interior Ministry, thereby explaining their poor quality.) To his closest colleagues (Del Valle and Zenteno), Bernal has confessed that if he does not become the Secretary of the Interior Ministry, he will ask to be admitted to the FZLN.[11] What should we do?

P.S. that says goodbye:
Olivio just left saying, "*Adiós Compañero Subcomandante Sup.*" What? Why is this happening to me? I, who always dreamed of imitating a James Bond introduction, like in his first movie, and saying "My name is Marcos, Subcomandante Marcos . . ."

Vale with nuts.[12] *Salud*, and "What is that which shines in the highest halls?"[13]

Sup Marcos

The Sup hiding under a bed, not because he's afraid of being killed, but because, he says, the bed is much too wide, especially when one is alone . . .

* * *

---

9 The ruins of the Templo Mayor, the main temple of Tenotchtitlan, are today a museum. Mexico City's Zócalo and federal and local seats of government were built around it.
10 The September 16 celebration of Mexican Independence by hundreds of thousands in the Zócalo was marked by an exceptionally large show of military force.
11 During the PRI's XVII Assembly in Mexico City (September 20-22, 1996), party statutes were changed to favor candidates with over ten years of party militancy or having previously held electoral office, a move ostensibly designed to reduce favoritism.
12 Throughout these stories Marcos often signs off with *vale de nuez,* a play on *vale otra vez,* usually translated as "*vale* once again."
13 The first line in García Lorca's poem "*Muerto de Amor (a Magarita Mansa),*" from *Romance Gitano.*

225

The Seashell and
The Two People

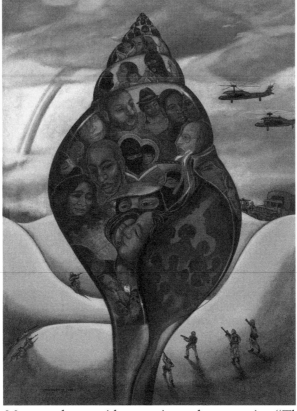

Durito sends Marcos a letter with a treatise and two stories. "The Seashell" is Durito's theory on the CND and the construction of the first Aguascalientes. "The Story of the Two People" is for inclusion in Durito's forthcoming book *Stories for a Sleepless Solitude.* The letter appears during a phase of the negotiations between the Zapatistas and the Mexican Government that involved "tripartite" talks among the EZLN, COCOPA and CONAI, aimed at creating an Implementation and Verification Commission for the San Andrés Accords signed the previous February. On November 7, 1996, two weeks after this communiqué was written, the formation of such a Commission was announced and was to be installed in San Cristóbal. But less than a month after the announcement, the Government reneged on its commitment to the Accords, and the effort to form such a Commission was abandoned.

First published in *La Jornada*, October 24, 1996. Originally translated by Cecilia Rodríguez.

October 23, 1996
To: International and National Civil Society
From: Sup Marcos

Madam:[1]

Yeah, it's us again. But don't be disturbed. Not yet. Now we write to thank you for the disturbing joy that took Comandanta Ramona and, with her, all of us, to the center of Power in Mexico. We've seen some of the images of those days when the entire Mexican political system trembled as our most powerful weapon passed. And we also learned about the National Indigenous Congress and about its frank call to the struggle summarized by the subversive banner of "Never again a Mexico without us."[2] Yes, that "us" is an invitation difficult to resist. Well, I believe what's next is, "Never again a world without us." Don't you think? Of course, everything turned out fine. And you are right; it was like a party. Of course it must have ruined more than one person's lunch, but you know that such things happen.

Do you know what? Something very strange is happening in this country. When you show no signs of life and wrap yourself up in problems you believe to be only yours, Power smiles and leaves everything for later, but the moment you engage in speaking and in taking to the street and in dancing, the supreme government is overcome with a strong urge to dialogue and to show it is serious about wanting to resolve the problems. No, I don't know why this happens, but it's so nice when you go out and dance to that little tune that goes like . . . what was that tune? Yeah, that's the one!

Well then, I also write to tell you that we continue in the dialogue, and today (I write these lines at dawn) we finished this first encounter they call "tripartite" because one is supposed to divide oneself into three in order not to lose sight of the local, the national, and the galactic. And speaking of galaxies, I'm going back to the ceiba. No, it's not that I'm afraid that Heriberto has eaten all the candy in my absence, or that Eva has organized feminist seminars with that Pedro Infante movie called *What Has That Woman Done To You?*[3] No ma'am, she's done nothing to me, that's just the name of the movie. Neither am I returning to the ceiba heights because I want to avoid Olivio's killer soccer kicks or Yeniperr's questions, and believe me, one is just as dreaded as the other. No, it turns out that . . .

---

1 In Spanish, "society" is a feminine noun, and thus the feminine form of address.

2 Despite government threats to arrest any Zapatistas who traveled outside Chiapas, Comandanta Ramona went to Mexico City for the founding meeting of the National Indigenous Congress (October 8-12, 1996). The sojourn of Ramona, who had become famous during the first negotiations of 1994 and had medical reasons for traveling to the capital, received much attention in the national and international press. See also "The Story of the Magical Chocolate Bunnies."

3 Pedro Infante starred in Ismael Rodríguez's 1951 film *A Toda Máquina 2 (¿Qué te ha dado esa mujer?)*.

well ... you know ... in the end, it's just that ... Haven't you heard the one about the October moon being bigger, etc., than all others? Yes, well it turns out that early the other morning I got by security and ... No ... Really, the only thing I caught was a cold so bad that every time I sneeze ... well, the shake-up of January 1st was nothing in comparison. Okay, the thing is, I escaped because when I am here they keep me inside four white walls where my friends don't come to see me, not from time to time, not one-by-one, not two-by-two, not from six to seven. I got out, and before I was captured by security I managed to catch sight of a moon, which reminded me of another moon two years ago ...

And on that dawn, like this one, the moon was a solitary breast vanishing behind the nocturnal hand of desire. But on this dawn I re-read Durito's last letter, and I should warn you, Durito has a marked tendency for philosophical discourse, so along with the letter comes what follows and is self-explanatory only from its title because it's called ...

The Seashell of the End and the Beginning (Neoliberalism and Architecture or the Ethics of the Search versus the Ethics of Destruction)

In the Lacandona, in the southeastern Mexican State of Chiapas, there is a deserted village surrounded by well-armed military posts. The name of this abandoned village was Guadalupe Tepeyac. Its inhabitants, indigenous Tojolabales, were expelled by the Mexican government's army in February of 1995, as the federal troops attempted to assassinate the leadership of the Zapatista Army of National Liberation.

But it isn't the painful exile of these indigenous people, who paid for their rebellion by living in the mountains, that I wanted to talk to you about. I wanted to talk to you about an architectural masterpiece that was born on the outskirts of the then-living Guadalupe Tepeyac in July and August of 1994. Illiterate for the most part and with a third grade education among the most "educated" of them, the Tojolabal architects raised in 28 days, a structure capable of holding 10,000 participants in what the Zapatistas called "The National Democratic Convention." In honor of Mexican history, the Zapatistas called the place of the encounter "Aguascalientes." The giant meeting place had an auditorium for 10,000 seated participants, a stage for 100, a library, a computer room, kitchens, lodgings, and parking lots. They say it even had an "area for holding any troublemakers."

Well, this is all rather anecdotal and one can learn more about it through other means (there are books, reports, photos, videos and movies from that time). What I want to point out now is a detail that went unnoticed by all those present at the 1994 Aguascalientes of Guadalupe Tepeyac (this Aguascalientes was destroyed in February 1995). The detail I refer to was so large that, ironically, it couldn't be easily discerned at first glance. It is this gigantic and unnoticed detail that is the subject of this essay.

It turns out that the auditorium and the stage were in the middle of a giant seashell going and coming, without end or beginning. Let me explain; don't get frustrated. The indigenous Zapatistas had raised a more or less conventional auditorium: a sort of stage that looked like the keel of a ship—a flat part in front with chairs, and a gallery with wooden benches (taking advantage of the slope of a hill).[4] All in all, nothing extraordinary. If anything was interesting, it was that the benches were mounted on forked branches and tied with vines. There was no metal in the gallery.

When they began to construct the lodgings, the library and other facilities, the indigenous Tojolobales of the Zapatista rebellion, now makeshift architects, began to construct houses in an apparent disorder that, or so thought the Sup then, were only scattered about the surroundings of the gigantic auditorium. It wasn't until he was assessing the capacity of each building, that the Sup noticed that one of the houses was "crooked," that is, it had an inexplicable break in one of its edges. He didn't pay much attention. It was Comandante Tacho, a Tojolabal, who asked him,

"What do you think of the seashell?"

"What seashell?" the Sup answered, following the Zapatista tradition of answers that are questions, the eternal game of the question to the mirror.

"Well, the one that surrounds the auditorium," answered Comandante Tacho as if he had said, "The day has light." The Sup only stared back at him and Tacho understood that the Sup did not understand what he meant, so he took him to the "crooked" house and showed him the roof where the cross-timbers made a capricious break.

"This is where the shell curves," he told him.

The Sup must have put on a "So?" face (similar to the one you must have now), which is why Comandante Tacho hurried to make a drawing in the mud with a stick. Tacho's drawing showed the location of all the buildings that surrounded the auditorium and yes, thanks to that break in the "crooked" house, the whole thing looked like a seashell. The Sup agreed in silence after looking at the drawing. Then Comandante Tacho left to see about the tarp that would cover the auditorium in case it rained.

The Sup was left standing there, in front of the "crooked" house, thinking that the "crooked" house was not really "crooked." It was only the broken curve of the seashell that needed to be drawn. He was doing that when a journalist approached him and asked, looking for a response of profound political content, what Aguascalientes meant to the Zapatistas.

"A seashell," answered the Sup laconically.

"A seashell?" he asked, and looked at him as if he hadn't understood the question.

---

4 This vision of the auditorium as a ship was a metaphor around which Marcos wove his opening address to the CND.

"Yes," he told him. And, showing him the point of the break of the "crooked" house, the Sup left.

Yes, I agree with you. The seashell of Aguascalientes could only have been discerned from above. What's more, only from a certain height.

I mean, you had to fly very high to discover the Zapatista seashell that was being drawn on these poor rebel lands. On one of its edges, there was a library and on another the old "safe house." The history of that "safe house" is similar to that of the EZLN in the Mayan indigenous communities. That little house was built far from the village, so no one would see them, the first Tojolabales who joined the EZLN. There they held meetings, they studied, and they gathered the tortillas and beans that they would send to the mountains where the insurgents were.

So, there was the Mayan seashell. The spiral with no beginning or end. Where does a seashell begin and end? At its most inner or outer part? Does a seashell go in or out?

The seashell of the Mayan rebel leaders began and ended at the "safe house," but it also began and ended at the library. The place of the encounter, of the dialogue, of the transition, of the search, *that* was the seashell of Aguascalientes.

From what "architectural" tradition did the indigenous Zapatistas borrow their idea of the seashell? I don't know, but surely the seashell, that spiral, is as inviting in coming as it is in going, and in truth, I wouldn't dare to say which part of a seashell begins or ends it.

Months later, in October of 1994, a small group from civil society arrived at Aguascalientes to complete the installation of electricity in the library. They left after a few days of work. That particularly cold and foggy morning, the moon was a promise upon which to rest the cheek and desire, and a cello bled a few notes at midnight in a light mist. It was like a movie. The Sup watched from a corner, protected by the shadows and the ski mask. A movie. The beginning or the end of a movie? After that group left, no one else returned to Aguascalientes until the party at year's end. Then they disappeared again. On February 10, 1995, air-transported, Federal troops took Guadalupe Tepeyac. The first thing they did when they entered Aguascalientes was to destroy the library and the safe house, the beginning and end of the seashell. Then they destroyed the rest.

For some strange reason, the breaking-point of the crooked house remained standing for several months afterward. It is said that in December of 1995, it fell only after other Aguascalientes were born in the mountains of the Mexican southeast.[5]

All of the above shows that the ethics of Power are the same as that of destruction, and the ethics of the seashell are the same as that of the search. And this is very important for architecture and for the understanding of neoliberalism. Right?

---

5 The "other" Aguascalientes were the five autonomous villages that hosted the Intercontinental Encounter in the summer of 1996: La Realidad, La Garrucha, Morelia, Oventic and Roberto Barrios.

That's how Durito's thesis ends, which, as you can tell, is only for academics. . .

So what is all this about beetles, seashells, and blushing moons? Well, the truth is that ten years ago on a morning in October, Old Antonio explained to me that a seashell is used for seeing within yourself and for jumping up, but I'll tell you about that on another occasion. I share with you now Durito's thesis because he's very demanding about what he means when he says, "Humanity should benefit from my great knowledge."

Yes, you're right. I also think that, for a beetle, he's very pedantic, but he argues that knights-errant are not pedantic, but simply knowledgeable about the strength of their arms and the size of their talent, especially when it comes to beating up scoundrels and picking on rogues.

And so madam, I say goodbye. We hope you don't forget that we're still [out] here. Well, we hope that at least you don't forget too soon.

Vale. Salud, and the unanswered question is: if one is inside the seashell, which way should one go? Towards the inside or the outside?

From the mountains of the Mexican Southeast
Subcomandante Insurgente Marcos
Mexico, October 1996

P.S. that fulfills its editorial duty – Oh! I almost forgot, in Durito's letter there is a story that, supposedly, I should add to his book *Stories for A Sleepless Solitude*, in the section called "Stories For Deciding." Here goes then, the story is called:

The Story of the Live Person and the Dead Person

Once there was a live person and a dead person.
And the dead person said to the live person,
"My, I envy you, so restless."
And then the live person said to the dead person,
"My, I envy you, so tranquil."
And so they were, envying one another, when suddenly, at full gallop, a bay horse at bay went by.
End and moral of the story: I reiterate that every final choice is a trap. It's necessary to find the bay horse at bay.

Don Durito de la Lacandona
(For fan letters, interview requests, carnations, and signatures of support for the "Beetle Anti-Big-Boots Society" please write to "Little Huapac Hole #69, Mountains of the Mexican Southeast (right next to where the Sup lives)." Please note for phone calls: if the answering machine doesn't pick up, don't worry. It's because I don't have one.)

Vale once again. *Salud*, and since we're talking about the traps of final choices everyone will agree with me that when it comes to choosing whether to come or go . . . it's always better to come . . .

The Sup with the flu and, obviously, something of a fever.

* * *

Forever Never

On November 29, 1996, COCOPA, CONAI, and the EZLN submitted a proposal for constitutional reforms to Mexico's Secretary of the Interior Emilio Chuayffet. The suggested reforms focused on autonomy and indigenous rights in the San Andrés Accords of February 1996. Despite Chuayffet's initial positive reaction, on December 5th he rejected the possibility of any constitutional reforms. In response, Marcos issues an urgent telegram calling for an intercontinental dance to create a rainbow. He also shares a letter from Durito that tells the story of "Forever Never." This communiqué marks the last appearance of Durito in the EZLN communiqués for a period of almost three years.

First published in *La Jornada,* December 8, 1996. Originally translated by Cecilia Rodríguez

December 8, 1996
URGENT TELEGRAM
For: National and International Civil Society
From: Subcomandante Insurgente Marcos
CCRI-CG of the EZLN

Madam:

Salud, greetings. Stop. Bow to you many times. Stop. Supreme government with amnesia. Stop. Forgotten agreements.[1]

Stop. Renewed excuses. Stop. Probable need for more Indian blood in order to refresh memory. Stop. Your presence is urgent. Stop. An intercontinental dance may serve to refresh memory. Stop. The grays hope to win. Stop. Rainbow needed urgently. Stop. If there is a dance I want one. Stop. Sigh. Stop. After you. Stop. Sigh. Stop. Hand in hand and hand on waist. Stop. Sigh. Stop. 1, 2, 3. Stop. Sigh. *Vale*. Stop. *Salud*. Stop. May the dance paint floor-to-ceiling. Stop and End.

The Sup, thinking telegraphically and naively, that the periods and hyphens mark a tune for dancing and a path for walking.

From the mountains of the Mexican Southeast
Subcomandante Insurgente Marcos

P.S. that announces the reappearance of a beetle remembered among so many forgotten agreements.

A letter from Durito arrived. He says he is returning in order to return the memory of the scoundrels who have come back for their jurisdictions. He says he may be a little late because Pegasus (his turtle, I mean, his mount) gets vertigo at high speeds (you know, those above 50 centimeters per hour), and because he has many gifts (among them a lock of hair which holds promise according to Durito). He also says someone should save him a dance, that with that "hand in hand and hand on waist" he has many hands left over and asks if he can put them (his hands, of course) where the sighs become stereophonic. He says other things, which morality and good behavior do not permit me to repeat if the stocks of the Lilliputian vendor are to keep their value (I mean what if we are sued).

Ah! He also adds a story whose text says:

The Story of the Forever Never

Once there was a he who was all night. Shadow of shadows, solitary step, he walked many nights in order to find her. Once there was a she who was all day.

---

1 On February 1, 1997, 10,000 Zapatistas marched through the streets of San Cristóbal demanding that the accords be respected. On March 4, COCOPA withdrew its constitutional reform proposal from legislative consideration.

Twinkle of wheat, pure dance, she walked many days in order to find him. They looked for each other much, he and she. The night pursued the day much. They both knew, he and she, of the search that could not be found. It seemed it would never happen, it seemed impossible, it seemed never, ever . . . . And then the dawn came, for him and her. Forever, never . . .

Tan-tan.

Durito's letter ended with this story. I, meanwhile, have already asked for sanctuary against being forgotten.

Vale made of nuts with nutmeg. *Salud*, and hope that the dawn will arrive soon and forever . . .

The *Sup* looking at a photo of Ché, which inexplicably, smiles. (Ché does, of course.)

* * *

The Hour of the Little Ones, Part I: The Return of ...

More than three years since he set out to visit Mexico City, Don Durito, now a pirate, returns to visit Marcos after a long voyage to Europe. In the fall of 1999, amidst increasingly violent repression against Zapatistas in Chiapas and against students in Mexico City on strike against neoliberal policies at UNAM, Marcos releases this five-part communiqué. These letters form part of a series known as "Siete Veces Dos" (Seven Times Two), emphasizing solidarity with other national and international struggles, and dealing particularly with various struggles of the little ones: flood and earthquake victims, Latinos in the United States, homosexuals and students.

First published in *La Jornada*, October 18, 1999. Originally translated by irlandesa.

October 12, 1999

For Don Emilio Krieger, who was always with the little ones.[1]

For the children of "El Molino" (of the Francisco Villa Popular Front) who lost their homes in a fire.[2]

In the letter box of time there are joys
that no one shall call for / that no one will ever
claim / and they will end up faded,
yearning for the taste of the elements
and nonetheless / from time's letter box
loose epistles will suddenly depart,
ready to settle into some dream
where chance fears are waiting.
—Mario Benedetti[3]

It's just barely raining, a humid and cold breeze. However, the beating of the rain against the mountain over the last few days has been so much and so strong that it has left her more than a little dented, and there are scars that have entirely ruined her skirt. But, well, after such a storm, this drizzle is welcome. It is the time of the rains. The time of the little ones.

A good man has died. What can one say when a good man has died? Some children, who fearlessly opened their homes to receive one thousand one hundred and eleven faceless ones, have lost their homes. What can one say when a child loses her home? One says nothing; one is only silent. Because many times sorrows are for keeping silent. Nonetheless, attempting some relief, the little ones from this side of the blockade extend their bridges, like hands, to where the good man is missing, and to where doors and windows are missing, to open up to the other forgotten and little one, the dignified and rebel other. They build their bridges to walk with others, to be close, to not forget. Perhaps that is why, unhurriedly, the shadow tenderly hones the first two letters of this fourth epistle, seeking to coax a smile amidst so much pain that is suffered there.

Down there, the candle reiterates its vocation as a beacon for that sailor in the mountain who, lost, navigates the shadows of dawn. Yes, let's go, but be care-

---

1 Emilio Krieger Vásquez, a nationally known constitutional lawyer responsible for many legal actions in defense of the poor and of human rights, died September 19, 1999. He founded the National Association of Democratic Lawyers or ANAD (Asociación de Abogados Democráticos), and was one-time president of the Federal Electoral Institute, or IFE (Instituto Federal Electoral). His public writings in defense of human rights and against the Salinas administration led to attacks on him and his wife in April 1994. He was invited to the Zapatista "Dialogue with Civil Society" in October 1998.

2 On September 22, 1999, a fire destroyed more than 800 homes in the community of El Molino in Mexico City.

3 See Mario Benedetti, *Buzón del tiempo* (Alfaguara, Madrid: 1999). See also Angélica Abelleyra's interview with Benedetti about the Zapatistas in *La Jornada* (May 12, 1997).

ful with the mud and those puddles. You're going slowly? Well then, I'll go ahead and from there I'll show you the way. Good, here I am. Yes. The shadow is alone once more. No . . . Just a minute . . . There seems to be someone else. That candle won't stop flickering! No, I'm not able to see who else is there, but it's obvious that there's someone, because the shadow is speaking to him. No, it must be refusing him, because it does nothing but repeat "no, no and no." Wait, I'll go over to that corner to see better. There, that's it. Hmmm. I believe our favorite shadow has gone crazy. No one can be seen around here. And it, with its 'no, no and no.' In short, it was to be expected, so much rain and so much early rising would drive anyone crazy. What? But I already told you no one was there! I should move closer? And if he sees me? All right then, slowly and discreetly. No, I tell you, there's no one. Just a minute! Wait! Yes, I can make something out now . . . There, in a corner! Yes! What a relief! It hasn't gone crazy, no. What happened is that it was so small I didn't notice it . . . What? Who is it speaking with? Well, then . . . you'll see. Do you really want to know? Yes? Well . . . well, with a beetle!

Durito!
Letter 4a

"No, no and no!" I tell Durito for the umpteenth time.

Yes, Durito has returned. But before explaining my repeated "no," I should tell you all the whole story.

Early the other morning, when the rain formed a stream right in the middle of the hut, Durito arrived onboard a can of sardines that had a pencil stuck in the middle, and, on it, a handkerchief or something like that, which I would later find out was a sail.[4] On the highest part of the mainmast, excuse me, of the pencil, a black flag was flying, with a fierce skull resting on a pair of crossbones. It wasn't exactly a pirate ship but, well, at least a pirate sardine can. The thing is that the ship, or the can, landed right at the edge of the table, and it did so with such a din that Durito came flying out and landed right on my boot. Durito composed himself as best he could and exclaimed,

"Today . . . today . . ." he turns around to look at me and says, "Hey, you, carrot nose! Tell me the date promptly!"

I hesitate, a bit for wanting to embrace Durito since he'd returned, another little bit for wanting to kick him for the "carrot nose" thing, and another bit more for . . . for . . . the date? . . .

"Yes! The date. That is, day, month, current year. Wake up, fool, for it seems that you're in the presidential debates! Give me the date!"

I look at my watch and say, "October 12, 1999."

---

4 Durito's plan to sail to Europe in a sardine can was first mentioned in January 1996 in "Durito to Conquer Europe."

"October 12? By my faith, nature imitates art! Good. Today, October 12, 1999, I declare discovered, conquered and liberated this beautiful Caribbean island that answers to the name of . . . of . . . quick, the name of the island!"[5]

"What island?" I ask, still disconcerted.

"What do you mean, what island, fool? Well, this one! What other one would it be? There is no pirate worth his salt without an island for hiding treasure and pain . . ."

"Island? I always thought it was a tree, a ceiba to be more precise," I say, leaning over the edge of the dense canopy.

"Well, you're deceived, it's an island. Where have you heard of a pirate landing on a ceiba? So, either tell me the name of this island, or your fate will be to serve as lunch for the sharks," Durito says threateningly.

"Sharks?" I say, with a gulp. And I argue, stammering, "It has no name . . ."

"'It Has No Name,' Hmmm. By my faith, that is a right dignified name for a pirate's island. Good, today, October 12, 1999, I declare the island of 'It Has No Name' to be discovered, conquered and liberated, and I name this individual of obvious nose my boatswain, first mate, cabin boy and lookout."

I try to ignore the insult, as well as the multitude of conferred posts, and I say, "So . . . now you're a pirate!"

"'A pirate?' Hell no! I am THE PIRATE!"

Just now I notice Durito's appearance. A black patch adorns his right eye, a red scarf covers his head, on one of his multiple arms a twisted little wire acts as a hook, and in another shines the little stick that once was Excalibur. Now, I'm not sure, but it must be some kind of sword, saber, or whatever pirates use. Besides that, tied to one of his several little feet he has a little branch as if it were . . . as if it were . . . hmmm . . . a wooden leg!

"And, so, what do you think?" Durito says as he makes a half turn so that all the elegance he has fabricated for his pirate's suit can be appreciated.

I ask him with care, "And so now you're called?"

"'Black Shield'!" Durito says pompously, and adds: "But you can put 'Escudo Negro' for those who aren't globalized."

"'Black Shield'? But . . ."

"Certainly! Was there not a 'Redbeard' and a 'Blackbeard'?"[6]

---

5 October 12th is officially celebrated as "Columbus Day" but is also known as *Día de la Raza*, or Indigenous Peoples' Day. On that day in 1992, protestors pulled down the public statute of the Conquistador Diego de Mazariegos in San Cristóbal de las Casas. This protest marked the first public appearance of the Zapatistas. See Neil Harvey, *The Chiapas Rebellion: The Struggle for Land and Dignity* (Durham: Duke University Press, 1998).

6 "Redbeard" or Khayr ad-Din Barbarossa (c.1483-1546) from Lesbos was the most famous of the Barbary Coast pirates of the 1500s. He fought Spanish and Portuguese incursions into North Africa, at first independently and then for the Sultan of the Ottoman Empire. "Blackbeard" or Edward Teach (c. 1680-1718) from Bristol, England operated out of North Carolina, in league with the Governor of that state, between 1716 and 1718.

"Well, yes, but . . ."

"Make no 'buts' about it! I am 'Black Shield'! Compared with me, 'Blackbeard' is barely gray, and 'Redbeard' is more faded than your bandana!"

Durito has said this brandishing sword and hook at the same time. Standing now, on the bow of his can of sardi . . . excuse me, of his vessel, he begins reciting the "Pirate's Song" . . .

"'With ten cannons on each side' . . ."

"Durito," I try to call him to his senses.

"'Wind at the stern, full sail' . . ."

"Durito . . ."

"'It does not cross the sea but flies' . . ."

"Durito!"

"What? A royal galleon is within our reach? Quickly! Unfurl the sails! Prepare to board!"[7]

"Durito!" I shout, desperate now.

"Calm down, don't shout or you'll look like an unemployed buccaneer. What's the matter with you?"

"Could you tell me where you've been, where you came from, and what brings you to these lands, excuse me, these islands?" I ask, more calmly now.

"I have been in Italy, England, Denmark, Germany, France, Greece, Holland, Belgium, Sweden, the Iberian Peninsula, the Canary Islands, in all of Europe." Durito has said all this delivering gestures to the right and to the left.

"In Venice, I ate with Dario one of those pastas that the Italians love so much, and that leave me i-m-m-o-b-i-l-e."

"Just a minute! Which Dario? You don't mean that you were eating with Dario . . ."

"Yes, Dario Fo.[8] Well, eating, eating, no. He was eating; I was watching him eat. Because, look, that spaghetti gives me a stomach ache, and even more so when they put 'pasto' on it."

"'Pesto,'" I correct him.

"'Pasto' or 'Pesto,' it still tastes like grass.[9] As I was telling you, I arrived in Venice from Rome after escaping from one of those "Temporary Detention Centers (for Immigrants)," that are a kind of concentration camp where Italian officials isolate—before expelling from the country—everyone that comes from other countries, and who are, therefore, 'different others.' Leaving wasn't easy—I had to start a riot. Clearly the support from those men and women in Italy who are against institutionalized racism was fundamental.[10] The fact is that Dario

---

7 These are the opening lines of the poem "The Pirate's Song" by José de Espronceda, a popular romantic poet of 19th-century Spain. See *Hispanic Anthology: Poems Translated from the Spanish by English and North American Poets*, Thomas Walsh, ed. (New York: G. P. Putnam's Sons, 1920).

8 Dario Fo, an Italian playwright and actor famous for his political farces, won the Nobel Prize for Literature in 1997.

9 In Spanish *pasto* literally means "grass. "

wanted me to help him with some ideas for a theatrical work, and I didn't have the heart to say no."

"Durito . . ."

"Afterwards I went on the march against the UN for the war in Kosovo."

"That should be 'against NATO' . . ."

"It's the same. The thing is that, after a series of misadventures, I set off to the Island of Lanzarote."

"Just a minute! The island of Lanzarote? Isn't that where José Saramago lives?"[11]

"Yes, well, I call him 'Pepe.' What happened is that Pepe invited me for coffee so that I could tell him about my experiences in the Europe of the Euro. It was magnificent . . ."

"Yes, I imagine that it would have been magnificent to chat with Saramago . . ."

"No, I'm referring to the coffee that Pilarica prepared for us. She really does make a magnificent cup of coffee."

"You're referring to Pilar del Río?"[12]

"The same."

"So, one day you're eating with Dario Fo, and the next you're having coffee with José Saramago."

"Yes, those days I was rubbing elbows with nothing but Nobel Prize winners. But I was telling you that I had a fierce argument with Pepe."

"And the reason?"

"Well, the prologue he wrote for my book. It seemed to me in bad taste that he would reduce me, the great and even-tempered *Don Durito de La Lacandona*, to the world of Coleoptera Lamellicornia."[13]

"And how did the argument end?"

"Fine, I challenged him to a duel, just as the laws of knight-errantry demand."

"And? . . ."

"And nothing, I saw that Pilarica's heart was breaking, since it was obvious that I would win, and I forgave him . . ."

---

10 The free passage of European citizens, part of the consolidation of the European Union, also mandated harsher treatment of non-European immigrants, resulting in protests both from the detainees and pro-immigrant, anti-racist activists.

11 José Saramago is a left-wing Portuguese writer who won the Nobel Prize for literature in 1998. Saramago has frequently traveled to Mexico and spoken out against government repression in Chiapas.

12 Pilar del Río, a Spanish writer and journalist, has written on the politics of Andalucian autonomy.

13 Durito is referring to José Saramago's prologue to the book by Subcomandante Marcos, *Don Durito de la Lacandona* (San Cristóbal de Las Casas: Centro de Información y Análisis de Chiapas, A.C., 1999). In biological taxonomy *coleoptera* (beetles) is one order of the class *insecta*. *Lamellicornia* is one cuperfamily of coleoptera.

"You forgave José Saramago?"

"Well, not completely. For me to forget the affront, he shall have to come to these lands and declare, at the top of his voice, the following speech: "Hear ye. Tyrants, tremble. Damsels, sigh. Children, rejoice. The sad and needy, be glad. Hear ye. Once more across these lands walks the ever grand, the magnificent, the incomparable, the well-loved, the long-awaited, the onomatopoetic, the greatest of knights-errant, Don Durito de la Lacandona.""

"You would force José Saramago to come to Mexico to say those . . . those . . . those things?"

"Yes, it seemed like a light punishment to me as well. But after all, he is a Nobel Prize winner, and I might need someone to do the prologue for my next book."

"Durito!" I chide him, and add, "Fine, but how was it that you turned into a pirate, excuse me, into THE PIRATE?"

"It was Sabina's fault . . ." Durito says, as if he were talking about a drinking buddy.

"You mean you also saw Joaquín Sabina?"[14]

"But of course! He wanted me to help him with the musical arrangements for his next record. But don't interrupt me. It happened that Sabina and I were bar hopping and chasing women in Madrid, when we reached Las Ramblas."

"But that's in Barcelona!"

"Yes, there's the mystery. Because a few minutes before we had been in a dive in Madrid, captivated by an olive-skinned beauty, an Andalucian from Jaén, to be more precise, and then I had to go and satisfy one of those biological needs they call 'primary.' That's when I mistook the doors, and, instead of the one for the 'water closet,' I opened the one to the street. And it turns out that it was in Las Ramblas. Yes, there was no longer any Madrid, nor Sabina, nor dive, nor olive skin, but I still needed a 'water closet' because a gentleman can't go about doing those things in just any corner. Ergo, I looked for a bar, trying to remember from when I used to hang out with Manolo . . ."

"I imagine you're referring to Manuel Vázquez Montalbán," I ask, ready to not be astonished by anything.[15]

"Yes, but it's too long a name, so I just call him 'Manolo.' Then I was anxiously, restlessly and feverishly looking for someplace with a 'water closet' when there appeared in front of me, in a dark alley, three gigantic shadows . . ."

"Bandits!" I interrupted, startled.

"Negative. They were three trash dumpsters, under whose shadow I calculated that I could do, intimately and discreetly, what I was thinking of doing in the 'water closet.' And so I did. So, with the satisfaction of the duty accomplished, I lit my pipe and heard, with absolute clarity, the twelve chimes from 'Big Ben.'"

"But, Durito, that's in London, England . . ."

---

14 See note in "Durito II"
15 See note in "To Lady Civil Society."

"Yes, it seemed strange to me as well, but what wasn't that night? I walked until I came to a sign that read 'Pirates. Wanted. No previous experience required. Prefer Beetles and Knights-errant. Information at The Black Speck bar.'" Durito lights his pipe and continues,

"I continued walking, looking for The Black Speck's sign. I was feeling my way, barely making out corners and walls, so thick was the fog that was falling over the alleys of Copenhagen that early morning . . ."

"Copenhagen? But weren't you in London?"

"Look, if you keep interrupting me with the obvious, I'll send you to the plank and from there to the sharks. I already told you that everything was quite strange, and if I had read the sign soliciting pirates in London, I was then looking for The Black Speck bar in Copenhagen, Denmark. I got lost for a few minutes in the Tivoli Gardens, but I kept on looking. Suddenly, on a corner, I found it. A pale light filtered from a solitary street lamp, barely piercing the fog, illuminating a sign that read 'The Black Speck. Bar and Table Dance. Special Discount for Beetles and Knights-Errant.' Not before appreciating the high regard and affection they hold in Europe for beetles and knights-errant . . ."

"Maybe because they don't suffer from them," I barely murmured.

"Don't think that the irony of your murmurings escapes me," Durito says. "But, for the good of your readers, I will continue with my narrative. There will be time enough to settle accounts with you.

"I was saying that, after appreciating the great intelligence of the Europeans for recognizing and admiring the greatness that some of us beings possess, I entered this bar in Montmartre, close to 'Sacre Coeur' . . ."

Durito stays silent for a moment, waiting for me to interrupt him by saying that that is in Paris, France, but I say nothing. Durito nods with satisfaction and continues:

"Once inside, a purple haze invaded the atmosphere. I sat down at a table in the darkest corner. It didn't take a second for a waiter, in perfect German, to tell me, 'Welcome to East Berlin,' and, without saying anything else, left me what I took to be the *carte* or menu. I opened it, and it consisted of one single sentence: 'Pirates in training, second floor.' I went up a staircase that was just behind me. I reached a long corridor flanked by some windows. Through one of them the canals and 400 bridges that raise Amsterdam above the 90 islands could be seen. In the distance the 'White Tower' could be seen, which reminds the Greeks of Salonica of the extremes of intolerance. Still along the corridor, further ahead, another window offered a view of the curved peak of the Swiss Matterhorn. Further along could be made out the miraculous stones of the Irish Blarney Castle that give the gift of words to whomever kisses them. On the left, rose the bell tower of the main Square in Bruges, Belgium. Following the corridor, before coming to a dilapidated door, a window looked towards the Plaza of Miracoli, and, by stretching one's hand a bit, one could touch the swooning incline of the Tower of Pisa.

"Yes, that corridor looked out on half of Europe, and I wouldn't have been surprised if there had been a sign on the door that said 'Welcome to the Maastricht Treaty.'[16] But, no, the door didn't even have a sign on it. What's more, it didn't have a latch. I knocked, and nothing. I pushed the heavy sheet of wood, and it gave way without difficulty. A mournful creaking accompanied the opening of the door . . .

"I then entered a room that was in partial darkness. Inside, on a table full of papers, an oil lamp poorly illuminated the face of a man of indefinite age, a patch covered his right eye and he had a hook for a hand that pulled at his whiskers. The man's gaze was fixed on the table. Nothing was heard, and the silence was so heavy that it clung like dust to the skin." Durito brushed the dust off his pirate suit.

"'Now there's a Pirate,' I said to myself, and I moved towards the table. The man didn't move at all. I coughed a bit, which is what we educated gentlemen do to attract attention. The pirate did not lift his gaze. Instead, a little parrot (that I just then noticed on his left shoulder) began reciting, with such excellent intonation that even Don José de Espronceda would have applauded, the line that goes: 'With ten cannons on each side, wind at the stern, full sail, it does not cross the sea, it flies, a swift sailing brig.'"[17]

"'Sit down,' he said. I don't know if it was the man or the parrot, but the pirate, or the one I supposed was a pirate, handed me a piece of paper without saying a word. I read it. I will not bore your readers or you, so I will tell you, to summarize, that it was an application to join the 'Great Brotherhood of Pirates, Buccaneers and Terrors of the Sea A.C. of C.V. of R.O.' I filled it out without delay, not without, of course, underlining my status as beetle and knight-errant. I handed the paper to the man and he read it in silence."

"Upon finishing, he looked at me slowly with his one eye and told me,

"'I was waiting for you, Don Durito. Know that I am the last true, living pirate in the world. And I say "true" because now there are an infinite number of "pirates" in financial centers and great government palaces who steal, kill, destroy and loot, without ever touching any water save that found in their bathtubs. Here is your mission (he hands me a dossier of old parchments): find the treasure and put it in a safe place. Now, pardon me, but I must die.' And as he said those words, he let his head fall to the table. Yes, he was dead. The parrot took flight and went out through a window, saying, 'The exile of Mitilini is dead, dead is the bastard son of Lesbos, dead the pride of the Aegean Sea.[18] Open your nine doors, fearsome hell, for there the great Redbeard will rest. He has found the one who will

16 The Maastricht Treaty, which established the European Union in 1993, marked an important step toward the creation of a neoliberal Europe. It laid the basis for the creation of a Europe-wide monetary union and common currency (the Euro) by requiring member governments to impose anti-wage austerity as a condition for full participation. The Treaty guaranteed the free movement of capital and, along with the Schengen Agreement, unified the EU's policies for restricting the movement of labor.

17 From the poem "The Pirate's Song." See note 7.

follow in his footsteps, and the one who made of the ocean but a tear now sleeps. The pride of true Pirates will now sail with Black Shield.' Below the window, the Swedish port of Gothenburg spread out, and, in the distance, a *nyckelharpa* was weeping . . ."[19]

"And what did you do?" I asked, now completely immersed in the story (although a bit seasick from so many names of places and locales).

"Without even opening the dossier of parchments, I retraced my steps. I went back down the corridor and down to the Table Dance-Bar, I opened the door and I went out into the night, right onto the Paseo de Pereda, in Santander, on the Cantabrian Sea. I headed towards Bilbao, entering Euskal Herria. Near Donostia-San Sebastian, I saw young people dancing the *Eurresku* and *Ezpatadantza* to the rhythm of the *txistu* and drum.[20] I climbed the Pyrenees and came to the Ebro River once more between Huesca and Zaragoza. There I managed to find a vessel and I continued on to the delta where the Mediterranean receives the Ebro, in the midst of the roar of the Vent de Dalt.[21] I climbed Tarragonia again on foot, and from there, to Barcelona, passing by where the famous Battle of Montjuic took place."[22] Durito pauses, as if to gather speed.

"In Barcelona, I set off on a freighter that carried me to Palma de Mallorca. We headed southeast, skirting Valencia and, further south, Alicante. We sighted Almeria, and, far off, Granada. Throughout Andalucia, a flamenco song set palms, guitars and heels in motion. A giant *zambra* accompanied us until, after doubling back by way of Algeciras, we crossed Cadiz, and at the mouth of the Guadalquivir, 'voices of death sounded,' coming from Cordoba and Seville.[23] A

---

18 This passage refers to Barbarossa who was born in Mitilini on the island of Lesbos in the Aegean Sea and wound up in Constantinople as the Admiral of the Sultan's fleet.

19 A *nyckelharpa* is a traditional Swedish stringed instrument played with a bow and keys that slide under the strings.

20 *Eurresku* (or *aurresku*) is an open circle dance with individuals performing spectacular and difficult steps in the center of the circle. *Ezpatandantza* is a kind of canopy dance, usually performed with swords or staffs. The *txistu* is a small, four-fingered flute played with the left hand while the right hand beats a drum (*taboril*) with a drumstick.

21 *El Vent de Dalt* means, literally, the Wind from Above. A strong wind blows down the Ebro River Valley from the Pyrenees to the coast of Catalonia. The zone upstream from the Ebro's delta is known as the "upper river" (*rebera de Dalt* in Catalan); the wind that roars through the delta is known as *El Vent de Dalt*.

22 Tarragonia is a region in Catalonia south of Barcelona. During the Thirty Years War, the Spanish king Philip IV sent an army to Catalonia to draw the province into war against the French. The Catalans, however, revolted, declared a Republic and allied with the French. When the Spanish army tried to subdue the rebels in Barcelona they were decisively defeated by the Catalans in a battle at Montjuic on January 26, 1641.

23 A *zambra* is both a gypsy party and a slow sensuous dance of Moorish origins now claimed by both Flamenco and belly dance. "Voices of death sounded near Guadalquivir" is a line from Federico García Lorca's poem "The Death of Antoñito El Camborio." See also note in "Durito Names Marcos His Squire."

cante jondo called out, 'Go to sleep now, Durito, beloved son of the world, leave your aimless wandering, and end your beautiful dance.'[24] We could still just make out Huelva, and then we headed to the seven main Canary Islands. There we made landfall and I gathered a bit of sap from the tree they call 'Drago,' good, they say, for the ills of body and soul. That's how I arrived at the island of Lanzarote and had the altercation with Don Pepe, which I've already related to you."

"Uff! You've traveled far," I say, weary from the mere telling of Durito's travels.

"And what I've left out!" he said, proudly.

I ask,

"Then, you are no longer a knight-errant?"

"Of course I am! The 'pirate' thing is temporary. Only while I carry out the mission entrusted to me by the deceased Redbeard."

Durito keeps staring at me.

I think: Whenever Durito stares at me like that it's because . . . because . . .

"No!" I tell him.

"'No' what? I haven't even said anything to you," says Durito, feigning surprise.

"No, you haven't said anything to me, but that look doesn't mean anything good. Whatever you're going to tell me, my answer is 'no.' I have enough problems as a guerrilla to get involved now as a buccaneer. And I'm not crazy enough to set sail in a sardine can!"

"'Pirate,' not 'Buccaneer.' It's not the same thing, my dear and large-nosed cabin boy. And it's not a sardine can, it's a frigate and it's called 'Learn From the Mistakes of Others.'"

I ignore the insult and reply,

"'Learn From Others' Mistakes'? Hmmm, strange name. But, in the end, 'Buccaneer' or 'Pirate,' or whatever it is, it means trouble."

"As you wish, but, before anything else, you should carry out your duty," Durito says solemnly.

"My duty?" I ask, letting down my guard.

"Yes, you should communicate the good news to the entire world."

"What 'good news'?"

"Why, that I've returned. And it doesn't have to be one of those long, dense, and boring communiqués with which you torture your readers. What's more, so as not to run any risks, I have a draft here."

Having said that, Durito takes a paper out from one of his bags.

I read and re-read. I turn to look at Durito and start with the 'no, no and no' that begins this tale.

In order to not bore you any more, I'll tell you that Durito was trying to get me to release a letter or communiqué destined for national and international civ-

---

24 *Cante jondo* is type of flamenco song characterized by its mournful rhythm and tone.

il society, announcing that Durito had now returned.

Of course I refused, since I had to respond to the letter sent to us by those participating in the International Civil Commission for Human Rights Observation (CCIODH), asking us to grant them the same trust which we gave them in 1998, to receive them and give them our word, since they would soon come for a new visit.[25] Here it is then:

Zapatista Army of National Liberation
Mexico, October of 1999
To the International Civil Commission of Human Rights Observation

Brothers and Sisters:
In the name of the children, women, men and elders of the Zapatista Army of National Liberation and of the Indigenous Communities in Resistance, I am communicating to you that it would be an honor for us that you visit these lands. You have our trust; you will be treated with the respect you deserve as international observers, and you will not have, on our part, any impediments to your humanitarian work. We will also be pleased to talk with you. We await you.

Vale. Salud, and remember that here, in addition to dignity, mud also abounds.

From the Island that 'Has No Name,' excuse me,
From the mountains of the Mexican Southeast

Subcomandante Insurgente Marcos
Mexico, "Learn From the Mistakes of Others" Frigate

Beware: Postscripts follow.

P.S. that extends its arm for twisting.
It so happens that, following my repeated negatives, Durito convinced me, offering me part of the treasure. Yes, we have reviewed the parchments, and there's a treasure map. Of course, we still need to decipher them, but the prospect of an adventure is irresistible.

And Durito's text? After arduous negotiation, we agreed that it would go as a postscript. Ergo, here follows the . . .

---

25   The Comisión Civil Internacional de Observación por los Derechos Hermanos (CCIODH), an organization of 230 activists from 13 countries, began to investigate Mexico's human rights record in 1997 with special attention to the situation in Chiapas. The first visit took place February 16-28, 1998 and was followed by a report to the European Parliament. The second visit took place November 15-25, 1999. In keeping with a more general campaign to exclude foreign observers, the Zedillo administration denied FM3 visas (non-tourist) to many of the CCIODH delegates.

P.S. for National and International Civil Society
Madame:

It is my honor to communicate to you the super-duper [that's what Durito's text says] good news, the gift that will cause young and old to rejoice. Let the great financial centers tremble! Let panic reach the palaces of great and false gentlemen! Let those from below celebrate! Let the most beautiful maidens prepare their finest gowns and let the spring of their wombs sigh! Let good men tip their hats! Let children dance with joy! The best and greatest of pirates [crossed out in the original], excuse me, of knights-errant that the world has ever known, has returned! Don Durito de la Lacandona! (copyrights reserved) [that's what Durito's text says]. Hooray for humanity! Our most heartfelt condolences to neoliberalism. He is here, the great, I mean 'great,' gigantic, marvelous, superlative, hyper-mega-plus, super-califragilisticespialidocious [that's what Durito's text says, the one and only, the incomparable, he, THE, Don Durito de La Lacandona!

Yessssss! [that's what Durito's text says].

End of Durito's text (from which I totally distance myself).

Well then. Durito is back now. (Sigh). I don't know why my head began to ache.

Vale. Salud, and does anyone have an aspirin?

The SupPirate (extraordinarily handsome with the patch over his right eye) (punsters, abstain).[26]

---

26 The Spanish for "patch over the eye," *parche en el ojo,* is also a slang expression for sodomy.

The Hour of the Little Ones, Part II: Those from Below

For all those who are little and different:

soon will come those crazed with power
refined/disloyal/a bit cannibalistic
owners of the mountains and the valleys
of the floods and the earthquakes
those standard-bearers sans standard
charitable and mean
clothing letters favors demands
sheathed in the letter box of time
      —Mario Benedetti[1]

This and the remaining letters in this series were first published in *La Jornada*, October 21, 1999. Originally translated by irlandesa.

1 See *Buzón de tiempo* (Alfaguara, Spain: Santillana, 1999). This and other poems from this volume were published in *La Jornada* on September 13, 1999 and are cited throughout this series of letters.

The storm is letting up a bit now. The crickets take advantage of its clearing and go back to sawing through the dawn. A great black hood covers the sky. Another rain prepares itself, even though the puddles down below report they're already full. Night comes with her own words now, and she takes from her side apparently forgotten stories. This is the hour of the story of those from below, the hour of the little ones.

Down below, the long wail of a snail calls, shadows respond with silence, snug is their armor, and hurried the black that cover their faces. The guards exchange passwords, and to the "Who goes there?" hope invariably responds, "The Homeland!" Night keeps vigil over the world of the forgotten. To do that she has made soldiers of what she remembers, and she has armed them with memory, in order to relieve the pain of the smallest ones.

Raining or not, down below the shadow without a face continues his vigil. Surely he continues writing, or reading, but, always, smoking that ever shorter pipe. Good, there's nothing to do up here, so let's visit the little house again. That way, if it rains again, we'll have a roof over our heads. Here we are. Damn! The mess is even more widespread now: papers, books, pens, old lighters. The shadow toils over his writing. He fills pages and pages. He goes back to them. He takes things out, he adds to them. On the little tape player, a very otherly sound, like music from a far-off land, in an equally distant language.

"Very otherly," I said. Yes, at the hour of the little ones, the other, what's different, also has its place. And that's what our visited shadow must have been thinking because I've managed to read "The Other" at the top of one of the pages.

But let's give him time to finish or to better define the bridge between what he thinks and feels and that elusive coquette that is the word. Well, he seems to have finished. Slowly he rises and slowly he goes over to the corner that serves as his bed. We're in luck, he has left the candle to keep vigil. Yes, a few pages have been conveniently left on the table. On the first page, we can read . . .

Another Letter, Another Broken Silence
Letter 4b

For the victims of earthquakes and floods.

The following letter was not written by me, I received it. Tumbling about in a little paper boat, a river of rainwater brought the wet pages and damp letters to my hut.

October 8, 1999, 4:45 am

Sup:

Here's something for you to distribute among your networks. Aside from the tragedy of nature, what hurts most is the criminal violence that, from the heights of Power, rains over a discouraged, crippled, ignorant, exhausted population full of pain. Let's do something for the more than 500,000 victims. These torrential rains have left children, old ones, men and women WITH NOTHING, especially the indigenous and *campesinos*, those condemned by this merciless and genocidal, ruthless and demagogic system. I am sharing with you a letter sent to me by a young woman with whom I was speaking yesterday morning; in it the harsh reality that batters us is felt:

Or, as took place in the Town called _____ (fill in the name of any affected community, the story is the same), visited by Zedillo and Governor _____ (fill in the name of any governor, they're all the same), and their entire information machine, with many trucks of supplies and aid, and as soon as the helicopters carrying them took off, they also pulled out taking the trucks with supplies, leaving just a few of them, which moves us to something more than indignation. In each Town they inform us that they're not giving us aid because they're aiding and attending to others who are more needy, not knowing that there is communication between all the Towns (via CB radio, which functions effectively, at least for learning about the situations in the Communities), and that's how we found out that there is no effective aid for any of the towns. Only a few report minimal and scant aid that is consumed as soon as it is received. In the particular case of _____ (name of an indigenous community)—and it would appear to be the case on all sides—the only thing that is needed is for the road to be restored, since the civil organizations will take charge to see that everything from the food to housing needs is set right. The concentration of the best and only means of communication (helicopters) causes the Government to become arrogant and to think that they are the only ones who understand and manage the situation. But the government machinery is insufficient for the opening and restoration of roads. Nonetheless, the officials in charge of that area do not turn to the Towns and Organizations that have the capability and the willingness to help.

_____ (name of state) needs to stop being the last state in the unfair and inequitable distribution of federal funds.

At the beginning of his administration, Zedillo said that he would put his social policies to the test in this state. He failed, because not only did he not manage to grant the state the resources necessary and sufficient for us to rise above marginalization and the thousand-year setback to which we have been subjected (it is no use mentioning that the primary problem of _____ (name of state) is impoverishment, and that everything else is its effects), but, moreover, he didn't do enough to safeguard that the little that arrives is administered well, and, finally, in the cases of disasters, neither was a satisfactory response established (although in the Media, they've been embellished and shown off).

The tragedy continues: the torrential rains were added to the earthquake. Just last night our promoters reported through CB radio an extremely serious situation that I'll sketch here: In _____ (indigenous community), 100 homes destroyed by the EARTHQUAKE and 80 swept away by the river, a helicopter brought them a minimal shipment of provisions, there are close to 250 sick children; in _____ (name of municipality) the Communities of _____ and _____ (names of indigenous communities) are destroyed, nothing has been brought to them, a helicopter landed just to greet them and then it left; in _____ (indigenous community) they only took a minimal amount of aid to the community of _____ (indigenous community) (a third of the Community was buried under a mountain), while the other nine communities are still without communication; in _____ (municipality), in addition to 70% of the housing having been left destroyed, the river swept away cornfields, coffee plantations and cut off roads, they have already been visited and they left them provisions (25 packets of meal, three boxes of water and 12 boxes of oil).[2] The situation is dramatic: not only has the emergency not been overcome, but it keeps getting worse: they lack medicine, clothing, blankets, non-perishable food, tarps. That is why we have joined four Organizations together in order to collect resources and pool donations. We are not going to stop. Not anymore.

The letter ends there. I mean, what can be read. The rest is smudged by water and with mud.

Durito, hanging from one of my chinstraps (thanks to his hook), has followed the reading attentively.

"What do you think?" I ask him.

"It's not the government's criminal irresponsibility that is surprising. Certainly they're not responsible for earthquakes and the rain, but it is repulsive how they have confronted the situation. The misfortune of those from below only serves them to appear on the front pages and in the subject lines of electronic news posts. But that's not what catches your attention; that was to be expected. The truly strong and impressive thing is that 'We are not going to stop. Not anymore.'"

"Yes," I tell him, "as if another silence has been broken."

"There will be more . . ." says Durito, dropping to my boot.

Outside, the morning is breaking through the dawn.

Salud. Salud, and, I agree, "not anymore."

The Sup, falling respectfully silent.

* * *

---

2 Torrential rains beginning in September and lasting through October affected over a million Mexicans in six states. The damages were further complicated by a 7.4 magnitude earthquake that struck off Mexico's Pacific coast on September 30th.

The Cave of Desire

ART: ERICA CHAPPUIS

Durito III

ART: JOHN DOLLEY

The Story of Dreams
ART: ERICA CHAPPUIS

The Story of the Bay Horse
ART: ERICA CHAPPUIS

Durito On Liberty

ART: ANITA PANTIN

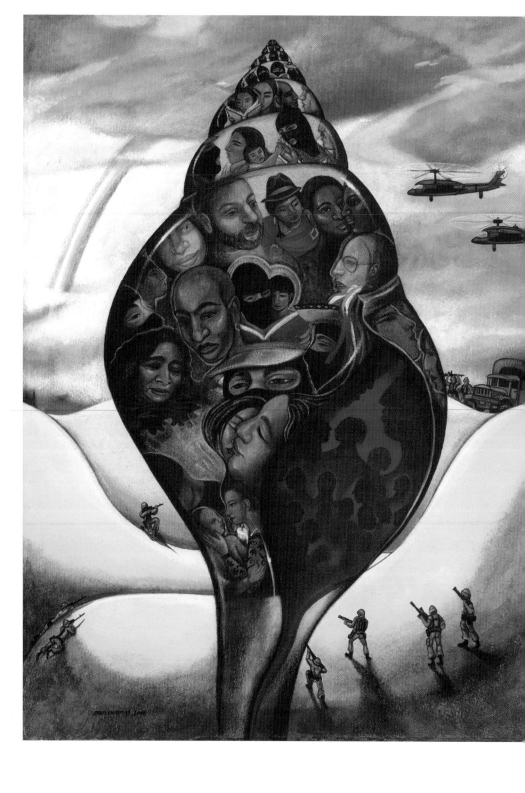

The Seashell and the Two People

ART: ERICA CHAPPUIS

Forever Never

ART: ERICA CHAPPUIS

The Hour of the Little Ones, Part 1

ART: ERICA CHAPPUIS

The Hour of the Little Ones, Part 2
ART: ERICA CHAPPUIS

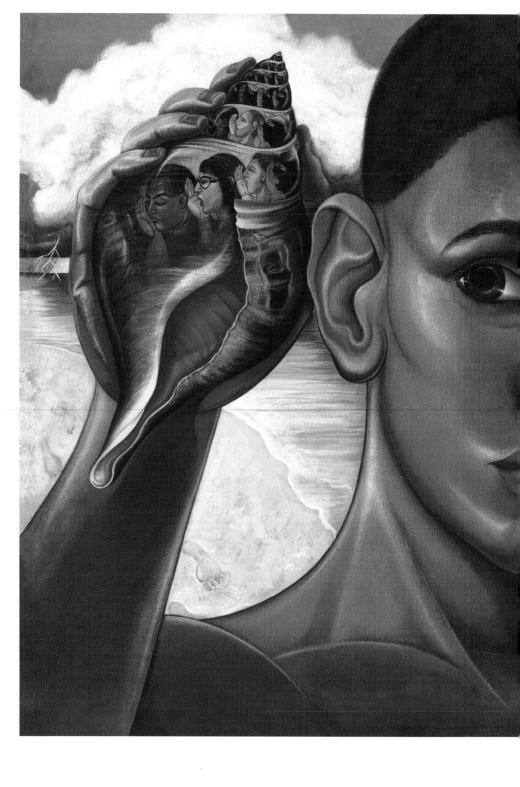

The Hour of the Little Ones, Part 3
ART: ERICA CHAPPUIS

The Hour of the Little Ones, Part 4
ART: ERICA CHAPPUIS

Chairs of Power and Butterflies of Rebellion
ART: JOHN DOLLEY

STORIES OF VIGILANCE BY CANDLELIGHT

The Hour of the Little Ones, Part III: The Undocumented Others

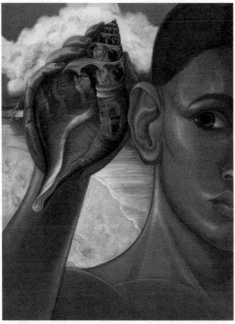

For the brown men and women in the United States:

we are the emigrants
the pale anonymous ones with the heathen and carnal century
on our backs where we accumulate the legacy
of questions and perplexities
   —Mario Benedetti

Durito says that, once over the border, a wave of terror strikes and pursues you. It's not just the threat from *la migra* and the *kukuxklanes*.[1] It is also the racism that fills each and every one of the corners of the reality of the country of the muddy stars and stripes. In fields, on the street, in businesses, in school, in cultural centers, on television and in publications, even in bathrooms, everything pushes you to renounce your color, which is the best way of renouncing one's culture, land, history, that is, surrendering the dignity which, being other, comes with the brown color of the Latinos in North America.

---

1 *La migra* is a common term for the Immigration and Naturalization Service, now called the Bureau of Citizenship and Immigration Services and housed within the Department of Homeland Security. *Kukuxklanes* is Marcos' Spanish phonological spelling of Ku Klux Klan, a paramilitary terrorist organization in the United States.

"Those brownies," say those who hide behind the classification of human beings according to the color of their skin, the crime of a system that classifies according to purchasing power, always directly proportional to the sales price (the more you sell, the more you can buy). If the little brown ones have survived the campaign of bleach and detergent by the Powers of the American Union, it has been because the "brown" Latino community (not just Mexican, but also Puerto Rican, Salvadoran, Honduran, Nicaraguan, Guatemalan, Panamanian, Cuban, and Dominican, to mention some of the shades in which the Latin American brown color paints North America) has known how to build a network of resistance without a name and without a hegemonic organization or product that sponsors it. Without ceasing to be "the others" in a white nation, Latinos carry one of the most heroic and unknown histories of this dying 20th century: that of their color, hurt and worked until it is made hope. Hope that brown will be one more color in the rainbow of the races of the world, and it will no longer be the color of humiliation, of contempt and of forgetting.

And it is not just the "brown" that suffers and is persecuted. Durito recounts that, in addition to his status as Mexican, the black color of his shell must be added. This courageous beetle was, thus, "brown and black," and was doubly persecuted. And he was doubly helped and supported, since the best of the Latino and black communities in the United States protected him. In that way, he was able to travel through the principal North American cities, as these urban nightmares are also called. He did not walk the routes of tourism, of glamour and marquees. Durito walked the streets of below, where blacks and Latinos are building the resistance that will allow them to be, without ceasing to be the other. But, Durito says, that's a story for other pages.

And now "Black Shield" Durito, or Durito *Escudo Negro* (if you are not globalized) has begun insisting that it is important that I announce, with drum roll and clashing cymbals, his new book, which he has titled *Stories of Vigilance by Candlelight*.

He now gives me a story that, he says, he wrote remembering those days when he traveled as a "wetback" or *mojado* in the United States.

"Above and Below are Relative . . . Relative to the Struggle that is Waged to Subvert Them"
Letter 4c (included in the story)

"It's a very long title," I tell Durito.

"Don't complain about the story or there'll be no treasure," Durito threatens with his hook. Here goes then:

Once upon a time there was a little floor that was very sad because everyone would walk over him and everything was above him. "Why do you complain?" the other floors asked him. "What else could happen to a floor?" And the little floor remained silent about his dream of flying lightly and winning the heart of the little cloud that, from time to time, would appear and pay him no mind. The little floor became more and more unhappy, and his sorrow was such that he began to cry. And he cried and he cried and he cried and he cried . . .

"How many times are you going to put: "and he cried'? Two or three would be enough," I interrupt Durito.

"No one is going to censure the great Black Shield Durito, much less a big-nosed cabin boy, and, even worse, with the flu," Durito threatens me while pointing out the terrible plank upon which the unlucky walks towards the bellies of the sharks. I give in silently. Not because I'm afraid of sharks, but because a swim would prove fatal to my perennial flu.

And he cried and he cried and he cried. The little floor cried so much that everyone and everything began slipping if they were standing or walking on him. And now he no longer had anyone or anything on top of him. And the little floor cried so much that he was becoming very thin and light. And, since he no longer had anything or anyone on top of him, the little floor began to float and he flew high. And he got his own way and now they call him the sky. And the cloud in question turned into rain and now she is on the floor and she writes him futile letters saying: "pretty little sky." Moral of the story: Don't look down on what is beneath you, because on the day you least expect it, it can fall on your head. And *tan-tan.*

"'*Tan-tan*'? Is the story over?" I futilely ask. Durito is no longer listening to me. Remembering his old days, when he worked as a *mariachi* in the East End of Los Angeles, California, he's put on a wide-brimmed *sombrero* and sings, off-key, the one that goes: "*Ay, ay, ay, ay, canta y no llores, porque cantando se alegran, cielito lindo, los corazones.*"[2] And afterwards, an out-of-tune shout of "Ay Jalisco, don't give up!"

Vale. Salud, and I believe we'll be late in setting sail. Durito has become determined to make modifications to the can of sardi . . . excuse me, to the frigate, so that it will look like a "low rider."

El Sup, *Órale Essse!*

P.S. of *wacha bato*: Can anyone help? Durito is determined that the menu on board will include chili dogs and burritos. Ah, *que carnal éssse!*[3]

---

2 "Ay, ay, ay, ay, sing and do not cry, because when you sing, pretty little sky, you bring joy to broken hearts." This line is from the song *Cielito Lindo* (*Pretty Little Sky*).

3 "Órale Essse," "wacha bato," and "a que carnal éssse!" are Caló phrases, meaning respectively, "Right on Dude!", "Check it out, man!" and "What a guy, man!"

The Hour of the Little Ones, Part IV: The Other . . .

So they lov'd as love in twain,
Had the essence but in one,
Two distincts, Division none,
Number there in love was slain.[1]

The True Story of Mary Read and Anne Bonny

For lesbians, homosexuals, transsexuals and transvestites, with admiration and respect.

While reviewing the parchments, I discovered a story that Durito is asking me to include in his new book, *Stories of Vigilance by Candlelight*. It is about a letter from an unknown sender (the signature is illegible). The addressee is also an enigma; although it is clearly named, it is not clear whether it is a he or a she. Better that you see it for yourselves. Upon my soul, if the lack of definition between the masculine and feminine is not quite explained in the epistle itself. The date is smudged, and we don't have the technology here to verify when it was written. But it also seems to me that it could have been as easily written centuries ago as weeks ago. You'll know what I mean. OK, then.

---

1 William Shakespeare, "The Phoenix and the Turtle," from the "Additional Poems to Chester's 'Love's Martyr,' or 'Rosalin's Complaint,'" in Howard Stauton, ed., *The Globe Illustrated Shakespeare, The Complete Works* (New York: Gramercy Books, 1979): 2321.

Letter 4d

You:

Pirate stories tell of two women, Mary Read and Anne Bonny, who disguised themselves as men and, as such, plowed through the seas in the company of other buccaneers, taking towns and vessels, hoisting the standard of the skull and cross-bones. It was the year 1720 and different stories have one or the other living and fighting the rough seas of those times. On a pirate ship, commanded by Captain John Rackam, they met each other. The stories tell that love blossomed, one thinking the other was a man, but upon learning the truth, everything returned to normal, and they went their separate ways.

It wasn't like that. This letter I write to you is the true story of Mary Read and Anne Bonny. The letter trusts in this other story, the one that will not appear in books, because they still persist in spinning the normality and good sense that everything has, and the normality of the 'other' goes no further than disapproving silence, condemnation or neglect. This is part of the story that walks along the underground bridges that the 'others' build, in order to be, and to be known.

The history of Mary Read and Anne Bonny is a history of love, and as such, it has its visible parts, but the greatest is always hidden, in the depths. In the visible part, there is a ship (a sloop, to be more precise), and a pirate, Captain John Rackam. Both ship and pirate were protectors and accomplices of that love that was so very 'other' and 'different' that the history from above had to cover it up for later generations.

Mary Read and Anne Bonny loved each other knowing they also shared the same essence. Some stories relate that the two were women, who, dressed as men, met each other knowing they were women and, as such, loved each other under the affectionate gaze of Lesbos. Others say that the two were men who hid behind pirates' clothes, and that they concealed their homosexual love and their passionate encounters behind the complicated story of women pirates disguised as men.

In either case, their bodies met in the mirror that discovers that which, for being so obvious, is forgotten; those corners of flesh that have knots that, when undone, inspire sighs and storms; places sometimes only those alike can know. With lips, skin and hands, they built the bridges that joined those alike, making them different. Yes, in whichever case, Mary Read and Anne Bonny were transvestites who, in the masquerade, discovered each other and met. In both cases, being the same, they revealed themselves to be different, and the two lost all divisions and became one. To the unconventionality of their being pirates, Mary Read and Anne Bonny added that of their "abnormal" and marvelous love.

Homosexuals or lesbians, transvestites always, Mary and Anne overcame with courage and boldness those whom 'normality' would put in chains. While men surrendered without putting up any resistance, Mary and Anne fought to the end, before being taken prisoners.

In this way, they honored the words of Mary Read. To the question of whether she feared dying:

She replied that, as to dying on the gallows, she didn't think it so cruel because, if it were not for that, all the cowards would become pirates and they would infest the seas to such an extent that the men of courage would die of hunger; that if pirates were left to choose their own punishment, they would have none other than death because their fear of it keeps some cowardly thieves honorable; that many of those who today swindle widows and orphans and oppress their poor neighbors who have no money in order to obtain justice would take to the seas to rob, so that the ocean would be full of thieves in the same way that the land is ...[2]

Homosexuals or lesbians? I don't know, the truth was taken to the grave with John Rackam when he was hung in Port Royal, November 17, 1720; and to the ship-wreck that cracked the sloop that served them as bed and accomplice. Whatever, their love was very "other" and great for being different. Because it happens that love follows its own paths and is, always, a transgressor of the law ...

I do my duty by telling you this story.

Adios.

(An illegible signature follows.)

There ends the story ... or does it continue?

Durito says that those who are different in their sexual preferences are doubly "other" since they are 'other' within those who are in themselves other.

I, a bit seasick from so much "other," ask him, "Can't you explain that a bit more?"

"Yes," says Durito. "When we are struggling to change things, we often forget that this includes changing ourselves."

Above, the dawn was about to change and make itself "other" and different. Rain followed, as well as struggle ...

Vale once more. *Salud*, and don't tell anyone, but I haven't been able to figure out how in the hell I'm going to fit into the sardine can (sigh).

El Sup, bailing water out of the frigate because, as you can imagine, it started to rain again and Durito says that bailing water is one of my "privileges."

---

2 *General History of the Thefts and Assassinations of the Most Famous Pirates*, Daniel Defoe, ed. (Madrid: Valdemar, 1999). Translation by Francisco Torres Oliver. For more on Mary Read and Anne Bonny, see Marcus Rediker, "Liberty Beneath the Jolly Roger: The Lives of Anne Bonny and Mary Read," in Margaret S. Creighton and Lisa Norling, eds. *Iron Men, Wooden Women: Gender and Seafaring in the Atlantic World, 1700-1920* (Baltimore: Johns Hopkins, 1996).

The Hour of the Little Ones, Part X: The Student Others

To the young university students on strike:

Sorrow takes hold of us, brother men,
from behind, from the side,
and it crazes us in the cinema,
it batters us in gramophones,
it thrashes us in beds, it falls straight down onto our tickets,
onto our letters . . .
    —Cesar Vallejo[1]

All night long, raining. Dawn arrives and still the rain is there, washing roads, hills, fields, paths, huts. It is like a pounding of urgent drops, and completely without order, falling on roofs, on trees, on puddles that are already full and, finally, onto the ground. Because that is how the hour of the little ones goes—disorderly, desperate, manifold.

1 Peruvian poet Cesar Vallejo, who was involved with communist and anti-fascist movements, died an illegal immigrant in Paris in 1938. The passage cited is from "Los Nueve Monstruos" ("The Nine Monsters"), which was included in the volume *Poemas Humanos*. See *Human Poems*, intr. by Clayton Eschleman (New York: Grove Press, 1968).

Down below ... we will have to wait to know what is going on down below, because now one cannot take a step without the mud seducing you and you end up kissing it with your entire body. Yes, it is rather complicated to define a fall this way, but it is raining so much that there is time for that and more. A fall ... There are times that one falls and there are times that one is fallen on. I mean, there are falls and there are falls.

What? Yes? The rain is slowing down? Yes, but the mud is not. Good, let's go, but slowly. It is dark. Perhaps there will not be anyone, or perhaps the shadow that concerns us has finally gone to sleep. Shall we have a look? Do you have a lamp? Fine. Hmmm. No, there is no one.

There is the usual disorder on the table. But today there is a different sheet of paper on it. At one side, a copy of *La Jornada* newspaper dated October 15, 1999. The headlines say "Riot Police and Strikers Clash on Beltway." A photograph takes up half the page. What? Do you want it described to you? Good, bring the light closer ... there ... Fine. It's in black and white. In the foreground there is a girl knocked down in the street, with her face bloody. Next to her, someone is being kicked by three riot police (two in the foreground and a third, between those two, half hidden by his shield and using his right hand to support himself while he's kicking). There are more details below: the photograph is by Rosaura Pozos, the girl on the ground is called Alejandra Pineda, and the person next to her, under the boots of the riot police, is her brother, Argel Pineda, one of the representatives of the General Strike Council. The scene is the South Beltway. In the photograph, the rest of the riot police (at least six more, if one carefully observes the number of helmets) are looking to the right of the photograph; only the last one in the scene is turned towards the pair of students, hesitating between continuing on ahead or joining the ones who are thrashing the young person on the ground.

More details? Good. At the back of the action of the blows against Argel and Alejandra, five men can be perfectly made out. Three of them are pointing their lenses (two are carrying still cameras and one a video camera) toward the right of the photograph. The other two are looking towards the scene of the kicking. One of them, with a checked shirt, is scratching his ear or holding something to his ear, the other is simply looking. Further back, far in the background, two vehicles can barely be made out: an automobile whose driver is blocked by the legs of the man who is just looking, and the front of another vehicle (probably a van), whose driver is looking in front of him, that is, to the left of the photograph. In the very far background, to the right, three "entertainment guides," whose texts cannot be read (that on the extreme right seems to be announcing a news program). In the same perspective, to the left, there is something that looks like a tower, of the type that has lamps or entertainment guides in its topmost part.

Good, I think that's all then. What did you say? The written sheet? What does it say? Yes, I'll read it ...

LETTER TO A PHOTOGRAPH
Letter 4X

Madame Photograph,

You will excuse me, but I was not able to see you until the dawn of the 17th day of October. No, do not think that I am reproaching you. I understand that, with so much rain, you have been delayed. Besides, the weight you carry is not at all light. You know? When I saw you, I felt a sadness here. Yes, I already know that there are photographs that hurt; I only wanted you to know that you are one of those.

If we go by the reporter's work (Roberto Garduño), we will have more means by which to read you. The girl, Alejandra Pineda, is a student at Preparatory School No. V, and her brother Argel is from the Faculty of Political Science, both from the UNAM. After the photograph (so we assume from the narrative), that is, after the blows from the riot police, Argel tries to help and to calm Alejandra, "who asked about her *compañeros*: How are they? They aren't hitting them more? My head hurts a lot, we don't want any more repression, we want free education." (*La Jornada*, October 15, 1999, p. 66). According to that reporter, and to some statements gathered by the same newspaper, the students were already withdrawing towards Ciudad Universitaria when they were attacked by the riot police.

What you speak with your image, and what the chronicles, reportage and statements describe, say some things to me. But—do you know?—there are other questions that are not answered by your image or the inside pages.

Then I would like you, Madame Photograph, to allow me to ask you a few questions. All right?

1. How old was Alejandra before the beating? 17, 18? And Argel? How old are they now?

2. If my eyes do not deceive me: the riot police are beating up Alejandra and Argel on the Beltway access road and not on the main lanes (which are the ones they were going to "clear")?

3. The riot police who are looking to the right in the photograph: are they looking that way in order not to see what their *compañeros* are doing? Or are they protecting the three who are beating up Alejandra and Argel, in order to prevent someone from coming and rescuing them? Further over there (to the right of the photograph), is another beating taking place? Are the students withdrawing?

4. The Mexico City government: is it beating up Alejandra for the crime of being Argel's sister? Is it beating up Argel for the crime of coming to Alejandra's aid? Is it beating up both of them for the crime of being "ultras"? Is it beating them because the cars are demanding free transit? Is it beating them because the polls demand it? Is it beating them to attract applause on Televisa and TV Azteca? Is it beating them for being young people? Is it beating them for being students? Is it beating them for being university students? Is it beating them so it can demonstrate that they govern with firmness? Pardon me, Madame Photograph, but I do not understand. Why are they beating Alejandra and Argel?

263

5. The women who congratulated Rosario Robles for having become head of the Mexico City government: did they also congratulate her for ordering the beating of Alejandra?[2] She: did she send Alejandra a kind word? Were they silent? Or did they say to themselves: "She deserved it for being rebellious"? What? Yes, excuse me, you would have no way of knowing that?

6. You, Madame Photograph, show at least three riot police hitting the student: why were only two brought before the authorities?

7. That billy club the riot policeman on the extreme right is carrying: is it an appeal to dialogue? A demonstration that the current government in Mexico City is "different" from the previous ones? Or is it merely the measure of the distance that separates words from actions?

8. Who is the man in the checked shirt talking to, if it's a cell phone he has at his left ear?

9. The driver of the car that is moving, who is not visible in the photograph: would he applaud the beatings the police are giving Alejandra and Argel?

10. What is it that Alejandra has under her body, other than blood, I mean? A poncho? A sweater? A piece of cloth? A jacket?

11. The driver furthest back: is he inviting us to do the same? To pass by in front of the photograph of bloody Alejandra and fallen Argel, without looking at them, without looking at her?

12. On page 69 of the newspaper in which you are the headline, there is another photograph (also by Rosaura Pozos, with the caption "Scene prior to the police clearing of the South Beltway"). In the foreground can be seen a young man, in a checked shirt, on his knees in front of a line of riot police. The young man has his backpack in front of his knees, and he is showing the riot police a book. On the police shields can be clearly read: "Public Security. Riot Police. Federal District." In the mid-ground, a woman with a hat. Further back, a cameraman. At the rear, trees and buildings. The questions . . .

12a. What is the title of the book the young man is showing the riot police?

12b. Is the young man on his knees saying something to the riot police?

12c. Was not Point Three of the list of demands from the National Strike Committee of the 1968 movement, I cite it verbatim, "Abolition of the Riot Police Force, direct instrument of repression, and no establishment of similar forces?" ("War Report," Julio Scherer and Carlos Monsiváis, p. 161)[3]

12d. Is the existence and operation of the Riot Police Force constitutional?

What do you say? This is something that should be asked of the other photograph? Good, you are right. Allow me some questions:

---

2 Rosario Robles replaced Cuahtémoc Cárdenas as President of Mexico City in 1999. Although a member of the PRD, she governed with an iron hand, often undermining popular mobilizations.

3 Julio Scherer García (and Carlos Monsiváis?) *Parte de Guerra: Tlatelolco 1968: documentos del general Marcelino García Barrigán: Los hechos y la historia* (Mexico, D.F.: Aguilar, 1999).

Do you remember that the reason for the march by the students was to protest the news coverage by TV Azteca and Televisa of the university conflict?

If you, Madame photograph, had not spoken: would we have remained with only the version that the electronic media and the Mexico City government gave out on the night of October 14 of 1999, in which the students were the aggressors, the police who intervened were all women, and only one student was injured ("nothing serious") by a "vehicle that ran over her"?

Do we have the right to expect that a government headed by the PRD would act differently?

Should we remain silent and not ask anything?

You know, Madame Photograph, that you justify "Letter 3A."[4] But you will see how much I would have wished that you had not verified that letter, but rather those who, in front of a hollow mirror, boast of being "proud officials of a democratic government like Mexico City's."

And you know what? Every time I look at you, Madame, I do not know why, but I am taken by an irresistible urge to pick up a rock and to hurl it far and break forever the silence that there, above, accomplice, remains quiet.

What? Yes, go on, Madame Photograph, continue on your way and continue asking. So inconvenient you are, Madame Photograph, such a busybody.

Vale. Salud, and I believe that what Alejandra had under her body is a flag. And I also believe that it was raised up, along with her.

The Sup, accumulating questions as if they were rain.

* * *

---

4 "Letter 3A" to Carlos Monsiváis, published in *La Jornada,* October 8, 1999, is part of the "Siete Veces Dos" series.

The Story of the Air
and the Night:
Insurgentas! La Mar in March

On International Women's Day, March 8, 2000, several thousand Zapatista women demanding rights for the indigenous and women, occupied the XERA radio station in San Cristóbal de las Casas for over 40 minutes. In their honor, Marcos speaks of the critical contributions of women to the Zapatista struggle. His comments include a personal tribute to La Mar, from whom he has drifted apart. Durito's advice on lovesickness leads Marcos to share with her the memory of Old Antonio's "Story of the Air and the Night."

First published in *La Jornada*, March 11, 2000. Originally translated by irlandesa.

INSURGENTAS!
(LA MAR IN MARCH)
Letter 6e, Mexico, March 2000

To those who fell,
To those who follow,
To those who shall come

There goes my warm letter,
a dove forged in the fire,
its two wings folded down
and the address in the center.
A bird that only wants
your body, your hands, your eyes
and the space around your breath
　　—Miguel Hernández[1]

The letters are late and they are not enough
to say what one wants.
　　—Jaime Gil de Biedma[2]

Juggling its nocturnal hat, the March hare is indecisive. It still does not know whether to rain, or to be content with leaving the sky stained with black ink. February has stayed behind, and with it its own disruptions of wind, sun and rain. It is now the women's March, from the 8th to the 21st, that of Zapatista women, of the *insurgentas*.

I have spoken before of the insurgent women, the *insurgentas*, of our being beside them, of their small and large acts of heroism. Every March 8th, we male insurgents face these women and give them a military salute. A small fiesta usually follows, with the meager resources of our mountain camps. The women have been in the mountains of the Mexican southeast from the beginnings of the EZLN. As time passed, more were to join that small delirious group, which the world would later know as the "Zapatista Army of National Liberation."

There are small, daily things that form part of guerrilla life, and they are like small dues that the mountain imposes on those who dare to be part of it. I know each and every one of those difficulties, and I know well that, for women, they

---

1　Spanish poet and dramatist Miguel Hernández fought on the Republican side of the Spanish Civil War until his capture by the fascists. He died in prison. This stanza comes from a poem titled "Letter." See Hernández, *Selected Poems*, Timothy Baland, ed., Timothy Baland, et. al., trans. (Buffalo: White Pine Press, 1989), 67.
2　Politically engaged, gay Spanish poet and essayist, Jaime Gil de Biedma was born in Barcelona in 1929 and died there of AIDS in 1990. The two lines open his poem "En Una Despedida," which was dedicated to "Jimmy Baldwin."

are double. Not because we impose them in that way, but rather because of things that come from other places and other times.

If one admires the fact that a person abandons their history and, as we say, "rises up," choosing the profession of insurgent soldier, they should stop and look at those who make that choice as women. Their admiration would be double. In addition to confronting a particularly harsh environment, the *insurgentas* must also confront a cultural code that, beyond the *mestizo*-indigenous division, designates spaces that are not for women (I mean attitudes, places, duties, work, responsibilities and the multiple etceteras added by a society built on exclusion). If an *insurgenta* thinks she has too much work with carrying, walking, training, fighting, studying and working along with the men, she is wrong. It could always be worse. And, in our case, it is worse to be in command.

Primarily indigenous, the EZLN carries with it not just the hope of something better for everyone; it also drags along the world's troubles and blindness that we want to leave aside. If, in the indigenous communities and in the cities, women must confront a world where being male is a privilege that excludes those who are different (women and homosexuals), in the mountain and as troop commanders, they must confront the resistance of the majority of the insurgents to take orders from a woman. If this resistance seemed to be substantially reduced during the 1994 combat, this does not mean that it has completely disappeared. The male will invariably think that he can do it better than his commander, if it is a woman. Something similar takes place in the villages, but I will limit myself now to speaking of the regular troops, of the insurgents . . . and of the *insurgentas*.

In the past, there had been just one merit promotion in the EZLN, that is, a promotion in military rank. An *insurgenta*, Maribel, rose from First Captain to Major of the Infantry. Now a major, Maribel is still short and dark, and she is still a woman. The only thing that has changed is that now she commands an entire regiment. To the problems that she faces in her new status as zone commander must be added those that correspond to being a woman.

Like her, other *compañeras*, with or without command, at arms and service, rigorously fulfill paying their dues of commitment and sacrifice, the same as all combatants. But, if the part least exposed to the glare of outside searchlights is that of the insurgent troops, the *insurgentas* add one more shadow to that of the ski-masks they wear: they are women.

And, I should say, they also add a superior level of heroism to ours, the men. We might not understand it (in spite of regulations and statutes, of the Revolutionary Law of Women, of talks and declarations), but we never stop appreciating it.

And alongside Maribel are other officers: in what we call "Health Services," there are the *insurgenta* Captains Oli-Ale (the woman with the most active years within the EZLN) and Mónica, and *insurgenta* Lieutenant Aurora.

There are more, officers and troops. Some, I have already mentioned, years ago, on an occasion like this one. Before them, there was Alicia, from the first group that founded the EZLN in 1983, and the first woman with troop command (the first in the mountains facing the problem of being a woman and commanding men). Soon after, Lucía arrived, the *insurgenta* author of the words to the Zapatista Hymn (and of many of the songs that are heard today at night in the mountains of the Mexican southeast).[3] And even before, there were Murcia (the first woman in the Zapatista guerrilla to fall in combat in 1974), Dení Prieto S. (fallen in combat in 1974), Soledad (fallen in combat in 1974), Julieta Glockner (fallen in combat in 1975) and Ruth (fallen in combat in 1983; she taught me how to shoot).

Through all of them, and with them, is Lucha, whom we call "the stainless steel *insurgenta*." More than 30 clandestine years cause Lucha's ski mask to shine among us in a special way. Today, in spite of the cancer that she hardly lets bother her, Lucha continues to be the first among our guerrilla women, and the best memory.

This March 8th, saluting our current *insurgentas*, we are saluting all those who preceded them and us, and who, in more than one sense, transcend us.

I shall tell you something about the name "*insurgentas*." The anecdote can be situated at any time and in any place in that unknown monotony of life in the mountains.

I found myself leading military training operations. Between exercise and tactical exercise, the guerrilla column was trotting to the rhythm of more-or-less obvious chants. I would shout, for example, "Who Goes There?" and the troops would respond in unison, "The Homeland!" That's how it was done and is done. In one of the chants of combat march the commander asks, "What are we?" and everyone responds, "*Insurgentes!*"

On that day that I am now recounting to you, half the column was made up of women. When I shouted "What are we?" I clearly heard, while the men were responding, "*Insurgentes!*" the women overcoming the men's voices with their shout of "*Insurgentas!*" I remained silent. I gave the men the order to "fall out." Then, facing just the women, I repeated, "What are we?" They responded strongly and firmly, without any interference, "*Insurgentas!*" I kept looking at them, disconcerted, and I noted a slight smile on their faces. I went back to the "What are we?" and they repeated, "*Insurgentas!*" I lit my pipe and smoked slowly, not looking at anything in particular.

I called them all to formation and told them, in so many words, "Today we learned that we are going to win. Any questions?" Silence. In a strong voice I ordered, "Attention! *Insurgentes!*" I turned around to look at the *compañeras*, and I added, "And *Insurgentas!* Fall out! Now!" The sound of the boots was, indeed, uniform. Thank goodness, I muttered to myself. They all went to the headquarters . . . men and women. I remained smoking, seeing how the afternoon, feminine as it is, was dressed as sea and lilacs, as *insurgentas*.

---

3 The Zapatista Hymn is based on the traditional *corrido* or ballad, "Carabina 30-30," made popular by Zapatistas during the Mexican Revolution of 1910.

The Zapatista *insurgentas* . . .

This time, I want to speak more about one of them. I can say this woman is one more of us, but for me she is not just one more, she is unique. La Mar is not a literary character—she is a woman, and she is a Zapatista. She was the architect of last year's national and international *consulta* (and an important part of each and every one of the peace initiatives these last six years). As frequently happens with the Zapatistas, her anonymity is double because she is a woman. Now, given that it is March 8th, I wish to make it clear that although most of the time it's my duty to be the public figure, many initiatives are authored, in their design and realization, by other *compañeros* and *compañeras*. In the case of the *consulta*, it was a Zapatista woman: La Mar. Just after March 21st, she picked up her pack and joined the unit . . .

One must also remember that the mobilization of women (in Mexico and in the world) was the backbone in that *consulta*: in the contact office (national and international), in the brigades, among the coordinators, on the voting tables, in the actions. Women—of all sizes, origins, status, colors, and ages—were the majority. And so, in order to salute the women who are fighting and, above all, those who are fighting and who are not seen, in many ways, the *insurgentas* appear in these lines. In order to celebrate them I have asked an old indigenous wise man to join me: Old Antonio, and the most intrepid and gallant knight these worlds have ever seen: Durito (alias Nebuchadnezzar, alias Don Durito de la Lacandona, alias Black Shield, alias Sherlock Holmes, alias Heavy Metal Durito, alias whatever else occurs to him). Well then, best wishes to the rebel women, to those without a face, to the *insurgentas* . . .

Love sickness

Below me again is March, its first three letters reiterating in these eyes that read in the golden light. Fito Páez accompanies me, giving a gift of a dress and my love, and on the little tape player he makes me move on with "There's nothing more I can say."[4] I take advantage of a gust of wind and I reach Don Durito, who is painstakingly sawing and nailing who-knows-what onto his sardine can. I know, I just said that it was a pirate ship. In fact, Durito just turned around and looked at me with sharpened daggers in his eyes when I wrote "sardine can," but I've only done so to remind the reader that Durito is now Black Shield (*Escudo Negro*), the famous pirate who shall inherit a truly difficult task from the deceased Barbarossa. Durito—excuse me, I mean Black Shield—arrived on a vessel that's called, for reasons still unknown to me, "Learn from the Mistakes of Others." Previously, Durito has proposed that I accompany him on a treasure hunt, but I've already recounted all that in another letter, so I shall not go on about it here. Now the thing is that, in this March of the sea, I've made my way to where Durito is working to see what he's up to and to ask him for guidance and advice.

---

4 Fito Páez is a singer and filmmaker from Argentina.

Durito is giving the last blows to what I suppose is a mast with a makeshift sail, and when I clear my throat to announce my presence, he says:

"Good, there it is. And now, with you in the bow, there will be no surprises to hinder us."

I give a melancholy smile and look at the vessel with indifference. Durito reproaches me: "It is not just any ship. It is a galley, a classic vessel destined for war around the 16th century. The galley can be propelled by sails or by the oars used by those 'condemned to the galleys.'"

He pauses and continues: "And, speaking of sails, might one know why sadness covers your face?"

I make a gesture to say, "It's not important."

Durito interprets it and says: "Ah! Love sickness."

He slowly puts the hammer and saw aside, disembarks, and taking out his little pipe, sits down next to me.

"I suppose, my future bowman, that what has you sad and distressed is in fact nothing other than a feminine being, a female, a woman.

I sigh.

Durito continues: "Look, my dear bathtub sailor, if the one who keeps thee sleepless is a woman, a particular one, then thy sickness is serious but a remedy possible."

I confessed: "It so happens that, yes, it is a woman, a particular one. She who is La Mar for many more reasons than the "Mariana" that names her. One unlucky day I drifted away from her and now I can't find the way or means to take refuge again in her moistness, to forget bad storms, well, to have her forgive me."

Durito takes a long puff and passes judgment:

"Great and serious are your faults and losses, but I can give you some counsel if you promise to follow my directions to the letter."

I said "yes" with an enthusiasm that made Durito jump with fright. He readjusts his eye patch as best he can and says: "It is necessary to resort to a spell. In love, the world is, as always, a puzzle, but it so happens that, if a particular male piece comes across another particular female piece, the pieces fit and take shape, and the puzzle spreads and teases faces, arms and legs.

"And breasts," I say, wringing the anguish I am feeling in mine.

"Good. What I am driving at is that the spell will only have an effect if she, La Mar in your case, is willing to submit to it. Otherwise, all will be futile. I mean, the spell will not work if the object of the spell is not aware that she is being charmed."

"A strange spell, this one."

Durito continues without paying me any mind: "Bring her a good memory, one of those that are good for seeing far ahead, one that shall make her lift her gaze and send it long and deep. Tell her to look ahead, not to the following day, not to next week, nor the coming year. Further ahead, beyond that. Do not ask her what she sees. Only look at her looking ahead. If you see that her gaze smiles with tenderness, then you will be forgiven, and there shall be wheat and sand and sea and wind, and you will be able to sail once again, and that, and nothing else, is what love is."

Durito picks up his gear once again and continues fixing the galley. The destination of the trip is still unknown to me, but Durito remains silent, letting me know that I should go and carry out what he has told me.

I wander through the dawn a bit more. I seek to find La Mar in bed. I know that you are thinking that I am speaking of just a bed, but here a bed is any bed or table or ground or chair or air, every time our shadow is copied in the other, never one, always two, but so close together. If it's not like that, then it's not a *vale*, you need two to talk about a bed. I think that if La Mar is sleeping, it would be a mistake to wake her up with this absurd story of the spell. Then it occurs to me that I should address the issue indirectly, approaching her while whistling some tune, commenting on the weather . . . or trying out a love poem.

But the problem, I intuit, is that a love poem holds a lock, an ultimate secret, that only a few, a very few, almost no one, is able to open, to discover, to free. One is left with the impression that what one feels for someone has already found its perfect, brilliant, complete formulation in someone else's words. And one crumples up the paper (or, in cybernetic times, decides to delete the file in question) with the commonplace in which feeling is made word. I don't know much about love poetry, but I know enough so that when my fingers turn to something like it, it seems more like a strawberry shake than a love sonnet. In short, poetry, and more specifically, love poetry, is for anyone, but not everyone has the key that opens its highest flight. That's why, when I can, I call on poets, both friends and enemies, and in La Mar's ear, I renew the plagiarisms that, barely stammered, seem to be mine. I suspect that she knows, in any case she does not let me know, and she closes her eyes and lets my fingers comb through her hair and her dreams.

I draw near and I think and I feel and I tell myself that such desires to return to the beginning, to start again, to return to the first stroke of the first letter, the "A" of the long alphabet of the company, to return to the first sketch that makes the two of us together and to begin to grow again, and, again, to sharpen the point of hope. There she is. She sleeps. I draw near and . . .

(. . .)

And all of this is to the point, or to the account, because, in this sea of March, everything seems to smell of desolation, of impasse, of incurable fall, of frustration. Because I am sure that it would seem strange to all of you that today I dare to prophesize the return of flags of all colors, populating, from below, fields, streets and windows. And I dare to do so because I look at this Zapatista woman, her tender insistence, her hard love, her dream. I look at her, and through her, and above all with her. I promise her and I promise myself, new air for those sister flags, banners, flyers, that disturb and keep the rich and poor awake, although for different reasons. I promise her and I promise myself, right in the middle of the most tedious night, another tomorrow; not the best, but definitely better. For this woman who, in the mornings and in front of me, pricks up her ears and puts on her pistol while telling me "here comes the helicopter" as if she were saying "they are knocking at the door." For this Zapatista, for this woman, and for many like her, who shoulder this so that the little good that remains does not fall, and in order to finally begin to build with that material that which today seems so far away: tomorrow.

Vale. Salud to all, and for her, a flower.

From the mountains of the Mexican Southeast
Subcomandante Insurgente Marcos

P.S. that fulfills the duplicity.
I am attaching here the memory that I gave to La Mar. This is how this Letter 6e achieves its double wing and undertakes the flight necessary for every letter. Over and out.

Story for a Night of Anguish

I tell La Mar that, for some reason that I can't manage to understand, Old Antonio might have read some of the German philosopher Immanuel Kant. Instead of becoming impassioned with xenophobia, Old Antonio took from the world everything good that the world made available, without regard for the land where it was born. Referring to good people from other nations, Old Antonio used the term "internationals," and he used the word "foreigners" only for those indifferent to the heart; it didn't matter that they were of his color, language and race. "Sometimes, even in the same blood there are foreigners," Old Antonio would say, in order to explain to me the absurd nonsense of passports.

But, I tell La Mar, the history of nationalities is another history. What I remember now refers to the night and its paths.

It was one of those dawns March uses to affirm its delirious vocation. A day with a sun like a seven-tailed whip was followed by an afternoon of gray storm clouds. By night, a cold wind was already gathering black clouds above a faded and timid moon.

Old Antonio had passed the morning and afternoon with the same calmness he was now using to light his cigarette. A bat fluttered about us for an instant, surely disturbed by the light which gave life to Old Antonio's cigarette. And like the bat, it appeared suddenly, in the middle of the night . . .

The Story of the Air of the Night

When the greatest gods, those who birthed the world, the very first ones thought about how and why they were going to do what they were going to do, they made an assembly where each one took out his word in order to know it and so that the others would know of it. Each one of the very first gods would take out a word and throw it into the center of the assembly, and there it bounced and reached other gods who grabbed it and threw it again, and so like a ball the word would go from one side to the other until everyone finally understood it. And then they made their agreement, the greatest gods who were those that birthed all things we call worlds. One of the agreements they found when they took out their words was that each path has its traveler and each traveler his path. And then they went about making things complete, or rather, each one with a partner.

That is how the air and the birds were born. There was not air first and then birds to travel it; nor were birds made first, and then air so that they could fly in it. They did the same with water and the fish that swim in it, the land and animals who walk it, the path and the feet that travel it.

But speaking of birds, there was one that protested much against the air. This bird said that it would fly better and more quickly if the air did not oppose it. It grumbled because, even though its flight was agile and swift, it always wanted to be more and better, and, if it could not be so, it said it was because the air became an obstacle. The gods became annoyed at how much he would fuss, this bird who flew in the air and complained of it.

And so, as punishment, the first gods took away its feathers and the light from its eyes. Naked, they sent him out into the cold of the night to fly blindly. Then his flight, once graceful and light, became disordered and clumsy.

But after many blows and mishaps, this bird managed to see with its ears. By speaking to things, this bird, or the bat, guides its path and knows the world that answers him in a language only he knows how to listen to. Without feathers to dress him, blind, and with a nervous and hurried flight, the bat rules the mountain night and no animal travels the dark air better than he.

From this bird, the *tzotz*, the bat, true men and women learned to grant great and powerful value to the spoken word, to the sound of thought. They also learned that night contains many worlds and one must know how to listen to them in order for them to come forth and flourish. The worlds of the night are born with words. Through sounds, they are made light, and there are so many they do not fit on the land, and many end up adapting themselves to the sky. That is why they say stars are born on the ground.

The greatest gods also bore men and women, not so that one would be the path of the other, but so that they would be, at the same time, the other's path and traveler. They were made different in order to be together. The greatest gods made men and women so that they would love each other. That is why the night air is the best for flying, for thinking, for speaking and for loving.

Old Antonio ends his story in that March. In this March, here, La Mar sails a dream where the word and bodies disrobe, they travel worlds without colliding, and love can take flight without anguish. Up there a star discovers an empty space on the ground and quickly lowers itself, leaving a momentary scratch in the window of this dawn. On the little tape player, Mario Benedetti, a Uruguayan of the entire world, says, "You all can go, I am staying."[5]

Another P.S. Did La Mar accept the spell? It is, as I know not who said, a mystery.

Vale once again. *Salud*, and March is, as usual, coming in very *loco*.

The Sup, waiting as always, that is, smoking.

* * *

---

5 This is the closing line to Benedetti's poem "A la izquierda del roble." Mario Benedetti, *Noción de patria. Próximo Prójimo* (Madrid: Visor Libros, S.L., 1998).

Off the Record: La Realidad

While Marcos writes to Pablo González Casanova, past rector of the UNAM and prominent member of the CONAI, Durito interrupts to hand him some political texts and then to lead him to some cookies. In an old sack hanging from a tree, Marcos finds among the rancid "Pancremas," various odds and ends, and two books: Lewis Carroll's *Through the Looking Glass*, and a book of political theory authored by himself.

P.S. proposing another window

(Off the record: La Realidad)
(Postscript to Letter 6c)
March 2000
To: Don Pablo González Casanova
UNAM, Mexico

Windows are like cookies: they are tasty and nourishing.
    —Don Durito de la Lacandona

First published in *La Jornada*, March 25, 2000. Originally translated by irlandesa.

Don Pablo:

I am sure that the epigram at the top of this letter will seem strange to you, and to its author even more so. It is not easy to explain, but I will try to do so. Everything began when . . .

Above, the sky stretches from horizon to horizon. It is stretched so much that its skin rips and light can be seen through the tatters. There is very little wind. Even so, a fleeting breeze brings me the echoes of some voices. I climb down from the ceiba and walk towards a little light covered by trees. It appears to be a small gathering or something like that. I approach and "in order to distinguish between the voices of the echoes, I stop and hear, among the voices, just one." The Mad Hatter and the March Hare are sharing tea while discussing with La Mar a poll that says that 90% of human beings prefer to celebrate their non-birthdays and to give up birthday parties. These things only happen in the mountains of the Mexican southeast. I am of the 10% who prefer to celebrate their birthdays, and so I was left without tea and without discussion.

Whatever it may be, the 21st is now hovering about on all the calendars, and for lack of tea there will be coffee and animal cookies. And, speaking of little animals, Zedillo's expanded cabinet (that is, his own and the one called—presumptuously—Labastida's "campaign team") overwhelms with its increasingly disreputable statements.[1] And it is not that the respectable has lost respectability, what is happening is that the number of Mexican men and women who are paying attention to what the Supreme One is saying is dwindling rapidly.

Durito, who when it comes to cookies, charges like a politician looking for his name on a ballot, appears at one of the edges of the table. I was writing a response to Don Pablo González Casanova (more of a postscript), when Durito, throwing eye patch, wooden leg and hook aside, exclaims-asks-exacts-demands, "Did someone say cookies?"

"I didn't say it, I wrote it. And don't get excited because they're animal cookies, and, I understand, they aren't among your favorites."

"Why do you always mix politics with things as noble as cookies? Besides, I know where there are some 'Pancremas' put away."

I immediately stopped writing.

"'Pancremas?' Where?"

"Nothing, nothing. If there's no tea, there are no cookies."

"But Durito . . . Okay, let's negotiate: I'll help you to work on the sardine ca . . . er, excuse me, the galley, and you tell me where the 'Pancremas' are."

Durito thinks about it for a minute. Then he asks: "Does that include swabbing the deck and bailing out the water in storms?"

---

1 Francisco Labastida Ochoa was the PRI candidate anointed to succeed Zedillo as President in the July 2, 2000 election. During his candidacy, Labastida visited Zinacantán where he claimed that in Chiapas there was no war with military maneuvers and exchanges of fire, only a "state of tension." See José Gil Olmos, "En Chiapas no hay balazos, sí un clima de hostilidades: Labastida," *La Jornada*, August 8, 1999.

"It includes it," I say, seeing that right now the sky has no room for clouds, and so I don't have to worry about any storms.

"Follow me," says Durito, and, getting down from the table, he embarks on a march through the mountains.

I took the lamp, although the moon made it unnecessary. We did not walk far. Durito stopped in front of a *huapac* and pointed to one of its branches. "There," he said. I looked towards where he was pointing and I saw a little hanging sack. It must have been an old "mailbox," left some time ago by one of our units. Durito sat down at the base of the tree, took out his pipe and began to smoke. I interpreted his silence and climbed the tree, untied the bag and climbed down with it. Upon opening it I saw that there indeed was a package of "Pancrema" cookies, a pair of AA batteries, a lamp that was now rusted, an old, worn book by Lewis Carroll (*Through the Looking Glass*), a Zapatista songbook . . . and a book of political theory whose author is Subcomandante Insurgente Marcos!

I don't remember having written any book on political theory. In fact, I don't remember having written any book, period. Certainly the idea of a long work, expounding on what we Zapatistas think about politics, has been floating through my head, but nothing has materialized. I began leafing through the book while Durito did a good job of polishing off the cookies. When I turned around, not even any crumbs of the "Pancremas" were left.

"You finished them all off?" I reproached him.

"You should be grateful. They were more rancid than the 'new' PRI." Durito looks at me and adds: "I can see that something is bothering you. You can confide in me, my dear disconcerted nose."

"Well I have just found this book in the mailbox. How is it possible, in an old mailbox in the mountains, to find a book that hasn't been written yet?"

"The solution to your problem is in the other book."

"Which one? The one by Lewis Carroll?"

"Of course! Check out Chapter Five."

And so I did. I'm not very sure, but I believe the answer would be in the following dialogue between Alice and the White Queen:

"That's the effect of living backwards," the Queen said kindly: "it always makes one a little giddy at first—"

"Living backwards!" Alice repeated in great astonishment. "I never heard of such a thing!"

"But there's one great advantage in it, that one's memory works both ways."

"I'm sure *mine* only works one way," Alice remarked. "I can't remember things before they happen."

"It's a poor sort of memory that only works backwards," the Queen remarked.

"What sort of things do *you* remember best?" Alice ventured to ask.[2]

278

"So I have in my hands a book that hasn't been written yet?" I said.

"That's the way it is. We are in one of those areas called a "window." I look at him in surprise.

"Yes," Durito says. "'Windows.' These places where one can see to the other side, be it what has happened, or what is going to happen. Here, for example, you can see what Zedillo's administration has been, and also see the chaos that it is leading to. Now the only stable thing is instability. There will be all kinds of problems."

"Well it seems they're getting there. You can already see the stock market is up in the clouds, and while not well understood, economic indices assure there will be no 'December error.'"

"Perhaps because it will happen in another month." Durito seems to take notice of my perplexity because he almost immediately adds, "You should understand." Durito looks at me doubtfully and corrects himself. "Okay, you should try to understand that . . . look, better that you read this that I'm writing." Durito hands me some written pages where it says:

Notes that try to explain what will happen just because when they happen just because.
Macro-economic Indices: Cosmetic Framing

In an election year, candidates are abundant, as are lies. One of the biggest is the one that sings the praises of an economic prosperity that is not to be seen anywhere. Blind to what the common people are suffering, government officials exhibit figures that say more in what they don't say. The high macro-economic indices are nothing but a macro cover-up for concealing the reality of the growth of poverty and the number of poor in our country. Facing the evidence that no one believes them, the government puts the achievements and the applause for the rapid and tumultuous sale of Mexico into the mouths of large financial centers. At business and government meetings (the most powerful club of national criminals), they congratulate each other for increased profits. Meanwhile, in Mexico's streets and countryside, survival becomes an everyday battle, and the price increases of basic products and services are reflected on the tables (less nourishment and quantity), in the streets (the number of the unemployed and under-employed are increasing), in small businesses (misery and closings), and in the countryside (increased emigration to the cities and to the American Union).

Even so, the cosmetic framing presents serious shortcomings. At the 13th Congress of the National College of Economists, Herminio Blanco, the Zedillo loyalist and Secretary of Commerce, faced criticism of his publicity campaign. Enrique Dussel, UNAM researcher, told him: "The 3,100 *maquilas* and 300 big national and foreign companies are 0.12 percent of the country's businesses, and they create only

---

2 Lewis Carroll, *Alice in Wonderland*, Donald Gray, ed. (New York: W. W. Norton & Co., 1992), 150-151.

5.6 percent of the jobs."[3] Noting that large corporations had not created productive linkages with small and mid-size industries (which are the primary source of employment in Mexico), the researcher had the sense of humor to point out to Señor Blanco: "These are facts, not globalphobia." (Ibid.)

In the great fraud called the "North American Free Trade Agreement" (product of the great Salinas lie), the immediate future is now being projected with the signing of a free trade agreement with the European Union. With a relish for modern cosmetics, the European governments are extending their hands to Zedillo without caring that his is covered with indigenous blood, without noticing that his government is the one that has the most ties with drug trafficking, and are closing their eyes to the lack of democracy in our country. The European Union's flexibility can be understood: what is at stake is a slice of the pie that is called, still, "Mexico." Due to the marvels of globalization, a country is measured by its macro-economic indices. The people? They do not exist; there are only buyers and sellers. And, within these, there are classifications: the small, the large and the macro. These last ones buy or sell countries. At one time they were governments of nation-states; today they are only merchants in search of good prices and substantial profits.

The Political Class And Their Organizers: The Clergy, The Army, The Media, Intellectuals, and International Organizations

If we have said before that the political class is increasingly less political and increasingly more business-like, in an election year cynicism takes on the overtones of a publicity "boom." The ones that "matter" are not the governed, but those who contribute to, or interfere with, the exercise of power. Convened by the Mexican political class, the high clergy, the army, the electronic media, the intellectuals and international organizations become "the great electors." Their respective interests receive the regime's benefits in an exaggerated way at election time. Citizens remain at the margins and their demands are reduced to electoral polls. The statements, counter-statements and comments to each other belong to the so-called "leaders" of an opinion that is increasingly closer to an agreement among cronies, and is increasingly removed from serious debate about ideas and programs.

The high clergy advances, with purported divine endorsement, in earthly intrigues. Teaming up with those who govern and/or those who aspire to govern, the Catholic hierarchy sees with satisfaction that its word has influence and bearing on government policies. While the lay state is nothing more than a shameful date on the calendar, the politicians and clergy share bread, salt, complicity and shamelessness in public and private meetings. It is not a mutual respect between

---

3 *El Universal*, February 9, 2000, Financial section, reported by Lilia González and Alberto Bello. *Maquilas* or *Maquiladoras* are assembly plants originally located on the U.S.-Mexico border and first developed under the Border Industrialization Program during the mid-1960s. Multinational corporations increasingly use *maquilas* throughout Mexico to provide low-waged labor to assemble electronic and automotive consumer goods.

different spheres, no. It is a symbiosis that allows some bishops and cardinals to be closer to the Mexico of Power than to common, everyday Catholics (the great majority of Mexicans). The Reform Laws? Pardon, my dear sir: isn't that the name of a street?[4]

In another arena, other "bishops" and "cardinals"—but from the intellectual Right—are fighting to occupy the space left by the supreme pontiff, Octavio Paz.[5] If one could in some way measure Paz' stature as an effective intellectual with and for power, it is measuring that of the dwarves who are fighting over his legacy. With Paz dies the last great intellectual of the Right in Mexico. Those who follow him might be of the Right, but they are far from being intellectuals. Still, the hierarchies of the intellectual Right in Mexico have their acolytes and, if it were necessary, their soldiers. In recent days, the intellectual front against the university movement suffered a serious setback. The blow came from an academic, an intellectual and leftist, called Pablo González Casanova. The UNAM researcher proved something fundamental: legality cannot supplant legitimacy. In the case of the UNAM conflict, "legality" (now other intellectuals have demonstrated that the entrance by the Federal Preventative Police into UNAM was illegal, as are prison trials against the imprisoned students) was converted into a means by which the senselessness of the violence received an honorary doctorate from the largest university in Latin America.[6]

If being a leftist was already something unforgivable in González Casanova, the fact of his working in accordance with his ideas was now too much. The "cardinals" of the intelligentsia sent their pawns (it seems that some of them even have first and last names) to cross swords with Don Pablo. Although they lost the battle, the intelligentsia of the Right does not lose sleep over that failed skirmish. Their decisive battles are not in the arena of ideas (they would surely lose), nor against progressive intellectuals. No, the ground to be conquered, the one they want, the one which some of them already enjoy, is at the side of the "prince," at the edge of his table, whispering praise into the ears of the great gentlemen of politics and money. Nonetheless, they have to do something to differentiate themselves from the buffoons swarming around government palaces. That is why they have their maga-

4 Following the Revolution of Ayutla of 1855, the liberal revolt that ousted Antonio López de Santa Ana, a series of legal reforms were enacted prior to the Constitution of 1857 to limit the power of the Church hierarchy and Mexican military, including the Ley Juárez (1855), Ley Lerdo (1856) and Ley Iglesias (1857). Many cities in Mexico have a street named La Reforma in honor of the revolt.

5 Poet and essayist associated with the PRI, Octavio Paz (1914—1998) was one of Mexico's most prominent intellectuals winning the Cervantes prize in 1981, the American Neustadt Prize in 1982 and the Nobel Prize for Literature in 1990.

6 Violating the autonomy of the campus, Federal Preventive Police, under the direction of Wilfredo Robledo, raided the University, arresting almost 1,000 student strikers in early February. The Federal Preventive Police was established as a special unit in response to the UNAM student strike under the leadership of the *Consejo General de Huelga* (General Strike Council). The strike for the abolition of educational reforms that sought to limit free public education began on March 12, 1999.

zines and television programs. The dead texts they sketch, their intellectual circles and their open spaces are not targeted at anyone but themselves. In these places they comment among themselves, they read among themselves, they "critique" among themselves, they greet each other, and, in so doing, they say to each other: "We are the conscience of the new Power, we are necessary because we say we are necessary; Power needs someone to set economic interests and their expenses to prose and verse; what makes us different from the buffoons is that we do not tell jokes, we explain them."

In this dwarf-like world of dwarves, the surface is a chessboard where bishops, kings, queens, pawns, knights and rooks conspire at the tops of their voices. Everyone knows who is going to win, what is important is not that, but rather which square they occupy and for how long. The racket deafens each of them, but the machine works. There are seven decades of a political system that is now called the "new PRI." The noise of the machine does not resemble that of gears grinding, each time it seems more like a publicity spot.

The problems begin when pieces enter that do not belong on that chessboard, when some strange object jams the gears, or when some interference obstructs the omnipotent "buying and selling"...

From the National News Page to the Entertainment Section?

The fundamental sound box of this Mexico of the powerful is the electronic media. However, far from being merely an echo of what the political class says, television and radio take on their own voice, and, without anyone questioning it, they become the primary voice. The great problems of the country do not define the national agenda, for that matter, neither do the political leaders. No, election campaigns and government agendas agree with radio and television programs. Electronic media does not broadcast news; it creates it, feeds it, makes it grow, annihilates it. The difference between party choices during elections is not based on the programs for the nation that one and the other support, but in the time slots they manage to secure in the media.

The ratings that matter are not of the television viewing public, but rather those that reside with the political class. The major part of the statements and declarations by the main political actors do not deal with real situations, but lead news stories. Thus, the "up-to-the-minute" issues covered by the media are those that they have selected. In the great theater of Mexican politics, the politicians are the actors and simultaneously the spectators. Radio and television carry out the roles of director, screenwriter, producer, lighting designer, stagehand and ticket taker.

If it is increasingly difficult to speak of a single Mexico, during elections it is impossible. The existence of two countries is palpable: the one that exists in the headlines and the one that takes place "off the record," outside the news and exclusive stories.

Off the Record: Reality

While radio and television try, ineffectively, to present an image of "normalcy" at the Autonomous National University of Mexico, the enthusiasts for the "Rule of Law" exercised against social activists are surprised that the entrance onto the campus of Wilfredo Robledo's paramilitaries and the detention of hundreds of university students did not "solve" the conflict at the greatest university. The university movement is not over, nor is the pretender, De La Fuente, the rector.[7] The selective and piecemeal release of student prisoners (at great pains to leave a few still in jail) has not discouraged the struggle for the demand for free education and for a truly democratic university congress with authority to make decisions. At times disconcerted, the university movement remains firm in its demands for freedom for political prisoners, free education and the congress, while radio and television try to make sure that the headlines belong solely to those who have paid for airtime. The rest should be relegated to the police blotter or used as "filler." Who cares about the parents who are bleeding to death to demand the release of their children, if Esteban (Guajardo) Moctezuma and Emilio Gamboa are fighting on Labastida's team?[8] The same media that were once horrified by the CGH's vocabulary now get excited about the "crap-fart-sssh" of the election campaigns and about the profuse exchange of digital signals among the candidates.

But, if Reality takes place well outside the programming, every once in a while it takes a bite out of the Mexico of above and ruins macro-economic indices, news programs and candidates' agendas. In a corner of the other Mexico, a community decides to do without *telenovelas* and news shows; it confronts the police and defends a rural teachers school.[9] In El Mexe, Hidalgo, the protagonists are not education students, nor the police who went to crush them; they are the people.[10] People who had no space in the news save for the police blotter, a point in the candidate's rally, a number in the amount of sandwiches and sodas to be given out during the proselytizing tour. As it appears, it disappears. An avalanche of statements bury the fundamental fact (the "*Ya Basta!*" firmly exercised) and one other thing:

Chiapas? It might be on the agenda of the UN or other national and international non-governmental organizations, but not on the national one. In order to

---

7 Juan Ramón De La Fuente became Rector of the UNAM on November 12, 1999, following the sudden resignation of Francisco Barnés de Castro.

8 Esteban (Guajardo) Moctezuma and Emilio Gamboa, both prominent members of the PRI, held important positions in Labastida's election team. Moctezuma served as campaign manager while Gamboa was the campaign's director of communications. Gamboa's alleged ties to narco-trafficking while a top PRI official was the focus of some controversy.

9 *Telenovelas* are soap operas, primarily produced in Mexico, Venezuela, and Brazil, popular throughout Latin America and increasingly translated into a number of foreign languages.

10 On February 20, activists from El Mexe Teachers College in Tepatepec, Hidalgo freed 176 students illegally held by police following an early morning raid on the college. Protestors retaliated for the attack on the school by parading some 40 captured officers without their clothes in the main plaza.

prevent that, the croquette Albores spares no expense.[11] In one year, the croquette has spent 28 million pesos to prevent "Chiapas" from being the sour note on the news (*Proceso Sur*, Number 1, March 4, 2000). The man with the checkbook is the beloved son of TV Azteca: Manuel de la Torre, who just yesterday was destroying rural schools with his whirling helicopter.[12] And today he is trying to herd journalists as if they were cattle.

While the government insists it has made a great economic investment in Chiapas, it "forgets" to say that that the greatest expense is on publicity, paid journalistic notes, bribes in order to silence "disagreeable" news and to improve the federal army's battered image.

Between Albores' barking and Rabasa's braying, the army takes up new attack positions, it ostensibly reinforces its garrisons, planes and helicopters increase their flyovers and the war continues, now keeping a prudent distance from press headlines.

The Zapatista indigenous insist on the value of the word: the women in San Cristóbal on March 8th, the *coordinadoras* on March 21st, the residents of Amador Hernández, those from Amparo Agua Tinta, the Tzotzils of Los Altos, the Tzeltales of Las Cañadas, the Chols and Zoques of the North, the Mames of the Sierra. They all remember that there is a word that the government did not honor, the San Andrés Accords, and that there is no peace, nor justice, nor dignity for the Mexican indigenous.

Far from the front pages, from the electronic news programs, the Mexico of the people takes place in resistance, in patient waiting, in hope . . .

"What are they waiting for?"

I return the pages to Durito, saying to him: "That 'what are they waiting for?' Is it a question, a demand or a prophecy?"

"Look out the window," Durito tells me. I do so, and I see and I don't believe it.

"You mean that . . . ? Who would have thought?"

"That's how it is. Windows are like cookies: they are tasty and nourishing," says Durito while he sets out on the return . . .

With those words Durito ended his talk that early morning, Don Pablo. When I returned to the hut, I re-read your letter and began writing you these lines. I should try to explain to you that we Zapatistas see ourselves not only in the window on the left that you point out in your text. We believe we have

---

11 A nickname for Chiapas Governor Guillén, suggesting that he resembles the deep-fried dumplings known as croquettes.

12 Manuel de la Torre, the executive director of TV-Azteca's news program "Hablemos Claro" ("Speaking Clearly") and brother to the Chiapas Secretary of Agriculture, accompanied Dolores "Lolita" de la Vega, the program's news anchor, on a surprise visit to the community of La Realidad. The fully-equipped newsteam landed a helicopter provided by the governor on the patio of the community's school house. Tojolobal leaders forced the helicopter to leave, but its departure ripped through the roof of the schoolhouse, severely injuring a number of children.

opened another window, a window within the window on the left, that our political proposal is more radical than those that look out your window and that it is different, very "other." (Note: I did not write "better," just "different.") And I suppose that this letter was intended to explain to you (and to others) what that other window that we Zapatistas had opened consists of, according to us.

But it happens that everything will be in that book that hasn't been written, but which can be read in one of the "window zones" in the mountains of the Mexican southeast. So you will have to wait for that famous book to be written (which is nothing if not optimistic) and to be published (which borders on naïveté).

For the moment, Don Pablo, receive our greetings and send your next letter with, preferably, some "Pancrema" cookies (better if they are not rancid). Perhaps then I can convince Durito to take me to the lucky "window" again. Because in the book I haven't written (but which, I suppose, I will write), I only managed to read the dedication, and I didn't get any further because a damp tenderness prevented me from doing so.

Vale, Don Pablo. *Salud*, and taking a good look at it, a window is nothing more than a broken mirror.

From the mountains of the Mexican Southeast
Subcomandante Insurgente Marcos

* * *

Durito.com

Falling on the anniversary of the massacre at Acteal, the withdrawal of the last troops occupying the Zapatista community of Amador Hernández left the conflict zone still heavily militarized. During the withdrawal of the 250 remaining troops, Durito informs El Sup that he will change his name from "Don Durito de la Lacandona" to "Durito-dot-com."

> Zapatista Army of National Liberation
> Mexico
> December 22, 2000
> To the National and International Press:
>
> Ladies and Gentlemen:
> Here goes a communiqué on the recent troop withdrawal.
> When the soldiers arrived, they did so furtively; now they are withdrawing with a great public show. If peace does, in fact, arrive, it does not matter to us that they present as Zapatistas those who are not (the ones from ARIC), and the ones

---

First published by Sitio oficial de la visita del EZLN a la Ciudad de México www.ezlnaldf.org. Originally translated by irlandesa. See also "Carta del CCRI-CG EZLN Sobre El Reciente Retiro de Tropas," *La Marcha del Color de la Tierra, Comunicados, cartas y mensages del Ejército Zapatista de Liberación Nacional* (México, D.F.: Rizoma, 2001), 20.

who've waged the dirty war as great promoters of peace (the military).[1] It is a chameleon disorder, which navigates according to the way the media winds are blowing.

Vale. Salud, and may the end of the year also be the end of despair.

From the mountains of the Mexican Southeast
Subcomandante Insurgente Marcos
Mexico

P.S. Durito says he is going to change his name. It will no longer be "Don Durito de la Lacandona," but "Durito-dot-com." He says he's riding the wave of "business excellence" now.

Dialectic (or Self-Contradictory) P.S. where Durito says always no, none of that "dot-com," nor "excellence," nor "business." He says that during times of travel, what is needed is a sailor. La Mar agrees, and I look for some seasickness pills.

---

1 In one of a series of well-publicized photo opportunities, staged by then-Governor Albores, of alleged Zapatistas surrendering their arms, members of ARIC (*Asociación Rural de Interés Colectivo*, or Rural Association of Collective Interest) were presented as Zapatistas. (AP: April 2, 1999)

The Other Player

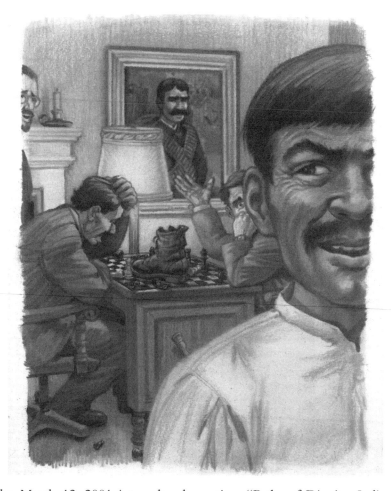

At the March 12, 2001 intercultural meeting, "Paths of Dignity: Indigenous Rights, Memory and Cultural Heritage," Marcos begins his presentation by complaining that Durito has repeatedly interrupted his preparation. Marcos also tells a story about the intervention of an indigenous man in a chess match. Leaving Marcos to talk about culture in the abstract, Durito exits to enjoy the rock concert held later that evening in the Zócalo.

First published on the Sitio oficial de la visita del EZLN a la Ciudad de México, www.ezlnaldf.org. Originally translated by irlandesa. See also "Ponencia del Subcomandante Insurgente Marcos, Encuentro Intercultural, Villa Olímpica, D.F.," *La Marcha del Color de la Tierra, Comunicados, cartas y mensajes del Ejército Zapatista de Liberación Nacional* (México, D.F.: Rizoma, 2001), 250-55.

March 12, 2001

A good midday to all:

We would like to express our appreciation to the community of the National School of Anthropology and History for offering us the opportunity to give our word alongside these people, who add their humanity to their power to give life to words, people who accompany a struggle that can only be recorded within the great battle for humanity.[1]

It is not simple to begin this talk.

Not just because the lights accompanying us are dazzling and leave very few dark spaces, the favorite place for the shadows that we are.

But also because an impertinent beetle has prevented me from preparing something poised and skillful, interrupting me with every kind of absurd and unintelligible thing.

Perhaps you have heard talk of him before, he calls himself "Don Durito de la Lacandona," and he has assigned himself the mission of, he says, righting injustice and offering succor to the needy and helpless. For some reason that I am not able to understand, Durito has decided that I fit into the category of the needy and helpless and, he says, my entire life is an injustice.

So you already know that what has kept me up all these days has not been the volume of Fox's contradictory statements, nor the death threats so generously lavished on us by the National Action Party. No, it's been Durito who has insisted that the bus is not a bus, but a vessel, and that the march in reality does not march, but sails, since it is the sea that gives it sustenance.

According to the little I was able to understand, Durito will attend the rock concert that will take place today in the Zócalo of Mexico City, in which, we are told, Joaquín Sabina, Maldita Vecindad, Santa Sabina and Panteón Rococó, as well as a good number of young men and women, will take part.[2]

But that is, as everything in this march, a story yet to be told.

In culture, Zapatismo has been able to find generous ears and echoes that voice their own dignity. In music, particularly in rock, in the visual and dramatic arts, in letters and in scientific analysis, we have found good people, humane people, who follow their own paths of dignity. And so we would like to take advantage of this event to greet all those men and women who struggle for humanity through culture.[3]

---

1 Marcos joined noted intellectuals José Saramago, Alain Touraine, Manuel Vázquez Montalbán, Bernard Cassen, Carlos Monsiváis, Elena Poniatowska, Carlos Montemayor and Pablo González Casanova at the panel discussion "Los Caminos de la dignidad: Derechos Indígenas, memoria y patrimonio cultural" convened at the Olympic Village Sports Center of the National School of Anthropology and History, or ENAH (Escuela Nacional de Antropología e Historia).

2 The concert, "Zapata en el corazón," had an estimated 90,000 Zapatista supporters, brigadistas and fans. Joaquín Sabina cancelled at the last minute. Although Marcos was rumored to attend, he did not join in the celebration.

3 For an important statement of the Zapatistas' appreciation for cultural workers, see "Today Ends the National Plebiscite for Peace and Democracy," in EZLN, *Documentos y comunicados 2*

In order to speak as Zapatistas about the paths of dignity, we will tell a story that is called:

THE OTHER PLAYER

Set in their studious corner, the players
move the gradual pieces. Until dawn
the chessboard keeps them in its strict confinement
with its two colors set at daggers drawn.
(...)
Eventually, when the players have withdrawn,
when time itself has finally consumed them,
the ritual certainly will not be done.
(...)
The player too is captive of caprice
(the words are Omar's) on another ground
where black nights alternate with whiter days.

God moves the player, he in turn the piece.
But what God beyond God begins the round
of dust and time and sleep and agonies?"
—Jorge Luis Borges[4]

This is the story:

A group of players finds itself engrossed in an important master chess game. An indigenous man approaches, observes, and asks what it is they are playing. No one answers him. The indigenous approaches the board and contemplates the position of the pieces, the serious, frowning faces of the players, the expectant attitude of those around them. He repeats his question. One of the players takes the trouble of responding: "It's something you wouldn't be able to understand; it's a game for important and wise people." The indigenous remains silent and continues to observe the board and the competitors' moves. After a time, he ventures another question: "And why do you play if you already know who's going to win?" The same player who responded before tells him: "You'll never understand, it's beyond your intellectual grasp. This is for experts." The indigenous doesn't say anything. He continues looking and he leaves. Soon after, he returns, carrying something with him. Without saying a word, he approaches the game table and places an old, mud-covered boot in the middle of the board. The players are confounded, and they look at him angrily. The indigenous smiles maliciously as he asks: "Check?"

(México, D.F.: Ediciones Era, 1995), 449-50. See also "From the Underground Culture to the Culture of Resistance," *La Jornada*, October 27, 1999.
4 "Chess," in Jorge Luis Borges, *Selected Poems*, Alexander Coleman, ed. (New York: Viking, 1999), 102-3.

End of Story.

Samuel Taylor Coleridge, an English poet from the cusp of the 18th and 19th centuries, wrote: "If a man were to cross through Paradise in a dream, and they gave him a flower as proof that he had been there, and if, upon awakening, he were to find that flower in his hand . . . what then?"[5]

In this March of Indigenous Dignity, we Zapatistas have seen a part of the map of national tragedy that is not at primetime on the radio and television news programs. Anyone present here can argue that this has no merit whatsoever, and that a march wasn't necessary in order to realize that the Mexico of below forms the majority in number and in poverty.

But I did not come to talk to you about poverty rates, constant repression, or deceptions.

On this march, we Zapatistas have also seen parts of rebel Mexicos, who see themselves and see others. That and nothing else is dignity. The Mexicos of below, particularly the indigenous, speak to us of a history of struggle and resistance that comes from afar and that beats in the today of each place. Yes, but it is also a history which looks forward.

From the mountains of the Mexican Southeast to the Zócalo of Mexico City, we Zapatistas have crossed a territory of rebellion that has given us a flower of brown dignity as proof that we were there. We have reached the center of Power and we find that we have that flower in our hands and the question is, as Coleridge wrote, "what then?"

Contrary to what the columnists of the political class might suppose, the question does not refer to what follows, but to what that brown flower means. And, above all, what it means for the future.

I know that in these times of modernity, where intellectual quotients are replaced by bank accounts, poetry by advertising spots, and science by verbal diarrhea, speaking of dreams can only sound anachronistic.

Nonetheless, the struggle of the Indian communities for their dignity is fundamentally a dream, indeed, it is a very otherly dream.

The indigenous struggle in Mexico is a dream that not only dreams the tomorrow that includes the color of the earth, also and above all, it is a dream that fights to urge the awakening of that tomorrow.

We Indian communities reappeared precisely when what denied us seemed stronger and more solid. And it's precisely what our dream already predicts—that the monuments that neoliberalism erects for itself are nothing but future ruins.

---

5 The full quote reads: "If a man could pass through Paradise in a dream, and have a flower presented to him as a pledge that his soul had really been there, and if he found that flower in his hand when he awoke—Aye, and what then?" See "Anima Poetae" (1816), in *Bloomsbury Biographical Dictionary of Quotations*, 1997.

Power wants to enclose the current indigenous struggle in nostalgia, chest-beating and the artisan "boom." It wants to strike out the Indian struggle within the framework of the past, something like "the past reaches out to us with unpaid accounts," to use the marketing language that is so fashionable. As if settling these accounts were the effective solvent to erase that past, and then the "today, today, today" that Fox used as an election platform and uses as a government program, could reign without any problem. The same "today" that neoliberalism has converted into a new religious creed.

If we warn that the indigenous movement wants to turn fashionable, we are not referring only to the publicity zeal that wants to envelope it.

After all, fashion is nothing more than a return to a past whose final horizon is the present, the today, nowadays, the fleeting moment.

In the struggle for dignity, there is a similar turn to the past, but—and this is fundamental—the final horizon is the future.

To put it in other terms, neoliberalism—nothing other than a fashion, that is, a turn to the past with the horizon of the present (thus the "neo" that gives the liberalism of yesteryear currency)—conceives of the current world as the only one possible, as the culmination of the ages. That's why Fox and others say that ultimately all progressive struggle ended with his reaching Power. His intellectuals and public relations advisors (that is, if there's any difference) shoot at the clock of history in order to stop time, and thus ensure that there is no other tomorrow than the one they are presiding over.

Neoliberal intellectuals, in contrast with their predecessors, have renounced the historic initiative and no longer announce the future. Not because they are unable to see it, but because they are afraid of it.

The Mexican indigenous struggle has not come to turn back the clock. It is not about returning to the past and declaiming, in an emotional and inspired voice, that "all previous times were better." I think they would have tolerated and even applauded that.

No, we Indian people have come to wind the clock and thus to ensure that the inclusive, tolerant and plural tomorrow—that is, incidentally, the only tomorrow possible—will arrive.

To do that, in order for our march to make the clock of humanity march, we Indian peoples have resorted to the art of reading what has not yet been written. Because that is the dream that animates us as indigenous, as Mexicans and, above all, as human beings. With our struggle we read the future that had already been sown yesterday, that is being cultivated today, and that can only be reaped if one fights, that is, if one dreams.

To the skepticism-made-State-doctrine, to neoliberal indifference, to the cynical realism of globalization, we Indian people have countered with memory, the word and the dream.

By launching into this fight with everything we have, the Mexican indigenous, as individuals and as a collective, have operated with a universally human

292

impulse, that of rebellion. It has made us a thousand times better than before and it has turned us into an historic force, not because of its prominence in books or monuments, but because of its ability to make history, like that, in lowercase.

The key to "The Other Player" is not in the old boot full of mud that interrupts and subverts the media chess game of the gentlemen of power and money, and the game that exists between those who have made politics the art of simulation and deception. The essential thing is in the smile that the indigenous smiles, and that he knows something. He knows that the other player, which is him, is missing and the other who is not him, but who is also other, is also missing. But above all he knows that it is not true that the fight has ended and that we have lost. He knows that it has barely begun. And he knows it, not because he knows, but because he dreams.

In short, we indigenous are not part of yesterday, we are part of tomorrow.

And given boots, culture and tomorrows, we remember what we wrote some time ago, looking back and dreaming ahead: "A boot is a boot that has taken the wrong path, and seeks to be what all boots long to be, that is, a bare foot."

And this is relevant because in the tomorrow that we are dreaming there will be no boots, nor jeans, nor soldiers, but bare feet, which is how feet should be when the morning is just beginning.

Thank you.

From the National School of Anthropology and History
Subcomandante Insurgente Marcos
Mexico

P.S. I know it might be disconcerting to some that, to speak of culture from the indigenous point of view, I resort to other voices—Borges and Coleridge in this case—but that is how I remind myself, and remind you, that culture is a bridge for everyone, above calendars and borders, and as such should be defended. So we say and say to ourselves: no to cultural hegemony, no to cultural homogeneity, and no to any form of hegemony and homogeneity.

* * *

The Story of the Little Dented Car

Just before Marcos and 23 *Comandantes* embarked on the March for Indigenous Dignity, Durito surprised El Sup disguised as a patrol car informing him that he would protect the Zapatista delegation during the march. Helping Marcos prepare a talk for children, Durito dictates "The Story of the Little Dented Car" about a wind-up toy that coped with the crisis caused by privatization.

First published by Sitio oficial de la visita del EZLN a la Ciudad de México, www.ezlnaldf.org. Originally translated by irlandesa. See also "Mensaje del Subcomandante Insurgente Marcos, ENAH," *La Marcha del Color de la Tierra, Comunicados, cartas y mensajes del Ejército Zapatista de Liberación Nacional* (México, D.F.: Rizoma, 2001), 278–281.

March 18, 2001
To the Boys and Girls of the Isidro Favela Neighborhood[1]

Through my voice the voice of the Zapatista Army of National Liberation does not speak.

Yes, you heard right, "the voice of etcetera," and it so happens that I was contemplating the walls in the room where we stayed yesterday, and I was looking for an idea or something that would wind me up to say a few words to you that would simultaneously be analysis, reflection, gratitude, invitation, etceteration, or something better than one of those games where everybody participates and there's joy and songs and dances, or at least as good.

But nothing. What came to me was something like that radio program where they say "boys and girls," or something. It occurred to me that just as Fox's public relations advisors tell him to imitate what we do, I could go out with a statement that I'm willing to fulfill the three conditions or that I don't want to supplant peace with commercials, or something along those lines.[2]

That's what I was up to, when the lights went out. The most incomplete darkness reigned around me. And I say "incomplete" because almost immediately there appeared, under the doorjamb, a kind of miniature Christmas tree that was moving laboriously. I checked the calendar, and it told me "we are in March, and in March there are no little Christmas trees."

Panic overtook me, but I overcame it because, given all that stuff about us Zapatistas being very brave, well, it wouldn't look good if I were to panic. So you won't be able to go around saying that I'm afraid of the dark, since we children really are afraid of the dark; that's why we Zapatistas fight so that all of us children can have light. But okay, that's another story.

I tell you, from under my door something appearing like a little Christmas tree was coming towards me. When it got close, I was able to make out that it wasn't a little Christmas tree, but one of those strings of colored lights being dragged by something that looked like a little dented car or a little flattened ball or . . .

"Little dented car your mama, and little deflated ball your mama!" screamed the thing that looked like a little dented car or a little flattened ball. I happen to like my mama very much so I turned on the lights in order to give . . . just desserts to . . . to whatever it was!

---

1 The Isidro Favela neighborhood surrounds the National School of Anthropology and History that hosted the Zapatista delegation during the March for Indigenous Dignity. The neighborhood and university have provided consistent and outspoken support of the Zapatistas.

2 Following the presidential succession of Vicente Fox, the Zapatistas announced their decision to participate in a renewed peace process only if Fox fulfilled three conditions: dismantling seven of the 259 military installations in the conflict zone; release of all Zapatista political prisoners; and acceptance of the San Andrés Accords. Fox, with the aid of the media, attempted to reduce the peace process to an agreement between himself and Marcos, and ultimately, into a media event with a commercial logo.

When I turned on the lights, surprise! I discovered that it was nothing more and nothing less than a grouchy beetle who calls himself "Don Durito de la Lacandona," although his real name is Nebuchadnezzar. He allows his friends to call him "Durito."

"Excuse me, Durito," I said to him. "But I didn't expect to see you around here. Why are you dragging that string of Christmas lights? Don't you know we're just barely into March?"

"Of course I know! If it were true that you are a Zapatista, then you'd know that we Zapatistas fight so that children can have Christmas whenever they want, whether in March or July, or a Christmas every month of the year . . ."

"Okay, okay. Why do you have those Christmas lights?"

"Because I've come in disguise."

"And what are you disguised as?"

"As a patrol car."

"A patrol car?"

"Yes, I'm in charge of guarding the safety of the Zapatista delegation, and I disguised myself as a patrol car so no one would realize that I am the great, the incomparable, the supreme Don Durito de la Lacandona! Completely digitized, guaranteed, and batteries included!"

"Digitized, guaranteed, and batteries included?" I asked.

"Yes, I'm into managerial excellence now," Durito answered, and continued:

"And tell me, dented carrot-nose, what are you doing?"

"A message or greeting to the children of this neighborhood, in order to thank them for welcoming us."

"Fine, step aside, this is a job for the indestructible Durito. I'm going to dictate a story to you. You'll read it to them, and it will be the delight of the young and old."

"But Durito . . ." I tried to protest.

"I don't want to hear any buts! Just write this:"

The Story of the Little Dented Car

Once upon a time there was a little wind-up car that no longer had a key with which to wind itself up. Or, it did have one, but there was no one to wind it up. And no one would wind it up because it was an old little car, and completely dented. It was missing a tire and, when it did work, it just went round and round.

The children didn't pay it much attention because they were into Transformers and Pokemon and Zodiac Knights and other things.

And so the little dented wind-up car didn't have anyone to wind it up. And one day the lights went out in the great city because the one person in charge had privatized the electrical industry, and the rich had taken the light to other countries, and the Transformers and Pokemon and Zodiac Knights wouldn't run anymore.[3] And then the little dented car said: "I have a key but I don't have anyone to wind it up." And a little boy heard him and wound him up and the little car began going round and round, and the little boy said: "And now?" "Not like that," said the little car. "Turn me upside down." The child did so, and he asked: "And now?" "Well, put a rubber band on the motor that's there." The little boy did, and the little car said, "Now wind me up and you'll see that light will be generated," and, yes, the little boy did, and there was light once again. This was repeated in all the homes where they had a little dented wind-up car, and, where they didn't, they continued without light. In the end the little car said: "That's just how you have to do it. Turn things upside-down so that the world will have light once again. *Tan-tan.*"

Moral: It's better not to let the electrical industry be privatized because, what happens if not everyone has a little dented wind-up car?

From the Isidro Favela Neighborhood,
Don Durito de la Lacandona (batteries included)
Mexico, March 2001

"Durito," I protested.

"What!"

"No one's going to like that story!"

"Why not? It's a good story, substantial, it doesn't need batteries and it's indestructible. And so I'm off, because Fernández de Cevallos is around and I have here a razor blade."[4]

Well, this is the story, boys and girls of the Isidro Favela neighborhood. I hope you've enjoyed it and that you understand now why the voice of the EZLN does not speak through my voice, but, in this case, the voice that speaks is that of a beetle by the name of "Don Durito de la Lacandona," who, he says, is devoted to helping the poor and challenging the powerful.

Vale. Salud, and if you see him around here, tell him to give me back the tobacco he took without telling me.

The Sup, sneezing.

* * *

---

3 The restructuring of the national electrical industry was justified by claims that Mexico would experience power shortages unless the nation privatized the Federal Electricity Commission (Comisión Federal de Electricidad) that provides over 90 percent of Mexico's electricity. Initiated by Ernesto Zedillo and vigorously pursued by Vincente Fox, the privatization efforts met strong opposition from the Mexican Electrical Workers Union, one of the nation's most militant and independent unions.

4 Throughout the march and the Zapatista's arrival in the nation's capital, prominent PAN Senator, Diego Fernández de Cevallos, publicly expressed his opposition to the San Andrés accords, the COCOPA proposal, and the Zapatista audience with the Congress, thus sabotaging Fox's attempts to meet the Zapatistas' conditions and, ultimately, the path of dialogue.

The Hand That Dreams
When It Writes

Following the arrival of the March for Indigenous Dignity in the Mexico City, Durito informs Marcos about how he used to make a living in the area around Azcapotzalco—one of the UAM campuses where the Zapatistas met with students. Durito also offers a short discourse on "doing politics" in which he mocks professional politicians, such as those who undermined the efforts of the Zapatistas to address the nation's legislators. Faced with consistent public support, the government capitulated and heard the Zapatista delegation on March 28, 2001.

First published by Sitio oficial de la visita del EZLN a la Ciudad de México, www.ezlnaldf.org. Originally translated by irlandesa. See also "Mensaje del Subcomandante Insurgente Marcos, UAM Azcapotzalco," *La Marcha del Color de la Tierra, Comunicados, cartas y mensajes del Ejército Zapatista de Liberación Nacional* (México, D.F.: Rizoma, 2001), 321-24.

March 20, 2001

Words of the EZLN at the Autonomous Metropolitan University, Azcapotzalco

Brothers and sisters of the UAM-Azcapotzalco,

Brothers and sisters of the neighborhoods of Northwest Mexico City:

You must all excuse me, but I have not managed to prepare anything special for this event. I have, therefore, resorted to the advice of a specialist in local issues, because, he says, he once worked in what was previously a refinery near here.[1]

As you are, surely, very knowledgeable about the history of the lands you walk, you will already know that I am referring to Durito, known (he says) at that time as "Heavy Metal Durito," and not exactly for his rock-and-roll talents, but because he would swipe scraps from the refinery and resell them as archeological pieces to Coparmex managers who, as everyone knows, are very knowledgeable about history, and have always been concerned with the preservation of historical patrimony.[2]

"It was really easy," Durito tells me. "They only had to see that the pieces were oxidized and rusted to be convinced that they belonged to an ancient civilization."

Durito studied at the UAM and was a professor there, and he had to engage in these things in order to pay for his tuition and supplement his salary.[3]

Durito became bored quickly because, he said, there was no glory in swindling imbeciles, and he thought it would be better to fight for the helpless. So he became a university worker and affiliated with the SITUAM.[4] They fired him when he tried to introduce the job category of "Beetle 'C', part-time worker." It was then that he moved from "AZCA," as he says, and went to other refineries that demanded his modest efforts and his precocious managerial initiative.

Durito, as everyone already knows (and if you don't know, well, you're spending your tuition for no reason), embraced the noble profession of knight-

---

1 The PEMEX refinery named "18 de Marzo" ("March 18") after the date of the nationalization of Mexican oil, was renowned for environmental and safety violations. Although Carlos Salinas was credited with its closure and conversion into a park, the closure was the result of protests by local activists and environmentalists, following a hazardous fire.

2 COPARMEX, the Confederación Patronal de la República Mexicana (Employers' Confederation of the Republic of Mexico) is a syndicate of Mexican industrialists formed in 1929.

3 In 1973 the Universidad Autónoma Metropolitana (UAM) opened three campuses: Azcapotzalco, Iztapalapa, and Xochimilco. UAM is the second largest university in Mexico City with an enrollment of 40,000 students.

4 The 7,000-member union Sindicato de Trabajadores de la Universidad Autónoma Metropolitana (SITUAM) walked out in February 1996 demanding a 100 percent wage increase. After a 43-day strike, the SITUAM ended the walkout on March 14, 1996, accepting a 16-percent wage increase PRI officials had insisted on all along.

errantry, and he learned a million-and-one arts, as well as a wealth of knowledge that would put the *Encyclopedia Britannica* and all its cybernetic links to shame, reducing it to the category of paperback dictionary with the brand name "The Crummy Inc., Ltd, TM," whose slogan is "The junk closest to your pocket."

It's here that I asked Durito if he knew why the "hardliners" in the Congress didn't want to engage in dialogue with the Zapatistas. And here is what he told me:

"My dear and flu-ridden peanut-nose . . ."

"It's not the flu, it's the IMECAS," I interrupted him.[5]

"So be it," Durito conceded. "Don't think those scoundrels deny you an ear and their word because of that hideous ski-mask, since it's common knowledge that you'd be even more hideous without it . . ."

Durito pauses so that all of you can start shouting that marvelous slogan that reconciles us with ourselves, that goes: "You are not ugly, you are not ugly!"[6]

Since the slogan is just a slogan, and reality is reality and nothing more, Durito presses on:

"You must find the reason yourself in what I am going to relate to you . . .

"The professional politician is accustomed to confronting life as if it were one of those pencils that almost no one uses anymore: the ones with lead at one end and an eraser on the other. Doing politics has come to be like that, a continuous writing and erasing, always trying to improve the line of the letters and their complex stringing together to make words, which is also how worlds are named. With the eraser they try to correct errors, to start each page over again, to embellish the letters, to refine the word, to decorate the world. The politician always strives to improve his penmanship, and he makes Power a magnificent pencil sharpener with which he files his words and makes them elegant and seductive. He amazes not a few, and some applaud him. But a pencil sharpener, as every student knows, in addition to sharpening the pencil, also uses it up. Soon it is so small that it becomes useless, and it ends up, like everything Power grinds down, in the wastebasket.

"Another pencil then takes its place, and the line of politics begins again. The intellectuals call the dead letters "democratic change." But Power is always ready to offer a pencil sharpener, and there will always be a wastebasket for the sharpened pencils of politics.

---

5 In an effort to gauge Air Quality Standards (AQS) in Mexico City, the government introduced IMECAS as a single measurement of combined air pollutants including carbon monoxide, nitrogen dioxide, sulfur dioxide, ozone, and lead. 100 IMECAS represents "clean" or "acceptable" air.
6 Throughout the march and at Zapatista appearances, crowds of supporters would shout: "*No están solos, no están solos*," ("You are not alone"). Marcos suggests that once his mask is removed and his countenance revealed the crowds would be forced to shout "You are not ugly" as a gesture of solidarity.

"The history of those who are the Power in politics only repeats itself: the words are the same, only the line of the letters changes, their slant, their flourishes, their size. But the words do not change, and, ergo, neither do the worlds.

"The problem, then, is not the beauty of the letters, but that words announce the worlds that, after leaving them behind, give birth to other words, and so on.

"For example, at times a pencil is not even necessary. At times it is enough for a hand to trace a name on the sea or the sand, that is a world in which there are two: the one who is named and the one who has in his hand the bridge that their mutual tomorrow creates."

"Did you understand?" Durito asks me.

"Sure," I respond. "It's better to use an automatic pencil, the kind that changes its answers."

"Good heavens! What strange and perverse wizard has cursed me by selecting you as my assistant? In truth I tell you, I have never known a companion so long of nose and so short of brains. Automatic pencil, my foot! Think, you dope!"

"A nib, then?" I insinuate timidly.

Durito exploded: "It's too much! I'm losing the best years of my life trying to educate a scoundrel like you! To the devil with nibs as well! And let's go, because we have to get to Azcapotzalco, and then to Iztapalapa, and afterwards to Xochimilco, where the ones who designed it divided up this university, thinking it would be easier to control that way. And you see now, divided and everything, Zapatista it is, and Zapatista it will be."

"Let's go, then," I say, resigned, but, without Durito noticing, I throw away the indelible ink marker with which I wrote in one of the bathrooms, "UAM-Azcapotzalco has two 'Z's' so that, even if they want to abbreviate it, it will always be Zapatista."

Vale. Salud, and don't think I didn't understand. The issue is not what you write with, but the hand that dreams when it writes. And that is what the pencil is afraid of, that is, the realization that it is not necessary.

From the Azcapotzalco Unit of the Autonomous Metropolitan University

Clandestine Revolutionary Indigenous Committee - General Command of the Zapatista Army of National Liberation

***

Chairs of Power and Butterflies of Rebellion

In this communiqué, Durito once again intrudes on his erstwhile companion as he struggles to fulfill his duties as spokesperson. Marcos had sent a communiqué to Angel Luis Lara, or "El Ruso," on the occasion of the inauguration of an Aguascalientes in Madrid. Meanwhile, Durito has converted one of his antennae into a satellite modem in order to download web porn. After registering his complaints that the porn he accessed did not have any beetles, he dictates to Marcos a tale about chairs. The allegory our knight-errant shares with his faithful squire underscores the virtues of a patient rebellion.

First published in *La Jornada*, November 25, 2002. Originally translated by Leslie López.

In the communiqué to El Ruso, Marcos made critical statements regarding the political and cultural repression against the Basque people. Spanish Judge Baltazar Garzon dismissed Marcos' critique, labeling his views on Euskadita Askatasuna (ETA) as uninformed support for terrorists, and challenged Marcos to unmask. In response, Marcos proposed a debate on the island of Lanzarote along with an *encuentro* titled "Give the Word a Chance," to be organized and attended by all the parties involved in the political struggle of Euskal Herra. Over 57 academics, journalists and artists joined the discussion by organizing a Civil Forum for the Word on December 22, 2002, as part of the preparation for the larger *encuentro* scheduled for April 22, 2003. ETA chafed at the Zapatista intervention and recommendation that ETA declare a ceasefire as a prerequisite for their participation. In a follow-up exchange the Zapatistas reiterated their right to speak their word, underscoring that they are informed about conflicts outside of Chiapas.

October 12, 2002
ZAPATISTA ARMY OF NATIONAL LIBERATION. MEXICO
For: Angel Luis Lara, alias El Ruso
From: Sup Marcos

Ruso, my brother: First of all, a hug. Second, a piece of advice: I think you'd do well to change your pseudonym; the Chechnyans might confuse you and then, that's right, goodbye Aguascalientes and goodbye to one of the best rockers of our day.

The date (October 12) on which I begin to write these lines is not accidental (nothing is accidental among the Zapatistas), nor is this absurd bridge which, today, I attempt to extend to where you are all working to prepare the inauguration of the Aguascalientes in Madrid.[1]

I'm sure it will all go very well for you and that the absence of that imbecile Aznar (the only thing he's lacking, as his name indicates, is to actually bray) and that constipated the little King Juan Carlos will go unnoticed, even in the magazine ¡Hola!?[2]

But tell all the men and women working with you in that heroic project that they should not be shy. A magazine called *Rebeldía* is about to come out (deported, surely), that will no doubt have a "society" page where you can insert a review that leaves the princess's wedding in the category of "children's parties."

Besides, the aforementioned magazine *Rebeldía* will surely be consistent with its principles and the first thing it will do is rebel against spelling rules, so don't invest too much in the advertising insert. By the way, if it includes photos it will

1 Information on the Madrid Aguascalientes can be found at www.aguascalientesmadrid.org.
2 Marcos is making a reference to *asno*, which translates as burro or ass. José María Aznar took the reins of power from Felipe "Felipillo" González, of the Socialist party, when he was sworn in as President of Spain before King Juan Carlos I in 1996.

be more expensive (unless it's porn) and the price, I am sorry to inform you, is not in euros but marks since they prefer a strong currency.

So no sniveling if royalty does not attend. Instead, I think, there will be plenty of men, women, children and elders, not just from the Iberian Peninsula, but from there above all else. If they are there, everything will be a success. But I should warn you that the police always come on the heels of success. Because the underdogs are just supposed to cry and resign themselves, as established in I-don't-know-what number proclamation that the crown emitted I-don't-know-when; and to the rhythm of the Civil Guard's clubs, everyone marches from their Aguascalientes to jail, or to the cemetery, which is the place that Spanish "democracy" has set aside for Iberian rebels.

I know well that those who attend the rebel party signified by an Aguascalientes will not be just from the Spanish state, but they will be the majority.

Transatlantic Canoes

We can't come, since we're planning to invade Europe shortly and as you can imagine, everyone here already has their baggage ready (well, if you can call two bundles of *tostadas*, a plate of rancid beans, two bottles of non-transgenic *pozol* and chile to taste "baggage"). However, nobody has a life preserver handy.

The best-prepared among us have packed some pills for seasickness and ask, innocently, if there will be "bathroom breaks."

But the worst is yet to come: it turns out I can't convince them that we're not going to get very far with *cayucos* (canoes made from hollowed tree trunks).

Of course we mustn't leave out the small detail that Chiapas does not have an Atlantic seaport and that, since we can't afford to pay the transit fee for the Panama Canal, we'll have to go all the way around the Pacific, by way of the Philippines, India and Africa, sailing north to the Canary Islands.

Because it would be in bad taste to arrive by land. We'd have to go through Mongolia, what's left of the USSR—where we'd have to be careful to say that we're on our way to see "The Russian" (El Ruso) and that they'll have to work it out—then Eastern Europe, passing through France to stock up on the "Chateau Neuf Du Pape, harvest of '69," (I'm even making puns with wines), then head through Italy and stuff ourselves with pasta, and then cross the Pyrenees. We're not daunted by the long walk, but so much exertion is hard on the uniform.

The enthusiasm builds among the crew to-be-almost as much as the vomit. As a matter of fact, I see one *compa* puking and I ask him why he's throwing up if we haven't even embarked yet.[3] "I'm in training," he says to me with that inexorable logic that reigns in the mountains of the Mexican southeast.

---

3 In the original spanish, Marcos uses "*gomitando*" from *gomitar* rather than the more colloquial "*vomitando*" or *vomitar*. In this instance, as well as throughout the communiqué, Marcos is being very explicit in differentiating between Spanish as it is spoken in Spain, including the words, slang, inflection, and rhythms, and the Spanish spoken in Mexico generally and Chiapas in particular.

Where was I? Oh yes! That we're not going to be able to go to the Aguascalientes inauguration because we're "in training," for the expedition as the *compa* said.

Of course, you shouldn't tell anyone that we're going to invade the Iberian Peninsula (stopping first in Lanzarote,[4] where we'll have a cup of coffee with Saramago and Pilar), because you know how the monarchy is, they get nervous so easily, and then go away on vacation with the princesses and the jesters (I'm referring to Felipillo González and Pepillo Aznar, who, as I said before, carries his penitence in his name).

Moreover, speaking badly of the monarchy could cost you. At the very least, they'll evict you from the premises, because of course you've gone and built the Aguascalientes in an "*okupás*" site, since the seat should pertain to people of dignity, and nobody doubts that there is more nobility in any *okupás* house than in El Escorial.[5]

Fuck! Now I've gone and messed with royalty again and I shouldn't, because when one messes with a garbage can one ends up smelling like shit, and you can't get rid of that odor, not even with those bottles of adulterated perfume they sell in El Corte Inglés.[6]

So, say yes to piracy but no to dispersion. Back to this monologue, which has the great advantage that you can't say a word, like when you are face to face with the meritorious Civil Guard who, if you permit me, is neither civil nor a guard. But everyone knows that the world of Power is full of incoherencies.

What? I'm off on another tangent? You're right, fuck, it's just that the mere perspective of missing the warmed-up Galician soup that you'll be ladling out because you don't have a cent left over for anything else, makes me, shall we say, restless.

Conquistadors and neoliberals

I was saying that the date of this letter is not accidental, that if I begin this document on the 12th of October to salute the Aguascalientes project, there's a reason.

In some sectors there is the erroneous idea that the situation of the indigenous peoples of Mexico is due to the Spanish conquest. And it's not that Hernando Cortez and the rest of those ruffians in armor and cassock who accompanied him were benevolent, but, compared to the current governing neoliberals, they are a bunch of charitable nuns.

From the men and women of dignified Spain we have only received words of fraternity, unconditional solidarity, attentive ears, and hands that help, that

---

4 Lanzarote is one of the seven major Canary Islands located only 60 miles off the coast of Africa in the Atlantic Ocean.

5 *Okupás* refers to a squat. El Escorial is the palace and library built by Felipe II of Spain in the late 16th century.

6 El Corte Inglés is one of Spain's largest department stores. There is also one in Mexico City.

greet, that embrace.

So excuse me, Father Hidalgo, but the Zapatistas now cry: "Down with the neoliberals! Up with the *gachupines!*"[7]

I imagine somewhere around there is a Catalonian band that plays *ranchera* music badly, but at work no one beats their rhythm.[8] And those from Galicia should come, and those from Asturias, from Cantabria, from Andalucía, from Murcia, from Extremadura, from Valencia, from Aragón, from La Rioja, from Castilla y León, from Castilla-La Mancha, from Navarra, from the Baleares Islands, from the Canary Islands and from Madrid.[9] To all of them, a great hug from us, and there's enough for everyone. Because with so many brothers and sisters, and all of them so great, our arms have grown from the strength of the affection we have for them.

What? I've left out the Basque Country? No, I want to ask you to let me make a special mention of these brothers and sisters.

Well do I know that that grotesque clown who calls himself Judge Garzón, hand-holder of the Spanish political class—which is as ridiculous as the court, but without its discreet charm (how has the duchess been? Just fine, baron, I don't miss that jester Felipillo at all because Pepillo is just as funny. By the way, you should zip up your fly, Baron, you don't want to catch a cold, which is the only thing you could catch in the court, etc.)—is carrying out real state terrorism that no honest man or woman could see without becoming indignant.

Yes, Garzón the clown has declared the political struggle of the Basque Country illegal.[10] After making a fool of himself with that idiotic story about nabbing Pinochet (the only thing he did was give him a paid vacation), he shows his true fascist vocation by denying the Basque people the right to struggle politically for a legitimate cause.[11]

And I don't say this just because. But here we have seen many Basque brothers and sisters. They were in the peace camps. They did not come to tell us what to do, nor did they teach us to make bombs or plan assaults.

Because here the only bombs are those of Chiapas, which, as opposed to those of the Yucatan, never rhyme.

And here comes Olivio to ask me if I will give him some of the chocolates

---

7 Father Miguel Hidalgo led the 1810 rebellion that would eventually result in Mexican Independence. *Gachupines* is a derogatory term referring to Spaniards and is commonly used in Mexico. However, it is not often used to refer to those Spanish exiles who arrived during the Spanish Civil War in 1937.

8 Ranchera music emerged after the Mexican Revolution and reflects a nostalgia for rural life.

9 These are provinces in Spain.

10 In the original, "clown" appears in English.

11 Baltasar Garzón received considerable public attention in 1997 for demanding the arrest of former Argentine military officers for the disappearances or deaths of over 300 Spanish citizens. He also demanded the arrest and extradition of Chilean dictator Augusto Pinochet for similar murders of almost 100 Spanish citizens. In October 1998, Pinochet was arrested by Scotland Yard and threatened with extradition to Spain. A British court subsequently ordered his release.

with nuts that they gave me because, it is rumored, I am veeery sick. And he recites a bomb of a poem for me.

"Okay," I say to him, noticing that the chocolates are already moldy. And Olivio deepens his voice as he recites: "Bomb, bomb, on my patio there's an orange sapling, and your sister sure is cute."

I'm not offended so much by the part about my sister, but rather by the lack of rhyme; nonetheless, I give Olivio the chocolates... but in the head, because I throw them at him while I chase him until I get tired, which is to say, a few steps.

What's more, here the only assaults are on good musical taste, like when I grab a guitar and intone, in my unmatchable baritone voice, the one that goes, "Every time I get drunk, I swear something happens, I go straight to see you and I get the wrong hammock."

Manu Chao is sure to give me a contract if he hears me.[12] Of course, as long as I don't have to pay for the two guitar strings that broke when, in a hand-to-hand combat with the insurgents I was singing that one about the schizophrenic cow. Or was it "Crazy Cow?" Well, if Manu is out that way, give him a hand and just tell him that we'll forgive him the strings when we see each other in the next station which, as everyone knows, is called "Hope."

And if Manu doesn't give me a contract, then I'll go with Amparo's group. Even though it might have to change its name, and instead of "Amparonoia" she'll call it "Amparofobia," since my critics are globalizing as well.[13]

Anyway, to be terrorists, the main thing we're lacking is the calling, not the means.

But, okay, so brothers and sisters of the Basque Country have been here, and they have behaved with dignity, which is how Basques behave. And I don't know if Fermin Muguruza is there, but I remember that once he was here, and they asked him where was he from, and he said "Basque," and they asked again, "French Basque or Spanish Basque?" Fermín didn't even miss a beat when he answered, "Basque from the Basque Country."[14]

I was looking for something to say in Basque to send my regards to the

---

12 Manu Chao, known for his fusion of different musical rhythms and explicit political lyrics, released his first solo album, *Clandestino*, in 1998, dedicating it to the Zapatistas. In 2000, Manu Chao performed for Zapatista communities in Chiapas. He now donates his royalties to the EZLN. Marcos is referring to "Esperanza," a song contained in Manu Chao's second solo album, *Próxima esta ción*.

13 Amparo Sánchez, lead singer of Amparonoia, traveled to Chiapas towards the end of 2000 only to return to Mexico City as part of the March for Indigenous Dignity in March 2001. Upon returning to Spain's alternative music scene, she organized Sound System in order to raise funds for the Zapatistas. Marcos is suggesting the change of name as a play on the word for anti-globalization activists in Spanish, "globalifóbicos" or "globofóbicos."

14 Fermin Muguruza has been the lead vocalist for the bands "Negu Gorriak," "Kortatu," and "Dut," dominating the Basque music scene by incorporating Basque folk music with the intense rage of punk and the fresh riddims of Dub, Hip Hop, Drum'n Bass, Reggae, and Ska, punctuated with lyrics always sung in Euskadi, the language of the Basque country.

brothers and sisters of that country, and I didn't find much, but I don't know if my dictionary is any good because I looked up the word 'dignity' in Basque, and the Zapatista dictionary says "Euskal Herria." Ask them if I am right, or if I should try again.

Finally, that which neither Garzón nor his epigones knows is that sometimes dignity changes into a puff fish, and woe be unto whoever tries to crush it.

Festival of rebellion

So I've said before that Aguascalientes should be a festival of rebellion, something which doesn't please any of the political parties.

"They are frauds," interrupted Durito.

"But wait Durito, I haven't even started talking about the Mexican political parties."

"I am not talking about those frauds, but rather about porn web pages."

"But Durito, we don't have Internet in the jungle."

"We don't have it? Sounds like the European Union. I have it. With some imagination and a little gum and duct tape I was able to convert one of my antennae into a powerful satellite modem."

"And could you let us know, postmodern knight-errant, why the porno web pages are a fraud?"

"Well, because there's not a single beetle, not even beetles with those little 'G-string' panties, or whatever they call them, much less naked beetles."

"Panties?"

"Of course! Fuck! Aren't you writing to Spanish purists?" asks Durito as he adjusts his beret.

"Panties?" I repeat, trying to avoid the unavoidable, which is Durito horning in on what I'm writing, a task for which he has more than enough hands and impertinence.

"Let's see, hmmm, hmmm," murmured Durito as he climbs up on my shoulder.

"Russian? Are you writing to Putin? I wouldn't recommend it, he might throw one of those gasses at you, that are even worse than the ones that you let loose when you eat too many beans.

I protest: "Look, Durito, let's not start revealing intimacies, because I have a letter here that the Pentagon sent asking for your formula for the development of ultratoxic gases."

"Ah, but I turned them down. Because my gas, like my love, can neither be bought nor sold, but is something I give freely, without concern for whether the recipients deserve it or not," says Durito with an Andalucian accent, which you really have to work hard at to get right.

After a pause, he adds: "And what is your theme for today, kiddo?"

"Nothing, *tío*, except rebellion and an Aguascalientes that they are going to open in Madrid," I answer, infected by the flamenco beat spreading through the air.[15]

"Madrid? Which Madrid? The Madrid of Aznar and the Meretorious? Or the irreverent Madrid?

"The irreverent one, of course. Although it wouldn't surprise me if Aznar wanted to stick his hooves in."[16]

"Magnificent!" Durito applauds, and dances in a way that might bring García Lorca back to life to compose his unknown and unpublished "Ode to the Epileptic Beetle."

When he finishes his dance, Durito delivers his orders: "Write! I'm going to dictate my speech to you."

"But Durito, you are not on the program. Come on, you haven't even been invited."

"I know, the Russians don't like me. But I don't care. Come on, write! The title is 'Rebellion and Chairs.'"

"'Chairs?' Durito, I hope you're not going to come up with another one of your..."

"Quiet! The idea comes from a little piece that Saramago and I wrote toward the end of the last century called 'Chair.'"

"Saramago? You mean the writer José Saramago?" I ask perplexed.

"Of course! Is there another one? Well, so what happened was, we drank so much that day that we ended up falling off the reiterated chair, and from the floor, I tell him, with all the lucidity and perspective of those on the bottom, 'Pepe, that little wine kicks worse than that mule Aznar—and he didn't say anything because he was looking for his eyeglasses.'"

"I told him, something is coming to me, hurry José, ideas are like kidney beans and sausage. If you're not careful, someone else comes by and eats them.

"Saramago finally found his eyeglasses, and then together we gave shape to that story, in the late eighties, if I'm not mistaken. Of course it is credited in his name only; we beetles struggle quite a bit with authorship rights."

I want to curtail Durito's anecdotes, and I urge him: "OK, I've got the title, now what?"

Chairs

Well, it's about how the attitude human beings have about chairs defines them politically. The Revolutionary (like that, with capital R) scorns ordinary chairs and says to others and himself: "I don't have time to sit down, the heavy mission commended to me by History (like that, with capital H) prevents me from distracting

---

15 *Tío* is a common slang term spoken in Spain meaning dude or guy. Marcos has captured the rhythm of the Spanish spoken on the Peninsula in the original text.

16 The more colloquial translation would be the English expression "stick his nose in," but this literal translation underscores Marcos repeated references to Aznar as a braying ass.

myself with nonsense." He goes through life like this until he runs into the chair of Power. He throws off whomever is sitting on the chair with one shot, sits down and frowns, as if he were constipated, and says to others and himself: "History (like that, with capital H) has been fulfilled. Everything, absolutely everything, makes sense now. I am sitting on the Chair (like that, with capital C) and I am the culmination of the times." There he remains until another Revolutionary (like that, with capital R) comes by, throws him off and history (like that, with small h) repeats itself.

The rebel (like that, with small r), on the other hand, when he sees an ordinary chair, analyzes it carefully, then goes and puts another chair next to it, and another and another, and soon, it looks like a gathering because more rebels (like that, with small r) have come, and then the coffee, tobacco and the word begin to circulate and mix, and then, precisely when everyone starts to feel comfortable, they get antsy, as if they had ants in their pants, and they don't know if it's from the coffee or the tobacco or the word, but everyone gets up and keeps on going the way they were going. And so on until they find another ordinary chair and history repeats itself.

There is only one variation, when the rebel runs into the Seat of Power (like that, with capital S, capital P), looks at it carefully, analyzes it, but instead of sitting there he goes and gets a fingernail file and, with heroic patience, he begins sawing at the legs until they are so fragile that they break when someone sits down, which happens almost immediately. *Tan-tan.*

"*Tan-tan*? But Durito..."

"No, no, never mind. I already know it's too dry and theory should be velvety, but my style is metatheory. Maybe I'll be accused of being an anarchist, but my speech is worth something as a humble homage to the Spanish anarchists of old. They are quiet heroes, and they don't shine less for it."

Durito leaves, though I'm sure he'd rather come.

OK, enough with the puns. What was I saying when that armor-plated impertinence interrupted me?

Ah! I was saying how Aguascalientes is a festival of rebellion.

And so, my dear Chechnyan, what is rebellion?

It could be enough for you to just take a look around at all the men and women who lent a hand in building that Aguascalientes, and at those who will attend its inauguration (not the closing assembly, because that will surely be done by the police) for you to get a definition, but since this is a letter, I should try to do it with words which, no matter how eloquent they might be, will never be as decisive as gazes.

And so it was, while looking for some text that might work, that I found a book that Javier Elorriaga lent me.[17]

---

17 Javier Elorriaga has served as a spokesperson for the FZLN and editorial advisor for *Rebeldía* magazine. See also note in *The Cave of Desire*.

The little book is called *New Ethiopia*, and it's by a Basque poet named Bernardo Atxaga.[18] In it there is a poem called "Butterfly Reggae," that talks about butterflies who fly out over the sea and have no place to rest because the sea has no islands or rocks.

Well, I hope don Bernardo will forgive me if the synthesis is not as graceful as his reggae, but it helps me say what I want to you:

Butterflies

Rebellion is like the butterfly who flies out towards that sea without islands nor rocks.

It knows that there will be no resting place, and yet it does not waver in its flight.

And no, neither the butterfly nor rebellion are foolish or suicidal; the thing is, they know that they'll have a resting place, that out there is a huge old island no satellite has ever detected.

And that big island is a sister rebellion which will set out just when the butterfly, that is, the flying rebellion, starts to falter.

Then the flying rebellion, that is, the sea butterfly, will become part of that emergent island, and will be the landing point for another butterfly already beginning its determined flight towards the sea.

This would be no more than a mere curiosity in biology books, but as I-don't-know-who said, the flutter of a butterfly wing is often the origin of the greatest hurricanes.

With its flight, the flying rebellion, that is, the butterfly, is saying NO!

No to logic.

No to prudence.

No to immobility.

No to conformism.

And nothing, absolutely nothing, will be as wonderful as seeing the audacity of that flight, appreciating the challenge it represents, feeling how it starts to agitate the wind and seeing how, with those drafts, it is not the leaves of the trees that tremble, but the legs of the powerful who until then naively thought that butterflies died if they flew out over the sea.

Yes, my appreciable Muskovite, it is well known that butterflies, like rebellion, are contagious.

And there are butterflies, like rebellions, of all colors.

There are blue ones, who paint themselves that color so that the sky and the sea fight over them.

And there are yellow ones, so that the sun embraces them.

There are red ones, painted that way by rebel blood.

---

18 A prominent Basque author, Bernardo Atxaga has published over 20 children's books. His collection of short fiction *Obabakoak* won considerable acclaim, including Spain's National Literature Award. His poetry has captured the attention of a number of musicians who have set his verse to music.

There are brown ones, who thus take the color of the earth with them over the waves.

There are green ones, which is how hope tends to paint itself.

And all are skin, skin which shines no matter the color it is painted.

And there are flights of all colors.

And there are times that butterflies from all over gather, and then there is a rainbow.

And the task of butterflies, as any respectable encyclopedia will tell you, is to bring the rainbow down closer so children can learn how to fly.

Speaking of butterflies and rebellions, it occurs to me that, when you are all in the circus, or in the trial, facing that clown Garzón, and you are asked what you were doing in Aguascalientes, you can answer: flying.

Even though they send you flying, deported to Chechnya, the laughter will be heard all the way to the mountains of the Mexican Southeast.

And a laugh, my brother, is as welcome as music.

And speaking of music, as far as I know, the dance of the crab has become fashionable in the governments of Mexico, Spain, Italy and France and consists, in broad strokes, of moving the hips and the arms counterclockwise.

And now that we're on hands of the clock, if you see Manuel Vázquez Montalbán, give him a firm handshake from us.

Tell him I've already learned that Fox asked him if he knew why Marcos and the Zapatistas were so silent, and he answered, "They're not silent; the problem is that you do not listen."

By the way, tell him that *butifarra* sausages are not like diamonds, in other words, not eternal, and the ones he sent were finished long ago, and that if he doesn't come up with, say with about five kilos, we are going to take him and Pepe Carvalho as hostages.[19]

No, actually, better not. Because they'll mistake us for terrorists and Bush, hand in hand with the UN, will throw another "humanitarian" war on us. Maybe he should send the *butifarras*, and in exchange I'll send him the recipe for Marcos' Special which, for good reason, His Majesty's chef (ha!) has asked me for to no avail.

OK, I'm signing off now. Don't hesitate to let me know what jail they put you in. I mean, for when we're out that way.

No, don't even think that it will be to set you free, but so we can make sure that you're well locked up, because all of you are totally crazy. Imagine, wanting to inaugurate an Aguascalientes in Madrid. Next you'll be wanting to create an autonomous municipality in prison.

Oh, and we won't be able to send you cigarettes. But *tostadas* and *pozol* we can do, which are as dignified as you are.

---

19 See note in "Hour of the Little Ones"

Vale. Salud, and if it's about reigning, then let rebellion reign.

From the mountains of the Mexican Southeast
Subcomandante Insurgente Marcos

P.S. Eva asks whether in the Spanish State (that's how she said it, seriously) they have VCRs because she wants to take her collection of Pedro Infante movies. I told her that you have a different system over there. She asked me: "What do you mean they have a different system? You mean they don't have a neoliberal government there?" I didn't answer her, but now I say to her: "Comandanta Eva, what else could there be?"

Another P.S.
Don't think that I don't know that rebels from Italy, France, Greece, Switzerland, Germany, Denmark, Sweden, England, Ireland, Portugal, Belgium, Holland and etc. are also going to be there at the Aguascalientes. Say hello to all of them, and tell them that, if they don't behave we're going. . . to invade them too. We are going to globalize moldy *tostadas* and rancid *pozol*. And then we'll see how the number of globophobes increases geometrically.

Vale again.

The Sup in training for the crossing, that is, puking the moldy chocolates with nuts that El Olivio left on the ground.

* * *

Apples and the Zapatistas

The last story of this volume marks Durito's first appearance in the editorial pages of *Rebeldía*, a new magazine from the Mexican left. Here Durito describes how the seeds sown by the Zapatistas will grow and bear fruit, giving sustenance to generations to come.

First published in *Rebeldía*, November 17, 2002.

Durito says that life is like an apple.

He also says that there are those who eat them green, those who eat them rotten, and those who eat them ripe.

Durito says that there are some, very few, who can choose how they eat an apple: either in a beautiful fruit arrangement, pureed, in one of those odious (to Durito) apple sodas, in juice, in cake, in cookies, or in whatever their gastronomy dictates.

Durito says that the indigenous people feel obligated to eat the rotten apple, that the consumption of green apples is imposed upon youth, that children are promised a beautiful apple all the while it's poisoned with worms of deceit, and that women are told they will be given an apple but only get half an orange.

Durito says that life is like an apple.

He also says that when a Zapatista is faced with an apple, he stands vigilant with his blade ready, and with a skillful slice, he cuts the apple in half.

Durito says that the Zapatista neither intends to eat the apple, nor is he interested in whether the apple is ripe, rotten, or green.

Durito says that while the heart of the apple is exposed, the Zapatista, with great care, removes the seeds, then tills a parcel of land and plants the seeds.

Next, says Durito, the Zapatista waters the little plant with his tears and blood, and guards its growth.

Durito says that the Zapatista will not even see the apple tree blossom, much less the fruit it will give.

Durito says that the Zapatista planted the apple tree so that one day, when he is not here, just about anyone would be able to cut a ripe apple and be free to eat it, either in a fruit arrangement, pureed, as juice, in a pie, or in one of those odious (to Durito) apple sodas.

Durito says that the Zapatista's problem is this: to plant the seed and guard its growth. Durito says that the problem for everyone else is to struggle to be free to choose how to eat the apple that will come.

Durito says that this is the difference between the Zapatistas and the rest of humanity: where everyone sees an apple, the Zapatista sees a seed, goes and cultivates the land, plants the seed, and guards it.

Outside of that, says Durito, we Zapatistas are like the kid next door. If anything, we're uglier, says Durito, while watching from the corner of his eye as I take off my ski mask.

Subcomandante Insurgente Marcos
From some dawn in the 21st century

* * *

Bibliography

Collections of Communiqués

EZLN, Documentos y comunicados, 1 de enero/8 de agosto de 1994 (México D.F.: Ediciones Era, 1994).

EZLN, Documentos y comunicados 2, 15 de agosto/29 de septiembre de 1995 (México D.F.: Ediciones Era, 1995).

EZLN, Documentos y comunicados 3, 2 de octubre de 1995/24 de enero de 1997 (México D.F.: Ediciones Era, 1997).

EZLN, Documentos y communicados 4, 14 de febrero de 1997/2 de diciembre de 2000 (México D.F.: Ediciones Era, 2003).

EZLN, *"Democracia, Sustantiva, Democracia Social: Propuesta del EZLN a la Mesa 2 sobre Democracia y Justicia en el Diálogo de San Andrés Sacamch'en de los Pobres,"* (México D.F.: Berbera Editores, n.d.).

Marta Durán de Huerta, ed., *Yo, Marcos* (México, D.F.: Ediciones del Milenio, 1994).

Zapatista! Documents of the New Mexican Revolution (New York: Autonomedia, 1994). Also available on line at: lanic.utexas.edu/project/Zapatistas/.

Ben Clarke and Clifton Ross, eds. *Voice of Fire: Communiqués and Interviews from the Zapatista National Liberation Army* (Berkeley: New Earth Publications, 1994).

Shadows of Tender Fury (New York: Monthly Review Press, 1995).

Subcomandante Marcos, *Cuentos para una soledad desvelada* (México, D.F.: Publicaciones Espejo, 1998).

Subcomandante Marcos, *Relatos de El Viejo Antonio* (México, D.F.: Centro de Información y Análisis de Chiapas, 1998).

Subcomandante Marcos, *La Revuelta de la Memoria: Textos del Subcomandante Marcos y del EZLN sobre la historia* (San Cristóbal de las Casas: Centro de Información y Análisis de Chiapas, 1999).

Subcomandante Marcos, *Desde las montañas del sureste mexicano* (México, D.F.: Plaza y Janés, 1999).

Subcomandante Marcos, *Don Durito de la Lacandona* (San Cristóbal de Las Casas: Centro de Información y Análisis de Chiapas, 1999).

Subcomandante Marcos, *Detrás de nosotros estamos ustedes* (México, D.F.: Plaza y Janés, 2000).

Juana Ponce de León, ed. *Our Word is Our Weapon: Selected Writings of Subcomandante Marcos* (New York: Seven Stories Press, 2000).

Daniel Barrón Pastor, ed., *La Guerra por la Palabra: A Siete Años de Lucha Zapatista* (México, D.F.: Rizoma, 2001).

Paulina Fernández Christlieb and Carlos Sirvent, eds., *La marcha del E.Z.L.N. al Distrito Federal* (México D.F.: Ediciones Gernika, 2001).

La Marcha del Color de la Tierra: Comunicados, cartas y mensajes del Ejército Zapatista de Liberación Nacional (México D.F.: Rizoma, 2001).

Interviews

Subcomandante Marcos y Adolfo Gilly, *Discusión sobre la historia* (México, D.F.: Taurus, 1995).

Yvon Le Bot, *El sueño zapatista* (Barcelona: Plaza y Janes, 1997).

Manuel Vázquez Montalbán, *Marcos: El señor de los espejos* (México, D.F.: Aguilar, 2000).

Marta Durán, *El Tejido del Pasamontañas, Entrevista con el Subcomandante Marcos* (México, D.F.: Rizoma, 2001).

Subcomandante Marcos, "The Punch Card and the Hourglass," interviewed by Gabriel García Márquez and Roberto Pombo, *New Left Review 9* (May/June 2001), 69–79.

Internet Archives of EZLN Documents

Chiapas95, www.eco.utexas.edu/facstaff/Cleaver/chiapas95.html

Chiapas Media Project, www.chiapasmediaproject.org

CIEPAC: Center for Economic and Political Research for Community Action, www.ciepac.org/bulletins

Enlace Civil, www.enlacecivil.org.mx/

EZLN Ya Basta!, www.ezln.org/

Frente Zapatista de Liberación Nacional, www.fzln.org.mx

Global Exchange, www.globalexchange.org/campaigns/mexico/chiapas

Irish Mexico, Group Zapatista Index, flag.blackened.net/revolt/zapatista.html

Mexico Solidarity Network, www.mexicosolidarity.org

Schools for Chiapas, www.mexicopeace.org

SIPAZ: International Service for Peace, www.sipaz.org

Pamphlets, Illustrated Books and Photo Collections

Subcomandante Marcos, *Zapatistas in Their Own Words* (London: ds4a,1994).

Daniel Cazés, ed., *Chiapas, El alzamiento* (México D.F.: La Jornada Ediciones, 1994

Subcomandante Marcos, *The Story of Colors* (El Paso: Cinco Puntos Press, 1996).

Subcomandante Marcos, *La Historia De Los Colores*, Colección El Viejo Antonio 1, n.d.

Subcomandante Marcos, *La Historia De Las Preguntas*, Colección El Viejo Antonio 2, n.d.

Subcomandante Marcos, *La historia de la espada, el árbol, la piedra y el agua,*

Colección El Viejo Antonio 3, n.d.

Subcomandante Marcos, *La historia de los sueños*, Colección El Viejo Antonio 4, n.d.

FZLN, "Siete piezas sueltas del rompecabezas mundial," México D.F., 1997.

FZLN, "Fuerte Es Su Corazón: Los Municipios Rebeldes Zapatistas," México D.F., 1998.

FZLN, "Acuerdos sobre Derechos y Cultura Indígena, Mesa 1 de los Diálogos de San Andrés Sacamch'en," México D.F., February 1999.

FZLN, "Declaraciones de la esperanza," México D.F., 1999.

FZLN, "Los Zapatistas y la manzana de Newton," México D.F., 1999.

FZLN, "Hacia el Segundo Encuentro Continental Americano," México D.F., 1999.

FZLN, "Siete preguntas a quien corresponda (Imágenes del neoliberalismo en el México de 1997)," México D.F., 1999.

FZLN, "Qué Hacer Ante Un Proceso Penal, Manual," México D.F., 2000.

Open Media Pamphlet Series, "To Open a Crack in History," October 1999.

Open Media Pamphlet Series, "Letters From Our Silence," April 1999.

Open Media Pamphlet Series, "I Scatter Flowers of War," August 1999.

Open Media Pamphlet Series, "On East Timor and Amador Hernández," September 1999.

AGIT Press, "Navigating the Seas, EZLN Communiqués (December 22, 1997–January 29, 1998)," n.d.

AGIT Press, "Memory From Below, EZLN Communiqués (January 29, 1998–March 28, 1998)," n.d.

AGIT Press, "Masks & Silences, April–July 1998," n.d.

CAT, "Now and Then: Voices of the Mexican Revolutions," n.d.

Mexico Solidarity Network (Montreal), "Communiqués of the Zapatista Army of Liberation, January '96–August '96," n.d.

Cecilia Rodríguez, "I Ask That a Small Piece of Your Heart be Zapatista," (El Paso: National Commission for Democracy, n.d.).

Margen, "20 Years Before," Los Angeles: *evidentes panfletos*, n.d.

Austin Class War, "Second Declaration of La Realidad," 1996.

Pablo González Casanova, "Causas de la Rebelión en Chiapas," México D.F., n.d.

Martín Salas, et. al., eds., *Chiapas: rostros de la guerra*, (México D.F.: Publicaciones Espejo, 2000).

Chiapaslink, "The Zapatistas: A Rough Guide," (London: Calverts Press, 2000), www.chiapaslink.ukgateway.net/ch0.html.

Irish Mexico Group, "Chiapas Revealed," Dublin, 2001. www.struggle.ws/mexico/pdf/revealed1.html.

Arturo Kemchs, *Chiapas: Caricaturas por la paz* (México D.F.: Editorial Planeta Mexicana, 2001).

Edited Works

Rosa Rojas, ed., *Chiapas, y las mujeres que?* Tomo I (Mexico, D.F.: Editiones La Correa Feminista, Centro de Investigacion y Capacitacion de la Mujer A.C., 1994).

Rosa Rojas, ed., *Chiapas, y las mujeres que?* Tomo II (Mexico, D.F.: Editiones La Correa Feminista, Centro de Investigacion y Capacitacion de la Mujer A.C., 1995).

Raúl Trejo Delarbre, ed., *Chiapas: la guerra de las ideas* (México, D.F.: Editorial Diana, 1994).

Elaine Katzenberger, ed., *First World, Ha Ha Ha! The Zapatista Challenge* (San Francisco: City Lights, 1995).

John Holloway and Eloina Peláez, eds., *Zapatista! Reinventing Revolution in Mexico* (London: Pluto Press, 1998).

Chiapas volumes 1-11 (México, D.F.: Ediciones Era y Instituto de Investigaciones Económicas). Available online at www.multimania.com/revistachiapas/

Midnight Notes Collective, *Auroras of the Zapatistas: Local and Global Struggles of the Fourth World War* (New York: Autonomedia, 2001).

Tom Hayden, ed., *The Zapatista Reader* (New York: Thunder's Mouth Press, 2002).

Christine Eber and Christine Kovic, eds., *Women of Chiapas: Making History in Times of Struggle and Hope* (New York: Routledge, 2003).

History

John Womack, *Rebellion in Chiapas, An Historical Reader* (New York: The New Press, 1999).

Thomas Benjamin, *A Rich Land, A Poor People: Politics and Society in Modern Chiapas* (Albuquerque: University of New Mexico Press, 1989; rev. ed. 1996).

Kevin Gosner and Arij Ouweneel, eds., *Indigenous Revolts in Chiapas and the Andean Highlands* (Amsterdam: CEDLA, 1996).

Dan La Botz, *Democracy in Mexico: Peasant Rebellion and Political Reform* (Boston: South End Press, 1995).

James Cockcroft, *Mexico's Hope: An Encounter with Politics and History* (New York: Monthly Review Press, 1998).

Monographs & Essays

George Collier, *Basta! Land and the Zapatista Rebellion* (Oakland: Food First Books, 1994).

Lynn Stephen, "The Chiapas Rebellion," *Radical America* 25:2 (June 1994): 7-17.

Gustavo Esteva, *Crónica del fin de una era* (México, D.F.: Editorial Posada, 1994).

Alexander Ewen, "Mexico, The Crisis of Identity," *Akwe:kon Journal* 9:2

(Summer 1994): 28-40.

Bill Weinberg, "Zapata Lives On: A Report from San Cristobal," *Akwe:kon Journal* 9:2 (Summer 1994): 5-12.

Ronald Nigh, "Zapata Rose in 1994, the Indian Rebellion in Chiapas," *Cultural Survival Quarterly* 18:1 (Spring 1994): 9-13.

George Collier, "Roots of the Rebellion in Chiapas," *Cultural Survival Quarterly* 18:1 (Spring 1994): 14-18.

Gary Gossen, "Comments on the Zapatista Movement," *Cultural Survival Quarterly* 18:1 (Spring 1994): 19-21.

Frank Cancian and Peter Brown, "Who is Rebelling in Chiapas?" *Cultural Survival Quarterly* 18:1 (Spring 1994): 22-25.

Andrew Reding, "Chiapas is Mexico: The Imperative for Political Reform," *World Policy Journal* 11:1 (Spring 1994): 11-25.

Luis Hernández Navarro, "The Chiapas Rebellion," in *Transformation of Rural Mexico* 5 (San Diego: Ejido Reform Research Project, Center for U.S.-Mexican Studies, University of California San Diego, 1994).

Antonio García de León, "Chiapas and the Mexican Crisis," *NACLA* 29:1 (July/August 1995): 10-13.

Sylvie Deneuve and Charles Reeve, "Behind the Balaclavas of Southeast Mexico," (August 1995): 1-11. Online at flag.blackened.net/revolt/mexico/comment/balaclava.html.

John Ross, *Rebellion from the Roots* (Monroe: Common Courage Press, 1995).

Philip Russell, *The Chiapas Rebellion* (Austin: Mexico Resource Center, 1995).

Noam Chomsky, et al., *Chiapas Insurgente: 5 Ensayos sobre la realidad mexicana* (Navarra: Txalaparta Editorial, 1995).

María Fernanda Paz, "Searching for Root Causes: A Historical Background Sketch of the Protagonists of the Zapatista Uprising," *Identities* 3:1-2 (1996): 235-252.

James Petras and Steve Vieux, "Both Innovation and Revolutionary Tradition: Lessons of the Chiapas Uprising," *Against the Current* 10:6 (January/February 1996): 5-7.

Adolfo Gilly, *Chiapas, la razón ardiente: Ensayo sobre la rebellion del mundo encantado* (México, D.F.: Ediciones Era, 1997).

Katerina, "Mexico is Not Only Chiapas Nor is The Rebellion in Chiapas Merely a Mexican Affair," *Common Sense* 22 (December, 1997), 5-37. Online at www.geocities.com/CapitolHill/Lobby/2379/tptg1.htm.

Peter Poynton, "Mexico: Indigenous Uprisings, Never More a Mexico Without Us!" *Race and Class* 39:2 (October-December 1997), 65-73.

Carlos Montemayor, *Chiapas: La rebelión indígena de México* (México, D.F.: Editorial Joaquín Mortiz, 1997).

Richard Roman and Edur Velasco Arregui, "Zapatismo and the Workers

Movement in Mexico at the End of the Century," *Monthly Review* 49:3 (July–August 1997): 98–116.

Alejandro Guillermo Raiter and Irene Inés Muñoz, "Zapatista Discourse: What is New," *Common Sense* 21 (1997): 18–30.

Adolfo Gilly, "Chiapas and the Rebellion of the Enchanted World," in Daniel Nugent, ed., *Rural Revolt in Mexico, US Intervention and the Domain of Subaltern Politics* (Durham: Duke University Press, 1998).

Neil Harvey, *The Chiapas Rebellion: The Struggle for Land and Democracy* (Durham: Duke University Press, 1998).

Julio Moguel, *Chiapas: la guerra de los signos del amanecer Zapatista de 1994 a la masacre de Acteal* (México D.F.: La Jornada Ediciones, 1998).

Arij Ouweneel, "'Welcome to the Nightmare': Thoughts on the Faceless Warriors of the Lacandona Revolt of 1994 (Chiapas, Mexico)," in Kees Koonings and Dirk Krujit, eds., *Societies of Fear: The Legacy of Civil War, Violence and Terror in Latin America* (London: Zed Books, 1999).

Bill Weinberg, *Homage to Chiapas: The New Indigenous Struggle in Mexico* (New York: Verso, 2000).

John Ross, *The War Against Oblivion* (Monroe: Common Courage Press, 2000).

Thomas Benjamin, "A Time of Reconquest: History, the Maya Revival, and the Zapatista Rebellion in Chiapas," *American Historical Review* 105:2 (April 2000): 417–450.

Carlos Tello Díaz, *Rebelión de las cañadas: Origen y ascenso del EZLN* (México D.F.: Águila, León y Cal Editores, 2000).

Rachel Neumann, "We Make the Road by Walking: Lessons from the Zapatista Caravan," *Monthly Review* 53:2 (June 2001). Online at www.monthlyreview.org/0601neumann.htm.

Vicki Larson, "Brief Impressions from Chiapas," *Monthly Review* 53:2 (June 2001). Online at www.monthlyreview.org/0601larson.htm.

Midnight Notes, *Auroras of the Zapatistas: Local and Global Struggles of the Fourth World War* (New York: Autonomedia, 2001).

Rosalva Aída Hernández Castillo, *La Otra Frontera: Identidades múltiples en el Chiapas poscolonial* (México D.F.: Centro de Investigaciones y Estudios Superiores en Antropología Social, 2001).

Xóchitl Leyva Solano, "Regional, Communal, and Organizational Transformation in Las Cañadas," *Latin American Perspectives* 28:2 (March 2001): 20–44.

June C. Nash, *Mayan Visions: The Quest for Autonomy in an Age of Globalization* (New York: Routledge, 2001).

Lynn Stephen, *Zapata Lives! Histories and Cultural Politics in Southern Mexico* (Berkeley: University of California Press, 2002).

Postmodern Rebellion

Roger Burbach, "Roots of the Postmodern Rebellion in Chiapas" *New Left Review* 205 (May/June 1994), 113-124.

Ana Carrigan, "Chiapas, The First Postmodern Revolution," *The Fletcher Forum* 19:1 (Winter/Spring 1995), 71-98. Republished in Juana Ponce de León, ed. *Our Word is Our Weapon: Selected Writings of Subcomandante Marcos* (New York: Seven Stories Press, 2000), 417-443

Daniel Nugent, "Northern Intellectuals and the EZLN" *Monthly Review* 47:3 (July/August 1995), 124-138.

Roger Burbach, "For a Zapatista Style Postmodernist Perspective" *Monthly Review* 47:10 (March 1996), 34-41.

José Rabasa, "Of Zapatismo: Reflections on the Folkloric and the Impossible in a Subaltern Insurrection," in Lisa Lowe and David Lloyd, eds., *The Politics of Culture in the Shadow of Capital* (Durham: Duke University Press, 1997), 399-431.

Women

"Interview with Ramona and Ana María," Turning the Tide 7:5 (September-October 1994), 13-14.

Rosalva Aída Hernández Castillo, "Reinventing Tradition: The Women's Law," *Akwe:kon Journal* 9:2 (Summer 1994), 67-70.

Rosa Rojas, ed., *Chiapas, y las mujeres que?* Tomo I (México, D.F.: Editiones La Correa Feminista, Centro de Investigacion y Capacitacion de la Mujer A.C., 1994). English translation online at www.eco.utexas.edu:80/Homepages/Faculty/Cleaver/begin.html

Rosa Rojas, ed., *Chiapas, y las mujeres que?* Tomo II (Mexico, D.F.: Editiones La Correa Feminista, Centro de Investigacion y Capacitacion de la Mujer A.C., 1995).

Diana Banjac, "Rape in Mexico: An American is the Latest Victim of the Repression," *The Progressive* (January 1996), 18-21.

Lynn Stephen, "Democracy for Whom? Women's Grassroots Political Activism in the 1990s, Mexico City and Chiapas," in Gerald Otero, ed., *Neoliberalism Revisited: Economic Restructuring and Mexico's Political Future* (Boulder: Westview Press, 1996), 167-186.

Claudia Von Werlhof, "Upheaval From the Depth: The Zapatistas, the Indigenous Civilization, the Question of Matriarchy and the West," *International Journal of Comparative Sociology* 38:1-2 (June 1997), 106-130.

Rosalva Aída Hernández Castillo, "Between Hope and Adversity: The Struggle of Organized Women in Chiapas Since the Zapatista Uprising," *Journal of Latin American Anthropology* 3:1 (1997), 102-120.

Christine E. Eber, "Seeking Justice, Valuing Community: Two Women's Paths in the Wake of the Zapatista Rebellion," *Working Paper* #265 (March 1998), Women in International Development, Michigan State University.

Neil Harvey, "The Zapatistas, Radical Democratic Citizenship, and Women's Struggles," *Social Politics* 5:2 (Summer 1998), 158-187.

Rosalva Aída Hernández Castillo and Lynn Stephen, "Indigenous Women's Participation in Formulating the San Andrés Accords," *Cultural Survival Quarterly* 23:1 (Spring 1999), 50-51.

Erika Jones, "Indigenous Women in Chiapas Claim Their Rights," *Sojourner: The Women's Forum* (August 1999).

Christine Eber and Christine Kovic, eds., *Women of Chiapas: Making History in Times of Struggle and Hope* (New York: Routledge, 2003).

Autonomy

Araceli Burguete Cal y Mayor, "Chiapas: Maya Identity and the Zapatista Uprising," *Aba Yala News* 8: 1, 2 (Summer 1994), 6-11.

Evon Z. Vogt, "Possible Sacred Aspects of the Chiapas Rebellion," *Cultural Survival Quarterly* 18:1 (Spring 1994), 34.

Duncan Earle, "Indigenous Identity at the Margin: Zapatismo and Nationalism," *Cultural Survival Quarterly* 18:1 (Spring 1994), 26-30.

Jeffrey W. Rubin, "Indigenous Autonomy and Power in Chiapas: Lessons from

Mobilization in Juchitán," in *Transformation of Rural Mexico* 5 (San Diego: Ejido Reform Research Project, Center for U.S.-Mexican Studies, University of California San Diego, 1994).

Héctor Díaz-Polanco, *La rebelión Zapatista y la autonomía* (México, D.F.: Siglo Veintiuno Editores, 1997).

Lynn Stephen, "The Zapatista Opening: The Movement for Indigenous Autonomy and State Discourses on Indigenous Rights," *Journal of Latin American Anthropology* 2:2 (1997), 2-41.

George Collier, "Reaction and Retrenchment in the Highlands of Chiapas in the Wake of the Zapatista Rebellion," *Journal of Latin American Anthropology* 3:1 (1997), 14-31.

Shannan Mattiace, "'¡Zapata Vive!': The EZLN, Indigenous Politics, and the Autonomy Movement in Mexico," *Journal of Latin American Anthropology* 3:1 (1997), 32-71.

Lynn Stephen, "Redefined Nationalism in Building a Movement for Indigenous Autonomy in Southern Mexico," *Journal of Latin American Anthropology* 3:1 (1997), 72-101.

Héctor Díaz-Polanco, "Acteal and Autonomy," *Against the Current* 13:2 (May/June 1998), 20-22.

Gustavo Esteva, *Grassroots Postmodernism: Remaking the Soil of Cultures* (London: Zed Books, 1998).

Luis Hernández Navarro, "The San Andrés Accords: Indians and the Soul," *Cultural Survival Quarterly* 23:1 (Spring 1999), 30-32.

Patrick Cuninghame and Carolina Ballesteros Corona, "A Rainbow at Midnight: Zapatistas and Autonomy," *Capital and Class* 66 (Autumn 1998), 12-22.

George Collier, "Zapatismo Resurgent: Land and Autonomy in Chiapas," *NACLA* 33:5 (March/April 2000), 20-22; 24-25.

Tim Russo, "A Day in a Zapatista Autonomous Community," *NACLA* 33:5 (March/April 2000), 23.

Gustavo Esteva, "The Meaning and Scope of the Struggle for Autonomy," *Latin American Perspectives* 28:2 (March 2001), 120-148.

Xóchitl Leyva Solano, "Regional, Communal, and Organizational Transformations in Las Cañadas," *Latin American Perspectives* 28:2 (March 2001), 20-44.

Christine Eber, "Buscando una nueva vida: Liberation Through Autonomy in San Pedro Chenalhó, 1970-1998," *Latin American Perspectives* 28:2 (March 2001), 45-72.

Shannan L. Mattiace, "Regional Renegotiations of Space: Tojolabal Ethnic Identity in Las Margaritas, Chiapas," *Latin American Perspectives* 28:2 (March 2001), 73-97.

Radical Democracy

Karen Kampwirth, "Creating Space in Chiapas: An Analysis of the Strategies of the Zapatista Army and the Rebel Government in Transition," *Bulletin of Latin American Research* 15:2 (May 1996), 261-67

John Holloway, "The Concept of Power and the Zapatistas," *Common Sense* 19 (June 1996), (pages unknown). Online at aries.gisam.metu.edu.tr/chiapas/power.html.

John Holloway, "Dignity's Revolt," *Common Sense* 22 (December 1997). Online at aries.gisam.metu.edu.tr/chiapas/dignity.html.

Wildcat (Germany) and John Holloway, "Wildcat (Germany) Reads John Holloway—A Debate on Marxism and the Politics of Dignity," *Common Sense* 24 (1999), 58-75. Online at www.ainfos.ca/98/oct/ainfos00201.html.

Régis Debray, "A Guerrilla with a Difference," *New Left Review* 218 (July/August 1996), 128-37.

Joseph M. Whitmeyer and Rosemary L. Hopcroft, "Community, Capitalism, and Rebellion in Chiapas," *Sociological Perspectives* 39:4 (Winter 1996), 517-538.

Lynn Stephen, "Pro-Zapatista and Pro-PRI: Resolving the Contradictions of Zapatismo in Rural Oaxaca," *Latin American Research Review* 32:2 (1997), 41-70.

June Nash, "The Fiesta of the Word: The Zapatista Uprising and Radical Democracy in Mexico," *American Anthropologist* 99:2 (June 1997), 262-274.

Lynn Stephen and George Collier, "Reconfiguring Ethnicity, Identity, and Citizenship in the Wake of the Zapatista Rebellion," *Journal of Latin American Anthropology* 3:1 (1997), 2-13.

Lynn Stephen, "Election Day in Chiapas: A Low-Intensity War," *NACLA* 31:2 (September/October 1997), 10-11.

Karen Kampwirth, "Peace Talks, But No Peace," *NACLA* 31:5 (March/April 1998), 15-19.

Xochitl Leyva Solano, "The New Zapatista Movement: Political Levels, Actors and Political Discourse in Contemporary Mexico," in Valentina Napolitano and Xochitl Leyva Solano, eds., *Encuentros Antropológicos: Power, Identity, and Mobility in Mexican Society* (London: Institute of Latin American Studies, School of Advanced Study, University of London, 1998).

Gustavo Esteva, "The Zapatistas and People's Power," *Capital and Class 68* (Summer 1999), 153-182.

Kathleen Bruhn, "Antonio Gramsci and the Palabra Verdadera: The Political Discourse of Mexico's Guerrilla Forces," *Journal of Interamerican Studies & World Affairs* 41:2 (Summer 1999), 29-55

Stephan Gregory, "John Berger and Subcomandante Marcos: Peasants, Parables, and Politics," *Third Text* 52 (Autumn 2000), 3-19.

Josée Johnston, "Pedagogical Guerrillas, Armed Democrats, and Revolutionary Counterpublics: Examining Paradox in the Zapatista Uprising in Chiapas Mexico," *Theory and Society* 29:4 (August 2000), 463-505.

Monty Neill with George Caffentzis and Johnny Machete, "Towards the New Commons: Working Class Strategies and the Zapatistas," n.d. Online at www.geocities.com/CapitolHill/3843/mngcjm.html

Rosalva Aída Hernández Castillo, "Between Civil Disobedience and Silent Rejection: Differing Responses by Mam Peasants to the Zapatista Rebellion," *Latin American Perspectives* 28:2 (March 2001), 98-119.

Chris Gilbreth and Gerardo Otero, "Democratization in Mexico: The Zapatista Uprising and Civil Society," *Latin American Perspectives* 28:2 (March 2001), 7-29.

Kara Ann Zugman, "Mexican Awakening in Postcolonial America: Zapatistas in Urban Spaces in Mexico City," (PhD. diss., University of California Berkeley, 2001).

Encuentros

Lynn Stephen, "The Zapatista Army of National Liberation and the National Democratic Convention," *Latin American Perspectives* 22:4 (Fall 1995), 88-99.

EZLN, *Crónicas intergalácticas: Primer Encuentro Intercontinental por la Humanidad y contra el Neoliberalismo* (Barcelona: Collectiu de Solidaritat amb la Rebellio Zapatista, 1997).

Massimo De Angelis, "2nd Encounter for Humanity and Against Neoliberalism, Spain 1997," *Capital and Class* 65 (Summer 1998), 135-157.

Greg Ruggiero and Stuart Sahulka, eds., *The Zapatista Encuentro: Documents from the 1996 Encounter for Humanity and Against Neoliberalism* (New York: Seven Stories Press, 1998).

Human Rights

"Mexico, The New Year's Rebellion: Violations of Human Rights and Humanitarian Law During the Armed Revolt in Chiapas, Mexico," *Human Rights Watch* 6:3 (March, 1994).

Physicians for Human Rights and Human Rights Watch, *Mexico: Waiting for Justice in Chiapas* (Boston, 1994).

"Mexico at the Crossroads: Political Rights and the 1994 Presidential and Congressional Elections," *Human Rights Watch* 6:9 (August 1994).

Andrew Reding, *Democracy and Human Rights in Mexico* (New York: World Policy Institute at the New School for Social Research, 1995).

"Mexico: Labor Rights and NAFTA, A Case Study," *Human Rights Watch* 8:8 (September, 1996).

"Mexico: Torture and Other Abuses During the 1995 Crackdown on Alleged Zapatistas," *Human Rights Watch* 8:3 (February, 1996).

Centro de Derechos Humanos Fray Bartolomé de las Casas, *Ni Paz, Ni Justicia* (San Cristóbal de las Casas, 1996).

Human Rights Watch/Americas, *Implausible Deniability: State Responsibility for Rural Violence in Mexico* (New York, 1997).

John Ross, "Zapata's Children: Defending the Land and Human Rights in the Countryside," *NACLA* 30:4 (January/February 1997), 30-35.

Nikki Craske, et al., "Chiapas, Before It's Too Late…: A Report by an Independent Delegation to Chiapas, Mexico," (March, 1998).

Richard Stahler-Sholk, "The Lessons of Acteal," *NACLA* 31:5 (March/April 1998), 11-14.

Global Exchange, "On the Offensive: Intensified Military Occupation in Chiapas Six Months Since the Massacre at Acteal" (June, 1998).

Global Exchange, et al., *Foreigners of Conscience: The Mexican Government's Campaign Against International Human Rights Observers* (México, D.F., 1999).

Human Rights Watch, *Systemic Injustice: Torture, "Disappearance," and Extrajudicial Execution in Mexico* (New York, 1999).

Lynn Stephen, "The First Anniversary of the Acteal Massacre," *Cultural Survival Quarterly* 23:1 (Spring 1999), 27-29.

Shannon Speed and Jane Collier, "Limiting Indigenous Autonomy in Chiapas:

The State Government's Use of Human Rights," *Human Rights Quarterly*, 22:4 (November, 2000), 877-905. Online at muse.jhu.edu/journals/human_rights_quarterly/v022/22.4speed.html

Militarization

Stephen J. Wager and Donald E. Schulz, "Civil-Military Relations in Mexico: The Zapatista Revolt and Its Implications," *Journal of Interamerican Studies and World Affairs* 37:1 (Spring 1995), 1-42.

Martha Patricia López A. *La Guerra de Baja Intensidad en México* (México, D.F.: Plaza y Valdés, 1996).

Francisco Pineda, "La guerra de baja intensidad," in Andrés Barreda, et. al., *Chiapas* 2 (México, D.F.: Ediciones Era, 1996), 173-195.

Graham H. Turbiville, "Mexico's Other Insurgents," *Military Review* (June-July 1997), online Internet www.cgsc.army.mil/milrev/English/mayjun97/turb.htm.

James Rochlin, "The Indigenous and Mexican Security: Chiapas and Southern Mexico," in Redefining Mexican "Security," *Society, State, and Region Under NAFTA* (Boulder: Lynee Rienner Publishers, 1997), 57- 97.

Donald E. Schulz, "Between a Rock and a Hard Place: The United States, Mexico and the Challenge of National Security," *Low Intensity Conflict & Law Enforcement* 6:3 (Winter 1997), 1-40.

Democracy, Human Rights, And Militarism In The War On Drugs In Latin America (Guatemala: The Transnational Institute, The Bolivian Documentation and Information Center, and Inforpress Centroamericana, April 1997).

CONPAZ, Fray Bartolomé de Las Casas Human Rights Center, CONVER-GENCIA, *Militarization and Violence in Chiapas* (México D.F.: Impretei, 1997).

Luis Hernández Navarro, "The Escalation of War in Chiapas," *NACLA* 31:5 (March/April 1998), 7-10.

Andrés Aubry and Angélica Inda, "Who Are the Paramilitaries in Chiapas?" *NACLA* 31:5 (March/April 1998), 9.

Luis Hernández Navarro, "Mexico's Secret War," *NACLA* 32:6 (May/June 1999), 6-10.

Lincoln B. Krause, "The Guerrillas Next Door: A Short History of Mexico's Armed Revolutionaries from the 1960s to the EZLN Uprising of 1994," *Low Intensity Conflict & Law Enforcement* 8:1 (Spring 1999), 34-56.

Andrew Selee, "From Elite Violence to State Violence: The Origins of Low-Intensity Conflict in Chiapas," *UCLA Journal of Latin American Studies, Generation* 99 (Winter 1999), 1-12. Online at www.generation99.org/journal/Chiapas.htm

Inés Castro Apreza, "Quitarle el agua al pez: la guerra de baja intensidad en Chiapas (1994-1998)" in Andrés Barreda, et. al., *Chiapas* 8 (México, D.F.: Ediciones Era, 1999), 123-141.

Gustavo Castro and Onécimo Hidalgo, *La Estrategia de Guerra en Chiapas* (México D.F.: 1999).

CIEPAC, CENCOS, and Global Exchange, Siempre Cerca, *Siempre Lejos: Las Fuerzas Armadas en México/Always Near, Always Far: The Armed Forces in Mexico* (México D.F.: 2000).

Graham H. Turbiville, "Mexico's Multimission Force for Internal Security," *Military Review* (July/August 2000).

Graham H. Turbiville, "Mexico's Evolving Security Posture," *Military Review* (May-June 2001). Online at fmso.leavenworth.army.mil/fmsopubs/issues/mexico_evolve/mexico_evolve.htm

Environment

James D. Nations, "The Ecology of the Zapatista Revolt," *Cultural Survival Quarterly* 18:1 (Spring 1994), 31-33.

George A. Collier, "The Rebellion in Chiapas and the Legacy of Energy Development," *Mexican Studies/Estudios Mexicanos* 10:2 (Summer 1994), 371-382.

Neil Harvey, "Rebellion in Chiapas: Rural Reforms, Campesino Radicalism, and the Limits of Salinismo," in *Transformation of Rural Mexico* 5 (San Diego: Ejido Reform Research Project, Center for U.S.-Mexican Studies, University of California San Diego, 1994).

Philip Howard and Thomas Homer-Dixon, "Environmental Scarcity and Violent Conflict: The Case of Chiapas, Mexico," *American Association for the Advancement of Science, University of Toronto* (January 1996).

Naomi Adelson, "The Environmental Roots of the Chiapas Uprising," www.wws.princeton.edu/~jpia/1997/chap7.html.

Víctor M. Toledo, *La Paz en Chiapas: Ecología, luchas indígenas y modernidad alternativa* (México, D.F.: Ediciones Quinto Sol, 2000).

Andrés Barreda, "What Lies Beneath," *NACLA* 34:4 (January/February 2001), 38-40.

Electronic Fabric of Struggle

Harry Cleaver, "The Chiapas Uprising: The Future of Class Struggle in the New World Order," *Riff-Raff: attraverso la produzione sociale* (Padova), marzo 1994, pp. 133-145; *Impaction* (Tokyo) No. 85, 1994, pp. 144-160; *Common Sense* (Edinburgh) No. 15, April 1994, pp. 5-17; *Canadian Dimension* (Winnipeg), Vol. 28, No. 3, May-June 1994, pp. 36-39; *Lonnsslaven* (Oslo), #5, Spring-Summer 1994, pp. 6-7 (excerpt); *Studies in Political Economy*

(Toronto), No. 44, Summer 1994, pp. 141-157; *África América Latina. Cuardernos.* (Madrid) Número 18, 2a/1995, pp.71-84.

June Nash, "Press Reports on the Chiapas Uprising: Towards A Transnationalized Communication," *Journal of Latin American Anthropology* 2:2 (1997), 42-75. Online at www.eco.utexas.edu/facstaff/Cleaver/chiapa-suprising.html

Harry Cleaver, "The Zapatistas and the Electronic Fabric of Struggle," in John Holloway and Eloína Peláez, eds. *Zapatista! Reinventing Revolution in Mexico* (London: Pluto Press, 1998), 81-103.

Harry Cleaver, "The Zapatista Effect: the Internet and the Rise of an Alternative Political Fabric," *Journal of International Affairs* 51:2 (Spring 1998), 621-640. Online at www.eco.utexas.edu/faculty/Cleaver/zapeffect.html.

David Ronfeldt and John Arquilla, *The Zapatista Social Netwar in Mexico* (Santa Monica: Rand Arroyo Center, 1998).

David Slater, "Rethinking the Spatialities of Social Movements: Questions of (B)orders, Culture, and Politics in Global Times," in Sonia Alvarez, et al., eds., *Cultures of Politics, Politics of Culture: Re-visioning Latin American Social Movements* (Boulder:Westview Press, 1998), 380-404.

Gustavo Lins Ribeiro, "Cybercultural Politics: Political Activism at a Distance in a Transnational World," in Sonia Alvarez, et al., eds., *Cultures of Politics, Politics of Culture: Re-visioning Latin American Social Movements* (Boulder: Westview Press, 1998), 325-352.

Harry Cleaver, "Computer-linked Social Movements and the Global Threat to Capitalism" (1999). Online at www.eco.utexas.edu/faculty/Cleaver/polnet.html.

Judith Adler Hellman, "Real and Virtual Chiapas: Magic Realism and the Left," in Leo Panitch and Colin Leys, eds. "Necessary and Unnecessary Utopias," *Socialist Register* 2000 (Suffolk: Merlin Press, 1999), 161-186.

Harry Cleaver, "The Virtual and Real Chiapas Support Network: A Review and Critique of Judith Adler Hellman's 'Real and Virtual Chiapas: Magic Realism and the Left,' Socialist Register, 2002,'" n.d., 1-41. Online at www.eco.utexas.edu/faculty/Cleaver/anti-hellman.html.

Justin Paulson, "Peasant Struggles and International Solidarity: The Case of Chiapas," in Leo Panitch and Colin Leys, eds., "Working Classes, Global Realities," *Socialist Register* 2001 (New York: Monthly Review Press, 2000), 275-288.

Judith Adler Hellman, "Virtual Chiapas: A Reply to Paulson," in Leo Panitch and Colin Leys, eds., "Working Classes, Global Realities," *Socialist Register* 2001 (New York: Monthly Review Press, 2000), 289-292.

Globalization

Massimo De Angelis, "Globalization, New Internationalism and the Zapatistas," *Capital and Class* 70 (Spring 2000), 9-35.

Manuel Castells, Shujiro Yazawa, and Emma Kiselyova, "Insurgents Against the Global Order: A Comparative Analysis of the Zapatistas in Mexico, the American Militia and Japan's AUM Shinrikyo," *Berkeley Journal of Sociology* 40 (1995-6), 21-59.

David Slater, "Spatial Politics/Social Movements: Questions of (B)orders and Resistance in Global Times," in Steve Pile and Michael Keith, eds., *Geographies of Resistance* (New York: Routledge, 1997), 258-276.

Sarah Hilbert, "For Whom the Nation? Internationalization, Zapatismo, and the Struggle Over Mexican Modernity," *Antipode* 29: 2 (April 1997), 115-148.

Massimo De Angelis, "Global Capital and Global Struggles: The Making of a New Internationalism and the Zapatista's Voice," *l'acéphale* (October 1997). Online at www.acephale.org/encuentro/globintr.html.

George Yúdice, "The Globalization of Culture and the New Civil Society," in Sonia Alvarez, Evelina Dagnino, and Arturo Escobar, eds., *Cultures of Politics, Politics of Cultures: Re-Visioning Latin American Social Movements* (Boulder: Westview Press, 1998), 353-379.

Markus S. Schulz, "Collective Action Across Borders: Opportunity Structures, Network Capacities, and Communicative Praxis in the Age of Advanced Globalization," *Sociological Perspectives* 41:3 (1998), 587-616.

Ana Carrigan, "Why Is the Zapatista Movement so Attractive to Mexican Civil Society?" *civreports journal* 2:2 (March-April 1998), 1-22.

John Berger, "Against the Great Defeat of the World Order: An Introduction," *Race and Class* 40: 2/3 (October 1998-March 1999), 1-4.

Aaron Pollack, "Epistemological Struggle and International Organizing: Applying the Experience of the Zapatista Army of National Liberation," *Working Paper* #295 (August 1999), Institute of Social Studies.

Luis Hernández Navarro, "Globalizing Liberation," *NACLA* 33:6 (May/June 2000), 4, 43.

Henry Veltmeyer, "The Dynamics of Social Change and Mexico's EZLN," *Latin American Perspectives* 27:5 (September 2000), 88-110.

Mike Gonzalez, "The Zapatistas: The Challenges of Revolution in a New Millenium," *International Socialism* (Winter 2000), 59-80.

Roger Burbach, *Globalization and Postmodern Politics: From Zapatistas to High-Tech Robber Barons* (London: Pluto Press, 2001).

Greg Fuchs, "Words as Weapons: James De La Vega, Subcomandante Marcos and Zapatasos!" *Clamor* 7 (February/March 2001), 78-81.

Mark T. Berger, "Romancing the Zapatistas: International Intellectuals and the Chiapas Rebellion," *Latin American Perspectives* 28:2 (March 2001), 149-170.

Neoliberalism: NAFTA, Plan Puebla Panama, and the FTAA

Kristin Dawkins, "NAFTA: The New Rules of Corporate Conquest," *Open Media Pamphlet Series* 24 (June 1993).

Neil Harvey, "Playing with Fire: The Implications of Ejido Reform," *Akwe:kon Journal* 9:2 (Summer 1994), 20-27.

Elaine Bernard, "What's the Matter with NAFTA," *Radical America* 25:2 (June 1994), 20.

Tom Barry, *Zapata's Revenge: Free Trade and the Farm Crisis in Mexico* (Boston: South End Press, 1995).

Gustavo del Castillo V., "NAFTA and the Struggle for Neoliberalism: Mexico's Elusive Quest for First World Status," in Gerald Otero, ed., *Neoliberalism Revisited: Economic Restructuring and Mexico's Political Future* (Boulder: Westview Press, 1996), 27-42.

Neil Harvey, "Rural Reforms and the Zapatista Rebellion: Chiapas, 1988-1995," in Gerald Otero, ed., *Neoliberalism Revisited: Economic Restructuring and Mexico's Political Future* (Boulder: Westview Press, 1996), 187-208.

Ricardo Grinspun and Maxwell Cameron, "NAFTA and the Political Economy of Mexico's External Relations," *Latin American Research Review* 31:3 (1996), 161-188.

Stephen D. Morris and John Passé-Smith, "What a Difference a Crisis Makes: NAFTA, Mexico and the United States," *Latin American Perspectives* 28:3 (May 2001), 124-149.

Videos, Films, Music

Chiapas, La Otra Guerra, Canal 6 de Julio, 42 minutes, 1994, videocassette.

La Luz Llegará, director Carmen Ortiz and José Luis Contreras, 1994, time unknown, Colectivo Perfil Urbano, videocassette.

Los Más Pequeños, Colectivo Perfil Urbano, 62 minutes, 1994.

Viaje Al Centro de la Selva, director Epigmenio Ibarra, 60 minutes, 1994, videocassette.

Zapatistas: The Next Phase, director Gloria La Riva, 1994, 23 minutes, videocassette.

Aguascalientes, la Patria vive. documentary, 56 minutes, 1995.

Las Compañeras tienen grado [Zapatista Women with Rank], director Guadalupe Miranda and María Inés Roque, 30 minutes, 1995, videocassette.

Corridos sin rostro/Ballads without a face, director Othelo Khanh, 1994, videocassette.

Chiapas Historia Inconclusa, director Cristián Calónico, 90 minutes, 1995, videocassette.

Chiapas, Diálogo bajo amenaza, Canal 6 de Julio, 47 minutes, 1995, videocassette.

Prado Pacayal, director Carlos Martínez, 26 minutes, 1995, videocassette.

Somos Indios, Cantos Mexicanos por la Democracia, Justicia y Libertad, Dedicado al EZLN, TechnoDisc Records, 1995, PCD 1126.

Todos Somos Marcos, Quihubo Videos, 1995, 10 minutes, videocassette; (distributed with *Prado Pacayal*).

The Tequila Effect, directors Jose Manuel Pintado and Gloria Ribe, 40 minutes, 1995, videocassette.

Un Grano Para Mi Hermano, Colectivo Perfil Urbano, 1996, videocassette.

Marcos Historia y Palabra, director Cristián Calónico, 90 minutes, 1996, videocassette.

The Sixth Sun, director Sal Landau, 1996, 56 minutes, videocassette.

Juntos Por Chiapas, director Cristián Calónico, 28 minutes, 1997.

Acteal estrategia de muerte, Canal 6 de Julio, 47 minutes, 1998, videocassette.

Chiapas, La Historia Continúa, director Cristián Calónico, 58 minutes, 1998, videocassette.

Del Dolor a la Esperanza, Colectivo Perfil Urbano, 64 minutes, 1998.

Zapatista, Big Noise, 60 minutes, 1998, videocassette and DVD.

A Place Called Chiapas, director Nettie Wild, Zeitgeist Films, 93 minutes, 1998, videocassette.

Por Estos Pies Que Aún Caminarán Mucho…, Bicycle Café Music, 1998.

Phyllis Ponvert, "Putting the Power of Video in the Right Hands: The Chiapas Youth Media Project," *Against the Current* 13:2 (May/June 1998), 22–23.

Freedom is Forbidden: A Zapatista Benefit Compilation, T4 Records, 1999, T4-07.

The Sacred Land, Chiapas Media Project, 2000, videocassette.

Oscar Chávez Chiapas, Ediciones Pentagrama, 2000, LPCD 416.

Chiapas: Historia y Dignidad, director Cristián Calónico, 81 minutes, 2001, videocassette.

The Silence of the Zapatistas, Chiapas Media Project, 2001, videocassette.

Storm from the Mountain, Big Noise, 2001, videocassette.

Los Nakos Va Por Chiapas, Discos Pentagrama, nd, PCD 265.

www.nodo50.org/raz/informacion/videos.htm